(1999)
1ST. Ed.
10,⁻

The Vices of Integrity

The Vices of Integrity

E.H. Carr, 1892–1982

———————◆———————

JONATHAN HASLAM

VERSO

London • New York

First published by Verso 1999

© Jonathan Haslam 1999

All rights reserved

The moral rights of the author have been asserted

Verso

UK: 6 Meard Street, London W1V 3HR

USA: 180 Varick Street, New York NY 10014–4606

Verso is the imprint of New Left Books

ISBN 1–85984–733–1

British Library Cataloguing in Publication Data

A catalogue record for this book is available from the British Library

Library of Congress Cataloging-in-Publication Data

A catalog record for this book is available from the Library of Congress

Typeset by M Rules

Printed by Biddles Ltd, Guildford and King's Lynn

In memory of Tamara Deutscher,
who understood

'Over everything there lies the divine ordination of things which we cannot indeed directly prove, but which we can sense . . . Belief in providence is the sum and substance of all belief; in it I cannot be shaken.'

Ranke to his son, 1873

'There is strong shadow where there is much light.'

Goethe, *Gotz von Berlichingen*, Act 1

'The littleness of the great have a fascination for the ordinary man. The cynically inclined, and not they alone, find satisfaction in discovering that the man of genius in everyday life behaves not better, but often a good deal worse, than the man in the street. And there is some consolation in the reflexion that in the contacts of genius with the ordinary man, or even with mere talent, our human sympathies are not always on the side of genius.'

E.H. Carr, 'The Two Russians', *Fortnightly Review*

Contents

Preface

The name E.H. Carr will be familiar to teachers and students of history from his provocative polemic, *What is History?* To specialists in Soviet history he will be remembered as the author of no less than fourteen intimidating volumes covering the Russian revolution from Lenin to Stalin. To the interested layman as well as those fascinated with nineteenth-century Russia he is the man who exquisitely portrayed Herzen and his circle in *The Romantic Exiles.* To the political scientist *The Twenty Years' Crisis* remains a classic. For many years he served his country as a diplomat and later as a controversial assistant editor of *The Times.* To family he was always 'the Prof.' To friends and collaborators he was simply Ted.

To most, however, he was an enigma, a distant and forbidding figure, more a demi-god (or demon) than a human being. Partly, though not entirely, for these reasons he attracted as much abuse as praise. Certainly no one has ever expressed indifference; and this should scarcely prompt surprise. Anyone as articulate as he, who pronounced on the most vital issues of the day with such vigour and ruthlessness, was bound to make innumerable enemies as well as allies. The one-time Trotskyist Max Eastman described him as 'a mild, quiet-hearted bourgeois with a vicarious taste for revolutionary violence'.[1] The late Sir Isaiah Berlin attacked him for having 'never concealed his dislike of liberals' and for not being averse to 'casting a protective mantle over extremists, however foolish or misguided he may think them to be . . .'.[2] Praise came easily from the lips of some distinguished colleagues. The classicist Moses Finley wrote of him as 'the most controlled intellect, I believe, that I have ever encountered'.[3] To Hugh Seton-Watson he always remained 'an object of admiration and gratitude'.[4] The American ex-Communist turned anti-Communist Bertram Wolfe simultaneously accused him of apologetics and

---

[1] *New York Times*, 27 August 1950.
[2] Review of E.H. Carr, *Studies in Revolution*, London 1951, in *International Affairs*, October 1951, p. 471.
[3] Finley to Betty Behrens, 6 November 1982.
[4] Seton-Watson to Behrens, 11 November 1982.

confessed to being 'filled with admiration' for his 'scholarship, industry and mastery of the materials'.[5] But whether as recipient of deserved and undeserved abuse or as the object of adulation he made too great an impact on his time to be passed over in silence: hence the need for a biography.

The author knew him from 1973. He long remained withdrawn and unforthcoming in almost every respect: kindly, witty, given to ironic observation, lapping up gossip, intensely loyal to those he respected but on occasion crusty and suspicious of questions unrelated to the work at hand, wary of intimacy, above all a loner. Everything about him intensified one's curiosity. Only in the last months of his cancer did he show a more vulnerable side.

Research was initially towards a purely intellectual biography but inevitably turned into something else. Berlin was the first to insist, in his inimitable way, that one had to treat the whole man. This turned out to be absolutely true. As Nikolai Berdyaev – one of Carr's favourite writers – wrote long ago: 'It is impossible to understand a scholar other than in relation to his personality. Every significant scholar is the product of a significant personality, from whose depths emerge the elements of creativity and from whose depths emerges the only explanation.'[6] To this one must add the equally important role played by the times through which he lived.

Carr died leaving next to nothing behind him that could assist the biographer. Other than the enormous mass of published work, there were only appointment diaries from 1925 to 1960 (we never found out what happened to the diaries that followed) and a handful of papers. This meant that the life had to be reconstructed *de novo*. It also explains why the text has taken over a decade to put together. It meant too that those who knew him at various phases of his life provided the documentary bases for the biography. Not everyone involved, indeed perhaps no one involved, will agree entirely with the result: neither those who loved and admired him, nor those who feared and hated him. Where Carr's papers are cited, the reader can consult the material at the Birmingham University archives, where I also hope to deposit photocopies of other correspondence and his appointment diaries. Elsewhere, where no provenance is given, the papers largely remain in private hands. Where no source is given, the author obtained the information from his subject at first hand or from members of the immediate family. Every endeavour has been made to avoid repeating hearsay evidence where sources could not be checked. Memory, we need to be reminded, is a continuous process of recreation rather than a static store of information.

Without the generous support and patience of Carr's son John, daughter-in-law Betty, step-daughter Rachel Kelly (and her husband Bill), this book would never have seen the light of day. Professor R.W. Davies, who collaborated on two volumes of Carr's *History of Soviet Russia*, was of

---

[5] Wolfe to Carr, 2 February 1960.
[6] N. Berdyaev, *Aleksei Stepanovich Khomyakov*, Moscow 1912, p. 30.

inestimable value throughout; though I know he does not share my perspective. And the late Tamara Deutscher, who helped so much, made me see by power of example that one can remain fond of and committed to a man whose weaknesses and views are not entirely one's own. She can unfortunately only be thanked with a posthumous dedication.

Others whom I must also thank include the following: the British Academy, for a small research grant, and for details of Carr's election to its fellowship; Andrew Rothstein, Professor Gabriel Gorodetsky (Tel Aviv University), and Professor Y. Taniuchi (Tokyo University), for giving me copies of their correspondence; Dr C. Abramsky; Lord Annan (King's College, Cambridge); the late Sir John Balfour (Foreign Office); Professor Michael Balfour; Dr John Barber (King's College, Cambridge); Emily Morison Bech; Emeritus Professor Lord Beloff; the late Professor Sir Isaiah Berlin (All Souls College, Oxford); Professor James Billington (Library of Congress); the late Dr George Bolsover (School of Slavonic and East European Studies, London); Professor John Brademas (New York University); Peter Calvocoressi; Lord Carr of Hadley; Churchill College archive; the late Sir Ashley Clarke (Foreign Office); College archives, University of Wales at Aberystwyth; Dr Valerie Cromwell (formerly of Newnham College, Cambridge); Russell Davies (University of Wales at Aberystwyth, archives); the late Winnie Elkin; Professor Sir John Elliot (Oxford University); Mr Tim Farmiloe (Macmillan's); Professor Sheila Fitzpatrick (University of Chicago); Dr David Foglesong (Rutgers University); the late David Footman (St Antony's College, Oxford); Tom Forde; Professor Jonathan Frankel (Hebrew University of Jerusalem); Dorothy Galton (formerly of the School of Slavonic and East European Studies, London); Professor Israel Getzler (Hebrew University of Jerusalem); the late Lord Gladwyn (Foreign Office); Professor John Hazard (Columbia University); Phyllis Hetzel (Newnham College, Cambridge); Dr Christopher Hill (Balliol College, Oxford); Professor Keith Hopkins (King's College, Cambridge); Institute for Advanced Study archives (Princeton); International Institute for Social History archives (Amsterdam); the late Professor James Joll (London School of Economics); Dr Aileen Kelly (King's College, Cambridge); Dr Christopher Kelly (Corpus Christi College, Cambridge); Professor George Kennan (Institute for Advanced Study, Princeton); Sue Knowles (BBC Written Archives Centre); Professor François Lafitte (Birmingham University); Joan Lafitte (formerly at Political and Economic Planning); Professor Eugene Lampert (formerly of Keele University); Dr Peter Laslett (Trinity College, Cambridge); Lilly Library, Indiana University; Mr Iverach McDonald (of *The Times*); Professor Isabel de Madariaga; Professor Arno Mayer (Princeton University); Merchant Taylors' School archives (Miss Bakewell, Mr Woolley and Mr Mash); Professor Roger Morgan (European University, Firenze); the late Dr Christopher Morris (King's College, Cambridge); Mr Nigel Nicolson; Ms Jane O'Malley; Mary Pomery; Dr Brian Porter (University of Wales at Aberystwyth); Lady Cynthia Postan; Sir Victor Pritchett; Public Record Office, Kew; the late Sir Frank

Roberts (Foreign and Commonwealth Office); the late Dr Robson (Trinity College, Cambridge); Rockefeller Foundation Archive (Tarrytown, New York); Professor Sir Martin Roth (Trinity College, Cambridge); Denis Routh (formerly of All Souls College, Oxford, and University of Wales at Aberystwyth); Royal Institute of International Affairs; the late Professor Hugh Seton-Watson (School of Slavonic and East European Studies, London); Professor Quentin Skinner (Christ's College, Cambridge); Dr Jonathan Steinberg (Trinity Hall, Cambridge); Dr Zara Steiner (New Hall, Cambridge) and Professor George Steiner (Churchill College, Cambridge); Professor Paul Streeten (New York); Professor Hugh Stretton (University of Adelaide); the Reverend Geoffrey Styler (Corpus Christi College, Cambridge); Trinity College, Cambridge, archives; Emeritus Professor Robert Tucker (Johns Hopkins University School of Advanced International Studies); Professor Richard Ullman (Princeton University); University College, London, archives; the late T.E. Utley (*Daily Telegraph*); the late Michael Vyvyan (Foreign Office and Trinity College, Cambridge); Ella Wolfe (Stanford, California); Emeritus Professor Donald Cameron Watt (London School of Economics).

Corpus Christi College, Cambridge
March 1999

1

A 'Singular' but Promising Upbringing

Edward (Ted) Hallett Carr was born in Upper Holloway, a rapidly expanding north London suburb, on Tuesday 28 June 1892 to Elizabeth Jessie (née Hallett) and Francis Parker Carr. It was a very humid day. From that evening unusually severe thunderstorms continued until the early hours of Thursday morning. Nearly every elm on Hampstead Heath and Parliament Hill fields was scorched by lightning.[1] The political climate was no less electric. Ulstermen were in revolt. Prime Minister William Gladstone was bent upon Home Rule for Ireland, a policy condemned in no uncertain terms by *The Times* as 'an impudent imposture and a fraud upon the nation.'[2] Gladstone dissolved Parliament and called an election to secure an effective majority in the House of Commons. The domestic political consensus forged in the Victorian era had irreparably broken under the immense weight of the Irish problem. Other difficulties arose. No longer the workshop of the world, though still its banker, Britain now faced a working class that was organizing to force a redistribution of the nation's wealth. Yet few saw these signs as indicative of a larger problem. To established opinion Gladstone seemed prompted by some obscure, perverse and mischievous delight in upsetting a self-evidently successful social order.

The bases for that order were so designed as to secure maximal capital accumulation. The *Financia Times* confidently extolled 'the investing spirit and wealth of the age', and looking abroad could find hardly a country 'which has not benefitted to a greater or less extent through the renewed activity of the human race'.[3] Income was saved rather than spent so that successive generations could pass on ever increasing amounts of capital. Within this order the Carrs were not untypical representatives of the 'rather respectable, well-to-do but parsimonious bourgeoisie'.[4] The family line most probably

---

[1] *The Times*, 30 June 1892.
[2] Editorial, ibid., 29 June 1892.
[3] 'Finance in 1889', *Financial Times*, 1 January 1890.
[4] Carr to Tamara Deutscher, 28 August 1974.

originated in Scandinavia. The name derives from the Middle English *kerr*, meaning brushwood or wet ground, from the Old Norse *kjarr*. Viking settlers subjected the northeast of England to extensive colonization in the centuries prior to the Norman invasion.[5] It is here that we find Ted's ancestors in the late Middle Ages. George Carr was a merchant, sheriff in 1450 and eight times mayor of Newcastle. The Carrs made a successful living in commerce as merchant adventurers in the fifteenth and sixteenth centuries. But they chose the losing side in the Civil War (1640–46) and, evidently as a consequence, slipped dramatically down the social scale. Mathew Carr, born in 1693, after the Restoration, found work as a humble anchorsmith in Sunderland. A branch of the family then moved south through Yorkshire and by the end of the eighteenth century Ted's great-grandfather, a saddlesoap turned blacking manufacturer, had set up house in Barnet: at that time in the countryside north of London. His son Robert was born nearby in Highgate in 1819 and sired four sons of whom Francis Parker – Ted's father – was the youngest and therefore the poorest.

We know little of Francis. Apparently he had 'a great reputation in the family for being very clever – a wrangler [scholar] at Cambridge . . . and a chess player of considerable repute'.[6] Francis's part of the business – writing ink – produced a steady income, sufficient to rear a middle-class Victorian family. But no great wealth was accumulated, and for one simple reason: he lacked ambition. Indeed, the house where Ted was born – 62 Gladsmuir Road, Upper Holloway – was, as it is still, only a modest semi-detached villa typical of the era and the area. His parents had moved into the newly built home on his mother's pregnancy, at a time when most of the other side of the street was still under construction. Their neighbours were a schoolteacher and a retired congregational minister, not untypical of the rest of a street in which clerks, typists, journalists and hosiers had finally attained a comfortable suburban existence with the security of their own modest property. Most could afford a resident servant, where space allowed.[7] Upper Holloway trailed behind Highgate and the more princely elevations of Hampstead in the social hierarchy. Beyond Hampstead stood open country, embracing villages such as Finchley and Hendon to the north.

The family was 'middle middle class, and very Victorian', Carr recalled. 'They never to my knowledge went abroad in their lives.'[8] And the home into which he was born was perfectly secure and normal – except for one fateful peculiarity: the presence of the dominant maiden aunt Amelia, Jessie's sister, who very much needed a focus for her starved affections; an example of what Carr later and tellingly described as 'that Victorian horror, the

---

[5] J. Geipel, *The Viking Legacy*, London 1971, p. 199.
[6] *Autobiographical sketch*, composed in 1980 for Tamara Deutscher, at her request. In the author's possession.
[7] *Census return*, 1891: Islington, District 9, 1a, street index 9.
[8] Interview with P. Scott, 'Revolution without the Passion', *Times Higher Education Supplement*, 7 July 1978.

dependent relative.'[9] When younger brother Frederick was born on 24 June 1895 Jessie was in bad health. Amelia seized a unique opportunity and snatched little Ted for herself.[10] Francis was too unassertive to stop her and by the time Jessie had recovered, they were faced with a fait accompli. Abrupt deprivation of his mother's attention at the tender age of three compounded the problem that all children have when siblings appear. Many years later Ted would dwell on the impact of this unfortunate early experience. On one occasion he confessed: 'Yes, you are of course right to say that my emotional life has always been a bit askew – due, if any purpose is served by recollecting this now, to my singular upbringing.'[11]

His brother and sister both saw Ted as the favoured one of the three yet, looking back, he saw himself as having been an isolated child. Indeed the degree of alienation he felt from his parents is apparent from the fact that he omitted all reference to them in his *Who's Who* entry later in life. And when a friend once suggested that she and Ted were 'like orphans' in old age, he quickly identified with that image: 'I think I can see how it fits in my case. The platitude that the old return to childhood has some force.'[12] A timid child, he grew up with two 'secret fears': 'loneliness and coldness'.[13] He very much longed to be loved. Yet at the same time he learnt to suppress the greater part of his emotions. The reserve he displayed inevitably distanced him from his peers. He found it almost impossible to talk directly about his feelings, yet he could express them eloquently on paper. Years hence the only way friends and members of the family could tell he was distressed was by the way he walked. Outbursts of raw emotion quite literally made him feel ill. 'Physical sea-sickness I've never suffered from,' he confessed years later. 'But I appear to succumb to emotional sea-sickness when rocked sharply and violently up and down.'[14]

From all this it would be a mistake to infer that Amelia maltreated him. On the contrary she gave him the sense of direction in his life that an unambitious father and an infirm mother were unable to provide. She also spoilt him, even to the point of learning Latin to help him with his schoolwork. And these studies soon formed a safe haven from the tempestuous seas of uncontrolled emotion. His younger sister, 'the Ike', born on 22 January 1900, used to recall that on return home from school aunt Amelia would bustle him up to her room for homework. That side of the relationship yielded rich returns; and brother and sister were no doubt jealous of all the special attention. But the plain fact was that aunt Amelia, no matter how loving, was not Ted's mother.

An odd one out within the family, he also came from a family largely

[9] Carr to Tamara Deutscher, 12 July 1973.
[10] Rachel Kelly, a step-daughter to Carr, to the author, 4 February 1985. This point is confirmed by John Carr, his son, as well as Tamara Deutscher, who heard it from Carr.
[11] Carr to Tamara Deutscher, 30 August 1982.
[12] Carr to Tamara Deutscher, 12 September 1978.
[13] Carr to Tamara Deutscher, 26 May 1975. Also, from a letter undated and sometime in October 1973: 'I sometimes get frightened of loneliness and of not being able to cope with myself.'
[14] Carr to Tamara Deutscher, 20 January 1973.

isolated within the community. 'I grew up . . . in a closed society of forty or fifty relatives', he recalled years hence.[15] This was a feature he readily seized upon in his biography of Dostoevsky: 'The lack of playmates in his childhood left equally visible traces on his life and work. It would sound paradoxical to speak of the isolated childhood of one who was brought up with six brothers and sisters in a three-roomed flat, but isolated the family certainly was; it had no social life; all its activities and reactions were domestic, not external.'[16] This was also true of the Carr household which, with the birth of two other children, had to move to more spacious accommodation not far distant at Ridsdale, Crouch Hill, Hornsey North. The extended family usually gathered for Sunday lunch at the much grander house of Ralph Carr, Francis's brother, who lived in nearby Highgate. The rest of their social life was equally family-centred: a consequence of the fact that the family business included all but uncle Alfred. This had one trivial but notable result: the Carrs were collectively known for their own particular brand of humour, which made life a little difficult for those that married them.[17] Ted remembered that when he was young the family 'was accused of having "a warped sense of humour", because we laughed at things other people didn't find funny'.[18]

This was a very provincial background. The rest of the world intruded only through books. We know nothing of Ted's schooldays until he reached thirteen. Very tall and thin, with intelligent, penetrating eyes but weak sight and the slightly bulbous nose characteristic of most Carrs, he was a diffident child, not so much anti-social as taciturn, more interested in words than games; someone who instantly commanded respect rather than affection, but whose native wit easily won over brighter minds. His parents, true to one particular Victorian value, thrift, did not pay for his secondary education. Instead in 1905 Ted won a scholarship to Merchant Taylors', then a day-school recently transplanted from cramped quarters to a magnificent new set of Victorian Gothic buildings opened by the royal family at Charterhouse Square in central London. From Crouch Hill he commuted daily via the steam and sulphur of the Great Northern Railway to Aldersgate and a city that was notorious for pickpockets and other petty criminals.

Merchant Taylors' was a more than adequate destination, though it was undergoing something of a crisis as it was losing its market to the public schools opening in the fresh air of the countryside within easy reach of London. The headmaster John ('Pongo')[19] Nairn had been appointed in

---

[15] V. Mehta, *Fly and the Fly-Bottle: Encounters with British Intellectuals*, London 1963, p. 150. One has to exercise a little caution here. Carr did not believe the account of the interview to be entirely accurate, though Mehta, being blind, was undoubtedly sensitive to the slightest word and tone.

[16] Carr, *Dostoevsky (1821–1881): A New Biography*, London 1931, p. 13.

[17] Lord Carr to the author, 21 August 1984.

[18] Carr to Tamara Deutscher, 31 December 1973.

[19] The nickname is said to derive from the fact that he had the habit of grabbing boys idling in the corridor and pummelling them in the stomach, asking them why they were not outside in the fresh air.

1900 at the early age of 26 on the basis of his distinguished achievements as an undergraduate in classics at Trinity College, Cambridge, to which he had been elected a Fellow in 1896. He was visibly floundering, however. Due to inexperience, Nairn created something of a crisis with St. John's College, Oxford, which hitherto had provided a scholarship for the best students of classics from the school. But as a result of his refusal to compromise, from 1902 to 1911 the head monitor, normally the best classicist in the school and therefore destined for St. John's, was directed elsewhere.[20] The inspection by the Oxford and Cambridge Board in 1914 also concluded that the school hours were too short and the homework too long, and that the education of the majority was sacrificed so that a few could win classical scholarships to Oxford and Cambridge. The modern subjects had scarcely developed when Nairn arrived; here, however, he had made some limited progress. The school thus offered 'secondary education, and access to Oxford and Cambridge, to middle-class boys whose parents could not have afforded a public school education for their children.'[21]

It proved a challenge Ted had no difficulty in meeting. It was a world of starched white Eton collars, fashioned wide and low; any suit could be worn provided the cap with paschal lamb was in place, though seniors could and did wear bowlers. Boaters were worn in summer. Yet for all the apparent stiffness and conformity, this was unquestionably a time of unusual individuality; perhaps most evident from school photographs in which each subject posed for himself rather than as an undifferentiated member of the group. Moreover eccentricity seems to have been the second, if not the first, qualification for schoolmasters. At Charterhouse Square they generally had a reputation for being friendly as well as competent, though some were unbelievably pompous. Conway, a talented teacher of classics, left an indelible impression. One pupil recalls his arrival into the classroom to find a scrummage forming, which broke up immediately upon his entry. It prompted a typical outburst: 'When a Master comes into his classroom, and finds boys throwing each other about, the zone of augustness which ought to surround the Master is transgressed, and he is displeased and disgusted.'[22] The other teacher of classics, Bampfylde ('Bam'), a tall, dark, good-looking man who invariably wore a frayed black coat and a brown corduroy waistcoat, was universally adored, introducing pupils to the beauty of the Greek language and literature, which became one of Ted's best subjects. [23]

Intellectually self-confident, Ted frequently 'came out top of the class'[24]

[20] F. Draper, *Four Centuries of Merchant Taylors' School 1561–1961*, London 1962, chapter xvii.

[21] *Autobiographical sketch.*

[22] C. Mayne, 'Via Classics to the Special Sixth', *Old Merchant Taylors' Society News Sheet*, Summer 1967, pp. 26–8.

[23] Sir F. Leith-Ross, 'A Schoolboy at the Turn of the Century', ibid., Summer 1964, pp. 13–17.

[24] He recalled that he was 'invariably' top of the class, though the school records show differently: Merchant Taylors' School, *Election of Scholars, 1906–1908*.

and 'never doubted' his ability to do so 'in any subject except science, which
anyhow played no significant part in the curriculum'.[25] In June 1906 at the
end of his first year he carried home the form prize, a mathematics prize and
a divinity prize. Indeed, in ironic contrast to his later life, maths and scripture
initially attracted his highest performance; and he had an amazing ability to
cite scripture, though a skill rarely exploited, into his ninetieth year. But
there was of course a personal price to pay, at least in the lower forms: 'Boys
who always come out top of the class aren't very popular with their school-
mates';[26] and Ted certainly made matters worse by his open intolerance of
fools.

Commuting held some advantages. The older children tended to mimic
their fellow travellers and took to reading the morning newspaper en route to
school. Their awareness of the world around them was also greatly enhanced
by studying at the hub of the financial and political empire which had now
drifted to the right. Ted distinguished himself from his fellow pupils by supporting the Liberal Party. His father had voted Conservative in 1895 and
1900. But because he was 'an impassioned free-trader' and the Conservatives
shifted to industrial protection in the face of stiff competition from Germany
and the United States, he went over to the Liberals who were convinced free-
traders, taking Ted with him. Indeed, Ted recalled his father's 'logical
exposition of the merits of free trade and demolition of the absurd fallacies of
the "tariff reformer"' as his 'first insight into the processes of rational argument'. The Liberal triumph in the general election in 1906 was thus his 'first
political memory'. He became an enthusiastic supporter of Lloyd George's
programme of social reform – noting with surprise that his father 'stuck
firmly with the Liberals throughout the Lloyd George period' through thick
and thin. The only drawback was that 'at least 95%' of Ted's fellow pupils
'came from orthodox Conservative homes, and regarded Lloyd George as an
incarnation of the devil'. To Ted Lloyd George became a hero, a status maintained to the very end. The Liberals at school were thus a 'tiny despised
minority',[27] and this experience doubtless reinforced what was by now an
ingrained sense of isolation.

Only in the middle years of school did he develop an aptitude for classics
and benefit fully from 'a first-rate narrow classical education' at the hands of
Conway and 'Bam.' But once he took to the subject, there was no stopping
him. Classicists were encouraged to offer translations in their own time for
what was known as the 'Versions Book.' Ted's contributions outnumber all
others and are more than double those of Gilbert Murray, the second most
prolific and the leading classicist of the time. In terms of quality they surpass
succeeding generations of professional classicists.[28] It was also at the age of

---

[25] *Autobiographical sketch.*
[26] Ibid.
[27] Ibid.
[28] I am grateful to Alan Woolley of Merchant Taylors' for this information.

sixteen or seventeen that Ted was encouraged 'to read pretty thoroughly the classics of English literature' and 'became an omnivorous reader of current popular novels'[29] – Galsworthy being a particular favourite. It was unquestionably this combination of classics and fiction that laid the foundation for the extraordinary dexterity with which he could deploy the English language. At seventeen he won the general Greek scholarship prize, a prize for Greek verse (work done out of school) and a 'James Greaves' English literature prize.[30] He then sat for university entry. The successful products of Merchant Taylors' had invariably been destined for Oxford but, due to Nairn's unresolved dispute with St. John's College, Ted was instead encouraged to compete for a place at Cambridge. His father had studied mathematics at St. Catharine's. Ted later claimed he chose Trinity 'because it was the largest and the best college in the university';[31] it was no doubt Nairn – formerly a Fellow – who had convinced him that this was so.

At the age of seventeen and a half on 6 December 1909 he set off with the devoted Amelia as self-appointed chaperone to sit for his exams on the following day. They arrived in a city only in name: in fact, it was a small, provincial market town, paved with wooden blocks and noisy with horse-drawn vehicles pursued by small boys who scooped up the dung for the gardeners growing vegetables in the environs.[32] Despite the smog – when a northeasterly was not blowing through – Cambridge, and Trinity in particular, none the less stood as an impressive sight as an isolated outpost of learning in the depressed agriculture of the fens.

On return home Ted soon received good news from the genial and eccentric Master of Trinity, the bearded and burly Reverend Henry Montagu Butler, that he had won a classical exhibition worth forty pounds. It was, Butler informed him, 'only by the narrowest possible margin' that he had missed election to a full scholarship, 'and only then in the face of great competition'.[33] Ted did not intend coming up so soon anyway, and he was advised that he could probably secure a full scholarship at the examinations in the following year. In February Merchant Taylors' Company granted him a supplementary exhibition of thirty pounds per year.[34] And, finally, at examination in December 1910 he succeeded in winning the full scholarship. He received a flattering letter of congratulation from Montagu Butler: 'You have passed a capital examination, especially, though by no means exclusively, in Composition, and we have had great pleasure in electing you to an Entrance Scholarship. Your work was so good all round that I shall be by no means

[29] Ibid.
[30] Merchant Taylors' School, *Election of Scholars, 1909*.
[31] *Autobiographical sketch*.
[32] Tressilian Charles Nicholas (1888–1989), speech at a dinner at Trinity in 1988: *Cambridge Review*, June 1990, vol. III, no. 2309.
[33] Montagu Butler to Carr, 18 December 1909: *Carr Papers*. These are now deposited at Birmingham University.
[34] Letter from the Merchant Taylors' Company, 18 February 1910: ibid.

surprised if in time a University Scholarship falls to your lot. We all liked your English essay.'[35]

The additional year required thus formed the triumphal conclusion of Ted's school career and the opening of far wider horizons. In sport he was never as successful as in his studies. He played Fives for the school, mainly at doubles in the second IV. By May 1911, however, whether because of his rapid growth in height (well over six feet) or sudden loss of interest he 'Lost his form entirely.' 'Plays with his arm and not his wrist,' the team captain wrote. 'Seems to take a jump at the ball, often with the consequence that he misses it entirely.'[36] As a consequence he had to be dropped at the end of that season. On the Fives court his attention may have wandered, but where the exercise of words was concerned he was unfailingly quick on his feet. As president of the debating society – a somewhat light-hearted affair, more wit than substance – he took an active part in its proceedings. On 2 March 1911 he had proposed the motion 'That this House regards the influence of the modern stage as pernicious.' His tongue in cheek performance earned him a backhanded accolade in *The Taylorian* which indicated that his somewhat malicious sense of humour was by now well established: 'This [motion] was proposed by Mr. CARR, who showed clearly how much can be accomplished by use of abuse.'[37]

Ted was equally deadly in political debate. In January 1910 the Liberal Party which he supported had regained power but owed its continuing existence to the support of the votes of the Irish Nationalists in the Commons, who of course demanded Home Rule in return for their assistance. Asquith's government also sought to introduce a bill limiting the power of the Lords to veto legislation approved by the Commons. It was clear to the opponents of Irish independence that if that constitutional change succeeded, Irish Home Rule would then make it through Parliament. Speaking for the Unionists, Member of Parliament Lonsdale warned that 'any attempt to force Nationalist rule upon Ulster would be met by the most determined resistance . . . If this means civil war,' he added for good measure, 'the responsibility will not rest with them but with the Government . . . .'[38] In the parallel debate at Merchant Taylors' on 16 March Ted's Liberal credentials were on open display: he was avowedly in favour of independence. He accused the opposition – in the form of fellow pupil Mr Wade – 'of laying all kinds of charges – savagery, barbarity, disloyalty – at Ireland's door'. He 'then went on to deal with the question of religious animosity, saying that it was rather the Protestants who persecuted the Roman Catholics than *vice-versa*. Finally, Home Rule would not mean separation of Ireland from England, but a restoration of Irish nationality.'[39] His ideals were firmly established.

---

[35] Butler to Carr, 17 December 1910: ibid.
[36] *The Taylorian*, May 1911, p. 185.
[37] Ibid., p. 138.
[38] 6 February 1911: Hansard, *Parliamentary Debates*, 5th Series, vol. XXI, House of Commons, 1911, col. 84.
[39] *The Taylorian*, p. 139.

That summer was a double celebration. First there was George V's coronation on 22 June, for which Ted composed an ode that won him the Merchant Taylors' Company Medal: a truly dreadful piece of royalist panegyric, very much a product of its time, echoing the jingoism of Edwardian England, but showing a certain technical virtuosity in Latin, shades of Virgil and Trajan, and occasionally also real literary quality.[40] Ted swept the board at prize day[41] and, as head monitor – a position that went to the best regarded winner of a university scholarship – he delivered the Latin Oration congratulating the King and Queen on their coming coronation and welcoming the colonial representatives visiting England in honour of the event. He then took the leading role in Sheridan's *Scenes from St Patrick's Day*.[42]

There was absolutely nothing at this stage to suggest that Carr was anything other than the model product of a Victorian education, committed to God, King and Country. Indeed, for all the dramatic changes that were to occur during the years that followed, in some fundamental sense throughout his life he remained 'a good Victorian at heart'.[43] For his generation – at least from the middle and upper classes – this was a golden age. Over half a century later he reflected how the

doctrines of liberalism and individualism held virtually unchallenged sway. In Britain, progress towards their realization was the core of the now derided 'Whig interpretation of history.' The standard of living of the 'workers', of the depressed classes, was slowly rising. Beyond the civilized pale, primitive peoples benefited from the benevolent and nurturing supremacy of the white race. By the turn of the century some cracks had begun to appear in the seemingly solid structure. But these did not matter too much.

The world seemed a good place and was getting better. 'This country was leading it in the right direction. There were, no doubt, abuses but they were being, or would be, dealt with. Changes were needed, but change was automatically for the better. Decadence was a puzzling and paradoxical concept.'[44]

At the time Ted went up to Trinity in October 1911 this stable world was still intact. But the forces undermining it were reaching their zenith. In areas well beyond his limited range momentous discoveries were being made. Nineteen eleven was the year Rutherford (then still at Manchester) realized that the atom contained a nucleus. It was also the year Niels Bohr arrived at Trinity as an advanced student to work under J.J. Thomson at the Cavendish laboratories on Free School Lane. Only two years earlier the Frenchman Blériot had accomplished the first flight across the Channel in an aeroplane. And it was only a matter of time before these and other achievements were

---

40 Ibid., July 1911, pp. 202–3.
41 Merchant Taylors' School, *Election of Scholars, 1911*.
42 Merchant Taylors' School, *Order of Speeches, 1911*.
43 Carr to Tamara Deutscher, 17 May 1974.
44 *Autobiographical sketch*.

harnessed to the engine of war. In the wake of the Agadir crisis a month
after Carr arrived in Cambridge the Intelligence Department of the War
Office was busy in East Anglia making a minute return of anything of use in
time of war – horses, sites for camps, wells, farms and so forth. Some students
were to the forefront in anticipating disaster, though doubtless they were a
tiny despised minority.[45] On 31 October 1911 the Union Society debated the
motion: 'That in view of the serious nature of Anglo–German relations, this
House views with the utmost concern the recent appointment to the
Admiralty [of Winston Churchill]'.[46] Yet most, including Carr, considered
their future predictably promising, as it had been for their predecessors for
the better part of a century. Indeed, on arrival in Cambridge in 1911 he took
no interest in politics. 'The period of the great controversies was over.'[47]

That October there were fewer freshmen than usual, though Trinity
received the same number as the year before: 198.[48] Scholars as ever had first
pick of the rooms. Carr chose Great Court, a magnificent expanse since
Tudor times, crowned by an elaborate fountain at its centre. Later on – in
1914 – the millionaire heir apparent Nubar Gulbenkian acquired rooms just
above. Carr later recalled 'the kitchen porters staggering upstairs with the vast
trays of food for the banquets which he gave'.[49] Indeed, Gulbenkian got into
deep trouble when a visitor turned up unexpectedly to find champagne bot-
tles stacked high outside his rooms and reported this to his father, who
promptly reminded him that he was there for an education, not expensive
entertainment. Trinity was thus dominated by the upper classes and towered
over the rest of the university, as it still does, in terms of numbers and as a
result proved a rather anonymous experience which was only partly offset by
the creation of the *Trinity Magazine* in February 1914.[50] Hot and cold running
water had yet to appear, let alone central heating, far less women (beyond the
restricted confines of the new colleges for ladies). Students were forbidden to
'give, or join in giving, or take part in, an entertainment at a tavern or pub
room, without the permission of their College Tutor'. Gates were locked at 10
pm. Dinner in Hall was compulsory five nights a week. Proctors, flanked by
Bulldogs, were required to enforce the wearing of 'academical dress' and
prevent students smoking when so dressed. They were empowered to stop
members of the University 'engaging in any pursuits or practices which are
objectionable as being cruel, dangerous, liable to produce gambling, inconsistent with gentlemanly behaviour, or detrimental to good order'.[51]

Tuition or supervision was still a fairly recent innovation. 'Undergraduates

---

[45] *Cambridge Evening News*, 25 November 1911.
[46] Ibid., 1 November 1911.
[47] *Autobiographical sketch.*
[48] *Cambridge Evening News*, 7 October 1911.
[49] 'Note for the Secretary of the British Academy'. In the author's possession.
[50] Editorial, *Trinity Magazine*, no. 1, 25 February 1914.
[51] *The Student's Handbook to the University and Colleges of Cambridge*, Cambridge 1911, pp. 54–5.

were less looked after than now; a man saw his tutor twice a term, when he came up and when he went down, and that was that.'[52] Lectures were the dominant mode of instruction, though numbers in attendance were often small. Social life was conducted in sets, with scholars, for example, or oarsmen, congregating to the mutual exclusion of outsiders. 'There was no bar, no common rooms; one couldn't even have breakfast or lunch in hall but ordered them in one's room.'[53] It was a very competitive academic world in which Carr blossomed. As a freshman he distinguished himself in the examination for the university scholarship, and he was immensely excited by the highly stimulating intellectual milieu; above all, by 'the most powerful intellectual machine I've ever seen in action, A.E. Housman, whose effortless handling of obscure classical texts I enormously admired and should have liked to emulate.'[54]

Housman was an extraordinary figure. He had been appointed Kennedy Professor of Latin and Fellow of Trinity in the summer of 1911. The Vice-Chancellor of Cambridge described Housman as a 'brilliant' student from Oxford. In fact he had been a disaster. As a result he found employment in the upper reaches of the patent office (as did Einstein). But by a superhuman determination to succeed, he transformed himself into the leading classicist in the country and within a very short span of time shot from total obscurity to a Chair at London University and then Cambridge.[55] Any achievement has a price, however, and this magnificent achievement was bought at high personal cost. On his death *Trinity College Magazine* – anticipating an image projected on Carr in later life – described Housman as 'a remote and forbidding figure, a monument of learning, fastidious taste and embittered reserve'.[56]

Carr never entertained any illusion about acquiring intellectual intimacy with such a giant. But throughout his life Housman remained – as he did for others – the model intellect. One who attended Housman's lectures subsequently described them as 'austere both in matter and in manner . . . certainly nobody with tastes at all akin to his own could witness that easy command of the relevant learning, that lucid exposition and dispassionate judgement, without setting before himself a new standard of scholarship'.[57] Another former student, Enoch Powell, has described the manner in which Housman 'could indeed at times scarcely master his emotion sufficiently to read aloud the verses of Horace or Propertius, Catullus or Virgil, upon which he was about to comment'.[58] And Carr was at this stage of his life very

[52] Interview with P. Scott.
[53] Quoted in M. Kaplanoff, 'E.H. Carr – A Profile', *Trinity Review*, Lent 1973.
[54] *Autobiographical sketch.*
[55] R. Graves, *A.E. Housman: The Scholar-Poet*, Oxford 1981.
[56] Obituary, *Trinity College Magazine*, 30 April 1936.
[57] A. Gow, *A.E. Housman: A Sketch*, Cambridge 1936, p. 43.
[58] E. Powell, 'A.E. Housman', *Independent*, supplement, 27 January 1980, p. 46.

much taken with the asethetic side to classics. But what he acquired from
Housman were two rather different characteristics: a 'rather pedantic addiction to the minutiae of accuracy and precision' and a 'flair for cutting
through a load of nonsense and getting straight to the point'.[59] It is no accident that Housman's dictum 'accuracy is a duty and not a virtue'[60] found
repeated expression in Carr's advice to students and others when he finally
became a professional historian. Two other features they noticeably held in
common were a delight in irony and Housman's irresistible urge to mix acid
with his ink. Last but not least, as we have seen, Housman's formidable
reputation for aloof reserve and arrogance hid an extraordinary intensity of
emotion – something else that he and Carr shared. As Carr noted some sixty
years later: 'man (even A.E. Housman) cannot live by intellect alone.'[61]
The sense of not just intellectual but also emotional affinity with Housman
thus grew all the more as the years gained upon him.

Michaelmas 1911 was thus the culmination of great anticipation: Carr's
horizons were limitless. His youthful ambition and dedication were intimately
tied to a driving belief in progress, a belief strikingly apparent in the poem he
wrote in Latin hexameter for the Montagu Butler prize, which he won in
1912. The title issued for the competition at the end of May 1911 was 'Pennis
non homini datis' ('. . . on wings not given to man'),[62] a quotation from Horace
which referred to the myth of Daedalus, whose son Icarus perished in a fool-
hardy attempt to fly on wings designed by his father. Writing in the style of
Lucretius, Carr briefly recapitulated the story of Icarus, rapidly dismissing the
fable as unlikely, and pointing out, with typical bluntness, that in any case
Icarus did not get very far, which served him right. This was his prologue to
describing man's successive attempts at artificial flight, written just two years
after Blériot's great achievement. These attempts led to many lives lost, as in
war, where the besiegers who were knocked off the fortress walls and killed at
least formed a pile of corpses that others could mount to attain the ultimate
goal. So, too, did they deserve to be honoured. Men saw that clouds and
gases could rise; so they filled balloons with gas. But there were dangers; they
got burned or were buffeted by wind. So they took birds as a model. Motion
was required to stay aloft; so engines were needed. They fitted wings and a
rudder to take advantage of wind pressure. Thus, he concluded, there is no
limit to what man can attain, or the heights he can reach:

> . . . Non generi humano divinitus esse negatum
> Quicquam, aut terrigenis iter intercludier ullum.

Apart from his studies, Carr's time was spent in excited discussion, most

---

[59] Autobiographical sketch.
[60] Gow, Housman, p. 32.
[61] Carr to Tamara Deutscher, 5 October 1974.
[62] Cambridge University Reporter, 30 May 1911.

especially with another young undergraduate, Eric Farmer, who alone in the college was reading moral sciences (philosophy). With Farmer Carr 'discussed the meaning of life', and 'first heard the name of Hegel, on whose behalf McTaggart was conducting a popular rear-guard action against Russell and Moore'.[63] Whether it was his friendship with Farmer, who was homosexual, or with someone else, male or female, an emotional relationship grew into unreciprocated devotion, an infatuation never to be consummated and fraught with frustration, as the Latin epigram Carr composed for the Sir William Browne's Medal – awarded in 1912 – indicates:

'Either Caesar or No One'
To N.
Lest you ask me, my dearest, of how many lovers I am willing
to be one,
Receive this and store it up in your mind, N.,
I don't care whether you are holding on to three or three times
three thousand;
Either I shall be your one and only lover, or I shall be none.

To be in love with someone who has other lovers is stressful enough. But to be thus in love and simultaneously subjected to the unwanted attentions of a dominant maiden aunt threw Carr into the kind of emotional turmoil that, together with excessive hours of study, neglect of physical exercise, and the rather unwholesome damp Cambridge winter, ended in collapse with a severe case of rheumatic fever by the end of that first term.

His recovery was also impeded by the emotional storm that had broken upon him. Over a year after the illness was contracted, he was still hors de combat, convalescing in the Lake District. Montagu Butler wrote to him: 'The return of the Examination for the University Scholarship has led me to think rather specially of you. It must have been something of a trial to be kept from the Field of Battle in which you distinguished yourself so much last year as a Freshman.' He went on: 'I do hope you are getting solidly as well as rapidly stronger, and that the return of Spring in a few weeks may enable you thoroughly to enjoy hours in the sun. Whatever you do, don't *over*work with the brain while you are at all below your full powers. It is one of the worst mistakes we can make in our early years.'[64]

Not until the eminent physician Sir Bertrand (later Lord) Dawson was consulted did an improvement set in. Appointed physician-extraordinary to King George V, Dawson had exceptional clinical instinct and diagnostic ability, particularly in cases where physical and emotional problems were closely intertwined. 'The power to penetrate the patient's mind, to help that mind to unfold and to perceive where the burden presses most heavily – all that is part of diagnosis,' he wrote. 'The resulting confidence and inspiration in the

---

[63] *Autobiographical sketch.*
[64] Butler to Carr, 18 January 1913: *Carr Papers.*

patient's mind are part of the treatment.'[65] Aunt Amelia was the root of the problem. Once this was understood, Carr's recovery was certain, though he was not able to return to Trinity until Michaelmas 1914, after more than two years' absence. By then his friend Farmer had graduated and gone. Carr never saw him again until – unexpectedly – they met at a Trinity feast for old members in the early fifties.

The return to Trinity had prompted the critical decision to break with 'the woman': a decision that must have caused great anguish but to which he was driven by the determination to maintain good health; and, having reached that decision, he carried it through with surgical dispassion and precision. Amelia remained in the family household at Crouch End until Jessie died of cancer in June 1922. Francis was not assertive enough to demand her departure. That task fell to Ted, but it was a move supported by the rest of the family. She maintained contact with them until she eventually died on 15 September 1939, still exerting a distant pull on Ted's emotional stability even from beyond the grave, with devastating consequences for his married life. Many years later, in his seventies, he recalled his childhood and the stifling emotional impact of aunt Amelia: 'I suffered from a surfeit of the wrong kind of emotion, and have failed to establish a balanced emotional relation in which I could give as well as take . . . .'[66] On her death he duly disposed of her possessions. All that appears in his diary, on 12 November, is the laconic note: 'Looked through my old letters to the woman.' The letters were, unfortunately, meticulously destroyed.

The Cambridge to which Carr returned had altered dramatically. It was no longer so detached from the outside world. The magic was gone. War had broken out in August 1914 when Germany invaded Belgium in order to strike at the heart of France, thereby prompting British intervention. Hitherto, the very idea of a large-scale war had been to Carr and his generation 'an unthinkable monstrosity.'[67] 'I cannot feel that we in this island are in any serious degree responsible for the wave of madness wh[ich] has swept the mind of Chistendom,' wrote First Lord of the Admiralty Winston Churchill. 'No one can measure the consequences . . . we all drift on in a kind of cataleptic trance.'[68] In Cambridge the number of students dropped from 3600 to 1700. At Trinity the majestic Nevile's Court was turned into a field hospital. The Officers' Training Corps drilled in Great Court and there were troops billeted in some colleges. It was expected that the Germans might invade and that, should they do so, they would head for Cambridge because of its location at the centre of the eastern railway network. There was also, of course, a blackout: gas was no longer lighting the streets or courts, and candles illuminated

---

[65] Presidential address to the Medical Society of London, 16 October 1922: quoted in F. Watson, *Dawson of Penn*, London 1950, p. 11.

[66] Carr to Betty Behrens, 26 July 1966. In the author's possession.

[67] Carr, *From Napoleon to Stalin and Other Essays*, London 1980, p. 20.

[68] Churchill to Clementine Churchill, 28 July 1914: R. Churchill, *Winston S. Churchill*, companion vol. 2, part 3, 1911–1914, Boston 1914, p. 1989.

high table. Roads into Cambridge were blocked to prevent cars providing guidance to incoming Zeppelins. The war was thus never very far away. Sir John French had told Trinity Fellows most emphatically: '*When* they invade us, Cambridge will be the first place occupied, on account of the railways.'[69]

Undergraduates like Carr 'were left free to carry on their normal activities'.[70] He was lucky. His rheumatic fever had left him with an uncertain heart and that alone saved him from the tragic fate of his contemporaries in the barbed wire and blood-soaked mud of Flanders. He plunged back into his work with renewed vigour. He won the coveted Porson Prize for Greek verse translation and the Craven Scholarship all in those first few months after his return. 'It was what I expected from your first Examination for our Entrance Scholarship and, if possible, still more from the time you sent in that brilliant Platonic Dialogue for our College Prize', wrote Butler on the evening of 9 February 1915.[71] Some of Carr's essays have survived. They show an extraordinary capacity for digesting vast amounts of new information and turning it into a compelling narrative; independence of mind, boldness of judgement, a compelling logic; all wholly divorced from any expression of moral sentiment. For instance, he already showed a healthy – or, as Sir Isaiah Berlin would have said, unhealthy – respect for power. Witness these comments on the problem of reform in ancient Rome:

> The truth was clearly revealed that the only path to real reform was the concentration of greater powers than the constitution then allowed in the hands of a single individual. His [Tiberius Gracchus's] assassination also clearly revealed that such an individual must be backed by physical as well as moral force.

One might almost be reading about Lenin. Consider the following from an essay on armed force in Roman politics:

> It is a mistake to contrast Sulla and Caesar as reactionary and reformer; both were imperialists. It was the logical result of the introduction of force into Roman politics: civil violence must give place to the more powerful brute strength of an army, and a military monarchy is the inevitable sequel.

'Logic' and 'inevitability' were thus already staples in the Carr lexicon.

Carr's interest in politics and history had been relatively slow to mature compared with his mastery of language and literature. After the fireworks of Liberal reform and Lloyd George's battle with the landed interest, his interest in politics had waned. But his interest in history, hitherto never that strong, began to make headway as a result of the training he received in

---

[69] Henry Jackson, Vice-Master of Trinity, to Sir George Trevelyan, 18 October 1914: R. St. John Parry, *Henry Jackson, O.M.: Vice-Master of Trinity College & Regius Professor of Greek in the University of Cambridge – A Memoir*, Cambridge 1926, p. 96.

[70] N. Gulbenkian, *Pantaraxia*, London 1965, p. 55.

[71] Butler to Carr, 9 February 1915.

Greek and Roman history under 'a rather undistinguished classics don, who specialized in the Persian wars.' The don taught how 'Herodotus' account . . . not only contained a lot of pure mythology, but was shaped and moulded by his attitude to the Peloponnesian War, which was going on at the time he wrote. This,' Carr noted many years later, 'was a fascinating revelation and gave me my first understanding of what history was about.'[72] And it is this sense of the nature of history, so firmly set within him, that re-emerges from the distant past in the lectures he gave half a century later and which some conservative minds in their ignorance wrongly mistook for new-fangled radicalism from a diehard troublemaker.

The full range of insight and imagination appeared in his essays on such subjects as Plato and poetry. There exists an outstanding essay on the 'Influence of Religion on Greece.' It begins with a sweeping judgement of the type he always revelled in and unfolds in an effortless sequence of argument. 'If you can write such essays in examination,' his supervisor wrote, 'they ought to go a long way to gaining you distinction.' Indeed, it occasioned no surprise when, after sitting part two of the examinations in classics between 29 May and 2 June 1916, he took a first division with special distinction in the first class of the Tripos (historical section), after what amounted to only seven terms' work.

In retrospect the years that followed appeared wasted: had it not been for the war, Carr might have moved on to a fellowship in classics and remained at Trinity thereafter.[73] But the realities of the outer world intervened to remove him from the cloistered confines of academic life.

---

[72] *Autobiographical sketch.* Unfortunately there were too many dons who fitted Carr's description to identify who this was.

[73] In conversation with the author.

2

'Temporary Clerk' at the Foreign Office

Carr had never worried about the future. He knew he did not want to enter commerce, and he was not particularly attracted to any of the professions. 'Top classical scholars went into the top ranks of the civil service'; this was therefore not an unlikely destination. 'But I certainly never thought of the Foreign Office,' he confessed. 'My world was wholly insular, and uninterested in foreign countries. As a boy, I think I was once taken on a holiday trip to Boulogne.'[1] The war changed everything. Unfit for the military because rheumatic fever had weakened his heart, but eminently suitable for public service, Carr was among those drafted by John Tilley, the Chief Clerk of the Foreign Office, to compensate for the loss of those who had left for the front. The date was 5 June 1916.[2]

These and additional needs turned the wartime Foreign Office from an exclusive club, entry into which required a personal recommendation from the secretary of state, into a career open to all talents. This innovation did not go unchallenged. Tilley recalled that 'there were some of the older men who could not conceive of any good coming from a clerk who was not in the regular service'.[3] Indeed, one senior diplomat told the Royal Commission which reported in 1914 that the property qualification for entry should be maintained, on the grounds that the

> primary qualification for the Diplomatic Service is a capacity to deal on terms of equality with considerable persons and their words and works. Sometimes, very rarely, this capacity is given, on its highest form, by something which is hardly examinable – by very great intellectual powers. Ordinarily, however, this capacity is a result of nurture in an atmosphere of independence. Unfortunately, it is scarcely too much to say that the present constitution of society provides this atmosphere of independence only where there is financial independence. In a

---

[1] *Autobiographical sketch.*
[2] Tilley to Carr, 5 June 1916: *Carr Papers.*
[3] Sir John Tilley and S. Gaselee, *The Foreign Office*, London 1933, p. 180.

very few cases freedom of mind and character is achieved elsewhere, but then a great price, not measurable by money, has to be paid for it – how great a price only those who have paid it know.[4]

Similarly, in attempting to rebut the implication of the report that favouritism had operated in selection – witness the number of old Etonians in the service – Samuel Hoare, then still a diplomat but later Foreign Secretary, argued that 'If foreign policy is to be democratized, it is not by turning municipal scholars into Ambassadors that the end will be reached,' adding that 'If men with a certain kind of upbringing and education make the best diplomats, it is their services which the country should seek for its diplomatic affairs.'[5]

Such snobbery, so smoothly rationalized, weighed heavily against those who entered the Office in wartime. And it was not merely a matter of attitude. The assumption that members would have a private income continued to affect remuneration. Those who served at home were paid only 'enough to live on at a pinch'.[6] These aspects of the service were slow to change; far too slow for Carr, as it turned out. Elsewhere, however, the war had a more marked effect. It altered the distribution of power and responsibilities within the Office. Whereas prior to hostilities 'it was still the place where no junior clerk was supposed to concern himself with foreign policy or do much more than file papers and index the "Confidential Print", in the same sort of clothes as would be worn for an afternoon call in Belgravia' – 'stiff collars and cuffs, morning coat and striped trousers' – the outbreak of war meant that even the most junior clerk was now faced with substantial responsibilities. Sir Laurence Collier, a contemporary, recalls that 'we juniors had the chance of our lives'.[7] The Irishman Sir Owen O'Malley, also a junior, fondly remembers 'when we took the whole of the Norwegian mercantile marine in charter – a million and a half tons deadweight at seventy shillings a ton deadweight per month for an indefinite period. No bloody nonsense about having been at Radley and Magdalen about that I can assure you.'[8]

Apart from the War Department and the ciphering room, almost all the rest of the Office's work was done in the newly formed Contraband Department, a polite euphemism for the unit headed by Sir Robert Cecil that conducted economic warfare against the central powers. The department took up three vast reception rooms. As one participant recalls: 'The big reception hall on the first floor at the top of the stairs, now known as the "Locarno Room", became the Third Room of the Contraband Department, roaring

---

[4] Reservation by Arthur Boutwood: *Royal Commission on the Civil Service, Fifth Report of the Commissioners*, Command 7748, London 1914, p. 43.

[5] Ibid., p. 46.

[6] Ibid., p. 183.

[7] Sir Laurence Collier, 'The Old Foreign Office', *Blackwood's Magazine*, September 1973, vol. 312, no. 1883, pp. 256–61.

[8] Quoted in Z. Steiner, 'The Foreign Office and the War', *British Foreign Policy under Sir Edward Grey*, ed. F. Hinsley, Cambridge 1977.

with typewriters and full of people rushing about in a very undiplomatic state of hurry.'[9] Carr joined at a salary of two hundred pounds a year, 'almost a starvation wage' in middle-class terms.[10] 'It is not at present possible to state for what length of time your services will be required', Tilley told him in the letter of appointment dated 5 June 1916. But he could scarcely imagine that he would still be in the Office twenty years hence.

It was here, in the Northern Section of the Department, that Carr first came into contact with Russia, a major ally in the war against the central powers; his job was to protect the supply routes that ran by way of Sweden. It was a very minor role. As he noted in a minute written later in December 1917: 'Until recently the Contraband Department had little interest in Russia, except from the transit point of view, i.e. their sole object was to get goods into Russia, not keep them out.'[11] Indeed, it must have been more than a little deflating, while others were dealing with great issues of state and, still more, proving their courage on the front line, to have to deal with the export of items such as scotch herring, or 660 tons of pure olive oil (for use in Russian churches), in correspondence with an unlikely department called Explosives and Supply, Oil and Fats Branch. Indeed, his inability to tolerate fools gladly soon emerged in Carr's minutes. The Rubber and Tin Committee seemed incapable of coming to grips with the problem of rubber supplies – caught up in Norway and blocked by Sweden, whose neutrality favoured Germany – from transit to allied Russia: 'I am afraid,' he wrote in great irritation early in December 1916, 'we left it to the Ctee's intelligence to realize that if there had been any possibility of transiting this rubber, we should never have proposed any other course.'[12]

The revolutions in Russia saved the day, however, relieving Carr of boredom and throwing up a challenge. Tsarist Russia proved the weakest link in the allied chain. In March 1917 the monarchy collapsed after bread riots in the capital, Petrograd. Under the provisional government the Russians remained allies. Some in the west, however, looked with horror on the overthrow of the old autocracy. In the Contraband Department Carr was once again faced with the bureaucratic myopia of the Rubber and Tin Committee, who wanted to reverse the previously favourable treatment accorded Russia in the supply of strategic materials. 'This is a matter of our general policy towards Russia,' he wrote. 'As far as I am aware, we have not been adopting a more cautious and less generous attitude towards Russia in consequence of recent developments.'[13] But the price paid by the provisional government for maintaining participation in this unpopular war was a further revolution on 7 November

---

[9] Quoted in Steiner, 'The Foreign Office and the War', p. 521.

[10] Department of Information, Intelligence Bureau, 25 February 1918 and Committee on Staffs Report, 3 August 1918: *FO* 366/787.

[11] Minute dated 14 December 1917 on Sir C. Greene (Tokyo) to Foreign Office, 11 December 1917: *FO* 382/1421.

[12] Minute dated 9 December 1917: *FO* 382/843.

[13] Minute dated 22 May 1917: *FO* 382/1420.

1917 when Lenin and the Bolsheviks seized power. This was a critical turning-point in world history. As Carr acknowledged: 'it was the Russian revolution which decisively gave me a sense of history which I have never lost, and which turned me – long, long afterwards – into a historian.'[14]

At the time, however, the level of ignorance was so high that few took these dramatic events seriously. He recalls:

> At the moment of the revolution, a Russian trade delegation was visiting London, accompanied by a commercial attaché to the British Embassy in Petrograd, Peters, with whom I had several talks in the first few days of the revolution. Peters, like everyone else, believed that this was all a flash in the pan, and that the Bolsheviks could not last for more than a week or so – till reinforcements arrived. From the first, owing to some *esprit de contradiction*, I refused to believe this. I studied eagerly every bit of news, and the longer the Bolsheviks held out, the more convinced I became that they had come to stay. It was a lucky hunch. I'm not sure how far I saw this at the time as a challenge to western society. But I certainly regarded the western reaction to it as narrow, blind and stupid. I had some vague impression of the revolutionary views of Lenin and Trotsky, but knew nothing of Marxism: I'd probably never heard of Marx.[15]

The Bolsheviks were taking Russia out of the war, and not only did they survive, but before long the British were laying plans for military intervention to overthrow the regime. Carr's sympathies were at this stage most definitely not with the Bolsheviks. The war against Germany was at its height, and Lenin had arrived in Russia with German assistance. The British Government had thus by December 1917 launched a de facto blockade. An enquiry from the makers of pumps and pumping machinery in Wolverhampton prompted Carr to advise that 'in the existing circumstances we should prefer that they should not accept or execute any further orders . . . for the present'.[16] His task had thus shifted from trying to get goods into Russia to trying to keep them out, a job that he had no qualms about undertaking. The Swedish Government, which had previously done its best to sabotage aid to Russia, now argued that Finnish food shortages justified the shipment of provisions to Finland. Carr regarded this as 'a piece of impertinence'[17] – in the past the Finns had supplied the Germans – though he was unceremoniously overruled. But further news soon came to his aid and in a minute written at the end of the year he wrote: 'We now definitely know . . . that most of the foodstuffs which we were kind enough to allow to be forwarded from Sweden to Finland have fallen into the hands of the Bolsheviks.' 'We do not want to feed the Bolsheviks, and if they are able to lay hands on any considerable consignments, they will probably pass on the surplus at a good price to their

---

[14] *Autobiographical sketch.*
[15] Ibid.
[16] Minute dated 21 December 1917: *FO* 382/1420.
[17] Minute dated 19 December 1917 on Wrangel (Swedish Legation in London) to Cecil, 15 December 1917: *FO* 382/1421.

German friends', he concluded.[18] And to those who argued humanitarian reasons for sending food aid to Russia, he gave a characteristically ruthless retort: 'I do not know much about our Russian policy, but I take it that while being outwardly polite to the Bolsheviks we should be only too glad to see them collapse. The thing most likely to cause their collapse is I take it hunger in Petrograd and Moscow, and if we supply food there, we shall be simply defeating our own ends.'[19]

The October Revolution put to an end British efforts to funnel trade to Russia. It took much less work to keep commerce out than find the means to lure it in. From late November 1917 Carr's time was thus less than fully engaged on Russian business; he was known to have an enormous capacity for hard work and since the Contraband Department's remit was almost impossible to implement with existing resources – control of all the trade routes in and out of western Europe and beyond – he was quickly deployed to oversee the Commission for Relief in Belgium (CRB) along with his residual Russian duties. The Commission had been set up by the allied powers as a humanitarian means for providing supplies to forestall hardship in occupied western Europe. It operated on a selective basis that aimed both to avoid supplementing the German war effort and to sustain the overall blockade. This necessitated diplomatic contact with the Germans, who were inevitably interested in encouraging the resulting shipments as a means of breaking the blockade; the difficulty was that of ensuring that when the aid came into occupied Europe, the Germans would not then appropriate native resources and use the aid to supplement what they had taken from the occupied population. Proposals for supply would be sent to the Commission's director for Europe in London, William Poland, who would then submit them to the Contraband Department for approval. Carr took initial responsibility for those decisions taken in the name of the secretary of state. His minutes in the CRB files show both his dry sense of humour and his hard-nosed approach to matters of state.

Regular meetings were held in Paris between British, French and Belgian representatives to coordinate policy. In January 1918 a decision was reached to cut the line of credit to the Belgians. No proper minutes appear to have been kept. The Belgians then wrote claiming no such decision had been made. Carr commented: 'The Paris conferences seem to be conducted, & important decisions taken, in a style for which it would be hard to find a parallel outside comic opera or a school debating society.'[20] The Americans were the ultimate suppliers of relief aid, and Herbert Hoover was the real authority across the Atlantic; but the British jealously kept the ultimate decisions to themselves. The Germans were giving preferential treatment to Belgians working in their interests, thus breaking the spirit of the understanding on

---

[18] Minute dated 31 December 1917 on Sir E. Howard to Balfour, 13 December 1917: ibid.
[19] Minute for Sir Eyre Crowe, 29 December 1917: ibid.
[20] Minute dated 31 January 1918: *FO* 382/2024.

relief. The British planned to protest to Berlin and then take counter-measures, which would inevitably mean cutting supplies to those Belgians favoured by the German authorities. The State Department offered no objection but questioned the suggestion of retaliation by the British. Carr's response was suitably dismissive and revealed London's customary response to US preferences: 'The double position of Mr. Hoover makes it difficult for the Americans to express decisive views on points of this sort, & it is therefore usually best to proceed without consulting them . . . I don't like the suggestion of bluff without intending to carry out.'[21] This position became policy two weeks later.

Carr took a similarly unyielding stance vis-à-vis the Netherlands, a neutral power. The Dutch always resented the trans-shipment of supplies destined for Belgium through their territory. The fact that they were less deserving because they had not been subjected to attack and occupied had evidently escaped their attention. On 10 April 1918 the Dutch minister of agriculture, Posthuma – not one of London's favourites – threatened not to allow supplies through if his country were not given half of the shipment. Carr's response to the ultimatum was vehement. He minuted:

> If we once permit the Dutch to use transit of C.R.B. goods as a lever & a bargaining instrument against us, we shall place ourselves in exactly the same helpless position in which we stood vis-à-vis Sweden at the time when we had to transit goods to Russia.
>
> If on the other hand we take a firm stand, I believe that Dutch public opinion which is I understand genuinely interested in the Relief will discountenance a policy of stoppage & compel the Govt. to continue to let supplies through.
>
> We shall undoubtedly have to face strong opposition, but if once we submit to this threat & make concessions our whole Dutch policy is going to be paralysed.
>
> I think we must *at once* give the Admty. [Admiralty] instructions to divert all Relief ships & not allow them to proceed to R'dam [Rotterdam]: *then* tell the Belgians, French & U.S. & point out necessity of taking a firm stand & putting out of court once for all the idea that we are prepared to admit Relief supplies to be a subject of bargaining.[22]

He took a similarly tough line with respect to the Serbs. He had objected to cattle being shipped to occupied Poland because the Germans intended to consume the milk drawn from the cows that were to be sent, but through lack of coordination and the gullibility of the British ambassador in Copenhagen the deal was done before London could step in and stop it. Proposals for shipments to Serbia triggered the following response: '. . . if we are unable to put a stop to serious abuses in the case of relief in Belgium, which is a highly civilized country with ample means of communication, near at hand, & with one

---

[21] Minute dated 1 March 1918 on Reading (Paris) to London, 25 February 1918: ibid.
[22] Minute dated 11 April 1918: *FO* 382/2026.

frontier in contact with a neutral power, we shall be absolutely without any guarantees worth having in the case of a *wild* & distant country like Serbia . . .'.[23] Carr had very soon absorbed the ethos that reasons of state override every other necessity.

In April 1918 – evidently now regarded as something of a Russian specialist though, not untypically for the Foreign Office, without any Russian to his name – Carr was transferred from the Contraband Department to the Northern Department, which dealt with relations with Russia and neighbouring powers. There he cut his teeth on dealing with the problems created by the Bolshevik revolution at the political level, working as the junior in a team of three, the others being 'regular F.O. officials'.[24] That summer the British led a war of intervention to overthrow the Bolshevik regime on the ostensible grounds that, having signed a separate peace with Germany, Lenin had closed the eastern front and therefore exposed allied forces to the entire brunt of the German onslaught. The irony was that the British still maintained an embassy in Petrograd; the Bolsheviks in turn maintained an informal mission in London, under Maxim Litvinov. The British in Petrograd were actively recruiting support for the overthrow of the regime in the capital and when, after an attempted assassination of Lenin, the Bolsheviks raided the British mission, naval attaché Captain Cromie was killed in attempting to defend it from attack. The British responded by locking up Litvinov and his party in Brixton prison. Under Lenin's instruction Commissar for Foreign Affairs Georgii Chicherin sought an exchange of British (and French) officials for Litvinov and company. Carr's hostility to the Bolsheviks and his native realism prompted him to dismiss the idea on the grounds that Chicherin could not be trusted.[25]

Russia was still a side-show, however, even with the advent of the war of intervention that summer. The war against the central powers was the critical issue, not finally resolved until 11 November 1918. News of peace had barely reached the Foreign Office that morning when the sound of crowds outside in adjacent Downing Street was heard through its windows. 'There were the wildest cheers,' recorded the young and idealistic diplomat Harold Nicolson, 'and then . . . they were silent – and they bared their heads and sang "God Save the King" – after which throughout the morning came cries and cheers from the parade . . .'.[26] But, for those in power, one set of complications resolved had given place to yet another. 'The vanquished nations, covering as they do the greater part of Europe and Asia, are plunged into anarchy, approaching in many regions to a complete dissolution of society', wrote Minister of Munitions Winston Churchill:

---

[23] Minute dated 24 November 1917: *FO* 382/1653.

[24] *Autobiographical sketch.* Carr dates this to several weeks after the revolution, but the documents indicate it was more like several months.

[25] Minute dated 10 September 1918: *FO* 371/3336.

[26] Nicolson to Vita Sackville-West, 11 November 1918: *Sackville-West Papers*, Lilly Library, Indiana University, 1918.

Over the four once mighty Empires of Russia, Germany, Austria and Turkey hunger reigns supreme. The structure of their governing institutions has been completely shattered; the whole system of their industrial life is paralysed, all those vast intricate processes by which great cities are fed and warmed, by which industries are maintained, by which trains are made to run and ships to put forth upon their voyages, are either completely arrested or are working in feeble and fitful spasms.

All the Rulers have been cast down, all the governing classes have been utterly discredited. New and untried men, destitute of experience, have been tossed by the waves of revolution on to this or that pinnacle of rock, where they cling precariously and desperately till they are engulfed in the surges of another billow . . . . A permanently ruined Germany means a permanently impoverished Britain. Russia in anarchy means Europe in convulsion; and Europe in convulsion means Asia in disturbance and America in distress.[27]

Nicolson, too, was depressed and feared the emergence of Bolshevism in Britain and France. 'We expect it at any moment in Holland', he wrote.[28]

A speedy peace settlement to stabilize the situation was thus an urgent requirement. The conference would be held in Paris, a conference to which the Bolsheviks, of course, were not invited. The Permanent Under Secretary at the Foreign Office, Lord Hardinge – maliciously caricatured by Nicolson[29] as 'so pompous that he almost fell over backwards'[30] – was an ex-Viceroy of India and a protégé of King Edward VII, 'hardly the right person to engage in the rough-and-tumble of policy-making under a dynamic Prime Minister', Carr noted years later.[31] Hardinge chose eighteen officials to join the British delegation, including Carr, who was put into a section dealing with northeastern Europe: the Baltic, Scandinavia, Russia and Poland. Together with Michael Palairet he served as an assistant – 'junior bottle-washer' as he described it[32] – to the head of that section, Lord Howard of Penrith, hitherto ambassador to Sweden and regarded by others as 'the Russian expert'.[33] He made a favourable impression on Howard as one of the 'most helpful, able and pleasant younger secretaries in the Diplomatic Service';[34] before long he was being referred to proprietorially as 'my E.H. Carr'.[35]

---

[27] Cabinet Memorandum, 'The Unfinished Task', 19 November 1918: M. Gilbert, *Winston S. Churchill*, vol. IV, Companion, Part 1, Documents January 1917–June 1919, London 1977, pp. 417–18.

[28] Nicolson to Sackville-West, 10 November 1918: *Sackville-West Papers*, 1918.

[29] 'A clever little man' was how Carr described Nicolson over fifty years later: Zara Steiner's notes of an interview with him, 1973.

[30] Nicolson (Paris) to Sackville-West, 11 January 1919: *Sackville-West Papers*, 1919.

[31] 'Lloyd George, Churchill, and the Russian Revolution', *From Napoleon to Stalin and Other Essays*, London 1980, p. 32.

[32] *Autobiographical sketch.*

[33] Nicolson (Paris) to Sackville-West, 13 January 1919: *Sackville-West Papers*, 1919.

[34] Diary entry, November 1918: Lord Howard of Penrith, *Theatre of Life: Life Seen from the Stalls, 1905–1936*, London 1936, p. 275.

[35] Diary entry, 14 January 1919: ibid., p. 291.

Orders to proceed to Paris were unaccountably delayed. Howard's team did not leave with the main body of the delegation led by Hardinge until 8 January 1919. After a rough crossing they reached the Hotel Majestic on the Avenue Kléber at 11 o'clock that evening, a 'a vast caravanserai . . . constructed almost entirely of onyx for the benefit of the Brazilian ladies who, before the war, could come to Paris to buy their clothes.'[36] The hotel accommodated the entire British delegation which, besides the Foreign Office, numbered hundreds of officials, clerical assistants and secretaries. Work was done nearby at the Hotel Astoria. For those such as Carr, who were ardent admirers of Lloyd George and broadly, though never naively, favoured a new world order framed squarely within the liberal tradition, the conference proved a sobering experience. US President Woodrow Wilson's high-minded proposals met with relentless opposition from 'Tiger' Clemenceau, bent on revenge against Germany. The arch-manipulator Lloyd George typically played both ends against the middle but ultimately sided with France. The apparent indifference of the great powers to the aspirations of nations now demanding national self-determination shocked some with the spectacle of realpolitik in action. Nicolson described in a letter to his wife, the popular novelist Vita Sackville-West, the manner in which the 'wretched small powers' were 'brought in one by one and made to state their case. They are sat down opposite Clemenceau as if in the dock. It is an odd spectacle.'[37] Lloyd George would pull apart the reports of the specialists and reach decisions with the other leaders that paid scant attention to the territorial and ethnic realities which lay behind the maps they spread out over the floor at their feet.

The peace conference, Carr noted many years later, worked at several levels. First, there was the 'old level of national interest and the old diplomacy'. This was a line 'exclusively followed by the French and Italians'. Second, there was a level at which:

policy proceeded on the line of belief in self-determination, this taking the form of the rational argument that, if you wanted a lasting territorial settlement, you must have one which satisfied the peoples concerned. The contrast with the Congress of Vienna was constantly stressed. Both the British and the Americans purported to work on this level. But the whole thing was infinitely complicated, first, by the fact that neither the British nor the Americans had any notion of applying it to countries outside Europe where their own interests lay. A third and most important complication peculiar to the British was that they did not really believe in self-determination as such, but simply in the rights of small nations; and this was really a hangover from the old balance of power theory of supporting the weak against the strong, taking the form of the liberal doctrine that God is on the side of the small battalions. Very soon after 1918, Germany began to qualify in British eyes as a small nation which had to be bolstered up to counterbalance

---

[36] H. Nicolson, *Peacemaking 1919*, London 1964, p. 44.
[37] Nicolson (Paris) to Sackville-West, 1 February 1919: *Sackville-West Papers*, 1919.

France. This was, of course, the policy which had its short-lived triumph at Locarno.[38]

In addition, 'work went on on the basis of a belief in public opinion and democratic control of foreign policy.' The United States

> wholeheartedly believed in this because they never really needed a foreign policy. (Many years later, when a foreign policy became vital to the US, the phenomenon of McCarthyism was a necessary stage in convincing the Americans that they must not have opinions of their own about foreign policy.) The British half believed it and half did not. But it had been necessary to appeal to public opinion during the war, and Lloyd George used it in the election, but turned against it when he found Northcliffe used it against him. The whole business of the union of democratic control and the propaganda of the League of Nations was thoroughly disliked by the British policy-makers, though the League of Nations itself was acceptable so long as it could be fitted into the old scheme of the balance of power.[39]

Carr's reaction to events at the time indicates some moral sensitivity: 'it seemed to me (as to most English liberals) that we betrayed the liberal principles we had so loudly trumpeted during the war.' But this should not be exaggerated. At the time he 'brushed this off, partly with the bad excuse . . . that things done in wartime don't count, and partly with the belief that we should soon put things right'. [40] Signs of his idealism are evident from his work for Howard on the issue of nationalities in eastern Europe. The break-up of the old empires in Europe that Churchill so feared paved the way for fledgling nation-states. One major problem was, however, that the aspirant nations sought strategic frontiers which cut across the very principle of ethnicity they were using to justify their renaissance; and this was not the only difficulty which arose. Decades later, Carr summed up these complexities:

> Before they had finished their work, the peacemakers of 1919 had some inkling of the complications of the problem. They fully understood that the territorial intermingling of different peoples made the drawing of frontiers in Eastern Europe on the basis of nationality a matter of extreme difficulty. They understood in part that the objective marks of nationality were not always clearly defined, so that it was impossible to say dogmatically whether the Ukrainians were a separate nation or merely Russians speaking a variant dialect, and whether Slav-speaking Macedonians were Serbs, Bulgars, or just Macedonians. What they hardly understood at all was that, even where the objective marks of nationality were perfectly clear, the possession of these marks did not necessarily give the clue to the state of mind of the possessor. Mesmerized by the assumption that the principle of nationality and the principle of self-determination were indistinguishable in their results,

---

[38] Carr to Arno Mayer, 13 November 1959: Arno Mayer's personal correspondence.
[39] Ibid.
[40] Carr to Betty Behrens, 19 February 1966.

and by the fact that this assumption on the whole worked in Western Europe, politicians and propagandists alike were content to believe that the man whose mother-tongue was Polish or Serb or Lithuanian wanted to be a citizen of a Polish or Serb or Lithuanian state. Only where the 'lines of nationality' were not 'clearly recognizable', or where for some other reason the fate of an area was especially debatable, was the expedient of a plebiscite adopted.[41]

How were these conflicting aims to be squared? In a memorandum on 'Minority Nationalities', written on 20 November 1918, Carr's solution to this thorny issue was an unexceptional amalgam of pragmatism and liberal principle:

(1) The position of such Minority Nationalities in other States. The new States containing alien Minorities, must be given distinctly to understand either by a special declaration from the Allies or by the terms under which their State is constituted that they are only allowed, for reasons of geographical convenience, to incorporate in their State Minorities of different nationality on condition that such Minorities receive full civil and religious liberty and all the rights of citizenship.
(2) Inducements to such Minorities to migrate to their own national State. In general it is desirable that States should hold out inducements to their nationalities outside their borders to return to them, and in the case of countries ravaged by the War, there will probably be large vacancies for such settlers. On the other hand, any sort of compulsion is out of the question, and it does not appear that the Allied Govts can take any action at all in the matter beyond a friendly hint of the possibility of such a solution in the interests of future peace.[42]

One of the most awkward issues was that of the Jewish minority in Poland. It is here that Carr's path crossed that of Lewis Namier (né Bernstein), who campaigned vigorously from within the Political Intelligence Department (PID) of the Foreign Office against the Polish pogroms that were taking place during the Paris peace conference. A larger than life figure, 'an angular personality, relentless and sometimes over bearing in argument', he had migrated from Russian Poland to Britain in 1907 and then proceeded to turn himself into a loyal British subject, though he remained to the end of his life unalterably 'unconventional and un-English'. Namier studied at Balliol College, Oxford, and after military service in 1914–15 joined the PID. In retrospect Carr noted: 'The cause of the Ruthenian (or Ukrainian) peasant majority of East Galicia, and the attempt to save them from the fate – which befell them – of annexation by Poland, which was the chief preoccupation of Namier's period of service in the Foreign Office and at the Peace Conference, earned him the undying hostility of the Polish nationalists . . .'.[43] But Carr's first encounter with Namier found him

---

[41] Carr, *Conditions of Peace*, London 1942, p. 44.
[42] *FO* 371/4353.
[43] 'Lewis Namier', *From Napoleon to Stalin and Other Essays*, London 1980, pp. 186–7.

campaigning vigorously on behalf of the persecuted Jewish minority in Poland. He was not alone. The secretary and special delegate of the Jews of the British empire, Lucien Wolf, tackled Carr, whom he found 'very *boutonné*'[44] on these questions, for the first time in mid-March 1919. At the time Carr was very favourably disposed towards the successor states and disinclined to upset them – a natural consequence of his liberal world view. When, in January 1919, the Polish national committee under Piłsudski formed a government under the premiership of Paderewski and called on the great powers for diplomatic recognition, Carr unhesitatingly argued for immediate recognition. 'Assuming that the meeting of the Diet which is fixed for to-day confirms (as it almost certainly will) the statement that the Paderewski Govt is supported by a vast majority of Poles I see no reason why it should not be officially recognized at once', he wrote on 10 February.[45] And he argued against any special status for Danzig which might deprive Poland of full sovereign rights over the Baltic port, on the grounds that the city would gradually be polonized and this process should not be discouraged. He was not at all anti-semitic, either. Thus when Wolf called at the Astoria Carr seemed 'very glad' to see him, Wolf noted, 'and to get all the news I could give him about the Polish Jewish question'.[46]

In 'Observations on Proposals Regarding Cultural Minorities as far as they affect Poland', dated 14 March 1919, he estimated that the new state of Poland would have four and a half million Jews and two and a half million Germans. But he was extremely reluctant to placate Wolf and Namier to the extent of making special provisions particular to Poland on behalf of the Jews: 'Such special provisions would probably be more deeply resented by the Poles than general provisions applicable equally to other states in the same position.'[47] In direct contrast to Namier, who was obviously emotionally entangled in the whole matter, Carr tended – at first – to take a coolly dispassionate and even-handed view: 'In the case of the Jews,' he wrote,

> the Poles have followed the convenient practice of alternately regarding them as Poles or denying their right to be considered Poles as it suits their convenience, and the Jews have been more or less playing the same game. This should be put a stop to, and it is really in the long run in the interests of the Polish State that any Jew born in Poland or in the territories now ceded to Poland who wishes to obtain Polish citizenship should be allowed to do so. The same applies to Germans.[48]

---

[44] Entry, 9 September 1919: L. Wolf, *Diary of Peace Conference 14th January–12th October 1919*, University College, London, p. 606.
[45] Minute dated 10 February on a letter from the Polish National Committee to Balfour, 7 February 1919: *FO* 608/61.
[46] Entry, 15 March 1919: Wolf, *Diary*, p. 117.
[47] *FO* 608/61.
[48] Ibid.

Wolf was thus told that the allies 'did not care to take the risk of stipulating for guarantees which the League of Nations might refuse to apply, as, in that case, the Treaties would have no guarantee at all'.[49]

However, Carr's sympathies for the successor states, Poland in particular, came under immense strain as his dealings with them increased. Wolf found it reassuring that Carr 'did not seem perturbed by the tricks and threats of the Roumanians,' for instance, 'and said he thought the Supreme Council saw through them all.'[50] On one occasion in mid-June he told Wolf that the Poles had made no observations on the peace treaties: 'Carr said they had not uttered or written a word, from which he concluded that they had something up their sleeves.' He also 'said that for inexperienced diplomatists nothing was more fatal than the Polish atmosphere . . .'.[51] The ugly realities behind the struggle for power in eastern Europe began to corrode his sympathies for the re-emergent nations. The treatment of minorities reflected a larger problem. Lacking natural frontiers, the successor states proved rather too eager to expand their own boundaries in blatant disregard for the self-determination of others; and their hostility to one another was in certain instances no less than their hostility towards the Germans. Carr witnessed these events at first hand and responded with dignified disdain. The Poles were definitely the worse culprits. 'This was the period of Korfanty, Zeligowski and the disputes over Teschen and Eastern Galicia, not to mention the campaign of 1920 [to seize the Ukraine]. The picture of Poland which was universal in Eastern Europe right down to 1925 was of a strong and potentially predatory power.'[52] In June 1920 a tour of Danzig, Warsaw and 'the Eastern Plebiscite Areas' took him to Teschen, an area inhabited by Poles but within Czech frontiers, where Carr witnessed some bizarre petty banditry being conducted by both sides. 'In spite of occasional tragic incidents and a possible tragic conclusion,' he wrote, 'the situation in Teschen is pure farce and a salutary warning to any who may still be tempted to take the new nations of central and eastern Europe too seriously.'[53]

In May he had been taken on as British secretary to the New States Committee under James Headlam-Morley. Headlam-Morley, a classicist recruited into the PID, became 'a distinctive and important member of the British delegation . . .'.[54] He was as impressed with Carr as was Howard – 'most sensible and open-minded', he opined[55] – and for some years thereafter became something of a mentor to the rising young man. Work for the

---

[49] Entry, 7 June 1919: Wolf, *Diary*, p. 349.
[50] Entry, 8 September 1919: Wolf, *Diary*, p. 597.
[51] Entry, 16 June 1919: Wolf, *Diary*, p. 374.
[52] Carr to Isaac Deutscher, 27 November 1954: *Deutscher Archive*, Amsterdam, Institute of Social History, File 15.
[53] From Carr's notes: enclosure no. 505, 12 June 1920, *Documents on British Foreign Policy 1919–1939*, eds R. Butler et al., London 1960, pp. 698–9.
[54] Carr, 'James Headlam-Morley', *From Napoleon to Stalin and Other Essays*, London 1980, p. 165.
[55] Headlam-Morley to Namier, 10 February 1919: *Headlam-Morley Papers*, Churchill College Archives, Acc. 727, box 11.

committee was merely a logical continuation of Carr's work for Howard. And just as he had enthusiastically supported recognition of Poland, so too did he advocate the same for the Baltic states, Finland, Estonia, Latvia and Lithuania, which had formerly been a part of the Russian empire. The allied war of intervention had rescued them from Bolshevism. The issue was whether to grant them recognition. To a consistent liberal, support for national self-determination was the only course of action. In mid-April the American representative on the Commission on Baltic Affairs, Dr Samuel Eliot Morison, found out that Carr considered Britain had already recognized Finland *de facto* and believed that 'she should *de jure* . . .'.[56] At dinner with him later, on 19 June, Carr – uncharacteristically – boasted that 'at the Five [the Supreme Allied Council] when Finnish Independence [was] recognized, Hardinge was his gramophone!'[57] Zealous for the rights of the Baltic states, Carr was therefore indignant when 'some War Office General' argued that granting diplomatic recognition would be futile since 'sooner or later either Russia or Germany will gobble them up'.[58] And there in the archives is a minute on a telegram from General Gough in Helsinki to the Chief of the Imperial General Staff on 25 July 1919. 'I hope that the Peace Conference may yet be induced to recognize, if not the final, at least the provisional, independence of the Baltic states', Carr wrote.[59]

As the Paris peace conference proceeded, allied forces in Russia had become increasingly bogged down in the first of several conflicts to save exhausted and, it seems, largely indifferent populations from the perils of Bolshevism.[60] Carr had no sympathy for what appeared a futile enterprise. He was therefore acutely frustrated, not least because, like other members of the Foreign Office under Lloyd George's premiership, 'nothing I did or wrote had any importance at all'. But he did 'warmly' approve Lloyd George's resistance to War Minister Churchill's[61] schemes for finishing off the Bolsheviks, and 'was disappointed when he gave way (in part) on the Russian question in order to buy French consent to concessions to Germany on Upper Silesia, Danzig and reparations'.[62] Lloyd George, he recalled, 'had no faith in these Russian adventures; but, in order to please a section of his supporters, he momentarily surrendered the reins to the most dangerous member of his team, Mr. Churchill; and he afterwards showed unnecessary relish in liquidating the unhappy consequences of his colleague's policy'.[63]

Indeed, as early as February 1919 the Prime Minister's secretary, Philip Kerr, argued against Churchill's advocacy of a policy of open war against the Bolsheviks on the grounds that 'it must lead to the Peace Conference taking

---

[56] Entry, 15 April 1919: *Morison Diary*, Harvard. I am grateful to Dr Fogelson for this reference.
[57] Entry, 19 June 1919: ibid.
[58] *Autobiographical sketch.*
[59] Carr's minute on Gough (Helsingfors) to CIGS (War Office), 25 July 1919: *FO* 608/186.
[60] For the detail: R. Ullman, *Britain and the Russian Civil War*, London 1968.
[61] Churchill moved from Munitions to War in November 1918.
[62] *Autobiographical sketch.*
[63] Review under the name of John Hallett of General Wrangel's memoirs, *Fortnightly Review*, January 1930.

charge of Russian affairs, & if they do that it will end in revolution in the West.'[64] Lloyd George readily agreed. 'An expensive war of aggression against Russia is a way to strengthen Bolshevism in Russia & create it at home. We cannot afford the burden', he advised Churchill.[65] But this left Carr and others on the delegation in Paris in the dark. Carr's instincts were those of Lloyd George. He thought that the counter-revolutionary forces should be kept at arm's length and he vividly remembered 'spending a weekend writing a memorandum on the inadvisability of recognizing Kolchak [who headed the provisional government opposing the Bolsheviks in the Far East], only to learn on Monday that the Big Four had decided to offer him recognition on certain conditions'.[66] This was April 1919. The Foreign Office archives contain his argument: 'This is one of the minor inconveniences of the present policy of drift in Russia. In any case it would be inopportune to recognize Kolchak as long as there is the possibility of a decision being taken to cease supporting the anti-Bolshevik elements in Russia – in which case Kolchak would collapse at once.' Unfortunately for Carr the foreign secretary did not agree. More importantly, Lloyd George himself was won over to that position. As Morison noted in his diary: 'Carr says [the] exchange of notes with Kolchak [was] started by Foreign Office people who had always been pro-K., and that L.G. [Lloyd George] supported it as [he was] alarmed by [the] anti-Bolshevist movement in England, esp. Parliament.' Carr himself noted, a decade later, that:

> The vacillating character of British policy . . . was mainly due to domestic issues . . . . It was not the only occasion on which Mr. Lloyd George himself judged rightly, but had not the courage of his convictions. He had no faith in these Russian adventures; but, in order to please a section of his supporters, he momentarily surrendered the reins to the most dangerous member of his team, Mr. Churchill; and he afterwards showed unnecessary relish in liquidating the unhappy consequences of his colleague's policy.[67]

In the event Kolchak 'havered over the conditions, and the Bolsheviks defeated him before the plan got any further'. Although by no means sympathetic to the Reds, Carr's impatience with the existing policy was expressed in a minute dated 28 May 1919:

> There is much in the present Allied policy in Russia which justifies the charge of hypocrisy. Our original intervention in Russia was alleged to be directed against the Germans. Against whom is it directed now? If against the Bolsheviks, all the talk about non-intervention is simply absurd.
> There are only two honest courses to pursue (1) to cease fighting the Bolsheviks,

---

[64] Kerr to Lloyd George, 15 February 1919: Gilbert (ed.), *Churchill*, p. 532.
[65] Lloyd George to Churchill, 16 February 1919: ibid., p. 539.
[66] *Autobiographical sketch.*
[67] Review of Wrangel.

or (2) to declare war on them and cease talking about non-intervention.

The present disingenuous policy which tries to reconcile two contradictory ideals can do us no good in the long run.[68]

As ever the clear voice of reason, Carr showed no deference to the kind of unhappy compromise integral to the political process in a democracy; in this respect he resembled George Kennan, US diplomat and accomplished Russianist of the next generation, whose emotional absolutism similarly never came to terms with the distasteful relativism of democratic political life.

In July 1919 Carr's scepticism drove him to press his views even more forcefully in a minute appended to a despatch from Archangel:

> This is an essay on the theme – which has long been too obvious to require demonstration – that Russia is incapable of reconstructing herself. The task before us is not merely that of 'restoring' Russia but of governing her when restored. My only doubts are (a) whether for the next twenty years or so we are likely to have sufficient energy, men or let alone all the money to undertake such a formidable task; (b) whether, if we were prepared to undertake it, our present policy would be the best method to adopt.[69]

Lloyd George reached the same bitter conclusion independently, re-reading the parliamentary debates on the war of intervention against revolutionary France in the 1790s. Indeed, the lesson of that time was that intervention did more harm than good, acting as the catalyst that brought Napoleon Bonaparte to power, and resulting in the great war that lasted till 1815 and the introduction of income tax into Britain. With the collapse of substantial opposition to the Bolsheviks in Russia and with growing political unrest at home (a policemen's strike, severe industrial unrest on the Clyde and a growing trade union campaign against the war in Russia), Lloyd George – with an eye, as always, to the domestic front – overruled diehards like Churchill in the governing coalition and pulled British troops out by the end of the year. A few years later Carr concluded, with customary asperity:

> it is no longer possible for any sane man to regard the campaigns of Kolchak, Yudenich, Denikin and Wrangel otherwise than as tragic blunders of colossal dimensions. They were monuments of folly in conception and of incompetence in execution; they cost, directly and indirectly, hundreds of thousands of lives; and, except in so far as they may have increased the bitterness of the Soviet rulers against the 'white' Russians and the Allies who half-heartedly supported them, they did not deflect the course of history by a single hair's breadth.[70]

Lloyd George's decision to pull out confirmed Carr's high opinion of the Prime Minister. 'All in all,' he wrote later, 'none of the Versailles statesmen

---

[68] *FO* 608/178.
[69] Minute, 16 July 1919: ibid.
[70] Review of Wrangel.

had a better record for foresight and common sense than Mr. Lloyd George.'[71] And nothing annoyed him more in old age than the trivialization of Lloyd George in a television drama. But what did the war of intervention amount to? How did these decisions fit into the proceedings of the Paris peace? The place of the Russian revolution in the scheme of things continued to puzzle him to the very end. When called upon to think back and reflect upon those times at the end of the fifties he noted:

> I rather waver myself between the two extremes of things, that it was subconsciously very important indeed, and of thinking that it made very little difference, and the appeals made to it by Hoover and Lloyd George were merely excuses to get support for policies which they favoured on quite other grounds. On the whole I feel that the first alternative is too clever in anticipation of what happened in the second World War, and that the second alternative seems the nearer as far as Paris was concerned.[72]

To Carr, the war was 'an immense disaster'. His indignation at the unfairness of the allied treatment of Germany, 'whom we cheated over the "Fourteen Points" and subjected to every petty humiliation' was shared not only by 'many'[73] in the British delegation to Paris but also by most liberals and socialists, and later made it difficult to see Hitler in realistic terms, when he sought expansion in the name of national self-determination. In a typical comment made in reviewing a book on *The Spirit of British Policy* by Kantorowicz (a German) on 18 July 1931, Carr openly condemned the war guilt clause of the Versailles treaty that had been imposed on Germany and argued that 'we should like to see the German case equally well stated by some English writer.' He and his generation had grown up in a 'pro-German tradition'. 'In the early years of this century,' he wrote later, 'unstinting admiration for Germany and everything German was common form in this country; even as late as 1911 and 1912 desperate attempts were still being made, with very little encouragement from the other side, to keep up Anglo-German friendship', And 'except perhaps for a short time in the first world war' – when 'Germans were Huns, who raped women and tortured children' – he had never succumbed to anti-German sentiment.[74] Moreover his natural empathy for the Germans was compounded by the behaviour of the successor states of eastern Europe. The balkanization of eastern Europe was, he now wrote, 'a step, though for the moment it seems a retrograde one, in the progress towards a higher civilization. But for this progress to become apparent,' he argued, 'we shall have to wait till one of the great powers has

---

[71] 'Mr. Lloyd George Defends His Course in the Versailles Negotiations', *Christian Science Monitor*, 18 January 1939.
[72] Carr to Arno Mayer, 13 November 1959: Arno Mayer's personal correspondence.
[73] *Autobiographical sketch.*
[74] *Christian Science Monitor*, 18 July 1931; 'The Puzzle of Anglo-German Relations', BBC Radio, 20 May 1952.

recovered sufficient strength to put the central European house in order.'
That is to say, the successor states would pull themselves together only once
they faced a common external threat. He was still a firm believer in their independence. The liberal foundations had most certainly been badly shaken by
war and its aftermath; but they had yet to collapse.

A vengeful peace signed at Versailles in May 1919, Carr decided none the
less to remain in the diplomatic service. He had enjoyed the experience in
Paris enormously. But it was the work rather than the social whirl that surrounded the conference which interested him. The only exception was in
June when, after the official celebrations following signature of the treaties in
the Hall of Mirrors at Versailles, 'some of the Delegation went out and as far
as I understand,' wrote Headlam-Morley, 'indulged in a little mild mafficking.
Even Carr took his Miss Dougherty out . . . '.[75] The excitement of being
actively at the centre of world events and the undoubted glamour that still
attached to the profession ensured that he would stay on in the service for the
time being. Technically he was merely a 'temporary clerk' and as such he
received a salary below his rank. But he received recognition for his work at
the conference in the form of a CBE awarded on 1 January 1920. He was also
asked to stay on in Paris as part of a very small unit that serviced British representatives at the Allied Conference of Ambassadors, 'entrusted with the
task of handling all minor current questions of the execution of the peace
treaties'.[76] Carr's immediate superior was Orme Sargent, a diplomat of the
old school with a sharp mind and a capacity for shocking cynicism, whom
Carr much admired. Sargent certainly had considerable respect for his junior
helper and only many years later, when Carr advocated appeasement of
Stalin's Russia, did that give way to disparaging judgements.

Not given to sociability, Carr nevertheless took an attentive interest in the
opposite sex. It was in Paris, apparently during the 'relatively colourless and
uneventful interval after the turbulent period of upheaval and peace-making
in the first half of 1919 and before the shape of things to come in the post-war
world began to reveal itself in 1920',[77] that he fell in love with Lois Simpson,
then working for the British team as a clerical assistant. There was every
expectation that they would marry. But she was only temporarily beyond
reach of the parental home. On 30 November 1921 his position as third secretary was formalized and he was transferred back to London on 9 January
1922. He and Lois were now engaged to be married. But a mere fortnight
before the wedding she broke off the engagement. The presents were
returned and she refused to see him. It is not at all clear whether this
Dickensian disaster resulted entirely from her own volition or under cumu-
lative parental pressure. Carr was heartbroken. In those days one could not

[75] Sir James Headlam-Morley, *A Memoir of the Paris Peace Conference 1919*, ed. A. Headlam-
Morley et al., London 1972, p. 180.
[76] Carr, 'The Groundwork of History', *Times Literary Supplement*, 4 September 1948.
[77] Ibid.

simply call on the phone or turn up on the doorstep for an explanation. Lois never married. She outlived him and, decades later, in a room untouched by the present, leafing through photographs of him in Paris that were unfaded by the light of intervening years, she wistfully expressed her bitter regret.

Still an eligible bachelor, Ted craved affection. Chance then threw him into the company of engineer Gilbert Rowe (né Rosenbusch), a Jewish-American and by then a naturalized British subject. Together with Carr and a lawyer named Walbrook, he worked on the allied commission for the division of property formerly belonging to the German state in the free port of Danzig. Rowe was quite a character, much given to the pleasures (and sins) of the flesh. On more than one occasion this led him to contract venereal diseases, with the result that his wife Anne would refuse to sleep with him. Anne was drawn to Carr, who was a sympathetic and attractive alternative to her wayward husband. Carr was by then in his early thirties; Anne was eight years older than he and was already a mother of three. She was wilful and stimulating company. Coming from a family notoriously given to tactless remarks, she was mild by comparison with the others.[78] The daughter of a farmer and something of a tomboy, tall and vivacious with an imposing manner, she had been a rebellious student of economics at Newnham College, Cambridge, from 1908 to 1911, the year that Carr came up. There she had shown herself to be indifferent to petty social convention. Her initial gravitation to Rowe, whom she had married during war work in the United States in 1916, was thus entirely consistent with the thrust of her character. Carr was, of course, about as different from Rowe as one could imagine. He was clearly fascinated with this whirlwind that blew into his life: a quiet introvert more at home with books than people irresistibly attracted to the lively extrovert who broke through his native reserve. What they shared was a quickness of mind and common political beliefs: both were Lloyd George liberals.

By the end of 1924 he and Anne were in love. The decision to marry was unfortunately prompted by Rowe's suicide. It is not clear whether the suicide was caused by Anne's decision to leave him because he had contracted gonorrhoea for the umpteenth time, but certainly knowledge that she had turned to someone else to rebuild her life must have tilted a very delicate balance towards despair. The marriage was also hastened by Carr's posting as second secretary to the British legation in Latvia. He had already acquired something of a reputation as a Baltic specialist but the decision was also very much a matter of money. As a 'temporary clerk' it made good sense to benefit from the subsidies entailed in an overseas posting rather than paying rents or a mortgage in London.

The decision to move to Riga marked a turning-point in Carr's professional as well as his personal life. It could scarcely have seemed so at the time,

---

[78] John Carr to the author (no date).

however, for the city was a diplomatic backwater: the only consolation was that revolutionary Russia loomed on the horizon. Since Carr had last attended to Soviet affairs in the confusion of 1919 the revolution had survived and apparently prospered. By the mid-1920s the economy was back to prewar levels of production and Moscow had emerged from the diplomatic isolation imposed upon it after the war of intervention. Problems remained, however. Carr's posting at Riga came at a critical moment in relations between London and Moscow. The newly elected Conservative government led by Stanley Baldwin reacted against continued Bolshevik attempts to subvert the empire by engineering the isolation of the Soviet Union. In China – the second greatest concentration of British overseas investment – the Russians were stirring up anti-British feeling. In Britain itself they sought to sustain the miners' strike and, later, the General Strike in May 1926. In London, pressure was mounting towards a breach in relations.

Riga was on the periphery. Its only claim to fame – though one was not to talk about it – was as the centre for Secret Intelligence Service (SIS) activities throughout eastern Europe. The SIS was then primarily focused on anti-Bolshevik operations all over the globe. Carr knew the two people who headed the Riga station: 'Both were British ex-residents in Russia, who had lost their fortunes in the revolution; their narrowness and bigotry far exceeded that of the comparatively sophisticated people in the F.O.'[79] Despite the SIS presence, the Latvians did not merit full embassy status. Britain's envoy was only a minister by rank. Sir Tudor Vaughan was a bluff and uninspiring product of the old school, whose tastes – much to Carr's disgust – ran to the *Daily Express*. Still the Liberal, Carr subscribed to the *Manchester Guardian*; in stark contrast to later life, when he read the *Daily Telegraph* on the grounds that a capitalist paper could not afford to get the facts wrong.

On 22 January 1925 he and Anne were married. There was no time and no need for a honeymoon. Prior to departing from Harwich on the evening of Friday the twenty-third he 'Spent [the] day wandering about St. Albans and searching for a flag for Vaughan.' After a very smooth crossing to the Hook, he and Anne embarked on a train bound for Berlin where they moved into a wagon-lit. The couple reached Riga 'punctually at 10pm' on the twenty-fifth. They were met by the Leepers, whom the Carrs were to replace at the Legation. Vaughan gave them supper. The subsequent fortnight was spent settling in, leaving calling cards and slipping into an easy way of life that began pleasantly enough but inevitably palled after four years: an incessant round of ping-pong, gossip and bad opera (a form of music that Carr came to loathe). Taciturn at the best of times, the insistent demands of social life inevitably strained his patience. 'Even in my better days,' he recalled, 'I could not bear parties that began at 7.30 and ended at 11.30. When I had to suffer a lot of these in Riga, I took to bridge for the only time in my life, because this was

---

[79] *Autobiographical sketch.*

often a permissible alternative to polite conversation.'[80] Anne did not share these anti-social instincts; on the contrary, the life of a diplomat's wife was a veritable tonic to the system.

The household in place and social life under way, Anne left for England in April to collect her three children. Ted took a month's leave on 1 May and they returned together to Riga at the beginning of June. Instant fatherhood and no honeymoon were tests the relationship easily met. Winnie Elkin, one of Anne's oldest friends from the days at Newnham who visited them at Riga, recalls that they were 'certainly very happy'.[81] Ted had at last found a focus for his affections and someone to care for him. And on 12 November 1926 the marriage was sealed when Anne – at the advanced age of forty-two – gave birth to a boy, John, who now joined the three from Rowe's marriage: Rachel (born 1917), Philippa (1919) and Martin (1921). Of these Ted was fondest of Rachel, an ebullient extrovert with many of her mother's qualities; she appears in his diaries as 'the Child'. Martin, a gentle and charming boy, never really commanded his affections; Philippa was too excitable and disruptive a force to become her stepfather's favourite.

These were always remembered as 'probably the easiest and most carefree' years in his life. There were drawbacks, however, particularly to a mind as demanding as Carr's: 'Riga was an intellectual desert. A bunch of rather second-rate diplomats and a few local notabilities engaged in party-giving and party-going . . . spiced with occasional bits of émigré gossip about Russia. It was excessively boring'.[82] Work at the sleepy legation scarcely taxed his mind. He took up golf (very briefly) and tennis and swimming – to strengthen his groggy heart – in the summer months. More significantly, he also began learning Russian to occupy his time. Riga was ideal for this purpose. 'The "man in the street" and in the country speaks German,' he noted. 'But the same man will be ready enough to talk Russian and not at all resent being addressed in that language.' There was certainly little point in learning Lettish, though he was still steadfast in his defence of their national rights: 'It is scarcely decent for those who have comfortable seats inside to shout to those who are still struggling in the doorway that these new languages are a nuisance.'[83] The Balts thus raised his moral sense. But it was the Russians that attracted his interest: they were 'different' – that is what intrigued him.

Before long he immersed himself in this new found interest. On 28 September 1925 he began taking Russian lessons from a somewhat unreliable Russian priest 'whose name I have not tackled', he noted with evident impatience.[84] Thereafter he had only twelve Russian lessons, each lasting an entire afternoon, before taking an examination to qualify for a diplomatic service

[80] Carr to Tamara Deutscher, 22 February 1973.
[81] Winnie Elkin to the author, 22 January 1984.
[82] *Autobiographical sketch.*
[83] Carr to Austen Chamberlain, 30 October 1926: *FO* 371/11736.
[84] Entry, 28 September 1925: *Carr Diary.*

allowance on 21 May 1926 (awarded on 27 June). He never really learned to speak with any fluency and his accent remained poor (in contrast to his French). But his tough training in classics paid off. Soon he was reading Russian literature at an amazing speed. He began with Tolstoy, moved on to Turgenev – whose *Hunter's Sketches* he never really liked – tried Pushkin and, after seeing a performance of *The Brothers Karamazov* at the Russian Theatre in Riga on 26 November 1926 – 'difficult to follow' – he seized upon Dostoevsky. As he wrote later: 'Posterity will have the last word, but at present seems likely to rate the rugged heights and depths of Dostoevsky above the pleasant rolling plains of Turgenev.'[85] Turgenev was in fact too westernized for his newly acquired exotic taste. And if Russian literature offered 'glimpses of a different kind of civilization and a new way of thinking',[86] Dostoevsky opened up an entirely new world of exotic ideas and moral dilemmas.

While he was burying himself in Russian books, relations between Britain and the Soviet Union were rapidly heading towards a crisis as a result of Soviet involvement in the Chinese revolution against British imperialism (1925–27). British diplomats responded by ostracizing their Soviet counterparts – at Buckingham Palace garden parties they were left alone with their tea and sandwiches: a particularly devastating device by which, it was hoped, their spirit would be broken. Not that Carr was at this stage at all sympathetic to the Bolsheviks. In a letter to a friend he attacked a recently published book, *Life under the Soviets*: the author could be 'with some justice called pro-Bolo . . . . If he had been content to say that the Red Terror was no worse than the White Terror had been at other critical periods, it might possibly have been true and would not in any case be demonstrably absurd; but he tries to suggest that the Red Terror existed mainly in the heated imaginations of the other side . . .'.[87] Carr tried to maintain a balance between 'pro' and 'anti'. He certainly thought fears of the Bolsheviks excessive and somewhat ridiculous. His diary entry on 10 February 1927, at the height of tension in relations with Moscow, betrays both his scepticism about the Bolshevik menace and his contempt for Vaughan: 'Minister stayed in bed, either because a woman told him yesterday he was going to be assassinated by the Bolos, or to avoid the German play – couldn't make out which.'

He typically chose this critical moment to pay his first visit to Moscow. Following the necessary enquiries in London and Moscow, he obtained visas at the Soviet consulate in Riga on 1 April. Borrowed Baedeker in hand, he left for Moscow by the 11.05am train three days later. He arrived on the afternoon of 5 April and was met by Peters – the man who had told him in 1917 that nothing would come of the Bolshevik revolution – and taken to the legation. We have no record of his impressions but, after touring the usual sights, we

---

[85] Carr, 'Turgenev and Dostoevsky', *Slavonic Review*, June 1929.
[86] *Autobiographical sketch.*
[87] Carr to Bernard Bourdillon, 25 January 1929: RIIA archives, Carr membership file.

know that he returned to Riga on 10 April, his curiosity further strengthened by what he had seen. Some six weeks later Britain broke off relations with Moscow: but war was not an option London could afford. The only drama relating to the breach that touched Carr personally was on 11 June, when the local SIS archives were moved into the legation; a move that elicited outrage from the diplomats, accustomed to propriety, and a firm response from London resolutely refusing to discuss the matter.

Russian literature was in the meantime subverting Carr's receptive mind. 'What appealed to me about Russia was that it was so entirely different. They thought in an entirely different way from the conventional world in which I had been brought up. Theirs was not really the same world as ours.'[88] On leave in London for two months from mid-November 1927 he spent the greater part of the time reading in the London Library. He also looked in at the Reading Room of the British Museum only to discover that 'they have plenty of pre-war Russian stuff but not much since'. These forays appear fairly aimless: there is no indication of any particular project in mind, though it was at this time that he 'acquired an overwhelming desire to write'.[89] The first sign that the writer was emerging is when he wrote from Riga on 13 May 1928 to Professor Bernard Pares, the pioneer of Russian studies in Britain, whom he had met at a Chatham House lecture on Russia, offering 'something on Dostoevski for [the] Slavonic Review', which Pares edited.[90] The answer was no: someone else was working on Dostoevsky. Undeterred, Carr continued rummaging around the bookshops of Riga with a projected biography of Dostoevsky in mind. On 20 September he began an article on Turgenev and Dostoevsky for Pares; this was eventually published in June 1929.[91] By then other pieces had already appeared in print.

In every other respect he was merely marking time. Attempts to get transferred from Riga had resulted in nothing. But it was undoubtedly the high degree of boredom that the Riga posting generated that accelerated his determination to write. 'I imagine that a transfer will probably be my fate before long', he wrote philosophically to Headlam-Morley.[92] The only glimmer of hope for the future was his writing. He took leave again on 6 December but arrived in London alone. 'My wife isn't coming this time,' he wrote to a friend, 'as our English nurse has left and it is difficult to leave the children under purely local superintendance.'[93] Anne had rapidly settled in at Riga and asserted her position as the wife of the first secretary with customary

---

88 Interview with P. Scott, 'Revolution without the Passion', *Times Higher Education Supplement*, 7 July 1978.

89 'Notes for the Secretary of the British Academy' (no date).

90 Entry, 13 May 1928: *Carr Diary*.

91 'Turgenev and Dostoevsky', *Slavonic and East European Review*, vol. VIII, no. 22, June 1929, pp. 156–63.

92 Carr to Headlam-Morley, 29 September 1928: *Headlam-Morley Papers*, Acc. 727, box 41.

93 Carr to Bernard Bourdillon, 23 November 1928: RIIA archives, Carr membership file.

forcefulness, even where it was indelicate to do so. On one occasion, as reported to Nicolson by Joseph Addison, 'there was a dreadful row with Mrs Carr, wife of the first and only secretary. She said that a woman whom Jo [Addison] had asked to his ball wasn't respectable. She repeated that remark behind Jo's back – and he sent for her husband and said she was never to come to the Legation again.'[94]

On leave, Carr stayed at his father's in Crouch End. On going up to the London Library he found, to his delight, a 'lot of new Russian books'. Visits to the Library were punctuated by trips to the Foreign Office to lobby for a new posting. On one dispiriting occasion he spoke to Selby, the foreign secretary's private secretary, 'who seemed surprised to hear I had been years in Riga'.[95]

For any aspirant writer, getting to know the right people is half the battle. Carr's literary contact was Lias, a diplomatic correspondent of the *Christian Science Monitor* and, unlike Ted, somewhat given to wishful thinking. They had met in Riga's small social circle. In London that December Lias introduced Carr to Braithwaite, editor of the *Monitor*, and to the young Victor Pritchett, once also – briefly – a foreign correspondent for that paper. Carr had read a few of Pritchett's reviews and was curious about one of his novels: 'he thought it had a "mean" view of human beings,' Pritchett recalls; 'I thought of him as the friendly tutor.'[96] Pritchett was then review editor of the *Spectator* and was greatly interested in Russian literature, much in vogue after the war. It was through him that Carr began reviewing: the first appeared under the title 'The Jewish Raskolnikov' on 16 March 1929. It drew on what were by now his extensive researches on Dostoevsky.

Thereafter his diaries tell little of wife or family, let alone of his work as a diplomat. Writing had taken over – for the rest of his life. And the tireless persistence with which he pestered editors with a singularly uninspired article about the construction of the Kiev railway station testifies to a relentless determination to get into print. Ironically it was at this moment, when his writing began bearing fruit, that he received the happy news on 17 March 1929 of his transfer to the Foreign Office. 'After returning from my week-end in Warsaw,' he told a friend, 'I found a telegram transferring me with the usual pressing urgency of all F.O. decisions to the Central European Department. I am pleased with my destination, partly as I'm very fond of Sargent [who now headed the department].'[97] As expected, it turned out that there was no urgency at all – this appears to have been Sargent's means of bringing a favourite back under his wing. Carr had intended to bring the family over to England for the summer and had been making enquiries about suitable accommodation. 'The housing problem therefore becomes not one for the

---

[94] Nicolson to Sackville-West, 21 September 1928: *Sackville-West Papers*, 1928.
[95] Entry, 17 December 1928: *Carr Diary*.
[96] Letter to the author, 11 July 1983.
[97] Carr to Bourdillon, 20 March 1929: RIIA archives.

summer,' he wrote to a friend, 'but for three years or ad infinitum. I fear it means the suburbs, inner or outer, as anything nearer is too expensive and anything further impossible for daily travel.' On 20 March he wrote to Headlam-Morley for help. 'The problem now before me is where to live, i.e. to find a place where houses aren't too dear and communications aren't too bad. Among the most likely suggestions which have been made are Hampstead, Blackheath and Wimbledon. I'm writing to friends in the first two.' What he wanted from Headlam-Morley was help with Wimbledon – could he send particulars of houses to await his arrival at the Foreign Office? He expected to be home about 1 April and wanted to get on with the job as quickly as possible. 'The house we want must have 3 sitting rooms and 5–6 bedrooms and be – I think – not more than half a mile from stations.' He was open to purchase or rental.[98] By the time Headlam-Morley replied – he had been away – and offered Carr his own place at £4,500, an offer had already been made on 1 Vanburgh Park Road West, Blackheath. Carr then returned to Riga to pick up the family (he hated packing and moving – that was always left to his wife) and – aside from the children emptying the contents of their stomachs over the side – the trip went smoothly. Before long they were all nestled in Blackheath and Carr had recommenced life as a commuter.

The Central Department focused on Germany: war reparations were once again at the top of the agenda; but Carr was not to be distracted from his academic pursuits. A typical diary entry on 28 June 1929 reads: 'Nothing exciting at the F.O. Collected a lot of books on Chekhov from L.L. [London Library].' At the Foreign Office his literary sideline went unseen. He usually wrote under a pseudonym, such as John Hallett (his mother's maiden name). He was in fact leading two distinct lives and, of these, diplomacy was of the lesser interest. On 15 July the extrovert John (Jock) Balfour joined the department but was soon acutely disappointed by Carr's withdrawn manner. 'We did work for a time . . . in the same room,' he recalled, 'but he kept himself and his brilliant intellect to himself. I have seldom met a person who was so aloof from his fellow men.'[99] Indeed this impression is confirmed by Pritchett: 'He struck me as an isolated man . . . as having hidden or repressed feelings.'[100]

It is not possible to identify precisely when Carr began to write the biography of Dostoevsky. By the late summer of 1929 he had already completed most of the research. Certainly by mid-August writing was under way. In September he 'Started on Dostoevsky in Siberia and the first marriage', completed the following month. And by early November he was working on *Crime and Punishment*. Pares had written suggesting a meeting with Prince Mirsky, an emigré, then teaching Russian literature at London University. Pares's idea was that Carr should take a PhD, evidently on the basis of his research on Dostoevsky. But any such hopes were dashed when Mirsky proved unreceptive.

---

[98] Carr to Headlam-Morley, 20 March 1929: *Headlam-Morley Papers*.
[99] Sir John Balfour to the author, 26 January 1983.
[100] Pritchett to the author.

After what Carr described as 'an amusing talk', the idea was quietly buried: 'a strange creature', he confided defensively to his diary.[101]

By the end of December 1929 the early chapters of *Dostoevsky* were in order. Carr sent a piece on 'Dostoevsky and epilepsy' – which has withstood the test of time – to Pares, who wanted sample chapters.[102] He had four typed up early in February 1930, and by mid-month he had reached the last decade of Dostoevsky's life. All this effort was interspersed with commuting to Whitehall, where a six-day week was mitigated by a light workload and extremely flexible working hours: few began until 11am. He was also doing a good deal of 'hack reviewing' and wrote general literary articles for Carter at the *Spectator* and Dickson at the *Fortnightly Review*. Both activities brought in much needed extra income: the Crash of 1929 had reduced his capital as it had that of others. Finally, on 30 March he 'wrote most of the final chapter of Dostoevsky', completing it on 10 April 1930. Not that Carr ever worked in strict chronological order: during composition he darted about, filling in the pieces of the jigsaw as they emerged from his research, until the final pattern matched his initial conception.

Towards the end of May he took some chapters along to Pares, but he had also hired a literary agent – just in case Pares let him down – and the agent sent samples to Heinemann and Constable, Gollancz, and Faber and Faber. It was a hard-fought battle to secure publication: the Great Depression had cut demand. But perseverance was never a problem; neither was self-confidence. Carr certainly needed both. His career at the Foreign Office remained in limbo. On 17 October he had a talk with Sargent about the possibility of taking the job held by George Bland since 1919: that of private secretary to the Permanent Under Secretary; but nothing came of it.[103] An invisible ceiling hung over his career and, for an ambitious young man, the frustration became all too evident. As a 'temporary clerk', his salary was still below the norm for his rank. Carr raised the matter with Sargent on 22 May and a meeting was arranged with Permanent Under Secretary Robert Vansittart but nothing was to be done: Treasury intransigence saw to that. He was, however, offered a transfer to the League of Nations section to replace William Strang, who was off to Moscow now that relations had been restored by the MacDonald Labour–Liberal coalition government.[104] Even the posting to the League was jeopardized when Sargent fought to retain him but Carr, eager to move onward and upward, 'defeated his scheme'.[105] By mid-June 1930 the transfer was effective.

The prospect of literary distinction filled a void in his life. Anne did not

---

[101] Entry, 19 November 1929: *Carr Diary*.
[102] Published as 'Was Dostoevsky an Epileptic?', *Slavonic and East European Review*, December 1930, pp. 424–31.
[103] Entry, 17 October 1929: *Carr Diary*.
[104] Entry, 30 May 1930: ibid.
[105] Entry, 16 June 1930: ibid.

share in this new enthusiasm, not least because she – and later Rachel – ended up doing all the typing and indexing. She would have much preferred to have become an ambassador's wife, to have some status in partial compensation for her husband's casual indifference to the affairs of the family. Pritchett caught the draught when invited to tea at Blackheath. Anne shocked him by mocking Ted's Russian interests.[106] There was, of course, another side to the picture. She had a lively, if unfocused, mind which was clearly under-used. For all her faults, she was also an extraordinarily generous soul. Rachel recalled 'how off-hand was the behaviour of many of E.H.'s colleagues and friends, even when she [Anne] was the hostess and she was interested in the subjects being discussed'. They were evidently unused to this demanding, liberated woman graduate, uncomfortable at being relegated to the periphery in social gatherings. Visitors were witnessing the outward signs of intimate tensions. Anne was perhaps more than a little jealous of her husband's new and all-consuming hobby, that took time and attention away from herself and her family. She was still the same but the man she married had changed and, in personal terms, not for the better. In a manner he kept throughout the rest of his life, Ted would work in the living room, scattering notes across the floor around his armchair, physically present but mentally distracted. When married to Gilbert, initially at any rate, Anne had had an active working life: as an inspector of the Board of Agriculture (1917–18) and then as a journalist and public lecturer (1918–20). At least when posted abroad she could busy herself with the diplomatic social round which she enjoyed to the same degree that Ted loathed it; and at an embassy she had a status comparable with that of her husband among the other wives. In Blackheath, however, she had to be content with humdrum suburbia and anonymity. She felt neglected and very much needed the attention that he now focused elsewhere, because, as her friend Winnie pointed out, 'though she was so warm-hearted, she had no real gift for making and keeping friends'; others found her 'too exhausting'.[107] Ted had found not merely fulfilment in writing but also something of an escape: retreating into a fortress of his own construction and leaving Anne down below, bombarding the battlements for attention.

The fate of *Dostoevsky* hung in the balance. Carr tinkered with the manuscript while he awaited a receptive publisher. Finally, on 25 June 1930, Pares 'Rang up and said he approved my Dostoevsky and would recommend it to Cape'. On 7 July Carr delivered it to Dorothy Galton, Pares's secretary. No sooner was the book done than (on Sunday, 13 July) he 'Began seriously looking at Bakunin', the Russian founder of anarchism, only to discover a few days later that Cape were 'No more encouraging than most publishers' about *Dostoevsky*. The bad news was confirmed on 16 September. Carr took the manuscript to Faber; they rejected it in January 1931. He tried Allen and Unwin,

---

[106] Sir Victor Pritchett to the author.
[107] Winnie Elkin to the author, 11 October 1984.

who wrote on 20 February asking to see him, 'but saying Dostoevsky isn't pub-
lishable': they had received a 'pretty damning report from one reader, but
promised to send to another'. Endurance won out when, on 7 April, he
received a letter from Unwin saying yes. Pares for some reason – perhaps
because he knew nothing about the subject – refused to write an introduction;
Mirsky obliged, even though he held no high opinion of the work.

The work is now difficult to judge. Carr's refutation of Freud's theory of the
causes of epilepsy in Dostoevsky has held up to current findings.[108] The biography reads smoothly and completes its mission very competently but it does
not offer much of a sense of Dostoevsky the artist. It does not even convey the
shattering impact Dostoevsky's entire outlook made upon Carr's own consciousness. It is too restrained to convey such a personal note; and whereas
almost all his other writings excited either considerable acclaim or fierce
condemnation (sometimes both), *Dostoevsky* came and went without attracting
much attention from anyone. In retrospect, Carr believed he had shown 'a
slightly liberalized and rationalized D[ostoevsky], which isn't quite true'.[109] It
was, after all, only a first work in a field hitherto completely unknown to the
author and based on a language mastered only on the eve of the research. In
his idiosyncratic introduction, Mirsky described it as 'the first life of
Dostoevsky, in any language, to be based on adequate material'. There was 'no
nonsense about Mr. Carr's book, and this is probably the first book on the subject (published outside Russia) of which so much can be asserted'. But Mirsky
was also sharply critical, particularly of the condescending generalizations
about the 'Russian mind' that peppered the work: signs that Carr's new
enthusiasm for this exotic world and his experience as a diplomat had yet to
extinguish all traces of his native Victorian provincialism. It could all too
easily be seen as the literary equivalent to a day trip to Boulogne.[110]

But there is far more to the biography than Mirsky could perhaps admit.
Carr places Dostoevsky in terms of not only his great contribution to literature – which he compares to that of Shakespeare – but also his keen portrayal
of key ethical, philosophical and psychological dilemmas in fictional form.
This is where Dostoevsky made the greatest impact on his biographer; the art,
as art, was secondary, and this is perhaps why Dostoevsky as artist emerges with
less clarity from these pages. It is in Dostoevsky's elemental and forceful rejection of what Carr describes as 'the orderly blight of rationalism'[111] inherited
from the seventeenth and eighteenth centuries that he has the greatest
impact. The best way of conveying this impression is to quote from
Dostoevsky's stream of consciousness in *Notes from the Underground*:

---

[108] See J. Frank, 'Freud's Case History of Dostoevsky', *Through the Russian Prism: Essays on
Literature and Culture*, Princeton 1990, chapter 9.
[109] Carr to Betty Behrens, 19 February 1966.
[110] This strange introduction was subsequently omitted by Carr from the new edition published
in 1962.
[111] Carr, *Dostoevsky (1821–1881): A New Biography*, London 1931, p. 318.

. . . anything can be said about world history, things that might enter the head of only the most disordered imagination. The only thing that cannot be said is that it's rational. You'd choke on the first word. And then there's another snag you keep coming across: such decent and sensible people keep appearing in life, such wise men, and such lovers of the human race who, throughout their lives, set themselves the very task of conducting themselves as properly and sensibly as possible, as it were to enlighten their neighbours for the very purpose of proving to them that it really is possible to live decently and sensibly on this earth. And so? It is well known that, sooner or later, towards the end of their lives, many of these people have betrayed themselves by committing some ludicrous act or another, at times even of the most indecent sort . . . . It is just his fantastic dreams, his abject foolishness that he wants to cling on to, solely in order that he can convince himself (as if it were absolutely necessary) that people are still people and not piano-keys, on which the laws of nature themselves are playing with their own hands, but are threatening to go on playing to the point where they would no longer be able to want anything beyond the directory. And besides: even in that case, even if he did turn out to be a piano-key, if that were proven to him by even the natural sciences and mathematically, he would still not come to his senses, and would deliberately do something to contradict it, simply out of ingratitude; just in order to assert himself.[112]

Thus in *Crime and Punishment*, the murderer Raskolnikov says he just killed, killed for his own sake, for himself alone.

Of course, Dostoevsky is a complex and contradictory figure, and the world takes from his writings whatever it is most in need of, at any one time. Dostoevsky's belief 'in the irrationality both of the world of phenomena and of human nature'[113] was, in his own life, counter-balanced by belief in God and an ultimate rationality: Raskolnikov mellowed by Sonia. But in the early twentieth century the counter-balance of Christianity looked less convincing. As Carr the atheist noted, 'Dostoevsky is in the position of one who has led the multitude to the edge of the precipice and, to preserve them from headlong destruction, has relied on a rickety fence of ancient half-rotten timber.'[114] He was speaking in general terms but might well have been talking for himself. Dostoevsky's legacy was destructive of old values but useless at replacing them – if one did not seek salvation in religion. This left man living entirely for his own sake, and driven by elemental and self-destructive forces ultimately outside his conscious control. Carr immediately saw a straight line of continuity through to Nietzsche's *Superman*, which he had read some years before – most likely as a student: 'Is not man's highest obligation to his own self? and is not his highest vocation the development and assertion of his own personality?' he asked, purportedly summarizing the essence of Dostoevsky's message;[115] perhaps summing up his own conclusions about life that were

---

[112] F. Dostoevsky, *Notes from the Underground and The Gambler*, Oxford 1991, p. 31.
[113] Carr, *Dostoevsky*, p. 322.
[114] Ibid.
[115] Ibid., p. 193. There is no record of his having read Nietzsche between 1925 and 1930.

merely latent tendencies before his reading of the great master. As he noted in a different context: 'Every biographer, however consciously and deliberately self-effacing, enters side by side with his subject into the biography which he writes.'[116]

Yet Carr's upbringing was too strongly fixed in the values of the Enlightenment for him to be able to abandon himself entirely to the world of the irrational. Nietzsche took irrationality to its logical conclusion; Carr did not follow him that far. Dostoevsky had opened the door from the secure world of Victorian rationalism and liberated his mind, but only to a limited degree. It gave him some moral legitimacy for indulging an egoism that had always troubled him. Conscience could now be dismissed. Unbound by convention, there was no higher being that could call him to account. 'I hate this conception of "ought";' he wrote years later in a tell-tale line, 'it's like "conscience".'[117] Rebellion could be justified. It was the Italian novelist Alberto Moravia who many years later, after a visit to the house where Raskolnikov was supposed to have done his deed, commented on the parallels between the Bolsheviks and Raskolnikov, the old woman and the bourgeoisie, Marx and Dostoevsky.[118]

Dostoevsky was thus a turning-point. It liberated Carr from the limitations of his own upbringing and sent him consciously in search of other beliefs that he could call his own. This search was never completed. As a younger man he had read Freud and this had had a dramatic effect on his awareness of the subconscious world, visible in the biography. Now the decisive influence was Dostoevsky. Later he would find himself drawn superficially to Marx. The round spectacles, the pin-stripe suit and the rolled umbrella concealed a mind in rebellion against his upbringing; henceforth it was only in externals that Carr remained loyal to Victorian convention. A further point needs to be made. When he looked back to the time of Dostoevsky's death, he commented: 'It was the threshold of an age of smaller men and faltering convictions, pre-eminently an age of transition.'[119] This reflected a growing preoccupation. Carr had never taken to religion. He was the last to join the crowd. It was not in his nature to sacrifice individual identity to a higher cause. Yet his cool detachment from the affairs of men, his confirmed scepticism in matters of faith, his imperturbable self-confidence, all in fact rested on a blind belief in progress. And this belief was under challenge.

Carr had reacted vociferously against the pessimism prevalent in western literature after World War I. From King's College, Cambridge, John Maynard Keynes's brilliant polemic against the postwar settlement – *The Economic*

---

[116] Carr, *From Napoleon to Stalin*, p. 184.
[117] Carr to Tamara Deutscher, 23 June 1974.
[118] A. Moravia, 'Marx e Dostoievski', *Un mese in U.R.S.S.: Opere complete di Alberto Moravia*, vol. 8, Milan 1976, pp. 3–9.
[119] Carr, *Dostoevsky*, p. 314.

Consequences of Peace, published in 1920 – brought home the failure of the allies to provide for a just peace that could also ensure prosperity. T.S. Eliot's poem *The Wasteland*, which appeared just three years later, in turn articulated the widespread spiritual fatigue draining the vital energies of the west since the war. Whereas the polemic from Keynes won Carr's wholehearted approval, the deep pessimism displayed by Eliot was anathema. It cut into the belief in progress which he saw as essential to the development of civilization. He was as much against nostalgia as he was against nihilism: 'it seems to me that the main trouble in 1919 and after was that we did not realize how far things had changed and how they were moving. We kept on thinking about getting back to normal – by which we meant getting back to pre-1914 or perhaps even to the good old days of Queen Victoria. We did not understand that we were living in a new kind of world, and we did not look in front of us to see what was coming.' Whereas others were drifting into cultural pessimism, he 'suddenly . . . had the great feeling that the world was moving, changing'.[120] His belief in progress thus came to be expressed as a compelling urge to anticipate future developments, to identify with the forces of change; and his gradual abandonment of conventional liberalism left him without firm moral foundations from which he could judge the values of the forces at work.

Carr's assault on cultural pessimism was launched on Saturday, 20 July 1929. It was a very hot day. He decided not to go up to the Foreign Office. Instead he spent the morning browsing in Greenwich library 'and afterwards wrote [an] article called "Age of Reason" on modern literary tendencies'. After initially rejecting it, the *Spectator* eventually published it on 26 April 1930. The focus of the attack was the nihilism of Marcel Proust:

> It was about the turn of the century that the trouble began. It did not come from the rebels or the radicals. . . . It came rather with men like Kipling and Rostand, men loyal to the core to the old traditions, men of genius – and yet men who somehow did not quite pull it off . . . . The great days of the glory of man and his achievements were numbered. The vein was petering out; in some strange way it no longer came off. It was, men said, the end of the Victorian Age . . . . It was once the vulgar ambition of mankind to make something out of nothing; Proust brought perfection to the more genteel pastime of resolving everything into nothingness.

The collapse of morale following the Great Crash added to his concern. 'As we know,' he wrote some thirty years later, 'the great depression had really started in the autumn of 1929, but nobody yet suspected that these were the initial stages of a major breakdown in our economic and in our political system – a breakdown which was finally to confirm the verdict of 1914 on the irretrievable collapse of the comfortable, prosperous, and relatively peaceful nineteenth-century world . . . we were still living in the afterglow of that world,

---

[120] Interview with P. Scott, *THES*.

not realizing that it was an afterglow, not knowing that the sun had already set.'[121] The nihilism in literature had its counterpart in political life. In a further article begun on 3 July 1930 and published as 'England Adrift' in the *Fortnightly Review* two months later, Carr speculated on this worrying trend:

> The prevailing state of mind in England today is one of defeatism or . . . scepticism, of disbelief in herself. England has ceased to have ideals or, if she has them, to believe in the possibility of their fulfilment. Alone among the Great Powers she has ceased to have a mission . . . . The government of the day has so little faith in its capacity to tackle the major problems of our generation that it invites the other parties to assist with their advice (imagine Mr. Gladstone invoking the assistance of Lord Beaconsfield!); and the principal opposition party, knowing full well there is no solution, declines the invitation and keeps its hands free to wash them of the consequences . . . we have no convictions beyond a vague sort of fatalism.

He contrasted the malaise in Ramsay MacDonald's Britain unfavourably with the spirit of progress prevalent in Stalin's Russia, a feature that made a significant impact on him and other doubting intellectuals in search of an alternative model of advance for society:

> The Russian preaches world-revolution and the establishment of the reign of pure communism at home and abroad. His ideal, like the ideals of Christianity, is vague and probably unrealizable; its strength lies in the driving power of the faith it imparts, and in the willingness of its adherents to submit to any material sacrifice and suffering in pursuit of their sacred goal.

In a review article published in September 1931 he elaborated further on this theme:

> You feel that these people have faith, and that it is this faith which, implanted in the masses, forces them to undergo the many privations which the Five Year Plan entails . . . . They have discovered a new religion of the Kilowatt and the Machine, which may well prove to be the creed for which modern civilization is waiting.
>
> This new religion is growing up on the fringes of a Europe which has lost faith in herself. Contemporary Europe is aimlessly drifting, refusing to face unpalatable facts, and looking for external remedies for her difficulties. The important question for Europe at the present time is not whether the Five Year Plan will be completed in four years, not whether the steel production of the Soviet Union will overtake that of Great Britain and France, or whether the output of Soviet factories is up to Western standards; but whether Europe can discover in herself a driving force, an intensity of faith, comparable to that now being generated in Russia. If not, her chances of recovering seem small.[122]

Unfortunately, this was also the context in which Carr later saw Adolf Hitler: the man who came to put the Germans back on the road; that was what was

---

[121] 'Memories of the League of Nations', broadcast printed in the *Listener*, 25 April 1952.
[122] Review of *Moscow Has a Plan* in *Fortnightly*, September 1931.

deemed the most important. Where precisely the road was going somehow slipped all too easily from critical view, as did the fate of other vehicles that were driven into the ditch to make way for them. Not that he thought Britain should emulate these countries: in Russia, economic planning had yet to prove itself. But he felt strongly that his own country had to shake off the widespread and debilitating torpor:

> We shall begin once more to believe in ourselves, to find creeds worth defending, causes worth fighting for, missions worth fulfilling. The fashion of indifference and the cult of futility will pass away; and we shall cease to be defeatists. But in the meanwhile we need a faith – or at any rate a passable fetish.

The painful re-examination of the safe assumptions in which he had been reared coincided with Carr's assignment to the League of Nations section at the Foreign Office. It is difficult in retrospect, given the subsequent sad hisory of that failed organization, to convey the sense of hope that it gave rise to in the years 1924 to 1930 (when, of course, it went unchallenged about its business). 'In those years,' Carr recalled, 'the League was rapidly becoming the focus of everything that mattered in international affairs; and each successive Assembly seemed to mark some progress in what has come to be known as the "organization of peace".'[123] In the course of his duties he attended the League's eleventh annual assembly at the Palais des Nations in Geneva in September 1930. The League was dangerously out of touch with reality, though Carr recognized this only after the first major postwar international crisis broke:

> The would-be luxury hotels at Geneva, with their Victorian or Edwardian decorations and furnishings, where the delegates to the League slept and ate and worked, were full of busy self-confidence; and no delegation was busier or more self-confident than the British delegation. It was headed by Arthur Henderson, the then Foreign Secretary, and Mr. Dalton and Mr. Noel-Baker were among its leading members. The Labour Government had been in power for more than a year and was making its mark on the world. There was much talk of making the League of Nations the focus of Labour foreign policy, of making good the rather contemptuous attitude to the League said to have been adopted by the previous Conservative Government, and generally of raising British prestige at Geneva. By way of doing this, three large British cars were driven out to Geneva for the use of the delegates so that they might be spared the indignity of travelling from the hotel to the meeting place of the assembly in Genevese taxis. Under the very shadow of the greatest economic crisis in modern history we were still living in the spacious days of the nineteen-twenties.[124]

Still wafted by utopian breezes, the powers at Geneva drafted amendments to the League Covenant for an absolute veto against resort to war. This idea

---

[123] 'The League in Perspective', *Spectator*, 25 September 1936, p. 485.
[124] E.H. Carr, 'Memories of the League of Nations', *Listener*, 25 April 1952.

never succeeded because the Japanese refused to cooperate – the reason why became only too evident a year later when they ran amok all over Manchuria during the 'Black Assembly' of 1931. But neither Carr nor any of his colleagues really understood what was going on. 'On looking back, what strikes me now as odd is that it never entered the heads of any of us that a man with a tank does not waste time looking around for gaps in a rickety old fence. When the time came, it was clear enough that the fence could not keep out a jeep – let alone a tank; it would scarcely have kept out a perambulator.'[125]

The debates over free trade at Geneva also enhanced his growing awareness of the relativism of western values. He recalled

> some of the debates about the economic crisis, which seemed to spell the bankruptcy of capitalism. In particular I was struck by the fact that everyone professed to believe that tariff barriers were a major cause of aggravation of the crisis, but that practically every country was busy erecting them. I happened to hear a speech by some minor delegate (Yugoslav, I think), which for the first time in my experience put the issue clearly and cogently. Free trade was the doctrine of economically powerful states which flourished without protection, but would be fatal to weak states. This came as a revelation to me [like the revelation at Cambridge of the relativism of historiography], and was doubly significant because of the part played by free trade in my intellectual upbringing. If free trade went, the whole liberal outlook went with it.[126]

The true depth of his disillusionment became clear as soon as he burst into print under his own name after leaving the Foreign Office several years later.

Meanwhile, partly out of curiosity, partly because his official position ruled out topics of current interest, Carr returned to nineteenth century Russia as the focus of attention of his subterranean literary life. It was, however, by no means clear what precisely he was to write next. *Dostoevsky* was still being hawked around the publishing circuit when he set to work on Bakunin, the father of Russian anarchism. By 20 July 1930 he had already 'Practically finished [the] first chapter'. But for some reason – perhaps because publishers were unenthusiastic – he dropped Bakunin in the spring of 1931 and turned his attention to that other great figure from the Russian revolutionary tradition, Alexander Herzen. It was while in Riga that he had first read Herzen 'in a collected edition of his works he picked up in a secondhand book-shop'.[127] It was this material that Carr turned into one of his most celebrated studies (which in retrospect he typically described as 'frivolous'), *The Romantic Exiles*. 'Some of this needs to be read with indulgence', he wrote decades later. 'I was still very young at 40.'[128]

---

[125] Ibid.
[126] *Autobiographical sketch.*
[127] From the back cover of the Penguin edition of *The Romantic Exiles* (1949 edition).
[128] Note to Tamara Deutscher in an edition of the book that Carr gave her.

Herzen formed a part of 'that brilliant generation of the 'forties, which had left Russia in the plenitude of faith and hope, and which . . . thirty years later, found scattered and unhonoured graves in French or Swiss or English soil'.[129] Their lives were thus spent in political disappointment, 'tragedy tinged with futility', debarred from their own society and 'coming from a country whose philosophical equipment and fashionable modes of thought were twenty years behind those of Europe . . . '.[130] It was less the politics or the philosophy than the people that captured Carr's attention, though he ingeniously intertwined the two. Bakunin, like Herzen, is thus portrayed as 'not merely . . . a Romantic by conviction; he was a Romantic by temperament'.[131] Carr was equally interested in the influence on his subject of George Sand as that of Jean-Jacques Rousseau. He portrayed these exotic Russian revolutionaries with great empathy and even greater irony, an irony which some of his subjects (notably Herzen) would themselves have much appreciated, were he describing anyone but them.

The book is really quite unlike anything else Carr ever wrote. It has an energy to it and a fluidity that makes it more like a novel than a biography. It reveals a compelling fascination with people, their foibles, their motives, their passions. At the same time, the aloofness and cynicism integral to the diplomat undoubtedly enhanced the critical differences in character that separated him from these exotic creatures. Yet, for all that, the utopian and romantic elements lurking beneath the immaculate Foreign Office façade also enabled him to see something of these revolutionaries from the inside. This is easily overlooked. It was a feature of his character that was instantly spotted by Lewis Namier, with whom, as we have seen, Carr first became acquainted in the wartime Foreign Office, and who was soon to become one of the most noted, feared and – later – scorned historians of his age. 'Perhaps I have always been a romantic,' he recalled after Namier's death many years hence. 'Namier said this when I wrote *The Romantic Exiles* and *Bakunin*.' And, later, when his own marital problems came close to driving him to despair, Carr would talk about these concerns under the semi-transparent veil of a discussion of the lifes and loves of *The Romantic Exiles*.[132]

The effort put into *Bakunin* was thus not wasted: it became the foundation for a full-length biography some years later. It also had the curious side-effect of giving Carr the idea of writing a novel, 'of which the theme was the impact of an outrageous and flamboyant character modelled on Bakunin on a conventional English group'.[133] But even by his athletic standards, the novel was hastily written. Pritchett read the manuscript and thought little of it; indeed, so little that he cannot even remember having read it. On 25 April

---

[129] *Romantic Exiles*, p. 421.
[130] Ibid.
[131] Ibid., p. 258.
[132] I am grateful to Sheila Fitzpatrick for this information.
[133] *Autobiographical sketch.*

1932 Carr received a letter from Gollancz refusing publication. Years later he threw the manuscript away. The work on Herzen, however, made great strides and fitted in well with his official duties. League affairs took him to Geneva regularly each autumn for the annual session. Herzen's surviving daughter Natalie lived in Lausanne – a steamer's distance from Geneva. Carr made several trips to see her: the first on 6 September 1931; the second only a week later. He had many conversations during which she imparted a great deal from her memory. These trips, and access to letters from the Herzens that he obtained from Marcel Herwegh – the rival family – in Paris, brought the book to life in a way denied *Dostoevsky*.

Somehow Carr continued effortlessly juggling two careers. The crisis created by the Japanese occupation of Manchuria, which began on 18 September 1931, introduced an unaccustomed air of reality into the sterile debates on disarmament at Geneva: 'A[nne] went to [a] Disarmament meeting in [the] evening where there was nearly a riot', he noted wrily in his diary on 27 November. His commitment to the ideals of the League was by now threadbare. The great powers argued that unless it was acknowledged that China was in a state of war with Japan, which the League – at least at the outset – did not, then article 16, which provided for sanctions, could not come into effect. In June 1932 the Belgian delegate attempted to patch up this gaping hole with the suggestion that, instead of a state of war, the mere existence of aggression should be taken as the sufficient condition for action. It was well intended but entirely missed the point, as Carr noted. In a minute dated 24 June he wrote: 'The object is laudable; but it may be doubted whether the present reluctance of members of the League to recognize that a state of war has arisen would not be matched by an equally strong reluctance to admit the existence of aggression against "territorial integrity and existing political independence".'[134] His experience at Geneva effectively toppled another liberal idol. There were not many yet left to fall.

Geneva had, however, proved a godsend to his writing. The troubling world of diplomacy for the time being hastened his escape into the 'Nineteenth Century Portrait Gallery', which was complete by Christmas 1932. After receiving Natalie Herzen's opinion, he despatched it to Gollancz on 20 January 1933. It took them less than a week to accept it. Finally his work was gaining swift recognition. It appeared in print on 27 March at the princely sum of eight shillings and sixpence. By then he was committed to a new project that excited none of the enthusiasm that his previous work had done. As he had written on its subject in *The Romantic Exiles*:

The drab, respectable monotony of Marx's domestic existence . . . affords a striking contrast to the many-hued, incalculable diversity of the Romantic Exiles. In them Romanticism found its last expression; and though there remained a

---

[134] Minute dated 24 June 1932 on Bourquin (Belgian delegation) to Cadogan, 18 June 1932: *FO* 371/16476.

handful of dare-devil Terrorists in Russia and of picturesque anarchists in western Europe, the revolutionary movement, as the years progressed, took on more and more of the grim, dogmatic, matter-of-fact characteristics of the later Victorian age. In the person of that typical Victorian savant Karl Marx, it entered a phase whose vitality has not yet altogether exhausted itself.[135]

His ambition was still to publish a full biography of Bakunin. The preface to *The Romantic Exiles* referred to 'that amazing energumen of revolutionary anarchism – a figure at once subhuman and superhuman' whose 'meteoric orbit touches and intersects at regular intervals the circles of *The Romantic Exiles*'. 'Bakunin deserves a volume to himself,' he wrote, 'and I plead guilty to an ambition to write it at some future time.'[136] Unfortunately it was difficult to drum up enthusiasm elsewhere. Carr wrote to the greatest living expert on Bakunin in the west, Max Nettlau, who was, however, extremely proprietorial about the object of his research and affection. He had published a great deal on the subject and was, he claimed, contemplating the composition of a full-length biography (in French) himself. And when he read reviews of *The Romantic Exiles*, he feared that Bakunin would be given the same treatment. As he put it to Carr:

> No doubt you know all this, but somehow these wicked foreigners, unless fully recognized like Mazzini, have always to be presented to the ordinary public as moderate fools or eccentrics at least and the heroes, if they are wealthy men, surrounded by a worthless crowd . . . . The reviewer praises your delicacy and discretion, but with all that, such works seem to cater for curiosity, not for study; they deal with the weak sides of men whose strong sides the public ignores and does not care for.[137]

The publishing world was equally unenthusiastic. Carr recalled:

> I drew a blank everywhere, and began to get rather desperate. Finally, I got an introduction to a man in Dents [evidently Richard Church]. He was more friendly than the rest, but agreed with them that nobody wanted a book about Bakunin. He did, however, want a biography of Marx (there was some publicity at the time about the approaching 50th anniversary of his death), and if I would write one, he would give me a contract and publish it. I succumbed to the temptation, not reflecting that I knew nothing about what was really important in Marx. I read the first volume of *Capital*, not understanding it at all, the *1st Brumaire* and the *Gotha Programme*, a life of Lassalle and a lot of subsidiary material, and set to work. It was a foolish enterprise, and produced a foolish book.[138]

The biography was both highly opinionated and ill-informed. But, as with *Dostoevsky*, the importance of *Karl Marx: A Study in Fanaticism* lay not in the

---

[135] Carr, *The Romantic Exiles*, London 1933, p. 423.
[136] Ibid., pp. 8–9.
[137] Nettlau (Vienna) to Carr, 3 October 1933: *Carr Papers*.
[138] *Autobiographical sketch.*

final product, but in the impact of the research on the author. This much is apparent from an article he wrote in the *Fortnightly* in March 1933:

> There are now few thinking men who will dismiss with confidence the Marxian assumption that capitalism, developed to its highest point, inevitably compasses its own destruction. The idea is once more abroad that the capitalist system has received notice to reform or quit.[139]

Several months later he argued: 'There is a point up to which we are all Marxists now. We all seek to explain political history in terms of the underlying economic realities.'[140]

There is no evidence that he had read Marx's *German Ideology*, but he was significantly affected a few years later by Karl Mannheim's *Ideology and Utopia*, which draws upon and extends some of the basic notions underlying Marx's thesis. Those ideas clarified the lesson he had drawn from the speech delivered by the Yugoslav foreign minister at Geneva, in which he had attacked the self-serving nature of Britain's case for free trade. This lesson was the manner in which 'the opinions of political and economic groups reflected their status and their interests'. Carr was thus 'more interested in Marxism as a method of revealing the hidden springs of thought and action, and debunking the logical and moralistic façade generally erected around them, than in the Marxist analysis of the decline of capitalism. Capitalism was clearly on the way out,' he recalled years later, 'and the precise mechanism of its downfall did not seem to me all that interesting.'[141]

Carr could never truly be called a Marxist. The view he expressed in the *Sunday Times* in May 1936 in an article on 'The Origins of Liberalism' remained the view he retained for a lifetime:

> The assumption that the division of mankind into propertied and propertyless classes is the fundamental division in the modern civilized world is simply not correct; and, in particular, it is not correct where the dividing line between propertied and propertyless is a constantly shifting one, or where it is not a line at all, but a broad belt of small property-owners whose interests and affiliations lie now on one side and now on the other.[142]

He was writing as a small property-owner.

Research on Marx took him back to the old haunts: the London Library and the British Museum Reading Room. At the Museum he met and lunched with the young Jane Tabrisky (later Degras), then very much the convinced Marxist in contrast to her later years. He noted enthusiastically in his diary: she 'knows everything about [the] Marx material'.[143] Before long he was

---

[139] John Hallett, 'Karl Marx: Fifty Years After', *Fortnightly*, March 1933.
[140] John Hallett, 'Nationalism: The World's Bane', ibid., June 1933.
[141] *Autobiographical sketch.*
[142] 'The Origins of Liberalism', *Sunday Times*, 24 May 1936.
[143] Entry, 6 December 1933: *Carr Diary.*

absorbing all she had to offer and was farming out to her drafts for criticism. Tabrisky thus became the first in a long line of helpers that Carr casually recruited throughout decades of research and writing on books that took him well beyond the broad compass of his considerable expertise. By early March 1934 the first proofs of the Marx biography had arrived; and, at a pace that publishers now seem to find impossible even to approximate with high technology, it appeared in the bookshops in May. The public was not ecstatic, though George Bernard Shaw quickly identified a fellow debunker. The story is that Shaw sent him a collection of essays with a note of congratulations, but did not put any stamps on the package. When the postman demanded the surcharge, Carr characteristically refused, not knowing who had sent it. The postman, habitually a master of discretion, was unable to contain himself and pointed out that when he saw who the sender was, Carr would change his mind; which, of course, he did. Buoyed up by such unexpected recognition from such an Olympian figure, he replied on 28 August and enclosed a copy of *The Romantic Exiles*.

The problem remained of securing publication of *Bakunin*. Dents mulled over specimen chapters, now some few years old, but appeared none too enthusastic. Victor Gollancz, who had published *The Romantic Exiles*, was prepared to take a 150,000 word *Bakunin*, but no more. On 29 February 1935 Carr lunched with Namier, now a self-described Tory radical and Professor of History at Manchester University. Carr had enormous respect for Namier: an 'exotic figure', who 'towered over his contemporaries'.[144] Namier promised to get Harold Macmillan to publish the manuscript in the series he was editing. And at the end of March he finally rang up relaying 'not v[ery] good terms' from Macmillan, then a fairly modest family firm. After weighing it up for a few days, Carr accepted the offer; Macmillan thereafter published almost all his work.

As we have seen, Carr's rise to literary and academic fame was scarcely meteoric. Success was almost immediately followed by setback. No sooner were Macmillan's committed to *Bakunin* than he received the dispiriting news that Gollancz were remaindering *The Romantic Exiles*, but he barely hesitated. At the end of April he bought Honeypots, near Woking, Surrey, a large rambling house in the country with several acres of land. The family moved in that summer. The move greatly improved Anne's life. Born a farmer's daughter, she made the most of a large garden, enjoyed entertaining, developed a social life of her own and took up voluntary work.

By then, work on *Bakunin* had become an all-consuming passion, interrupted only by regular forays into the three-and-a-half acre garden with a pair of shears: 'Chopped the laurel hedge and worked on Bakunin in Sweden . . . . Busy on the hedge and Bakunin . . . Bakunin and hedge-cutting.'[145]

---

[144] 'Lewis Namier', a review of Julia Namier's *Lewis Namier.* Carr, *From Napoleon to Stalin*, chapter 23. The Namier biography became one of his favourite books, not least because Namier was one of his favourite friends.

[145] Entries, 2, 6 and 8 July 1935: *Carr Diary*.

Increasingly, work at the Foreign Office had become a trying distraction from the main task at hand. Carr had been promoted to the rank of first secretary on 14 August 1933 which certainly alleviated his financial position; but there was still no prospect of rectifying the salary anomaly. He had also come to blows with the Permanent Under Secretary, who saw a conflict with Hitler's new Germany as inevitable. On Carr's view, Britain had no interest in blocking what he still took to be Germany's rightful quest for complete national self-determination. Ironically it was the vestiges of his crumbling liberalism that provided a moral prop for his increasingly vociferous advocacy of appeasement; but more of that later.

It was at this critical point in Carr's Foreign Office career that the University College of Wales at Aberystwyth advertised a vacancy for the Woodrow Wilson Chair of International Politics, the first Chair of its kind in Britain, hitherto filled by prestigious scholars – among them, Alfred Zimmern, later Montague Burton Professor of International Relations at Oxford, and Charles Webster, later Professor of International History at the London School of Economics – as well as by academics of less consequence. It was, as he later described it, a 'fancy chair',[146] offering a number of perquisites including a generous travel budget. On Sunday 3 November 1935, with Britain's relations with Fascist Italy on the verge of war over Mussolini's invasion of Abyssinia, Carr submitted his application for the Chair. The awkward and uncomfortable dichotomy in his life could now hopefully be brought to a swift conclusion – at the expense of the Foreign Office. From Aberystwyth, he would be free to write extensively on international affairs and attack those opposed to appeasement without official hindrance.

Up to this point, family matters had been allowed to drift quietly into the background. A dark cloud had, however, emerged on the horizon that autumn when Anne fell seriously ill. She had developed a growth on her groin and on 30 September she consulted a family friend, Dr Turnbull of St. Mary's Hospital, Paddington. He advised her to consult a surgeon. The following day the consultation took place and a biopsy was recommended. This was done before the week was out. The news was frightening: the growth was malignant. Ted was visibly distraught.[147] Anne was hospitalized in Hampstead under the care of Sir Stanford Cade. It was impossible to remove the sarcoma through surgery. Instead she underwent nearly two months of intense radio-therapy which, Cade later confessed, would have been enough to kill anyone less tough. But survive she did: the treatment proved a complete success – no recurrence in her lifetime until her death in 1961 – and, on 22 November, Ted had her driven home.[148] Unfortunately, the crisis over, he then lapsed into comfortable indifference, at the very moment when the after-effects of the therapy were beginning to exacerbate Anne's ill temper.

---

[146] Interview with P. Scott, *THES*.
[147] Winnie Elkin to the author, 22 January 1984.
[148] He never succeeded in learning to drive, despite several attempts.

3

Advocate of Appeasement

The Woodrow Wilson Chair of International Politics at Aberyswyth had been founded in 1918 by Lord David Davies and his sisters, Gwendoline and Margaret. All three made equal contributions to the endowment that paid 60 per cent of the cost of the Chair; the University paid the remainder. The trust deed defined the subject as 'political science in its application to international relations with special reference to the best means of promoting peace between Nations'.[1] It thus reflected the determination of liberals and social-ists after World War I to prevent another such catastrophe. These aims were interpreted narrowly as a commitment to the League of Nations. The early occupants of the Chair, international lawyer Alfred Zimmern and diplomatic historian Charles Webster,[2] shared this philosophy. Evasion was easier in the 1920s than the 1930s; and easier for a historian than for an international lawyer or a political scientist. The international system had broken down under the combined pressure of Japanese aggression, Hitler's denunciation of the Versailles Treaty, and – before long – the Italian invasion of Abyssinia. As a consequence, opinion began to polarize between the League's ardent supporters and its disillusioned opponents.

These were the unpropitious circumstances in which the Chair had fallen vacant after the resignation of Professor Jerome Greene. Lord Davies had objected to Greene's views and demanded a veto over the new appointment. The advisory board for the Chair sat as the selection committee: Ifor Evans, the College Principal, sat as chairman ex officio; Lord Davies represented the College Council; Professor E.A. Lewis represented the College Senate; Lord Granville was nominated by the foreign secretary; Professor Gilbert Murray represented the League of Nations Union; General Sir Neill Malcolm was

---

[1] Ifor Evans, 'Lord Davies, The Wilson Chair; and the Presidency of the College', February 1941: University College of Wales, Aberystwyth, archives – *P/CR/D/18*.

[2] Webster's views are perhaps less widely known. But Carr later wrote of him: 'when he gets away from history he is apt to be pompous and discursive, and to have bees in his bonnet (mainly of the L[eague] of N[ations] U[nion] variety).' Carr to Newton (BBC), 26 August 1938: E.H. Carr Talks I 1936–1947, BBC Written Archives Centre, Caversham Park.

appointed by Chatham House; and the Warden of All Souls, W.G.S. Adams, represented Oxford University. Over fifty candidates were considered. The committee decided to interview four, on 24 January 1936: W. Arnold Forster, no academic but a prominent publicist for the League cause; Herbert Butterfield, then a very promising history lecturer at Cambridge; historian of eastern Europe C.A. Macartney; and Carr.

On the basis of the interviews all agreed to eliminate Butterfield, though we have no idea why. Four of the members spoke against Arnold Forster on the reasonable ground that he had never attended university and was essentially a publicist. Murray, who had been Forster's most vigorous backer, decided to withdraw his support. Infuriated, Lord Davies adamantly refused to follow suit. This left Macartney and Carr; Macartney had in fact marginally more votes. Both names went to the College Council for a final choice. Evans leaned very much towards Carr. Davies, bent on victory at any price, began to pull strings via the League of Nations Union to win back Murray's vote for Forster. He failed. Furthermore the Misses Davies showed no inclination to back their brother in his lone crusade. When the Council met on 6 March 1936 Davies submitted his own minority report with the preposterous claim that Forster possessed 'qualifications equal, if not superior, to those of the other two candidates', emphasizing that the decision now rested with the Council alone. But he was overruled. By now Professor at the London School of Economics, Webster was among those academics on the Council who insisted that the decision be made on academic and no other grounds. The Council thus came down in favour of Carr, appointing him on a salary of one thousand pounds a year. Whereupon – legend has it – the enraged Lord Davies stormed out of the meeting leaving his fishing tackle behind.[3] He then attempted to force a crisis by resigning as College President. On 30 April 1936 news of his resignation and the reasons behind it appeared in *The Times*; but this was only the first in a series of skirmishes that would take place sporadically over the next decade – a war that Davies would eventually win.

By the end of April Carr had cleared his desk at the Foreign Office. He must have done so with a certain amount of regret, even though his career had not advanced as rapidly as he had had every reason to expect. Although his native diffidence had won him few but firm friends, he commanded a certain respect: he was regarded as one of the brightest of his generation.[4] And Lord Gladwyn was most impressed by the fact that Carr, at the modest rank of a first secretary, could call upon the services of a typist to dictate an account of their conversations on the German problem.[5] This was, of course, an issue on which he was most outspoken. Under the nom de plume of John Hallett,

---

[3] Morgan Jones, formerly Registrar of the College, present at the meeting: Brian Porter to the author, 14 May 1984.
[4] Interview with Sir Frank Roberts, 11 February 1983.
[5] Interview, 16 November 1983.

while still in the Foreign Office, he had in January 1933 written critically in the *Fortnightly Review* of the Treaty of Versailles which 'compelled' the Germans 'to subscribe to the most ruthless and sweeping moral condemnation in history . . .'. Germany had in the meantime gained a temporary recovery in the 1920s but with the burden of reparations payments postponed, not removed. The Great Depression then thrust the country once again into 'gloom and despair'. Hitler was bidding for power: '. . . it is difficult to say whether posterity will regard Adolf Hitler as its hero or its chief villain. It is already clear, however, that he will be its most characteristic and most striking figure.' Stresemann had tried in the twenties to restore Germany's dignity by bringing the country back 'on terms of equal friendship, into the company of the Great Powers'. But 'Hitler had to face a situation in which this endeavour seemed to have failed, in which, despite every effort, equality had proved unattainable by friendly means – a situation, moreover, where moral despondency was aggravated by the widespread physical distress of the economic crisis.' Thus he had 'abandoned the policy of the velvet glove, and deliberately sought to exploit the sentiments of hatred which Stresemann had striven to exorcize . . . Jews, capitalists, Communists and foreigners . . .'. For Carr, the 'crucial point about Hitlerism' was 'that its disciples not only believe in themselves, but believe in Germany. For the first time since the war a party appeared outside the narrow circles of the extreme Right which was not afraid to proclaim its pride in being German. It will', he wrote in an act of faith, 'perhaps one day be recognized as the greatest service of Hitlerism that, in a way quite unprecedented in German politics, it cut across all social distinctions, embracing in its ranks working men, *bourgeoisie*, intelligentsia and aristocrats. "Germany, awake!" became a living national faith.'[6]

What marked Carr out after Hitler's accession to power was less his strong sympathy for the Germans – common to most liberals (witness Lloyd George's visit to Hitler) – than the ruthlessness with which he pressed home his position. Carr incisively argued, as did others, that Germany be permitted to expand into southeastern Europe. In a minute on a despatch from the British embassy in Berlin written on 30 January 1936 he argued:

> Since I think everyone is now agreed that it is dangerous to sit indefinitely on the safety-valve, and that Germany must expand somewhere, I feel that there is an over-whelming case for the view that the direction in which Germany can expand with a minimum of danger or inconvenience to British interests (whether political or economic) is in Central and South-Eastern Europe . . . .[7]

It is said that he fell out with Permanent Under Secretary Vansittart over the appeasement of Germany. Vansittart was, indeed, notoriously Germanophobe.

---

[6] John Hallett, 'The Prussian Complex', *Fortnightly Review*, January 1933, pp. 37–45.

[7] Minutes dated 30 January 1936 on Phipps (Berlin) to Vansittart (London), 22 January 1936: *Documents on British Foreign Policy 1919–1939*, 2nd series, vol. XV, ed. W. Medlicott et al., London 1976, footnote pp. 619–20.

But this was not the sum total of his views. He returned from a visit to Berlin early in October 1936 and told Nicolson that the Germans' 'capacity for violence' was 'terrifying'. 'But luckily,' he is reported to have added, 'their one obsession is Russia and Communism and their one desire to make friends with us.'[8]

Be that as it may, Carr was certainly one of the most articulate exponents of the appeasement of Germany and the desire to leave the Office was not least prompted by the determination to publicize those views. In these circumstances Aberystwyth could scarcely have found a more forceful opponent of League principles. His attitude was epitomized in a diary entry on 7 March 1936: 'Germans enter Rhineland. Home to lunch.' And this was certainly not something he came to regret in later life. 'I remember clearly,' he wrote decades hence, 'that I refused to be indignant about Hitler's re-occupation of the Rhineland in 1936 (which coincided with my exit from the F.O.). This was a rectification of an old injustice, and the Western Powers asked for what they got.'[9] Of course *The Times*, the *Daily Herald*, the *News Chronicle* and the *Evening Standard* all took a similar line. But as events began to demonstrate more clearly that their judgements had been mistaken, Carr characteristically clung all the more resolutely to his initial position. He was nothing if not tenacious.

Thus what Lord Davies feared came to pass with a vengeance. On Friday 13 March, not given to superstition, Carr left for Aberystwyth in the company of Ifor Evans on the 6.10pm from Paddington, a route that was to be all too familiar in the coming years. What he discovered on arrival was a provincial seaside town, a proud and tightly knit chapel-going community, entirely alien to a cosmopolitan ex-diplomat in search of intellectual stimulus. Anne visited the college to enquire about courses in the arts department for Rachel, then aged eighteen, and Philippa, then sixteen; but Ted and Anne soon concluded that they could never live there and Rachel instead went on to read history at her mother's college in Cambridge. The family had moved into Honeypots only a year before and Anne was adamant that Aberystwyth was no improvement on suburbia, however dull. On returning, Carr wrote to his publisher Harold Macmillan, by now the up and coming young progressive Conservative MP for Stockton, announcing his new appointment and explaining: 'the fact that the best of these chairs in the country is located in Wales is, of course, due to Lord Davies; but fortunately the obligations of residence are extremely small!' This would 'leave me freedom to write and lecture on foreign affairs, which is what I have long wanted to do'.[10]

The decision not to move to Wales meant he had to commute from Woking to London, at times staying overnight at the Oxford and Cambridge Club (to which Headlam-Morley had introduced him) when there was additional

---

[8] Conversation, 8 October 1936: Nicolson to Sackville-West, 9 October 1936: *Sackville-West Papers*, 1936.
[9] *Autobiographical sketch.*
[10] Carr to Harold Macmillan, 17 March 1936.

business at Chatham House, and leave for Aberystwyth by the 11.05am on Tuesdays. There he would stay at the Marina Hotel on the seafront for two nights, during which he would not bother to shave, and return to London by the 10.15am on Thursdays. Since Carr could work in any conceivable condition – even out on the deck of a liner in a gale – this presented no problem. At College the duties were light. He found 'stimulation' in teaching, but to his regret there were few students; international politics was not a fully-fledged degree course, which was another frustration, and Carr failed in his bid to set up a complete department. Furthermore, it had been twenty years since he had graduated, and his bland assumption that students at Aberystwyth would work as hard as classical scholars at Trinity had in 1911 proved unfounded. The majority were from another world: the surrounding constituency was more interested in hill-farming techniques than the turmoil of international politics on the other side of the mountains.

His teaching obligations amounted to a mere two lectures a week to the students – both on Wednesday morning – and one public lecture – that afternoon – delivered in the Examination Hall of the Old College to a large and motley collection of students and townsfolk. One colleague of that era who attended regularly remembers him as the best academic lecturer he had ever heard. The remainder of the teaching was conducted by a lecturer: Dennis Routh, a Fellow of All Souls, a young man with a sharp mind and a ready wit, someone Carr found both congenial and stimulating company.

Naturally the abrupt career shift disrupted work on *Bakunin*, though not quite as much as one might have expected. In mid-March 1936 – with the manuscript 'getting near its end' – Carr had decided to delay completion until the appearance of an edition of Bakunin's works then in progress in Moscow, and expected out before the end of the year. An added distraction was the writing of a short text outlining the course of international relations since 1919 – originally projected as *The World since the Peace Treaties* – an idea mooted by Evans, who wanted it in Welsh for the university press, mainly for the adult education programme. Carr was free to publish in English, too, and approached Macmillan with the suggestion that 'there might be a big demand for such a book (elementary, of course, and not more than *50,000* words) not only for W.E.A. purposes, but also for sixth forms of schools (particularly in girls' schools, where they now all study "current events")'.[11] By the end of March, Macmillan had a synopsis; by mid-May he had the introduction and the first three chapters. Carr had first tried them out on daughter Rachel, who typically offered the firm advice that 'what the sixth form hates in textbooks is anything which savours of "writing down" to them'. That summer he also committed himself to taking up research 'probably on some aspect of British policy since the war' – a decision deferred until the autumn. By then he had finished the new text, a compact and lucid history, which was published as *International Relations since the Peace Treaties* on 6 January 1937, two

---

[11] Ibid.

months before the more controversial Bakunin finally reached Macmillan.

Although Carr restrained himself in expressing his advocacy of appeasement and went out of his way to appear even-handed, the text did emphasize
that the Versailles settlement 'was imposed by the victors on the vanquished,
not negotiated by a process of give-and-take between them', that the Germans
were treated to 'unnecessary humiliations' which only encouraged the belief
'now universal in Germany and . . . tacitly accepted by a large body of opinion
in other countries, that the signature extorted from Germany in these conditions is not morally binding on her'. He was equally cautious and subtle in
getting the message across on the BBC. It was on the advice of Ifor Evans that
the Corporation had hired Carr for talks programmes from October 1936. He
was by no means a scintillating speaker; he sounded too didactic and heavy-
going for the man in the street, and friends told him that 'they could almost
hear me waiting for the clock to move on before I uttered my next word.'[12]
But the style of delivery was one thing, the content and architecture of the
talks quite another.

Delivering a superbly sculptured broadcast on the first anniversary of Hitler
entering the Rhineland on 9 March, etched in the language of common
sense and buttressed by (loaded) rhetorical questions, he expressed due sympathy with the French security dilemma which explained the draconian
conditions they had insisted upon against the Germans in 1919. His 'impartiality' seemingly established, he rapidly went on to undermine the very
principle that Paris (and now Moscow, in an abrupt about-turn) was using to
safeguard its security: namely, the sanctity of international agreements. In
entering the Rhineland, Hitler had torn up two treaties: the Versailles Treaty,
and the Locarno Pact of 1925. The latter, unlike the former, had been freely
negotiated by Germany and had provided – courtesy of the British
Government – a mutual guarantee for both France and Germany against
aggression from the other party. Indeed, the very proposal for Locarno could
be attributed to a German initiative. Hitler had thus struck a blow not merely
at a dictated peace but also at the sanctity of treaties.

Did that matter? Carr went on to argue, with elegant deviousness, that
even in domestic law no contract is recognized as valid if signed under intim-
idation. 'Some contracts will be set aside by the state on what are called
grounds of general policy or the public interest. Sometimes the state will lay
down certain rules to which contracts must conform.' He cited the Rent
Restriction Acts as an example, all to demonstrate that 'in every day life the
sanctity of contracts isn't by any means unlimited.' Having undermined what
most would have accepted as a settled assumption, he then deftly drew the listeners on to his own assumptions, without their quite noticing it. 'Now the
difficulty in the international world is that you haven't got any organization
which has power to override an international treaty either because of the

---

[12] Carr to John Pringle (BBC), 5 February 1937: E.H. Carr Talks I, BBC Written Archives
Centre.

conditions in which it was concluded, or because it is contrary to the general policy or the public interest, or for any other reason.' The listener is thus carefully manoeuvred into lumping Versailles and Locarno into one pot together without any due distinction: there is not anyone to rule on contracts; even the Permanent Court of International Justice at the Hague has no power to rule that some clause or other 'is contrary to the general interest, and therefore null and void'. The League of Nations simply was not interested in doing so. The listener is thus left with the clear impression that since there is no one to arbitrate, it is up to each country to choose which treaties it cares to abide by and that they are within their rights to do so. Having effectively removed ethical and legal considerations from the case, Carr went on to dispose of the practical reasons for stopping Hitler.

It did 'look to the plain man as if we should have been under an obligation to go to France's help if she had called upon us; and in that case we might have found ourselves at war with Germany in a cause of which, at the bottom of our hearts, we didn't really approve.' However, he wanted listeners to reflect on the changing nature of war. 'It is commonly said that in the next war there *won't be* any civilians; and we all understand what that means. But I'm not sure that people have yet reflected very much on the effect which this change must have on the question of international treaties when these treaties contain an obligation, as they often do, to go to war if certain circumstances arise.' And this meant governments had to carry public opinion with them on questions of war and peace. Moreover, in 1914 they had not fought to defend the treaty guaranteeing Belgian independence nearly a century before; they had fought because the security of Belgium was regarded as vital to 'our own national independence'. 'A good many of us certainly remember the signing of the Locarno treaty and were old enough to have an opinion about it at the time. But, if a year ago, Great Britain had had to go to war on the strength of the Locarno Treaty, the war would have swept into its clutches a whole generation of young people to whom Locarno was only something they'd read about in books . . .'.

Instead, Carr suggested the possibility of making it a rule 'that any such agreement should have to be reviewed by Parliament say, every ten years, so that every fresh generation will have to consider what its obligations are and express its opinion about them'.[13] What, of course, he omitted to mention was the possibility that the failure to defend the sanctity of treaties against someone like Hitler might ultimately lead Germany to threaten British interests and security, that sometimes legal principles actually coincide with the national interest; but to say that would have irreparably weakened his case and, anyway, he simply did not believe it.

The BBC broadcast showed just how brilliant a propagandist Carr could be. Release from diplomatic duties had enabled him to develop further the skills which would later bring him into the editorial offices of the most powerful

---

[13] 'Hitler Enters the Rhineland', broadcast 9 March 1937. In the author's possession.

organ of opinion in the country. The use to which he put those tremendous skills is, of course, another matter. Even his producer found the point that 'most people' were 'not very upset' by the German occupation of the Rhineland a little hard to take.[14]

The late 1930s thus saw Carr active on several fronts: managing projects at Chatham House, teaching at Aberystwyth, external examiner for the Cambridge History Tripos, propagating his political views in the media, all accomplished alongside his regular academic writing, which by no means suffered as a result. *Bakunin*, for example, had proved a serious challenge, requiring original research from a variety of documentary sources in other languages and a good deal of revision. None the less, it duly appeared on schedule by the end of 1937, an authoritative and eminently readable work which filled a major gap in the literature, particularly in exploring Bakunin's personal life and demonstrating the link between his childhood and his later political activities. Hitherto, there had existed only the manuscript biography by Max Nettlau that was unavailable to most of the public and was some forty years old; a very partisan book by Steklov (whom Carr had met in Moscow); an extended essay by Izvolsky in French; and a biography in Russian by Polonsky, which had gone unnoticed.

Bakunin had a mixed reception. The young, ambitious and already influential Isaiah Berlin of New College, Oxford, praised it as 'a model of its kind, one of the best documented, best written, most important biographies of our time'. He faulted the author on several points, however; the most important being the lack of attention to ideological issues: Bakunin's influence on serious thinkers such as Herzen and Belinsky could not, he suggested, be reduced to the impact of personality, however overpowering that personality may have been. This approach, he argued, robbed Bakunin of his grandeur as a historical figure.[15] Yet Berlin was never entirely consistent on this point. Many years later he changed his mind about Bakunin and subsequently moved very close to Carr's position, though without acknowledgement, when he wrote that Bakunin 'has not bequeathed a single idea worth considering for its own sake; there is not a fresh thought, not even an authentic emotion, only amusing diatribes, high spirits, malicious vignettes, and a memorable epigram or two'.[16] Few, however, were so intimately interested in such exotic thinkers. Despite the criticisms in the review, Carr wrote to Berlin saying he was the only reviewer who knew something about the topic.[17]

It was, indeed, the personality of Bakunin rather than his politics that had originally inspired Carr's work. His complete agnosticism and emotional

---

[14] Pringle to Sir Richard Maconachie, Director of Talks, BBC, 24 February 1937: E.H. Carr Talks, BBC Written Archives Centre. This comment was made upon Ted's first draft of the talk.

[15] Berlin, 'The Father of Anarchism', *Spectator*, 31 December 1937.

[16] Berlin, 'Herzen and Bakunin on Individual Liberty', *Continuity and Change in Russian and Soviet Thought*, ed. E. Simmons, Cambridge, Mass. 1955, p. 498.

[17] Berlin to the author, 29 November 1995.

detachment, qualities Berlin had previously detected in the *Romantic Exiles*, inspired a delightful, if caustic, comment:

> Mr. Carr recognizes the magnitude and the fascination of the man he is describing; but being free from all political or emotional bias, he has instead developed the interest of a collector in an exceptionally odd and fascinating piece. He is a connoisseur of nineteenth-century revolutionaries as others of rare ivories or butterflies; and he treats them with the same delicate, well-informed, faintly proprietorial interest.[18]

Berlin was thus irresistibly attracted to Carr's work, while also troublingly repelled by it. A deep-seated ambivalence had taken root in his attitude towards Carr: he was both enormously stimulated by the sheer intellectual power of the man and at the same time profoundly disturbed by the evident lack of passion and warmth: an attraction of minds divided by temperament. They met and became acquainted as a result of the *Spectator* review. Yet, behind a façade of formal courtesies, changing political circumstances reinforced the elements of repulsion – Berlin the quintessential liberal and Carr the proto-authoritarian – and ultimately made them the best of enemies; so much so that, after Carr's death in 1982, Berlin could deliver harsh rebukes to his erstwhile rival, puzzlingly punctuated at regular intervals with the words, 'But, we were the best of friends.'[19] And while Berlin could find the humanitarian in Machiavelli, he would never even hear of the assertion that Carr had once been a liberal.

Berlin's was not the only critical reaction. Nettlau launched an unpleasant tirade, which did him no credit at all. The aim of the attack was directed at the same point made by Berlin – the author's apparent indifference to Bakunin's politics. This was also the criticism echoed by a more formidable voice, from across the Atlantic, that of Edmund Wilson. His review was unambiguously hostile: 'Cold Water on Bakunin'. It opened in a manner that left little doubt about what was to follow:

> Mr. E.H. Carr is an odd phenomenon – perhaps a symptom of the decay of Great Britain. A former member of the English diplomatic service, with an unusual equipment of languages, he now uses his knowledge of Europe to write the biographies of nineteenth-century revolutionists.[20]

What grated on Wilson – apart from Carr's nationality – was the 'simple amused condescension' he detected throughout the book and, indeed, throughout all his works. 'It has all the faults of his other books . . . the never intermitting British chill, which is always putting Bakunin in his place and

---

[18] Berlin, 'The Father of Anarchism'.
[19] In discussion with the author, 1983. Berlin later described theirs as a 'peculiar relationship' (Berlin to the author, 27 September 1995). But it remained a puzzle to him to the very end.
[20] Wilson, 'Cold Water on Bakunin', *New Republic*, 7 December 1938.

which gets on one's nerves with its ironical characterization of all Bakunin's projects as "interesting", all his ideas as "remarkable".' Part of the fault lay in the fact that Carr had no evident political position from which to engage Bakunin. Wilson, like Berlin, was therefore somewhat puzzled about his motivation:

> We wonder why he should have gone to the immense trouble of exploring these inaccessible materials and getting up these complicated subjects . . . merely in order to lift the eyebrow over them; and we ask ourselves whether Mr. Carr may not be simply a Foreign Office Englishman who has been led more or less accidentally through his knowledge of Germany and Russia to do some work in a historical field hitherto unexplored in English.

The more he wrote, the more indignant Wilson became: 'why should it be assumed that there is something intrinsically ridiculous or undignified about the movement for national workshops, the decisions of the International or the agitation in favour of the International carried on by the watchmakers of the Jura?'[21]

Wilson had a point. Carr was less interested in philosophical issues – certainly compared to Berlin. But Berlin and Wilson also missed something essential. It was not that Carr lacked passion; rather, it was suppressed. It was not mere intellectual drive, literary ambition, love of the exotic or pure whimsy that drew him into the coven of utopian revolutionaries. There was something deep within him that found them irresistible. He could not, at this stage, identify with their politics, which seemed wildly impracticable; he could, however, surreptitiously identify with their spirit of rebellion. They were the ultimate outsiders; Carr looked like an insider, but he had – somewhere deep within – become an outsider. What was missing was a true ideological cause to which this outsider could consciously attach himself. Instead, his energies as a closet rebel were channelled into support for Germany's right to challenge the peace settlement. The seeming detachment with which Carr now promulgated his views on international relations masked a deep and powerful, if only half conscious, emotional commitment.

The appointment to Aberystwyth had given Carr a prominent platform from which to pronounce on world politics. This platform and his second career as publicist gave him a deep sense of his own value, long denied him in the Foreign Office; only very rarely did the old feeling of being undervalued prompt a fierce retort. An instance of this occurred in 1938, when he was offered and accepted the role of interlocutor for a series of talks on the Mediterranean. Guy Burgess was involved at the BBC in settling the subsequent arrangements, for which Carr was paid handsomely. Burgess, for all his qualities, and the Russian Intelligence Services evidently appreciated them,

---

[21] Ibid.

was no paragon of organization. When the *Radio Times* appeared to announce the forthcoming talks, Carr's name was unaccountably omitted. Instead of assuming a natural mishap, Carr suspected the worse. 'I am definitely not prepared to take part in the series as an anonymous man in the street,' he wrote; 'nor was that the understanding when I was invited.'[22]

The only other Chair of international relations was held at the London School of Economics by Carr's colleague Charles Manning, a classicist and former Rhodes scholar from South Africa: a stimulating teacher, who hoped to create a science out of international relations; but a man who published nothing of substance that was not opaque. Carr always considered himself a friend, but found Manning's attachment to racial segregation peculiar in so cultivated a scholar. The main meeting ground for those interested in questions of international relations was neither Aberystwyth, of course, nor the LSE, but Chatham House in London's clubland, where diplomats, journalists and academics could meet in an informal setting. Carr had joined what was then the British (later Royal) Institute of International Affairs in October 1922, courtesy of Headlam-Morley, soon after his return from Paris. At that time, he had cited his interests as 'France, Germany, Austria, Russia and the ex-Russian states. China. Currency Questions.' To the question: would you be prepared to join in discussion? he wrote 'No. (member of the F.O.)' – which shows how little time has changed.[23] Chatham House did, however, provide weekly meetings, a small reference library and two bimonthly publications.

By 1936 the institute was in the hands of Professor Arnold Toynbee, another acquaintance from the wartime Foreign Office. Toynbee has rightly been described as 'a man of prodigious intelligence and equal industry'.[24] Aside from his magnum opus on the history of civilization, Toynbee edited and largely wrote the invaluable Chatham House annual surveys of world affairs which have provided many an academic with the raw material for work on the period. He was an anguished liberal, whereas Carr had resolutely broken with much of that tradition. As has been noted, 'Toynbee's faith – please mark that word – from the Peace Conference to the Abyssinian crisis lay in the liberal, rational humanism which underpinned the League of Nations. The failure of the League, more particularly of Britain and France, in that crisis threw him into violent despair.'[25] He lost his belief in the League and 'transferred it to God'.[26]

The Institute which Toynbee directed not only published its survey, it also sponsored collective studies of world events of a more analytical nature. Now that Carr was a professor – though he requested not to be addressed as

---

[22] Carr to Guy Burgess (BBC), 6 October 1938: E.H. Carr Talks, BBC Written Archives Centre; Burgess replied on 10 October in a mollifying letter of apology: ibid.
[23] Carr membership file: RIIA archives, October 1922.
[24] Unpublished but brilliant vignette by Peter Calvocoressi, quoted with the kind permission of the author.
[25] Ibid.
[26] Ibid.

such[27] – he was invited to take charge of some of these projects, including
that of the Nationalism Study Group set up by Garthorne-Hardy, who now
wanted to hand over to a competent chairman who was not anti-German. Its
secretary was the young Germanist, Michael Balfour – then a junior research
Fellow at St. John's College, Oxford. The group eventually produced a rather
modest pamphlet; but the work done eventually formed the basis for a slim
but pathbreaking book published in 1945 as *Nationalism and After*.

Carr wanted his friend Namier to speak to the group on Zionism and central Europe. 'I like Namier's mind,' he wrote later, 'though I do disagree with
most of his opinions, because it applies a sharp cutting edge to a lot of woolly
thinking.'[28] But Namier was a somewhat explosive personality. He and
Toynbee had evidently come to blows during the war in the Political
Intelligence Department of the Foreign Office; a difference of temperament
as much as of reason, perhaps. Toynbee later described Namier, for whom he
certainly had respect, as 'never quite naturalized intellectually'.[29] No less
important was the fact that Toynbee looked benignly on the Arabs, whereas
Namier was a Zionist. Thus instead of graciously accepting Carr's invitation,
Namier, always a somewhat fragile if overbearing ego, characteristically
launched a tirade against Chatham House for his not having been invited to
become a member of the group in the first place. He attacked the Institute
publications on Palestine and expressed particular dislike of Toynbee as 'pro-
Arab . . . a sentimentalist and a moralist, not a serious historian'. Carr was thus
placed in a rather embarrassing position. 'A good deal of this is, of course,
childish,' he wrote to Chatham House secretary Ivison Macadam, 'and you
have got to allow for this element in Namier, combined with his immense
intelligence and knowledge about international affairs. There is always an element of difficulty about co-operation with Namier, unless you know him
extremely well (as I do).'[30] It was a pity, but the group decided that on balance
they would prefer to do without him; and unfortunately the meagre results of
their work testify to the folly of the decision.

Carr's main preoccupation after surrendering *International Relations since
the Peace Treaties* to the publisher in January 1937 was a new project on 'Peace
and International Politics'. He thought of entitling it *Utopia and Reality*. This
was to be an introduction to international relations for the university student,

---

[27] Chatham House circular, 27 October 1936: RIIA archives. On 2 September 1950 he also
wrote to Harold Macmillan: 'Don't you think it is now time to drop the "professor" as I have
not been active in that capacity for three or four years?': Carr to Macmillan, 2 September
1950: Macmillan's company archives. There is also reference in a letter to Niuta Kallin of the
BBC to the fact that he was 'no lover of titles': Carr to Kallin, 7 July 1955: E.H. Carr File 2,
1948–1962, BBC Written Archives Centre. Later in life Carr insisted that Tamara Deutscher
address letters to him at home as 'professor' because when she failed to do so Betty Behrens
occasionally opened them in error. Betty thereafter unknowingly assumed that his preference was mere amour-propre: possibly a case of projection on her part.

[28] Carr to Betty Behrens, 16 December 1964.

[29] A. Toynbee, 'Lewis Namier, Historian', *Encounter*, January 1961, vol. XVII, no. 1, pp. 42–3.

[30] Carr to Ivison Macadam, 28 January 1937: RIIA archives, Carr membership file.

but fast became a devastating polemic directed against the ideals that overlay the Versailles peace settlement and were epitomized in the League of Nations; a polemic all the more acute for the fact that these ideals were once his own. Macmillan was, however, unhappy about such an abstract title, since he felt it would make it more difficult to sell.[31] The awkward compromise they settled on was *The Twenty Years' Crisis 1919–1939*, which has since given little idea as to what the book was actually about and has led unwary readers to confuse it with his previous text.

Carr finished the draft of the first chapter with characteristic speed and by early February this and the second chapter were in Routh's hands for criticism, which was usually aired in the train from Paddington and Oxford en route to Aberystwyth. Manning and Carr's more down-to-earth colleague from the Foreign Office, William Strang, also commented on these drafts. This illustrates the way Carr worked, certainly from the time of the Marx biography. Even in areas where he possessed sufficient expertise, his concern to get the facts straight and the analysis as precise and logical as possible demonstrated an extraordinary degree of self-discipline – not to say humility – all too rare in accomplished academics. He had internalized Housman's asceticism and blithely expected others to work to similar demands.

The book took an unusual length of time by his normal standards. There was, after all, nothing in the form of a text on the conduct of international relations that offered anything like the rigour required. The contract was signed in July 1938. Carr fully expected to complete the book by the end of the year. By May 1939, however, although 'virtually finished', he was still dissatisfied with the final chapter, not least because the international crisis was not yet over; and he was unsurprisingly anxious lest the book appear incomplete. 'Being an analysis of fundamental trends in international politics, it is not immediately topical', he wrote. 'But one cannot help feeling that something may happen which one can hardly help taking account of; and I am therefore reluctant to complete my MS till the last moment.'[32] At this stage, Carr prided himself on his realism. While those around him were taking moral positions on international affairs, he saw himself sustaining cool detachment. On 18 May he wrote to the more utopian Toynbee about Chatham House's *Survey of International Affairs* which, Carr argued, had grown too large, had lost perspective and 'balance'. Taking as an example its coverage of the Spanish civil war and reacting strongly against the high emotionalism whipped up by the left, he wrote:

It seems to me that a certain sympathy for Franco has been generated by the continual bombardment of the Government by the supporters of the other side. If you are continually told that you ought to support the Loyalists because they are democrats (which is untrue), or because they are a legal government (which is

---

[31] Carr to Harold Macmillan, 27 July 1939: Macmillan's company archives.
[32] Ibid., 31 May 1939.

humbug), or because British interests are at stake (which you do not believe, and which, in any case, you do not believe to be the real motive of your assailant), you will sooner or later get to dislike the Loyalists . . . .[33]

The Twenty Years' Crisis was a brutal and damning indictment of the utopian approach to international relations adopted by liberals and socialists since the Versailles peace. Since Carr had as a young man internalized those very ideals, the text was a form of exorcism of what was now seen as tainted and unjustified. It was his first onslaught against established liberal thought. He later explained it in slightly different terms:

> *The Twenty Years' Crisis* was written with the deliberate aim of counteracting the glaring and dangerous defect of nearly all thinking, both academic and popular, about international politics in English-speaking countries from 1919 to 1939 – the almost total neglect of the factor of power.[34]

Indeed, Carr set out to do for the understanding of international politics what Machiavelli had done for domestic politics; quite consciously so. As early as August 1930 he had expressed approval of Machiavelli's contribution in 'rudely' brushing aside 'the vague ideals of altruism and humanitarianism to which men did lip service and no more'.[35] 'Machiavelli's starting-point,' he noted in 1939, 'is a revolt against the utopianism of current political thought.'[36] 'The realists of the Renaissance made the first determined onslaught on the primacy of ethics and propounded a view of politics which made ethics an instrument of politics, the authority of the state being thus substituted for the authority of the church as the arbiter of morality.'[37] He argued:

> The teleological aspect of the science of international politics has been conspicuous from the outset. It took its rise from the great and disastrous war; and the overwhelming purpose which dominated and inspired the pioneers if the new science was to obviate a recurrence of this disease of the international body politic.[38]

It was, he stated, the 'hard ruthless analysis of reality which is the hallmark of science'.[39]

The book revolves around the distinction between utopia and reality, theory and practice, the intellectual and the bureaucrat. In Carr's view the intellectual tended towards the left 'just as naturally as the bureaucrat, the man of practice, will gravitate towards the Right'.[40] Now an academic, though

---

[33] Carr to Toynbee, 18 May 1938: RIIA archives, Carr membership file.
[34] Preface to the second edition, 15 November 1945.
[35] Review of a book on Machiavelli by Janni: *Fortnightly Review*, August 1930.
[36] Carr, *The Twenty Years' Crisis 1919–1939: An Introduction to the Study of International Relations*, London 1939, p. 81.
[37] Ibid., p. 31.
[38] Ibid., p. 11.
[39] Ibid., p. 13.
[40] Ibid., p. 26.

apparently unaffected by his own dictum, his aim was to impart the lessons of the bureaucrat to the intellectual camp. At the same time, Carr had no illusions about the seeming autonomy of the ivory tower. He also argued that intellectuals 'liked to think of themselves as leaders whose theories provide the motive force for so-called men of action'; but in reality their thought was 'conditioned by forces external to themselves'.[41] Thus the utopianism of the intellectuals all too often served more concrete material purposes, without the intellectuals themselves being aware of the fact; and the application of these ideals without regard to their base in real interests led to disastrous policies. Carr's aim was to unmask that utopianism and to show its hidden meaning.

The peace settlement of 1919 had suffered from lack of consciousness about the true roots of liberal ideals: 'the view that the nineteenth century liberal democracy was based, not on a balance of forces peculiar to the economic development of the period and countries concerned, but on certain a priori principles which had only to be applied in other contexts to produce similar results, was essentially utopian'.[42] Thus at least one object of the assault was the inefficiency produced by such naivety: 'The liberal democracies scattered throughout the world by the peace settlement of 1919 were the product of abstract theory, stuck no roots into the soil, and quickly shrivelled away.'[43]

This utopianism also presupposed a natural harmony of interests; but this assumed 'that every nation has an identical interest in peace, and that any nation which desires to disturb the peace is therefore both irrational and immoral'.[44] It is here that Carr's general assault on the self-interestedness of Anglo–American liberalism intersects with his case for appeasement. It was Britain that desired peace; the Germans who were bent on disturbing the peace. 'The common interest in peace masks the fact that some nations desire to maintain the status quo without having to fight for it, and others to change the status quo without having to fight in order to do so.'[45] The economic counterpart to this was free trade. Here Carr called upon his recollections of the Yugoslav foreign minister whom he had heard in Geneva attacking the self-interested sermonizing of the industrialized countries. 'The old "things-will-right themselves" school of economists argued that if nothing were done and events were allowed to follow their natural course from an economic point of view, economic equilibrium would come about of its own accord . . . . But how would that equilibrium come about? At the expense of the weakest.'[46]

---

[41] Ibid., p. 20.
[42] Ibid., p. 37.
[43] Ibid., pp. 37–8.
[44] Ibid., p. 67.
[45] Ibid., p. 68.
[46] Ibid., p. 74.

His was an assault on both the political and the economic underpinnings of the international system laid down largely under British influence during the heyday of liberalism in the nineteenth century. Its extraordinary originality and effectiveness is apparent even today to those who study international relations. Despite the fact that Carr aimed his argument as justification for appeasement, the work retains a more universal significance. No one had hitherto systematically analysed the conduct of international relations in such frighteningly realist terms. At the very least into the nineteenth century political philosophers – with the exception of the 'utopians' – had largely ignored international political behaviour and focused instead on the realm of domestic politics; a myopia currently reflected in the exclusively domestic orientation of even the most prestigious schools teaching the history of political thought. Carr's epitaph for Machiavelli stands as well for his own, written as it was after publication of *The Twenty Years' Crisis* and when the very outbreak of war had finally destroyed his own lingering illusions:

> Where Machiavelli is . . . most original and most modern is in his attempt to treat politics as an ethically neutral science, not as a branch of ethics. There is an element of technical efficiency in politics which is as independent of moral considerations as are the qualities of high explosives . . . . The greatness of Machiavelli is that he saw a part, though not the whole, of the truth about politics with unrivalled penetration.[47]

Of course, Machiavelli too was inspired by indignation at the incompetence of others; he too had ideals about the direction politics should take, as Carr duly noted.[48]

Therein lies the paradox of *The Twenty Years' Crisis*. Carr had banished the shibboleths of Victorian liberalism in the name of realism; yet vestiges of this liberalism had ultimately motivated his onslaught. It had failed to live up to his high expectations, it had been sold as a fake remedy. This would not have mattered in the slightest but for the fact that at least some of the evils that liberalism sought to expunge still incited his indignation. Carr was never a pure realist, if such a person ever existed – and he argued that they could not. His liberalism had been less the liberalism of Adam Smith or John Stuart Mill than of the era of radical reform under Lloyd George; it was a concern for the underdog, liberal radicalism or radical liberalism rather than that of the great tradition. In a sense, therefore, Carr was making the shift from a primary concern about political freedom to that of primary concern about economic and social welfare; and this was a shift essentially from liberal to socialist priorities, a shift reflecting the bitter experience of the Great Depression, which had made its impact even on young

---

[47] 'Is Machiavelli a Modern?' (a review of Butterfield, *The Statecraft of Machiavelli*), *Spectator*, 28 June 1940.
[48] 'In fact, Machiavelli is not so consistent', he noted. 'His realism breaks down in the last chapter of *The Prince*, which is entitled 'An Exhortation to free Italy from the Barbarians' – a goal whose necessity could be deduced from no realist premiss.' *The Twenty Years' Crisis*, p. 11.

Conservatives like Harold Macmillan. What Carr had exorcized from his consciousness was Mill's concern for the individual as against society; what he had no time for was bourgeois political democracy – it was inefficient. Others who had been affected in like manner – Oswald Mosley and, for a brief time, Harold Nicolson – drifted towards fascism; others still – one thinks immediately of the Cambridge spies like Kim Philby – had drifted to communism, at least in part in reaction to fascism. But Carr was the archetypal lone crusader, a Don Quixote without even a Sancho Panza.

There was thus something curiously moralistic about the new realist. While proclaiming a doctrine of ruthless realism he was in fact pushing for policies justified in moral terms. On the one hand he justified whatever the leading 'have-not' powers (like Germany) did on essentially moral grounds – for what else does the term 'have not' imply? On the other hand, he cut the ground from under those who argued for resistance to 'have not' demands not only on the basis of morality (they were 'haves') but also on the grounds that they should be 'realistic' about ends and means: they did not have the wherewithal to defend the status quo. Carr was only too aware of Francis Bacon's maxim: 'It is the solecism of power to think to command the end, and yet not to endure the means.' At the same time, however, it would be safe to conclude that he would never have written *The Twenty Years' Crisis* had he not mainly been concerned about the fate of Germany. Those who argue that he was *merely* obsessed with power, therefore, entirely miss the point; he was much more inconsistent in his thinking than they suppose, and in that sense much more human, too. But he did recognize that power had a peculiar quality of its own. It was not just a tool for whoever reached the top. It dictated certain necessities. This was a lesson that had become second nature to Carr as a diplomat.

The more foolish passages – and, given his skill with a pen, these views will never appear as extreme in print as they were felt in practice – were excised from later editions. Such instances occur in the chapter on 'Peaceful Change':

> In March 1939, the Prime Minister admitted that in all modifications of the [Versailles] Treaty down to and including the Munich Agreement, there was 'something to be said for the necessity of a change in the existing situation'. If, in 1935 and 1936, this 'something' had been clearly and decisively said, to the exclusion of scoldings and protests, by the official spokesmen of the status quo Powers, it might not yet have been too late to bring further changes within the framework of peaceful negotiation.[49]

He then unfortunately cited the Munich agreement as a model for negotiating peaceful change: corresponding 'both to a change in the European equilibrium of forces and to accepted canons of international morality'.[50]

For some, most notably Vansittart, a quick visit to Germany was sufficient to

---

[49] Ibid., pp. 281–2.
[50] Ibid., p. 282.

dispel any illusions that Hitler might be another Stresemann, bent only upon the restoration of the injustices imposed in 1919. For Carr, the opposite was the case. This was not least because he had an inherent tendency to go against the trend, but it was partly also due to a quick visit to the Soviet Union which had driven him to revise his otherwise positive impressions of the massive social and economic experiment taking place under Stalin's brutal direction. Not that Carr's illusions ever extended as far as the fatuous fellow-travelling fraternity such as Sidney and Beatrice Webb, whom he had occasion to mock gently in reviews. 'Mr. and Mrs. Webb', he wrote in February 1936, 'go through a whole chapter of verbal contortions to explain exactly why and how the Soviet Union is a democracy.' Their *Soviet Communism: A New Civilisation* was, he concluded, 'inconsistent and muddle-headed'.[51] The irony which so upset Edmund Wilson and annoyed Berlin was a necessary asset for a diplomat, and generally guarded Carr against the dangers of being hoodwinked by political phenomena (Hitler being a glaring exception). But, just as he had been impressed by the revival of German nationalist spirits with the rise of Hitler, so too had he seen in the fanaticism of the Five Year Plans a positive sign of Russia's future revival. He saw both regimes in common terms: the trend towards the corporate state; economic planning being its most novel feature.

'Fascism,' Carr wrote in May 1936, 'whatever its catch-words and slogans, is as revolutionary in essence as the Soviet system. The processes which have destroyed Liberalism in Russia, in Italy, and in Germany clearly have their root in the same necessity – the supercession of laissez faire by State capitalism.'[52] The link between that process and the New Deal, for example, in the United States was never lost on its Republican opponents, nor on some concerned liberals. In *The Good Society* Walter Lippmann advocated a return to liberalism and laissez faire. Carr attacked him:

> Seeking Utopias in the past is a strangely out-moded pursuit. History does not double back on its tracks; and the way out of our troubles is more likely to be found in a forward advance through the present phase of planned collectivism than in a return to the point where our ancestors are alleged to have gone wrong seventy or eighty years ago.[53]

Carr should have been more interested in Roosevelt's New Deal. Indeed he spent the first three months of 1938 in the United States, primarily visiting university departments that taught international relations, but also meeting the great and the good, including Lippmann. He even had tea at the White House with Mrs Roosevelt. Yet the United States appeared to pass through his consciousness leaving scarcely a trace behind.

---

[51] *Fortnightly*, February 1936.
[52] 'The Origins of Liberalism', *Sunday Times*, 24 May 1936.
[53] 'The Search for Utopia', *Spectator*, 24 December 1937.

Carr became more explicit about his newly acquired but as yet uncommitted interest in collectivism in 'Hitler's Gospel and Stalin's', published by the *Spectator* on 16 September 1938: 'The problem which confronts us today', he wrote, 'is . . . not a conflict of ideologies, but a world-wide phenomenon of which the totalitarian states are the most complete and uncompromising expression.' At this stage he still felt the need to express his reservations. Democracy was, he insisted, still ultimately more efficient: 'every regime needs the individual,' he argued, 'if not as an end, at any rate as an instrument, and the greatest survival power is most likely to be displayed by that regime in which the end and the instrument are most closely identified.' A year later, however, he found less need to distance himself from the new spirit of collectivism, and whereas others – such as G.D.H. Cole at Oxford – who took water with their Marx would seek to fudge the obvious association between social planning in democracies and the operation of the Leviathans further east, Carr typically chose to accentuate the similarities: 'the fact remains', he wrote, 'that the whole world is moving in the same direction, and that the resemblances in the economic structure of Soviet, Fascist and democratic countries are rapidly becoming quite as striking as the differences between them.'[54] Before long he was enthusiastically advocating a narrowing of their differences, while trying to preserve the essentials of individual liberty.

In choosing between the Fascist and Communist realities, Carr most definitely preferred Germany. Russia, where the show-trials had started in August 1936, increasingly disturbed him. On 28 August 1936 he published an article in the *Spectator* entitled 'The Twilight of the Bolsheviks'. It left no doubt about his reaction:

> The liberal friends of the Soviet Union, who took at its face value the new 'democratic' constitution announced for adoption by the All-Union Congress of Soviets next November, and persuaded themselves that the Soviet regime was really moving at last in the direction of liberty and toleration, cannot conceal their bewilderment. Even the more sceptical [Carr] have been horrified at this public reversion to terrorist methods.

He decided to see for himself.

The requirements of the 'fancy' Aberystwyth Chair meant that Carr had to present annual plans for foreign travel; he could spend up to four hundred pounds a year – a not inconsiderable sum in those days. He told the committee overseeing the Chair that he intended to visit Moscow during May–June 1937 via Berlin and Warsaw, probably taking in the Baltic states as well, 'to study on the spot how the situation in Eastern Europe is developing'.[55]

---

[54] 'Politics and Economics in Russia', *Spectator*, 1 September 1939.
[55] Minutes of Meeting of Wilson Chair of International Politics Advisory Board, 9 June 1936: College archives, Aberystwyth, R/DES/IP/3.

Contacting the Soviet embassy in London, he tactlessly asked ambassador Ivan Maisky for an introduction to the Communist International, which the Soviet Government had, since Lenin, pretended it had no control over. He had better luck at the German embassy; they gave him a series of introductions for his stay in Berlin. Finally on the afternoon of 1 May he and Anne embarked on the *Kooperatsiya* for Leningrad. Two days later they passed through the Kiel Canal and on the morning of the sixth the ship arrived off Kronstad, tying up at Leningrad at 9.15am. By eleven o'clock they had reached the Hotel Astoria in the centre of town, where they were met by Dickenson, the British vice-consul.

The subsequent five days were taken up sightseeing. Everything went according to plan until Carr unexpectedly encountered Prince Mirsky outside the hotel. Mirsky had, like a number of patriotic but misguided emigrés fooled by official propaganda, returned to the Soviet Union when conditions had been improving. By now, however, the terror unleashed by Stalin to wipe out all conceivable opposition and potential opposition was working its deadly way across the entire country, through party and state. Mirsky therefore pretended not to recognize Carr. But the latter, oblivious to the folly of his behaviour, foolishly persisted in trying to engage him in a conversation that may well have cost Mirsky his life. Any contact with foreigners without official permission, let alone unauthorized contact with a former British diplomat (and possible spy), was sufficient to ensure a death sentence; even the dentist at the US embassy was taken away to the camps. Sure enough, Mirsky was arrested and transported to a camp before the year was out. Carr did not realize the seriousness of the situation until his departure. Of course, Mirsky would probably have been arrested sooner or later anyway, as a former emigré; but this tragic incident in which he had been an unwitting agent of destruction ultimately brought home to Carr the real force of the terror and the real horrors of Stalin's despotism, which stayed with him for a number of years until the war altered his assessment of the Soviet Union.

He and Anne arrived in Moscow on 11 May 1937 and stayed at the Natsional, round the corner from the Kremlin. That evening was taken up with a coronation party at the embassy in honour of King George VI. Much time thereafter was taken up socializing with former diplomatic colleagues. He re-encountered Loy Henderson, formerly at the US legation in Riga and now on the staff of the embassy in Moscow, along with his Lettish wife. He then called on the Rossos at the Italian embassy; saw Neymann and Sabanin at the Commissariat of Foreign Affairs; managed to obtain access to the Marx-Engels-Lenin Institute where he met Adoratsky, 'frigid and stupid' (but probably frigid and stupid with fear); had lunch at the German embassy; paid a visit to the Society for Cultural Relations (where he saw Bakunin's biographer, Steklov); took an afternoon trip to a collective farm; and 'wrote a few lines of [an] article [for *The Times*], but couldn't work much'. People were not forthcoming. No one with any sense would say anything to a foreigner, even if obliged – on official duties – to be in the company of one.

Anne and Ted thus left for Warsaw on 1 June somewhat chilled by the Soviet experience. The Deputy Minister of Military and Naval Affairs Marshal Tukhachevsky had been scheduled to represent the Soviet Government at George VI's coronation but had, at the very last minute, been prevented from going on the grounds that he risked assassination. In fact it was only by remaining behind that he risked assassination – at Stalin's hands. Within days of the Carrs leaving for Poland, he was executed. The floodgates to the terror were now fully opened.

Looking back many years later he reflected on the impact this made upon him:

> The whole period of the purges was one of disillusionment and revulsion, the intensity of which was, I suppose, accounted for by my previous enthusiasm. I became very hostile to the USSR . . . .[56]

This was true only up to a point; but Carr was certainly deeply disillusioned. This much is apparent from the articles he wrote for the *Spectator* on 4 June and *The Times* (the first of three appeared on 5 July), plus an informal talk delivered at Chatham House on 12 October 1937. The piece in the *Spectator* is fairly evenly balanced, in that it refers to the improvements evident in Moscow since 1927 as well as the 'deep undercurrent of anxiety . . . discerned among those who are interested in anything more than existing from one day to the next . . . . Secretly, people wonder when the next big political trial is coming, and who will be arrested next . . . . The silent reign of terror . . . shows no sign of abating.'[57]

The articles in *The Times* do convey a certain disenchantment but nothing like to the extent later claimed. The first argued that the anniversaries of the regime's achievements 'are now eclipsed in the popular mind by the bloody reprisals of the past weeks'. The strongest condemnation is Carr's remark that 'The Soviet Union is governed by that kind of despotism which is customarily, though perhaps unjustifiably, labelled "Oriental".'[58] A second article refers to the 'victims of the Stalinist terror', though this does not lead him to a wholesale condemnation of the system;[59] but then, Carr never condemned any system wholesale; that would have contradicted his sense of history as progress. The rather negative view towards Moscow was sufficiently deeply ingrained to persist into the war, however. Reviewing Max Eastman's *Stalin and Socialism* in September 1940, which laid bare the horrors of socialism in the Soviet Union, Carr concluded decisively: 'Anyone who still thinks of Stalinist Russia as a model for this country to follow, and who still has a mind open to conviction, should find much to ponder in these pages.'[60]

---

[56] *Autobiographical sketch.*
[57] 'May in Moscow', *Spectator*, 4 June 1937.
[58] 'Twenty Years of Bolshevism: 1. A New Industrial Revolution', *The Times*, 5 July 1937.
[59] 'Soviet Theory and Practice: 2. A Retreat from Utopia', ibid., 6 July 1937.
[60] 'Stalin and Socialism', *Spectator*, 13 September 1940.

The Soviet experience put Germany in a better light. This is evident from an informal talk given to Chatham House that October:

> if to-day you compare Russia as it is to-day with Germany as it is to-day, Germany is almost a free country. I am sure I shall be taken to task about that, but that is my deliberate opinion, that is what I observed . . . the day after I arrived in Leningrad I met outside the hotel a man, a Russian, whom I had met in England and whom I knew quite well [Mirsky]. I was quite familiar with him, we had lunched together. I went up to him, and he pretended not to know me. In the end he had to admit he knew me and we got into conversation and he made embarrassed replies . . . which were quite obviously untrue, and in the end he turned away. I was simply dumbfounded, but I discovered . . . . The ordinary Russian intellectual has no right to talk to a foreigner, it is more than his life is worth if he was seen. This is a terrible position and Germany has not yet got to that pitch . . . . It does not mean that the German regime is more enlightened than the Russian regime, it means that in Germany there is still surviving a certain tradition of freedom which the Nazi regime has not been able to break down entirely.[61]

Indeed, in retrospect he confirmed that one 'result of my preoccupation with the Russian horrors was a neglect of what was going on in Germany'.[62]

A firm believer in progress but barely a liberal, Carr seized upon what he believed might be positive features in the totalitarian regimes. In his opinion any system that rebelled against laissez faire must have something to commend it and, not for the first time – and certainly not for the last – he rejected moral judgements:

> There is no reason to say that Russia is Left and Germany is Right. That is all complete nonsense, nor do I think it any use to talk of the wickedness of one side or the other, whether Hitler is wickeder than Stalin or the converse is true. The question of personal wickedness and good and bad fairies can be left to the fairy tale school of history which I hope is, today, nearly extinct.
>
> But let us look a little at the historical perspective. Both the German and Russian regimes, today, represent a reaction against the individualist ideology prevailing, at any rate in Western Europe, for the last hundred and fifty years . . . . The whole system of individualist laissez-faire economy has, as we know, broken down. It has broken down because production and trade can only be carried out on a nationwide scale and with the aid of State machinery and State control. Now State control has come in its most naked and undisguised form precisely where the individualist tradition was weakest, in Germany and Russia.[63]

We catch a glimpse of the ideas taking form in his mind about Britain's future: one of growing state control modified, unlike Germany and Russia, by the liberal tradition. This does not become more explicitly expressed until the

---

[61] 'Impressions of a Visit to Russia and Germany', 12 October 1937. In the author's possession.
[62] *Autobiographical sketch.*
[63] 'Impressions of a Visit'.

war, which itself hastened a process of statization that Carr believed must prove the way forward.

Thus the temporary condition of Russia and Germany was transformed into part of a longer term historical process, a homespun historical perspective that amounted to little more than a very doubtful rationale for inspired guesswork. 'The methods of the Tudor sovereigns, when they were making the English nation, invite many comparisons with those of the Nazi regime in Germany', he wrote in 1936.[64] Hitler was thus safely domesticated; to say the least, this inventive comparison concealed a moral judgement that has not withstood the test of time. It does, though, indicate a conservative Hegelian mode deeply ingrained in his thinking; of which more later. For the moment, one other aspect to all this is worthy of note. Carr's judgement of history was always strictly functional: he treated efficiency as more important than morality, detesting inefficiency (indeed, failure) of any kind; he was totally intolerant of the slightest display of incompetence. Perhaps this was not unusual in a man who had always striven for the very best in his work from childhood and who, sometime during youth (a habit recovered in declining years), took to Nietzsche and Spengler at regular intervals. In old age, even a meal served a few minutes beyond the appointed time made him irrascible. And only the suppression of spontaneous emotion and the development of intellectual prowess in a moral vacuum can ultimately account for the ruthlessness with which he could reach and sustain sometimes extraordinary opinions. The puzzle was how a man with such an absorbing interest in utopians, such a fascination with human foibles, could also be the man who advocated a collectivist order in which the first victim would likely as not be the very individualism that characterized his own life and every action. Unquestionably this reflected a deep dichotomy in Carr's own make-up that was never entirely resolved – and never could be, through the force of mere reason – into a unitary whole. He once wrote of Wyndham Lewis, scourge of wishful thinkers on the left: 'It is far easier to discover what he dislikes than what he stands for in the political world today.'[65] He could as easily have been describing his own awkward predicament.

By the autumn of 1938 Britain was already close to war. Although the Munich settlement at the end of September brought an illusory respite, Hitler's invasion of the rest of Czechoslovakia in March 1939 was seen in Britain as the prelude to a European war. Hitherto Carr's admiration for the 'realist' Neville Chamberlain was apparently undiminished,[66] though doubts had crept in, most notably about the wisdom of granting a unilateral security guarantee to Poland in April; Britain was in no position to defend the Poles without prior

---

[64] 'A Nationalist Abroad', *Spectator*, 29 May 1936. What exactly Geoffrey Elton would have made of such a statement boggles the mind.
[65] 'Talk about Nothing', *Christian Science Monitor*, 29 June 1936.
[66] Review of Chamberlain's *The Struggle for Peace*, *Times Literary Supplement*, 3 April 1939.

agreement with the Soviet Union. Not until July did Carr's safe assumptions begin to collapse, and even then not completely. Reviewing Winston Churchill's speeches of 1936–39 in the *Times Literary Supplement*, he described them as 'deliberately alarmist, and on the whole justifiably so'.[67] None the less, like a lot of others resigned to the inevitable, Carr cast about to see what part he might play in the coming conflict. His contacts on *The Times* since 1937 had brought him close to deputy editor Robin Barrington-Ward. Barrington-Ward's admiration for Carr was matched by that of Peter Fleming, on the foreign staff. Tom Jones, Lloyd George's éminence grise (and a power in Aberystwyth), had long been pressing for Carr's recruitment to the paper. The policy of appeasement had failed and *The Times* was, in Carr's words, 'in a mess'.[68] Editor Geoffrey Dawson's designated successor, Barrington-Ward, saw Carr as a likely assistant or foreign editor. The assistant editor took on a considerable range of administrative responsibilities. Besides his literary and analytical talents, Carr had distinguished himself at the Foreign Office by his 'administrative ability'.[69] Barrington-Ward lunched with him on 31 October and liked him. The editor, however, still had reservations.[70] Dawson had expressed the wish to retire before his sixty-fifth birthday, which fell on 25 October 1939, but when the time came he upset Barrington-Ward's plans – and also Carr's – by deciding to stay on.

Thus Carr had to look around for other work until something definite appeared at Printing House Square. Eventually, for lack of anything better, he threw in his lot with the organization of war propaganda, then located in the Foreign Office. Hitler had, in the meantime, secured the help of the Soviet Union in the coming conflict, and on 1 September 1939 his forces duly invaded Poland. Carr was then, ironically, putting the finishing touches to *The Twenty Years' Crisis*. On the following day, his diary reads: 'established in [the] Locarno Room of [the] F.O. with little to do: Kenney, Pratt, William [Strang], Moley [Sargent] etc. . . . Strange atmosphere of everyone running away from [the] war.' The entry that Sunday reads: 'Announcement of [the] declaration of war at 11.15'. On Monday: 'Went to [the] F.O. to take over.' Although not entirely unexpected, the news came as a body blow: 'it was of course Hitler who killed my liberalism,' he noted later. 'If liberal principles were right, we ought to have been able to apply them to the German question – and yet this led straight to appeasement.'[71] In fact, it led directly to war, which intruded yet again, cutting short another career but once more throwing up new challenges that, before long, would thrust Carr into a unique position from which to influence the postwar world.

---

[67] Ibid., 1 July 1939.
[68] Interview with P. Scott, *THES*.
[69] Lord Halifax, Preface to Carr, *Britain: A Study of Foreign Policy from the Versailles Treaty to the Outbreak of War*, London 1939, p. v.
[70] D. McLachlan, *In the Chair: Barrington-Ward of* The Times *1927–1948*, London 1971, p. 177.
[71] Carr to Betty Behrens, 19 February 1966.

4

At *The Times*

The outbreak of war on 3 September 1939 exposed the bankruptcy of Carr's line on appeasement as it did that of his model 'realist', Prime Minister Neville Chamberlain. But whereas August 1914 left intact his hopes for a return to prewar prosperity, the new conflict left him in a void: 'The war came as a shock which numbed the thinking process', he wrote in later years.[1] Toynbee fiercely attacked *The Twenty Years' Crisis* when it appeared in print soon after the outbreak of war on the grounds that it 'leaves you in a moral vacuum and at a political dead point'.[2] Indeed, there could be no better description of the sad state in which Carr found himself that fateful autumn.

He never accepted Toynbee's alternative; in his view, time spent diagnosing a disease was never time wasted. But 'this does not mean that we should refuse to work at developing the right remedies, and run after quack remedies which profess to cure every case, but in fact cure nothing at all, because they are not founded on a scientific diagnosis. I am afraid I regard schemes of world federation and collective security as quack remedies in this sense.'[3] Yet these tough words scarcely veiled Carr's own discomfort now that war had finally arrived. He was depressed; on his previous reckoning Britain was unlikely to win. On 14 September he wrote to his friend Ifor Evans from the Locarno room, the big reception hall on the first floor at the Foreign Office which had roared with typewriters at the service of the Contraband Department[4] just over two decades before:

> I confess that I did not, almost up to the last moment, really believe in the outbreak of war . . . now that the machine has begun to revolve, I don't see how it can be

---

[1] *Autobiographical sketch.*
[2] Arnold Toynbee to Norman Angell, 23 January 1940: *Toynbee Papers*, Bodleian Library, Oxford, box 1. Toynbee expressed similar sentiments in a letter to Carr which has unfortunately not survived, though its contents can be deduced from Carr's reply.
[3] Carr to Toynbee, 20 November 1939: ibid.
[4] Laurence Collier, 'The Old Foreign Office', *Blackwood's Magazine*, September 1972, vol. 312, no. 1883, pp. 256–61.

stopped, and I'm not therefore very optimistic: I'm even more afraid of the peace than I am of the war.

Meanwhile here I am in the Foreign Publicity Department of the Ministry of Information, sitting in this barn of a place at the F.O., waiting eventually to move to the headquarters of the Ministry of Information at the University [of London at Senate House]. The staff of this department is composed mainly of 'experts' and we badly want some good civil servants and organisers. The chaos in the Ministry as a whole is appalling.[5]

'Another silly departmental meeting', he confided to his diary a few days later. What he really wanted was a senior position at *The Times*, but Barrington-Ward could still offer nothing definite and by the end of September Carr learned that there was 'nothing doing'. His dissatisfaction was exacerbated by a significant drop in income. As he explained to Evans:

I understand the Ministry rates my services at £1000 a year. This looks as if it replaced my salary from Aberystwyth, but does not in fact do so for two reasons: (a) I was making a small but regular addition to my income by writing, mainly reviews – and this now goes entirely, or almost entirely; (b) I shall now have either to stay four or five nights a week at the Club or take a flat of some sort in town, as I do not think I can travel to and fro regularly with the black-out and restricted train service. At present, I'm staying with a colleague – just for this week.

He suggested Aberystwyth give him half-pay, so that he would not have to 'haggle' with the Ministry – 'the sort of thing I hate doing'.[6] This request initially met with a firm rebuff: Carr was reminded that he was on leave and therefore the college could only pay his superannuation. But Evans, true to form, eventually relented. This was not merely a matter of friendship; Carr was a not inconsiderable asset to Aberystwyth.

On 21 September the Ministry finally moved to Senate House. Carr's discontent continued. Even appointment as director of foreign publicity on 18 October proved a headache. The economic axe had fallen with the stricture that no new appointments could be made. Carr therefore sacked those he did not want in order to recruit those he did, including Dennis Routh. New battles ensued. The chief issue was over ultimate control of foreign propaganda. Those at the top of the Ministry wanted to keep it in their own hands. But no sooner had Carr been put in charge than a letter arrived from Foreign Secretary Lord Halifax 'demanding transfer of department to F.O.'[7] – a position Carr soon adopted as his own. This was 21 October 1939. But the prime minister sided with the Ministry.[8]

The ensuing bureaucratic battle sapped Carr's stamina and, as in the

---

[5] Carr to Evans, 14 September 1939: College archives, Aberystwyth: R/DES/IP/1 (8).
[6] Ibid.
[7] Lord Halifax to Lord Macmillan, 20 October 1939: Ministry of Information, *INF* (PRO) 1/859.
[8] Macmillan to Halifax, 26 October 1939: ibid.

past, nervous exhaustion found psychosomatic expression. On 22 February 1940 he suffered a 'mild attack of palpitations'. His heart had not troubled him since Riga. Not surprisingly he found these attacks 'very alarming'. But he 'was always told it was a nervous, not a functional disorder'. He told Evans: 'It was not a severe attack, and I am now back at the Office. But I was quite incapacitated for two or three days at the end of last week.'[9] Instead he relaxed and re-read old favourites: *Persuasion, Jane Eyre* and *Wuthering Heights.* On recovery he acted according to form: ruthlessly ridding himself of the conditions that had given rise to his ill-health. On Sunday 10 March he finished a memo on the transfer of the foreign publicity department to the Foreign Office: 'Depressed all day.' On the Monday he talked matters over with Gladwyn Jebb at lunch, saw his former colleague Alec Cadogan, who had replaced Vansittart at the head of the Foreign Office in 1937, and handed over the memo. Then on 16 March he wrote to Kenneth Lee, director general of the Ministry of Information, 'to force the issue'; but this simply prompted attempts to get rid of him.

His future at the Ministry in doubt, he wrote to Evans asking to return from leave. On 20 March Evans replied: 'I do not necessarily agree that "to throw yourself back on us at this stage of the academic year" would be a dirty trick.'[10] This was reassuring. But Aberystwyth was only a third and final option. His first preference was still *The Times*, alternatively the Foreign Office. The following day he had a 'long interview with Reith [the Minister], who disingenuously tried to get me to resign'. He then saw Campbell Stuart, a director of *The Times*, to ask him about prospects there. Scarcely able to contain his distaste for Reith, but lacking any support from his superiors – Monckton was 'helpless and wobbling' – Carr said goodbye on 29 March and was appropriately 'presented with *Don Quixote*' by his admiring subordinates, a gesture that amused him immensely.

Alec Cadogan was furious. 'Heard Ministry of Information were announcing Ted Carr's resignation,' he noted in his diary that day. 'Rang up Reith and said I couldn't have this. I knew nothing about it.'[11] For a while Carr held back from giving a clear 'no' to the Foreign Office; his eyes were still focused on *The Times*, though Ifor Evans expressed dissatisfaction at the idea that Carr should take a job in Fleet Street. Finally, in the sure knowledge that Evans had left him 'a free hand about Aberystwyth' and with only a 'hedging letter from Barrington-Ward', Carr belatedly handed Reith his resignation and wrote to Cadogan rejecting the offer to return to the Office. In retrospect Carr typically held no grudge against Reith. Reith 'recognized that I was no good at the job. Neither, of course, was he. No one really knew what we were meant to do.'[12] This did not much matter now that Barrington-Ward proved

---

[9] Carr to Evans, 27 February 1940: College archives, Aberystwyth.
[10] Evans to Carr, 20 March 1940: ibid.
[11] Entry, 29 March 1940: *Cadogan Diary*, Churchill College, Cambridge, 1940, acad 1/9.
[12] 'Revolution without the Passion', Peter Scott's interview with Carr: *Times Higher Education Supplement*, 7 July 1978.

'more forthcoming than on paper', though for the moment all that the deputy editor could offer was a job as leader writer. In fact a plot was afoot to unseat the editor, Dawson, and replace him with Barrington-Ward; this would then allow Barrington-Ward to take Carr on at the appropriate level. Carr accepted. It was second best, but it did give a measure of independence that would enable him to continue writing.

His tenure at the Ministry of Information had been something of an anomaly, a brief hiatus in Carr's new vocation as writer and publicist. Yet the time spent had not been totally wasted. He had set up a system of press attachés, a network to further foreign policy propaganda that works to this day. But in every other sense these were barren months: 'I . . . was content to follow the official line, and for a time stopped thinking at all. Nothing seemed to make sense', he recalled.[13]

The switch from government to journalism brought a renewed sense of purpose. Somewhat ashamed of the 'harsh "realism"' of *The Twenty Years' Crisis* and in need of something to fill the disturbing void, Carr decided to embark on a study of Britain's war aims and the problems of the postwar settlement. Now miraculously cured of sarcoma, Anne was working part time at the liberal–socialist think tank, Political and Economic Planning (PEP). There she introduced Carr to several bright young men whom he eventually recuited to *The Times*, including David Owen and François Lafitte, to write on social reform; he tried and failed, however, to induce Routh to leave PEP, to which he had fled from the Ministry of Information, and join him. But it was largely from these quarters that Carr found the ideas and ammunition with which to fight for a collectivist postwar order from his new vantage-point, at Printing House Square.

The tension that had precipitated his resignation from the Ministry predictably upset his health. On 14 May he had another attack of palpitations and for the next two weeks he had great difficulty putting pen to paper. The first leader thus did not appear until 28 May. It was innocuous enough, dealing with Sir Stafford Cripps's mission to Moscow, the aim of which was to weaken Soviet support for the German war effort; it was composed after a discussion of the matter with 'Moley' Sargent at the Foreign Office. The first indication of the new direction Carr's mind had taken did not become apparent until 21 June, with the publication of 'The German Dream'. Hitler was offering 'A Europe united by conquest'. 'There must and will be a new order in Europe', he wrote:

> But this cannot be achieved through the overweening ambition of one man or one country in defiance of the will of the majority of Europeans and of the whole world outside Europe. To speculate on better ways of building the new order would at the present time be to divert energy from far more urgent tasks. But two conditions must at least be fulfilled. The new European order cannot be achieved through

---

13 *Autobiographical sketch.*

conquest but only through co-operation, and it must unite Europe with the non-European world, not divide Europe from it.[14]

Such self-restraint did not last long, however. Once he had found his new voice, Carr began battling with Dawson and Barrington-Ward to put his views into print undiluted. Conflict arose from the fact that *The Times* was not just a newspaper. Its staff regarded themselves as something more elevated than mere journalists. Foreign governments firmly believed – not entirely unjustifiably – that in international affairs the paper was a mouthpiece of the Foreign Office, and this placed a powerful weapon in the hands of someone – like Carr – who sought to use the leader columns to determine the direction of government policy. Prime Minister Churchill, who had supplanted Chamberlain in April 1940, certainly did not expect to receive unsolicited advice and criticism on his conduct of the war from a professor, however learned, at Printing House Square. The restraining hand of Dawson and later Barrington-Ward therefore not infrequently censored Carr's more radical and dogmatic pronouncements. 'All the changes made were in the direction of toning down the sharpness of some of my conclusions,' he noted; 'the editor [Barrington-Ward, who took over in 1941] was a cautious man, who did not like to shock too many of the susceptibilities of his readers. Some of these changes I accepted more readily than others.'[15]

His new role buoyed his spirits and made him more outspoken than ever. His detestation of any kind of inefficiency prompted an unsolicited letter to R.A. Butler, then Parliamentary Under Secretary at the Foreign Office, on 8 July:

Since I left the Ministry of Information, I haven't felt that I ought to come and worry you, though there are several subjects I would like to talk about – including Russia – if you can spare me a quarter [of] an hour some time.

There is however one subject about which I feel I must write a word. It is one we discussed while I was still at the Ministry: the foreign broadcasts of the B.B.C. I am now writing some foreign news talks for them, so that I am seeing the outfit from a second angle. I can only say that, as I already suspected at the Ministry, the picture is one of incredible chaos and inefficiency. There is no central direction whatever. The only help or guidance I get is from the personal initiative of one individual, who is himself in despair owing to the completely muddled and aimless system . . . . The trouble is that none of the two or three people at the head of the Foreign Broadcasts have any idea whatever of organizing a rather big show. They are not bad people, but they are not equal to the job. Unless the F.O. is prepared to put a man of its own to clear up and organize the whole business, chaos will continue. The M[inistry] of I[nformation] are helpless because their relations with the B.B.C. are in the hands of an ex-B.B.C. official, who is an amiable but not a strong man, and cannot be expected to do the dirty on his former colleagues. And this is a dirty job, if it is done properly!

---

[14] 'The German Dream', *The Times*, 21 June 1940.
[15] Note to the author, summer 1982.

> Please don't give me away; I don't want to spoil such relations as I have with the
> B.B.C. or implicate those with whom I come into contact there.[16]

Before long he also found *The Times* inefficient; though it was not this but his
leaders that caused the greatest controversy.

The full impact of events had now hit home. The unexpected and rapid collapse of the west European democracies in the face of a devastating onslaught
from Berlin had persuaded Carr that the old international order could never
be reconstructed and that, in a distorted way, Hitler was bringing into effect a
revolutionary transformation of the European continent which, translated
into democractic practice, contained within it the seeds of progress. The first
leader that gave full vent to his new crusade appeared after editorial revision
on 1 July 1940. In contrast to 'The German Dream', this editorial, 'The New
Europe', picked up where *The Twenty Years' Crisis* left off. It argued that the first
lesson of the war was that 'the conception of the small national unit, not
strong enough for an active role in international politics, but enjoying all the
prerogatives and responsibilities of sovereignty, has been rendered obsolete by
modern armaments and the scope of modern warfare.' The collectivist order
that Carr had favoured but not advocated in the thirties was now translated to
the international system. His argument was basically economic: 'Europe can no
longer afford a multiplicity of economic units, each maintaining its independent economic system behind a barbed wire entanglement of tariffs, quotas,
exchange restrictions and barter agreements.' From here he glided back into
the domestic arena, drawing on his earlier enthusiasm for social reform under
Lloyd George, his later fascination with economic planning and his adoption
of the principles outlined by Keynes and later partly taken up by Beveridge:

> Over the greater part of Western Europe the common values for which we stand are
> known and prized. We must indeed beware of these values in purely nineteenth-
> century terms. If we speak of democracy, we do not mean a democracy which
> maintains the right to vote but forgets the right to work and the right to live. If we
> speak of freedom, we do not mean a rugged individualism which excludes social
> organization and economic planning. If we speak of equality, we do not mean a
> political equality nullified by social and economic privilege. If we speak of eco-
> nomic reconstruction, we think less of maximum production (though this too will
> be required) than of equitable distribution.

In conclusion, 'The European house cannot be put in order unless we put our
own house in order first.'[17]

These ideas were further elaborated in a draft memorandum after

---

[16] Carr to Butler, 8 July 1940: *Butler Papers*, Trinity College, Cambridge, RAB E3/3.

[17] 'The New Europe', *The Times*, 1 July 1940. In June 1941 Lord Beveridge was put in charge of
a Committee on Social Insurance and Allied Services. When Beveridge used Carr's arguments
concerning planning the peace and victory on the home front in his report of October
1942, the Cabinet delayed publication because the recommendations were regarded as too
revolutionary: J. Harris, *William Beveridge: A Biography*, Oxford 1977, pp. 419–20.

conversations with 'Moley' (on 19 July 1940) and Rex Leeper (24 July).[18] The draft was more explicit about Carr's intention to 'dovetail a domestic social policy into an international policy'. His aim was, above all, to offer 'something else than a return to the past'. He warned an audience at Chatham House:

> In a way I am a little alarmed when I find people thinking that somehow or other when the war is over we are going to get back our privileges and our comfortable life . . . . The fact is that in the nineteenth century this country was amazingly prosperous, owing mainly to the fact that we got ahead of the rest of the world in industrial development and we accumulated at that time a good deal of fat on which we have more or less been living ever since in the form of foreign investments, trade monopolies in many countries. Nearly all that has gone . . . we must, I think, be prepared for a more restricted and more strenuous and active life.[19]

And this meant economic planning, a form of socialism. The sacrifices entailed would require 'conscious adoption of the principle of social and economic equality'. This is what Carr meant when he indulged in hyperbole about World War II being 'in a sense a revolutionary war'. These basic themes – the need for radical transformation at home and the hopelessness of the small nation-state as a unit abroad – were further elaborated upon in the months that followed. In an interview with Collin Brooks on the BBC, Carr reasoned that the disaster that had occurred could be blamed on the backward-looking mentality epitomized in the often expressed hope of a return to normal:

> Well, this is all right if you are thinking of getting back your prewar 'bus service', or getting back to League football, or having all your family home again to Sunday dinner. But in the political world, this idea of getting back to normal is dangerous. The only normal thing about politics and economics is that they never go back to where they were – they are always moving on; and they move twice as fast in wartime as at any other time.[20]

But when he attempted to introduce these ideas into further *Times* leaders, he met opposition. A potted version of his original draft memorandum was presented to Barrington-Ward on 5 August. The plan outlined by Keynes the previous autumn[21] was unsatisfactory in Carr's view because it 'looked too much like a one-sided attack on wages'. He therefore warned against selecting from his own proposals those reforms which were acceptable to the right,

---

[18] *Carr Papers.*
[19] Ibid.
[20] 'Taking Stock: 1. How Did We Get Here? Discussion between COLLIN BROOKS and E.H. CARR', *Listener*, 30 September 1940.
[21] *The Times*, 14, 15 and 28 November, and 1, 6 and 16 December; reformulated into *How to Pay for the War: A Radical Plan for the Chancellor of the Exchequer*, London 1940.

while rejecting those acceptable to the left. He began in the most general way, emphasizing once more the need to break cleanly with the past:

> 'Freedom', 'democracy' and 'self-determination' no longer impress as slogans. They were worked to death in 1919 and failed to bring salvation. The demand is for a new society based on social and economic foundations.
>
> Socially, the weight of popular demand is for equality rather than for liberty. Somebody has well said that it is only for the prosperous that liberty means 'leave me alone'; for the others it means 'give me a chance'. Equality of opportunity is the form of liberty which requires stressing today.
>
> Economically, planning must take the place of laissez faire; the well-being of the community and not the price mechanism must be the governing factor in our economic policy, and planned consumption – an adequate standard of living for all – must be the basis of our system.[22]

What Carr outlined were broad proposals to raise standards of nutrition; increased house-building and public works; the creation of a national health service; fiscal measures including state family allowances; compulsory savings and a capital levy; compulsory education to the age of fifteen with the best children entered for public schools at fourteen, the others given primarily vocational training; if conscription were ended, then there should be 'a short period of compulsory physical training and camp life, combined either with military training or with some form of labour service'; the creation of 'standing foreign affairs and defence commissions which the ministers would meet from time to time for confidential discussion'; and, last but not least, in reconstructing Europe:

> We should take the line that frontiers and sovereignties have become relatively unimportant and must await economic reorganization. We cannot allow these things as in 1919 to get in the way of economic reorganization on a larger scale than heretofore. Neutrality divorced from power has been proved a myth – and a dangerous one at that; and we cannot set up again a system of small states wholly independent of one another and of their neighbours.[23]

But he had not changed his mind about world organization – nor really faced up to the contradictions in his own proposals on this matter: 'we should avoid like the plague all ready made schemes of political organization – League of Nations, Federal Union and so forth.' Instead he took what would now be called a 'functionalist' view of the process of integration:

> Our approach must be not through the medium of ideas, but through the concrete medium of economic planning. We shall need European commissions for relief, for transport, for agricultural and industrial reconstruction. If we have the energy to organize these things, power enough to enforce them, and supplies and capital enough (with American assistance) to get Europe economically on its feet, then we

---

[22] In the author's possession.
[23] Ibid.

shall find political forms shaping themselves by process of gradual growth to the needs of the new order.[24]

In retrospect these proposals sound remarkably familiar, for the obvious reason that many became reality, some via the Beveridge Report which appeared two years later, others through the legislation of the Attlee government or through the formation of the Economic Commission for Europe and, later still, the European Economic Community. Barrington-Ward wholly 'agreed with Carr:– planned consumption [sic], abolition of unemployment and poverty, drastic educational reform, family allowances, economic organization of the Continent, etc., but', he added, and this was a significant and ultimately contentious reservation, 'all this needs the right presentation.'[25]

The most celebrated leader that encapsulated Carr's basic ideas and led to conflict with Dawson was 'The Two Scourges'. Dawson had requested something along these lines on 26–28 November. But he was unhappy with what Carr turned in, despite the fact that it was eventually published in bowdlerized form on 5 December 1940. 'The great twin scourges which have most deeply touched the imagination and seared the conscience of the present generation are the scourge of war and the scourge of unemployment', Carr began. What precisely he thought would remove the scourge of war was left vague, largely because he so vehemently rejected the experience of the League of Nations and because his recently heightened awareness of the importance of power obliterated any abstract institutional prescriptions that anyone could devise. 'In the nineteen twenties,' he recalled, 'a series of bold – indeed over-confident – attempts were made to abolish war. They failed either because, like the Kellogg Pact, they remained purely negative, or because, like the League of Nations, they lacked the support of power on a worldwide scale and sought salvation in the barren accumulation of legal instruments and rules of procedure.'

What he now advocated in their place was a new international order based on a 'constructive' spirit: 'there is little doubt that we shall fail to achieve any effective international order, or any alternative to the horror of recurrent war, until we witness some such fundamental change, generally and reciprocally among the nations, in the scale of values.' Sacrifices had to be made, not so much of lives but of 'some of their profits and some of their wages to promote a common welfare in which they will eventually share'. There had to be an economic solution to war as for unemployment. Citing what had happened in Germany, Carr argued that the 'connexion between unemployment and war is not fortuitous'. Hitler had swept to power on seven million unemployed and war provided them with employment. On this simplistic, economistic argument Carr then constructed his case for curing unemployment as also

---

[24] Ibid.
[25] Barrington-Ward diary entry, 31 July 1940, as quoted in P. Addison, *The Road to 1945*, London 1977, p. 121.

the cure for war. As far as he portrayed it this was also a simple matter, and one that would not be rejected by today's social democrats. 'In 1940 the manufacturer forgoes profits, the worker forgoes trade union restrictions on conditions of employment, the consumer forgoes luxuries and lends to the Government to finance expenditure from which no material return is asked or expected.' If this had been done in 1930, a great deal of pain could have been avoided. Thus 'To formulate a social end, other than war, which will inspire such sacrifices is the cardinal problem of our time.' And the 'planning of peace calls for a leader who will have the courage and the vision to make the same appeal'.[26]

Dawson did not care for any of this, though with Barrington-Ward on Carr's side he was obliged to make some concessions. But he consistently obstructed Carr's attempts to radicalize further the editorial line on domestic policy. Although ten thousand reprints of 'The Two Scourges' were sold and demand for the paper shot up, Dawson was never pleased at the new direction the paper was taking. It was not too long before those on the right began to refer to *The Times* in its new guise as 'the threepenny edition of the *Daily Worker*'. Matters finally came to a head on 13 February 1941 when Dawson held back publication of a leader on 'Prospects of Recovery'. Carr took Barrington-Ward to lunch 'and talked sternly to him', intimating that he would resign if Dawson carried on in this manner. Barrington-Ward noted:

> He [Carr] complains of G.D.'s 'insincerity', by which he means the rather transparent conventions that G.D. employs to stave off discussion of political or social issues. He thinks that there has been a 'change of climate' with respect to his reconstruction articles. G.D. fobs them off or doesn't use them . . . He is not prepared to go on like this . . . I am much troubled and feel strongly the force of Carr's complaint. G.D. is not, I think, in real sympathy with the kind of article that Carr has been writing on home affairs, which has brought us so much credit. He does not seem to be aware that Carr is the ablest and best qualified man who has been near the paper for years. . . . I cannot stand by tamely and see him depart. I can't have G.D. queering my pitch for lack of a little imagination and perception.[27]

Barrington-Ward therefore took prompt action. First he counselled Carr to be patient. Next he tackled Dawson. But he was by no means successful. By early March no progress was in sight. Dawson had unsuccessfully 'tried to bamboozle' Carr on the 'Prospects of Recovery' article. On the sixth Carr went up to Printing House Square but wrote nothing. Instead he had a 'short talk with Dawson who made it clear that he wasn't interested in general articles'. He still did not tender his resignation. On the following day he learnt from his new friend and confidant, typographer Stanley Morison – who was

---

[26] 'The Two Scourges', *The Times*, 5 December 1940.
[27] Quoted in I. McDonald, *The History of* THE TIMES, vol. V: *Struggles in War and Peace 1939–1966*, London 1984, pp. 39–40.

'mad on' Carr[28] – that 'plans for felling G.D. are in train'. Morison was an unlikely figure: self-taught, with a Marxist background and Catholic convictions who had, through native intelligence and a natural gift for conspiracy, become something of an éminence grise at Printing House Square. The two men became good friends; Carr stayed at Morison's flat when he did not have to sleep over at *The Times* until he rented his own at Park West.

Carr stepped up pressure on Barrington-Ward while Morison plotted behind the scenes. He temporarily accepted restriction of his leaders to foreign affairs. In the meantime he wrote to Evans on 22 March 1941 explaining the situation vis-à-vis Dawson and suggesting that if no improvement were forthcoming he would stay on at *The Times* as a fulltime leader writer only until June 1941; thereafter he would come in only intermittently. But it is quite clear from the letter that Carr had every intention of succeeding at *The Times*; furthermore, he wanted to sort out the problem of his salary:

(a) when I left [the] M[inistry] of I[nformation] nothing else worth while opened in government service;
(b) I have every intention of returning to the functions of [the] Professorship, after the war;
(c) It would be intolerable to me in war to spend any substantial amount of my time lecturing to non-existent students or R.A.F. cadets;
(d) It would be equally intolerable to sit in pure academic seclusion writing long-term stuff: indeed I've never believed that, even in peace, anything useful can be written on politics by anyone wholly isolated from current realities;
(e) Hence I need something which gives me (i) the necessary contact with day-to-day affairs (ii) the sense that I am making some sort of contribution to the war – or at any rate to the peace (iii) a platform, other than the long-range one of book-writing, for getting some of my ideas across. *The Times* at [the] present moment comes nearer than anything else I've discovered to fulfilling these conditions.[29]

He therefore offered three options: first, maintenance of the status quo which, given that *The Times* was paying him forty to a hundred pounds a month, was unfair to the college; second, that *The Times* pay his entire salary, substituting for the income from the Chair; and, third, half-pay with *The Times* making up the difference. Evans generously but unwisely took the first option. It was only a matter of time before Carr's nemesis, in the form of Lord David Davies, learned of the deal and acted upon it, but in the meantime he had it both ways and progress at last began to be made at Printing House Square. On the night of 5 May 1941 proprietor John Astor took on the delicate task of removing the editor. He tactfully suggested that 'it might be unfair' to keep Dawson's duly appointed successor (Barrington-Ward) 'waiting indefinitely'. To lighten the blow Barrington-Ward 'begged' Dawson to take his time, in effect delaying departure by a few months. Dawson edited for

[28] Quoted in N. Barker, *Stanley Morison*, Cambridge, Mass. 1972, p. 391.
[29] Carr to Evans, 22 March 1941: College archives, R/DES/IP/1(8).

the last time on 30 September; by then, however, Carr was already in conflict with his successor over foreign policy.

On 22 June 1941 Hitler had, contrary to Stalin's expectations, launched a full-scale invasion of the Soviet Union. Since the terror and his visit to Moscow, Carr had distanced himself from Russia and Russian affairs. Yet it is striking that by the summer of 1940 he had drawn drastic conclusions about the future conduct of international relations, particularly with respect to treatment of the Soviet Union. However utopian on domestic issues, in matters of foreign policy Carr the realist was far from dead. On the contrary, the collectivism in international affairs that he advocated was intentionally vague and carried no great conviction. It was too hedged with qualification: 'we should avoid like the plague all ready made schemes of political organization – League of Nations, Federal Union and so forth. Political forms cannot be devised in advance, particularly by people as ignorant of the political climate of Europe as the Anglo-Saxons.' He had to sound vague because what he envisaged was essentially a revival of the great power concert that enforced peace through the greater part of the nineteenth century, perhaps also extended to economic matters. Carr's acute consciousness of the factor of power, now totally unencumbered by liberal baggage, led him to speculate upon the establishment of an international order that ruthlessly disregarded the rights of smaller nations. In the new scheme of things the 'small house must not be allowed, through its lack of fire-fighting appliances, to become a danger to its larger and better equipped neighbours', he argued in the 'Hazards of Neutrality' on 13 July 1940. He was even more explicit in the draft memorandum he gave Sargent and Leeper: 'I am not sure that the most important thing to small countries should be absolute complete independence. Does that mean liberty for them? What good does their independence do them? We see what has happened to small nations which were normally independent in this war.'[30]

Clearly Carr's assumption was that the top priority was to preserve the great powers from future fires, even at the expense of others; which was precisely the philosophy that underlay the betrayal of Czechoslovakia at Munich. It reflected the deference for power that had developed within him during *The Twenty Years' Crisis* and that had now dissolved the remnants of his youthful liberalism. And it was this, more than anything else, that – despite the Foreign Office's traditional lack of interest in the region – brought him into direct collision with former colleagues, indeed the government as a whole, and the east European governments-in-exile in particular.

The controversy arose from Carr's application of this ruthless philosophy to postwar plans for eastern Europe. The direction his mind had taken became evident from a talk to Chatham House on 14 August 1940:

---

[30] Document in the author's possession.

though it may be rather silly to attempt to make predictions of this kind . . . one must reflect as to what the position of Soviet Russia is likely to be at the end of the war. I think, myself, so far as the indications go at present, that she is going to remain neutral, she is not going to take one side or the other, and when we have beaten Hitler they will be sitting unexhausted and relatively strong where they are; and if the war ends with the collapse of Hitler I do not think that we shall probably be called on to have very much voice in what happens beyond the eastern frontiers of Germany, it seems to me that Russia, in her present mood, is going to take pretty effective care of that, unless we are prepared to go to war which I hope and believe we are not; and in this case we shall not have much to say for the moment about the destinies of Eastern Europe.[31]

The Baltic states were annexed by the Soviet Government in July 1940. These were the very states that Carr had once defended against great power priorities. Soviet annexation had a clear strategic rationale, once Germany had taken all of western Europe, but the notion that this was done through the will of the populations concerned was a laughable fiction. This, however, did not stop Carr from asserting that the decision to reunite these states with the Soviet Union reflected 'not merely pressure from Moscow but sincere recognition that this was a better alternative than absorption in a new Nazi Europe'[32] – which would not have reassured those shot or despatched to the Gulag. It is, of course, one thing to say a process is inevitable – and Soviet annexation surely was – but quite another to say a process is also desirable. To the unwary reader the elision was not necessarily obvious at first sight because of Carr's extraordinary verbal dexterity; and this not least made him such an effective propagandist.

Not surprisingly his editorial on the Baltic drew an angry response from Collier, now heading the Northern Department of the Foreign Office. He knew it was Carr, 'who used to work here but is not, in my view, a reliable guide on these subjects'. 'It may be arguable that on grounds of expediency we should turn a blind eye to these and many other proceedings of which we cannot approve; but, even so, we can surely do that without distorting the facts', Collier wrote to Barrington-Ward on 26 July.[33]

The German attack on the Soviet Union on 22 June 1941 came as a surprise to Stalin despite extensive intelligence reports anticipating the invasion. The Foreign Office, which had until recently dismissed talk of invasion as nonsense, was by then also expecting the attack. On 18 June Carr visited the Office and saw Alec Randell, Roger Makins, Ashley Clarke and Rab Butler. 'Everyone sure Germany is going for Russia', he noted in his diary. With the invasion a fact, Moscow became de facto an ally of London, and leaders that once implied the Baltic states were rightfully Russian now began to imply that eastern Europe should effectively fall into the Soviet sphere of influence at

---

[31] Ibid.
[32] 'Russia on the Baltic', *The Times*, 25 July 1940.
[33] Collier to Barrington-Ward, 26 July 1940: *FO* 371/24761.

the end of the war. Carr's state of mind can be gathered from his recollections thirty years later:

> In *The Times* I very quickly began to plug the Russian alliance; and, when this was vindicated by Russian endurance and the Russian victory, it revived my initial faith in the Russian revolution as a great achievement and a historical turning-point. It was obvious that the Russia of the second world war was a very different place from the Russia of the first – in terms of people as well as of material resources. Looking back on the thirties, I came to feel that my preoccupation with the purges and brutalities of Stalinism had distorted my perspective. The black spots were real enough, but looking exclusively at them destroyed one's vision of what was really happening ... I became increasingly interested in what the Russians had done, and how far this had any lessons for western society; and this tied up with my interest in the Marxist critique of capitalism and the bourgeoisie.[34]

This retrospective actually telescopes a process beginning in 1941 and not entirely completed until the end of the war. But its initial manifestations certainly began causing disquiet in Whitehall. If, as Carr suggested as early as 1940, the interests of the smaller states should concede to the interests of the great powers; and if, as he also suggested elsewhere, the Soviet Union would naturally seek to dominate eastern Europe, then, clearly, the price of the postwar peace would be paid by the states of eastern Europe, including those very Baltic states he had, as an idealistic young diplomat, once defended so vigorously against the cynicism of his elders. The irony was that the young Carr had reappeared in the Foreign Office in the form of the young Frank Roberts: an exceptionally sharp-minded diplomat who had yet to acquire the reputation of later years as the 'wicked wizard'. He dealt, as Carr had once done, with the Baltic states. Carr had lunch with him on 15 January 1942 to discuss the matter. It was as a result of this discussion that, on the following day, Carr sent him a memo that accurately reflected the views of General Gough in 1919, which he – then only twenty-eight and still a convinced liberal – had so vehemently opposed at the time:

> After the collapse of Russia and Germany the Baltic States enjoyed an almost accidental independence during the twenty years interregnum from 1919 to 1939. Apart from this interval in history it was always true that they would have fallen within the orbit either of Russia or Germany, and it is now more certain than ever in an age which has exposed the illusions of neutrality in Europe. The winning of the war means that they will fall within the orbit of Russia.[35]

What he omitted to mention, however, was what it actually meant to fall within the Soviet orbit. Without knowing the circumstances of the takeover in 1940 and its consequences, the unwary reader might easily believe it had no more significance than lying within a US or British sphere of influence. Carr

---

[34] *Autobiographical sketch.*
[35] Carr to Roberts, 16 January 1942: *FO* 371/32918.

thus created an illusion of equality in the manner in which the great powers would treat their protectorates. It is also not entirely impossible that he deceived himself as to the true implications of the policies he recommended. At the end of the war, he continued, Britain could be expected to dominate western Europe and to establish forward bases there. In turn 'Russia must be regarded as the chief arbiter of destinies in eastern Europe, in the peace settlement and thereafter.' As a logical corollary:

> It is . . . important for Britain that we should not stand committed to any particular view of territorial rearrangements in eastern Europe. If we agree in advance to specific solutions proposed by Russia, we shall by implication be committed to defend the justice of these solutions and their compatibility with the Atlantic Charter. If we oppose specific solutions, we are violating two fundamentals of a sound foreign policy: (a) by protesting against things which we shall be powerless to prevent, and (b) by offending a Power whose collaboration is vital to us.[36]

In a further memorandum, this time addressed to Barrington-Ward, he elaborated on this theme in a manner unfortunately only too reminiscent of the position he (and Barrington-Ward) had taken towards Nazi Germany; but a view which, in retrospect, was remarkably perspicacious:

> Before the war British prestige suffered from protesting in advance against things which, when they happened, we tamely acquiesced in because we had neither the power nor the will to prevent them.
> After the war Russian forces will probably march west at least as far as Berlin and dispose of Eastern Europe as they think fit. Is it conceivable that we shall have the power to interfere with them or that, even if we had the power, public opinion in this country (which, in large sections of it, shows signs of being almost frantically pro-Russian) would allow any Government to use it?[37]

It was an accurate prediction of what actually came into being; but the implication that Britain should have done nothing in the thirties and then nothing again in the forties has not withstood the test of time.

In order to convince a practising diplomat such as Roberts, Carr took the fact of British power for granted and argued more or less along the lines of a condominium with Russia, assuming British predominance over western Europe as a quid pro quo for Soviet dominance over the east. Barrington-Ward was a different matter, however. As a former appeaser, he assumed Britain's weakness in the postwar world. Carr therefore tailored his argument accordingly:

> The end of the war will leave two great powers on the Continent, Russia and Germany. We must not antagonize both simultaneously. They are natural antagonists so long as no third power tries to intervene in Eastern Europe. If we were to

---

[36] Ibid.
[37] Quoted in Barker, *Stanley Morison*, pp. 221–2.

oppose Russian policy in Eastern Europe after the war, we should quickly reconsti-
tute the German–Russian alliance.

We must give Russia a free hand in Eastern Europe if we wish to retain her as an
ally against Germany.[38]

His leaders in *The Times* on the subject were naturally more restrained –
Barrington-Ward was always at hand to tone them down if they made their
point too clearly – but they were certainly sufficiently explicit to convey certain signals about apparent British postwar thinking to the Russians and, of
course, to their future victims in eastern Europe. At the Foreign Office
'Moley' minuted: 'I assume that H.M.G. are definitely opposed to the policy
advocated by Professor Carr in *The Times* that we should tacitly disinterest ourselves from Central and South-East Europe, and that now and at the peace
settlement we should recognise all this part of Europe as falling within the
exclusive Russian sphere of influence.'[39] And this was certainly not the last,
nor the most forceful, minute on the subject.

When Carr argued that public opinion in Britain had become violently pro-
Soviet, he was a little disingenuous, since his own brilliant advocacy in *The
Times* had been and was still spreading such sentiment; and, given his argument that the existence of such sentiment bound the hands of the British
government and would prevent it adopting a policy of standing up to Soviet
expansion, he was actively forestalling one option that Sargent, Churchill
and others ultimately found to be the necessary course of action.

Had he restricted his pen to foreign affairs Carr's influence would have
been considerably less. But it was the fact that he advocated radical social
reform at home in conjunction with an assertively pro-Soviet stance abroad –
both of which found a strong echo among the general public – that made him
such a force to be reckoned with and such an object of fury in Whitehall. The
potent ideas that fertilized his leaders were expanded and extended into a
full-length book entitled, innocuously, *Conditions of Peace* – the title originally
used for a leader of 6 December 1940 – published early in 1942 in Britain and
the United States. He had begun writing in mid-May 1940. Progress was intermittent – interrupted by leader-writing, by duties as external examiner of
the Cambridge University History Tripos, activities at Chatham House and so
forth – but the manuscript was completed a little over a year later. As usual,
chapters in draft were farmed out to others to inspect and comment upon.
Barrington-Ward read the entire manuscript before it went to press in
September. In a sense the work was a continuation of *The Twenty Years' Crisis*,
an attempt to provide an answer to the dilemmas of those decades, to meet
Toynbee's jibe about offering no solutions. But in another sense – most
notably in its exploration of social democracy and planning – it represented
an entirely new point of departure. Carr saw planning not in the rigid terms

---

[38] Ibid.
[39] *FO* 371/33154.

of the planned economy visible in the Soviet Union but in the more general sense of economic controls apparent in the German war economy of World War I and the controls operating in Britain as he wrote. The Russians thus offered only one version of a larger type. In democratic countries, Carr argued, hostility to the methods used in Soviet Russia and Nazi Germany had 'hindered an impartial examination of the economic lessons of the policy pursued'. He continued:

> The Soviet regime introduced at an early date a system of planned production which in some quarters encouraged the belief that planned production might by itself provide a cure for our economic ills. In attempting to apply the precedent to Western Europe, it was, however, commonly forgotten that Russia was in a primitive stage of economic development, having a vast territory not yet fully exploited, a still rapidly expanding population, a low standard of living, no important exports other than raw materials, and a home market capable, even in staple commodities, of almost indefinite expansion – a combination of circumstances in which the possibility of overproduction scarcely existed. The German precedent was more instructive. Here planning was applied from 1933 onwards to a highly developed and industrialized economy which had in the preceding decade been subjected to the stimulus of intensive capital investment from abroad, and which had shown the symptoms of overproduction to a marked degree. The method adopted was a programme of planned consumption.[40]

What Carr meant by planned consumption was in fact public works; in other words, he was thinking very much in terms of a Keynesian solution to Britain's future economic problems, 'a mixed economy' in which basic industries and services would be autonomously run under ultimate government control, while luxury items would appear within a free market.

As usual, Carr rummaged in any cupboard for whatever he needed. The search for ideas was more intense than ever, and perhaps less discriminating. In the most general sense he borrowed some basic ideas from an unusual source, a book with the anodyne title *Dynamics of War and Revolution*. Published in 1940, its author, Lawrence Dennis, was the leading Fascist intellectual in the United States. The *Dynamics* was not a work that Carr skimmed through in his customary manner, but a book he returned to more than once in the course of writing. It was not untypical of him to take ideas wherever he found them, regardless of their provenance. It was a notable feature of his research in the thirties and just as much so in the postwar period. In this case, however, it laid his book open to attack unnecessarily, for the ideas he took from *Dynamics*, though not insignificant, were limited in import. *Conditions of Peace* opened with a backward and nostalgic glance at the 'civilized world on which the war of 1914 broke so suddenly . . . on the whole a prosperous and orderly world . . . a world of contented and reasoned optimism – a world which, looking back on the past hundred

---

[40] Carr, *Conditions of Peace*, London 1942, pp. 93–4.

years with pardonable self-satisfaction, believed in progress as a normal condition of civilized existence'.[41] But, having indulged this reminiscence, Carr
resolutely cast it all away. The 'first moral' for the victors was 'not to look backwards in search of principles to guide the post-war settlement'.[42] The second
was to drop the pervasive preoccupation with security: 'The political, social
and economic problems of the post-war world must be approached with the
desire not to stabilize, but to revolutionize.'[43] Thus the first chapter was entitled
'War and Revolution'. And it is here that the influence of Dennis is most notice-
able. Curiously for a best-seller produced during World War II, it presented
Hitler in the kind of domesticated manner that Carr always treated him. 'Hitler
has consummated the work, which Marx and Lenin had begun, of overthrow-
ing the nineteenth-century capitalist system,' he announced, returning to his
old theme of the late thirties. 'The same revolutionary forces are everywhere at
work and both sides are consciously or unconsciously impelled by them in the
same direction. The point at issue is not the necessity for a new order, but the
manner in which it shall be built.'[44] It was, indeed, a thoroughly unusual
approach to the subject. But then in wartime most of the population were in
need of something unusual, something new, some answers.

Dennis's work is not some extremist tract but a lucid and detached piece of
analysis which ends on a populist note. He defines revolution not in the usual
manner but as a massive upheaval that is not necessarily violent. Citing the
'industrial revolution' and the 'capitalist revolution', Dennis asserts 'the
times . . . are nothing if not revolutionary.'[45] His was a subtly contrived dia-
tribe against the status quo. It appealed to Carr for that very reason – Marx
served a similar purpose – as did its overt moral relativism. Dennis, too,
treated the Russian and German systems as manifestations of a larger single
process. It is therefore not surprising to find that at points he quotes *The
Twenty Years' Crisis*. Thus when Carr wrote of 'the contemporary revolution',[46]
this was meant in the most general sense. He argued – without any firm foundation of evidence – that great wars were 'commonly part of a revolutionary
process whose fundamental causes may be quite different from the immediate causes of the war'.[47] That contemporary revolution was, he argued, 'a
revolt against economic laissez-faire'.[48] It is here that he is at his most provocative and it was one reason why the book became a best-seller – the tide had
turned against the liberal philosophies prevalent since the Victorian era. The
great success of the book was matched by the ferocity of the reaction from
those most opposed to this 'revolution'.

---

[41] Ibid., p. ix.
[42] Ibid., p. xxxii.
[43] Ibid., p. 24.
[44] Ibid., p. 9.
[45] L. Dennis, *Dynamics of War and Revolution*, New York 1940, p. xviii.
[46] Carr, *Conditions of Peace*, p. 7.
[47] Ibid., p. 5.
[48] Ibid., p. 13.

The first assault on *Conditions of Peace* came from the indignant Rebecca West on 9 May 1942, in *Time and Tide*. West was the nom de plume of Cicely Fairfield – somehow being savaged by Rebecca seems more plausible than being savaged by Cicely – once a mistress of the celebrated socialist writer and notorious womanizer H.G. Wells, and now a literary critic and well-known author in her own right. *Black Lamb and Grey Falcon*, her best-selling story of travels in the prewar Balkans, had just appeared to rapturous applause. She was, by inclination, a conservative and monarchist; whether this was in reaction to Wells is not clear. Not surprisingly she loathed Carr's ideas. In a review she declared her sympathy with the Carr who showed 'tenderness and humour and intelligence' in *The Romantic Exiles* as opposed to the man who referred to 'all contemporary thought with the pain that a very respectable elephant might show on passing Monkey Hill', the man who subjected the foundations of society 'to a solemn questioning that spares nothing'.[49]

Some of her barbs were hopelessly wide of the mark. Her attack on Carr for arguing that existing political democracies were inadequate without extension to social democracy was signally weak and scarcely likely to win favour among those who had suffered grievously in the Great Depression without adequate welfare provision. Her argument that 'Democracy will not wash clothes . . . will not answer the telephone when the family is out' laid her open to accusations of snobbery and ignorance of the lives of the ordinary voter who never employed servants. But the accusation that Carr 'writes of self-determination and all its works with a peculiar whinnying scorn' struck close to the bone;[50] and, of course, there was always guilt by association – his use of Dennis did not escape her eagle eye: 'It is as odd for a serious English writer to quote Sir Oswald Mosley', she sniped.[51] It should occasion no surprise that the former London correspondent of *Kurjer Warszawski* rushed to write in expressing enthusiasm for West's 'knockout blow' against 'a man, whose power of doing mischief extends far beyond the pages of his books'. He rightly castigated Carr for the bland British middle-class assumption that the civilized world of 1914 'was on the whole a prosperous and orderly world'. But he went one step too far in accusing him of having made a 'disastrous intervention in favour of Nazi Germany at the height of the Sudeten crisis . . .'.[52] Since Carr was not even writing for *The Times* at that time, he demanded an apology and received one.[53] A curious footnote to *Conditions of Peace* is an entry in the diary of Beatrice Webb concerning Carr: 'He has apparently not read *Soviet Communism*, or other material about Soviet Russia.'[54] One cannot conceive of a more fulsome, though unintended, compliment.

---

[49] R. West, 'Notes on the Way', *Time and Tide*, 9 May 1942.
[50] Ibid., 16 May 1942.
[51] Ibid., 9 May 1942.
[52] Letter to the editor by F. Czarnomski, *Time and Tide*, 23 May 1942. The reference here is to the famous leader in *The Times* of 7 September 1938 demanding that Czechoslovakia concede the Sudetenland to Germany.
[53] Letters to the editor, ibid., 6 June 1942.
[54] B. Webb, *Diary*, British Library of Political and Economic Sciences, vols 55–7, 1941–43.

The second significant attack came from the House of Lords on 2 June. The speaker, Viscount Elibank, described him as 'a total appeaser of the first water'. What he most objected to, however, was Carr's leniency towards Germany. In order to preserve some chance of forestalling a further war of revenge, Carr favoured a policy that would reject the imposition of unilateral disarmament or division of the country, not least for overriding economic reasons. And the idea that Britain might hand over control of its colonies to international supervision made Elibank's blue blood boil: 'Professor Carr is indeed an active danger to this country and its future in the position which he holds, and if we were so foolish as to be guided by his views, we should certainly lose the peace, and all our sacrifices would be in vain.'[55] The attacks came not only from the right: from the somewhat lofty and judgemental heights of the independent left, George Orwell ranted at 'the general russophile feeling of the intelligentsia' and was indignant that, in addition, 'all the appeasers, e.g. Professor E.H. Carr, have switched their allegiance from Hitler to Stalin.'[56] Typically these harsh words in no way changed Carr's high regard for Orwell.

He was also under attack from a different but not unfamiliar direction. David Davies had finally found out that Aberystwyth was still paying him while he was also receiving the salary of an assistant editor at Printing House Square. On Christmas Eve 1942 Davies wrote to Ifor Evans attacking Carr and complaining that 'the College is helping to run and finance *The Times*.'[57] As the dispute rumbled on, Gilbert Murray, who had evidently been consulted by Evans, wrote to Carr none too sympathetically early in March. They met to discuss the matter, after which Murray wrote to Davies attempting to make a case for Carr, arguing that *The Times* was 'accepting his policy', and so forth.[58] Carr reacted angrily, pointing out to Murray 'the somewhat invidious position in which Lord Davies is seeking to place me'[59] – which prompted Murray to ask Davies not to circulate the contents of the letter[60] – and then wrote indignantly to Evans: 'Your friend G.M. has . . . made me for the first time seriously think of resigning the Chair . . . I have been warning well-meaning well-wishers how embarrassing it is to me to be to be credited with foisting a personal policy of my own on a supine and spineless Editor: nothing is more calculated to make my position difficult.'[61] Doubtless reinforcing his own instincts in the matter, Evans was alerted to the importance of keeping Carr

[55] Hansard, *Parliamentary Debates*, fifth series, vol. CXXIII: House of Lords 1941–42, London 1942, cols. 52–54.
[56] London Letter to *Partisan Review*, 17 April 1944: *The Collected Essays, Journalism and Letters of George Orwell: As I Please 1943–1945*, S. Orwell and I. Angus eds, London and New York 1968, p. 127.
[57] Davies to Evans, 24 December 1942: College archives, Aberystwyth.
[58] G. Murray to Davies, 31 May 1943: ibid.
[59] Carr to Murray, 12 June 1943: ibid.
[60] Murray to Davies, 14 June 1943: ibid.
[61] Carr to Evans, 12 June 1943: ibid.

happy by a telegram from Tom Jones, a key figure in the Welsh establishment, which said, inter alia: 'Professor Carr on *The Times* is worth several generals in the field . . .'.[62] A financial compromise was therefore settled which left Carr less well-off but David Davies temporarily silenced.

In *Conditions of Peace* Carr reiterated his condemnation of British foreign policy between the wars for 'its failure to establish any proper coordination between ends and means'.[63] Much of the book was taken up with the enhancement of British power through domestic reconstruction and the economic rehabilitation of postwar Europe, in large part – though not exclusively – to prevent that tragedy happening again. In the meantime, however, Britain would have to act in tandem with the United States – though not surrendering the initiative – particularly in the far east, develop the capacities of the commonwealth and empire and seek cooperation with the Soviet Union in Europe to sustain an effective counterweight to the likely resurgence of German power. Writing in 1942, he could make the assumption that the Baltic states would never be able to escape reabsorption into the Soviet Union, without necessarily making extravagant predictions about its future ability to project its power across the continent. Indeed, at this early stage of the war – with the Russians forced into retreat to the very walls of Stalingrad – he did not expect that the Soviet Union would necessarily be in a position to hold the balance of power at the close of hostilities. Just as there was a tendency to underestimate its military capability before June 1941, he wrote, 'so there may be a danger of exaggerating it in the closing stages of the war. Fifty years hence Russia may have become a great industrial Power. But at present,' he continued, 'Russian industrial development judged by Western standards is still limited; Russia is relatively weak in skilled industrial manpower in the Western sense of the term; her capacity for sustained military action beyond the limits of Russian or former Russian territory remains to be proved.'[64]

He was not alone in undervaluing Soviet power, though he was very soon arguing in the other direction. The Polish government-in-exile in London under General Sikorski favoured a modus vivendi with Moscow and had concluded a limited agreement on cooperation in July 1941. But Stalin insisted that the Poles recognize the Soviet Union's right to territory up to the so-called Curzon line, which included some large towns like Lvov with almost wholly Polish populations in a sea of countryside dominated by Byelorussians and Ukrainians. On this issue Sikorski refused to move; and in January 1942, for want of any alternative, Stalin conjured back into existence the Polish Communist Party – renamed, of course – that he had liquidated in 1938. The London Poles, blind to the impact of their position, clung to the same

---

[62] Telegram to Evans, 3 March 1943: quoted in *Aberystwyth Papers: International Politics 1919–1969*, ed. B. Porter, London 1972, p. 367.
[63] Carr, *Conditions of Peace*, p. 169.
[64] Ibid., p. 198.

fateful illusions about their bargaining power that had served them so ill since 1919 and steadfastly refused to compromise, with the net result that a postwar Poland run by Communists before long became Moscow's certain choice. Seeing the Red Army scattered before the German onslaught, the London Poles saw little or no reason to pander to Soviet postwar ambitions. They were therefore incensed when, on the eve of Foreign Secretary Anthony Eden's trip to Washington on 10 March 1943, *The Times* appeared with an article by Namier exposing the fallacies of prewar diplomacy for ignoring the importance of Russia and a leader by Carr, innocuously entitled 'Security in Europe', which took Namier's arguments one step further and argued for the appeasement of the Soviet Union in eastern Europe. Carr had been deeply disturbed since the autumn of 1942, when the signs first emerged, by the public resurgence of Soviet suspicions about malign western intentions. In leaders which argued – contrary to fact, though no doubt honestly believed – that past problems in Anglo–Soviet relations could be attributed largely to 'misunderstandings' and a 'gulf of mutual incomprehension', he had consistently and forcefully pressed for the British Government to make it 'clear to the world that Britain must stand shoulder to shoulder with Russia if the peace and freedom of Europe are to be established on a secure and impregnable basis'. It was a logical next step to demonstrate how this might be done. Carr chose 10 March 1943 on which to do so.

He opened with three lessons from Namier's article: first, that splendid isolation was no longer an option for British foreign policy; second, Russia's attempts to isolate itself had 'proved as futile and as disastrous as similar attempts by Great Britain'; and, third, that Britain had the 'same interests as Russia' in 'active and effective Russian participation in continental affairs; for there can be no security in Western Europe unless there is also security in Eastern Europe, and security in Eastern Europe is unattainable unless it is buttressed by the military power of Russia'. With the deftness for which his leaders became notorious, he went on to argue: 'A case so clear and cogent for close cooperation between Britain and Russia after the war cannot fail to carry conviction to any open and impartial mind.' The trouble was, of course, that the states of eastern Europe might feel they needed security against Russia. But this was an eventuality which Carr was unwilling even to consider, for he had already concluded, along with Namier: 'To suppose that Britain and the United States, with the aid of some of the lesser European Powers, could maintain permanent security in Europe through a policy which alienated Russia and induced her to disinterest herself in continental affairs would be sheer madness.' He therefore insisted upon 'ungrudging and unqualified agreement' between Britain and Russia. 'If Britain's frontier is on the Rhine,' he wrote, 'it might just as pertinently be said – though it has not in fact been said – that Russia's frontier is on the Oder, and in the same sense.' This did not have to mean domination of the countries between. 'The sole interest of Russia is to assure herself that her outer defences are in sure hands; and this interest will be best served if the lands between her frontiers and those of

Germany are held by governments and peoples friendly to herself. That is the one condition on which Russia must and will insist.' But did this not in fact amount to domination? Carr did not want to consider this question; he had already now moved to the belief that no one would have any choice, anyway:

> Everything goes to show that she [Russia] will be in a position after the war to shape the settlement on lines consistent with this conception of what her security demands. But it will make all the difference for the future of Anglo–Russian friendship whether these lines have been freely approved and welcomed by Britain in advance, or whether they are grudgingly accepted as a fait accompli after the victory has been won.

And in a message for Eden on his departure, he wrote that the 'other task of British foreign policy' was 'to interpret to the United States the common interest of Britain and Russia in European security and in the means of attaining it'.[65]

It should occasion no surprise to learn that the British Government took another view. At the Ministry of Information, for example, Minister Brendan Bracken, no doubt echoing his master's (Churchill's) voice, criticized the foreign policy of *The Times*, saying that they were 'all over the place', and described Carr in particular as 'loopy'.[66] The Polish government-in-exile was predictably infuriated, not least because of Namier, but also at the implications for Poland of Carr's line of argument. The Polish ambassador to Britain, Count Raczynski, said he knew who wrote the leader and 'knew what Carr's idea of Eastern Europe was, but it was not the idea of the Poles, and they knew very well what Russia would mean by friendly Governments'.[67]

It was not only the Poles who were provoked by the leader and Carr was obviously somewhat taken aback by the intensity of the criticism and the many diverse directions from which it came. Some saw it as a bid for Anglo-Soviet condominium in Europe. In a further editorial on 23 March, which was largely a curiously rambling discourse on the need for planned security in Europe, with comparisons to the exercise by the United States of the Monroe doctrine in Latin America, Carr resumed his position in less dogmatic terms and attempted to defend himself against the attacks made upon his views:

> This argument . . . does not invite Russia to ride roughshod over the interests and aspirations of smaller nations; on the contrary, it suggests the conditions in which a good neighbour policy, based on a sense of security and of assurance against external intervention, may become a reality in Eastern Europe. It does not involve a balancing of Britain's friendship with Russia against Britain's friendship with the United States; on the contrary, it is inspired by the profound and anxious conviction

---

[65] 'Security in Europe', *The Times*, 10 March 1943.
[66] 26 March 1943: W. Crozier, *Off the Record: Political Interviews 1933–1943*, ed. A. Taylor, London 1973, p. 352.
[67] 27 March 1943: ibid., p. 354.

that Europe, and not only Europe, will perish unless threefold concord between the United States, Russia, and Britain is fully maintained. It does not rest on the antic- ipation of a withdrawal of American military strength from Europe after the war – and still less on the desire for it; on the contrary . . . .[68]

However, his conclusion left no doubt – despite a series of qualifying clauses – that

while the organization of security in Eastern Europe, as throughout the world, will remain a matter of common and worldwide concern, the nucleus of military and economic power, which is the only effective instrument of security, must in that region, within the general framework, be provided primarily by Russia – the sole country east of Germany possessing industrial resources and development on a scale in any way equal to the task. This is a hard fact which cannot be overcome by wishful thinking or overlooked without dire peril.[69]

In April the discovery by the Germans of the bodies of thousands of Polish officers in shallow graves at Katyn in Byelorussia threw relations between the London Poles and Moscow into crisis. The former called on the International Red Cross to investigate. It is crystal clear that these men were murdered on the orders of Stalin and his henchmen during the Soviet occupation of Poland in 1940.[70] Carr may have had his suspicions but, whatever his under- standing, his leader on 'Russia and Poland' on 28 April 1943 suspended any such beliefs and focused instead on asking *cui bono?* Moscow had responded to the demands of the London Poles by breaking off relations with them. In precipitating the crisis, Carr judged them 'hasty and ill-advised':

Every Polish statesman and every Polish student of history knows that his country imperatively needs the friendship of at least one of her greater neighbours, east and west. No Pole today can contemplate deliberate cooperation with Germany . . . . Yet the action of the Polish Government ten days ago beyond doubt played, in fact though not in intention, directly into German hands . . . . Any Polish quarrel with Russia, whatever its origin, necessarily injures the cause both of Poland and of the United Nations.

These illusions about Stalin's good intentions were shared by many of Carr's former colleagues at the Foreign Office and, indeed, by Churchill himself. Such credulity with regard to Moscow's behaviour had grown to an unusual degree as the war proceeded. Witness Carr's trusting acceptance of Stalin's abolition of the Comintern that very month as a symbol of 'the renun- ciation of a policy which had in fact been abandoned long ago'. And this was a leader toned down by Barrington-Ward, who complained that 'The political

---

[68] 'Great and Small Nations', *The Times*, 23 March 1943.
[69] Ibid.
[70] For evidence from newly opened Russian archives: V. Abarinov, *Katynskii Labirint*, Moscow 1991; and N. Lebedeva, *Katyn: prestuplenie protiv chelovechestva*, Moscow 1994.

effects of what Carr writes are not always plain to him.'[71] A leader on 'Russia and the World' published on 21 February 1944 showed a degree of optimism that in retrospect seems hopelessly extravagant. Having warned that it was 'unlikely that any independent British or American initiative in countries bordering on Russia will be well received in the Kremlin', he asserted that there was 'no trace at all of Russian intention to claim any exclusive or preponderant part in the future shaping of the European settlement'. Citing, among other matters, the abolition of the Comintern, he went on to argue that 'Russia . . . is turning to the world around her in a new spirit of flexibility and open-mindedness.' There was in his mind 'no reason to doubt that this new flexibility will mark the approach of Russia to the problems of peace'.

Carr shared with many liberals from the Foreign Office the illusion that the Soviet Union would rapidly shed its messianic mission in favour of a purely state-oriented approach to international relations. The persistent way in which he – like General de Gaulle – always referred to 'Russia' and not the 'Soviet Union' was symptomatic. Dostoevsky never entirely undermined the residue of liberal rationalism in Carr's belief system. Although appreciative of the importance of ideology, he was always too much the rationalist to take fanaticism too seriously. It is partly for this reason that he misread Hitler; it is also why he misread the Soviet leadership in foreign affairs. This inbuilt resistance to the lure of ideology was also a safeguard, however. He was never as enthusiastically pro-Soviet in the myopic manner of others during the war. Indeed, he believed that 'the fog of mutual ignorance and prejudice' which had characterized relations between London and Moscow since 1917 was 'deepened rather than illuminated on the British side by a certain amount of that undiscriminating enthusiasm which lacks lasting quality and is a poor substitute for sober and critical appreciation'.[72] For him the issue was ultimately very much one of realpolitik. As he was never tired of repeating: 'Disaster lies ahead unless the principle of the relations of commitments to capacity is more firmly grasped and applied by the makers of British policy in the future than it has been in the recent past.'[73] If this were true for a power as extensive as the British empire, then it was all the more the case for the much diminished Poles.

The arrival of the Red Army on the borders of prewar Poland in January 1944 gave the resolution of these questions a new urgency, but the London Poles were still unwilling to budge. In vain Carr continued to plead from Printing House Square that the Polish exiles recognize the new balance of power: 'Polish policy after the last war was framed in the light of a concurrence of circumstances so unexpected that it might almost be called a freak of history –

---

[71] D. McLachlan, *In the Chair: Barrington-Ward of The Times, 1927–1948*, London 1971, p. 239. See 'End of the Comintern', *The Times*, 24 May 1943.
[72] 'Russia's Third Year', ibid., 22 June 1943.
[73] 'British Foreign Policy', ibid., 20 November 1943.

the simultaneous defeat and impotence of both Poland's great neighbours. Its inadequacy and its dangers for Polish security became apparent as soon as Russian and German strength began to revive.'[74] And in case the Poles thought the British might be sympathetic to their case, he recalled from memory the situation over twenty years before:

> ... Russia has made it clear that she does not accept the Russo–Polish frontier established under very different conditions in 1921. British opinion has never been happy about the equity of this line, which diverged very widely from the carefully considered recommendations put forward by the competent commission of the Peace Conference of 1919 . . . .[75]

With the swift progress of Soviet forces to the eastern bank of the Vistula outside Warsaw, the anti-Communist underground movement launched an insurrection (on 1 August 1944) in order to preempt the Soviet liberation of the Polish capital. But the uprising was ill-timed and insufficiently well-organized to succeed. Moreover the Polish resistance, having announced their anti-Soviet intentions, were denied Russian aid after they fell into difficulties. In a leader on the subject Carr described this tragic situation from all points of view. 'But,' he wrote, 'it is difficult . . . not to understand Russian reluctance to facilitate the supply of arms to men who are at the same moment proclaiming purposes plainly inconsistent with a friendly attitude towards Russia.' And his ultimate message was that the 'long and tragic record of the nineteenth century shows that the attempted intervention of western European Powers in relations between Poland and Russia, however well intentioned, has rarely brought credit to those Powers – or what is more important – advantage to the Polish nation . . .'.[76]

The dramatic collapse of the Warsaw uprising left the London Poles in an even worse bargaining position. British patience came rapidly to its limits. The intolerant outburst by General Sosnkowski, commander-in-chief of the Polish armed forces, blaming the failure of the uprising on everyone but those directly responsible, led to his dismissal. 'It is well known,' Carr wrote, 'that one of the exacerbating elements in the Russian–Polish controversy of the past eighteen months has been the presence in Polish military and official circles in this country of an influential group which made no secret of its anti-Russian opinions and missed no opportunity to disseminate them. Of this group GENERAL SOSNKOWSKI was, rightly or wrongly, reputed to be the leader . . .'. He thus expressed the hope that his removal might pave the way to 'a fresh approach to the problem of Polish–Russian relations'.[77] But these were idle illusions, and by the time the allies met at Yalta the fate of Poland was sealed. If there had been an opportunity to resolve the relationship, that had long

---

[74] 'A Step Forward', ibid., 15 January 1944.
[75] 'Poland and Russia', ibid., 8 January 1944.
[76] 'Cross Purposes', ibid., 31 August 1944.
[77] 'The Polish Dilemma', ibid., 2 October 1944.

ago disappeared; and the British were now reluctant to risk relations with Russia over what amounted to a fait accompli. In respect of Poland, Carr's leaders were not entirely at variance with government policy. The assumptions he held about the fortuitous manner in which the frontiers of prewar Poland had been shaped, and an awareness of Polish misdeeds with respect both to minority populations and in the collusion in Czechoslovakia's dismemberment, undoubtedly affected the outlook of others beside Carr. It was the intensity with which he argued the case for the continuation of the Russian alliance, and the remorseless logic with which he was thereby willing to dispense with the sovereignty of neighbouring countries in eastern Europe, that marked Carr out from the more wishful thinkers who believed that a peaceful postwar order might be obtained without payment of a tragic price.

What Carr was attempting from London was paralleled in Moscow by Deputy Commissar Maxim Litvinov, equally in the dark as to Stalin's true intentions. Recalled from the embassy in Washington in 1943, Litvinov was put in charge of a commission on postwar planning. But he was denied access to classified material and had no direct access to Stalin. However, he used his position to press his case for postwar collaboration with the west through the division of Europe along lines not entirely dissimilar to those proposed by Carr and his near equivalent in the United States, Walter Lippmann.

In a paper written between 4 August and 15 November 1944, 'On the Prospects and Possible Basis for Soviet–British Cooperation', Litvinov made the argument that Anglo–Russian conflict in the past had arisen largely from disputes in the east. Since that time the 'differences of regimes' had further complicated matters but, he argued, Britain had been seriously interested in an alliance in the mid-thirties. Now was the time to build on the existing alliance: Britain should be accommodated in Iran, Afghanistan and Sinkiang; Russia should be allowed control over the Dardanelles. A key problem was that of the balance of power in Europe. Britain needed to resolve this issue in close cooperation with Russia because of the growth of US power and the increased degree of friction between London and Washington:

> Such an agreement can be brought about only on the basis of an amicable delimitation of spheres of security in Europe on the principle of the closest neighbourly relations. The Soviet Union can consider as its maximum sphere of interests Finland, Sweden, Poland, Hungary, Czechoslovakia, Romania, the Slavic countries of the Balkan peninsula, and Turkey as well. Holland, Belgium, France, Spain, Portugal and Greece can undoubtedly be included in the English sphere.

Litvinov went on to cite Carr's leaders in *The Times* in support of this view.[78]

Soon after Litvinov began work on his report, Carr produced a leader on

---

[78] 'Sovershenno sekretno' (top secret), 15 November 1944, 'O perspektivakh i vozmozhnoi baze sovetsko-britanskogo sotrudnichestva', 1944. Komissiya t. LITVINOVA po podgotovke mirnykh dogovorov i poslevoennogo ustroistva: *Arkhiv vneshnei politiki Rossii*, F. s-t. Molotova, opis' 6, por. 143, papka 14.

'The British Role' which appeared on 12 August 1944. He argued forcefully that Britain should not hold back from assuring its postwar security in cooperation with other powers in anticipation of an attempt to merge all interests 'completely into a single, undifferentiated loyalty to a world organization so wide as to make it impossible to conceive it in any but the most abstract form, [which] must inevitably produce a reaction towards national isolation'. Instead he argued for Britain reinforcing its relations with both the Dominions and the states of western Europe, 'whose security is inextricably bound with her own and without whose friendship her policy must lack the necessary base for action in Europe'. He added: 'The cementing of relations between the British Commonwealth and the countries of Western Europe would be the complement to a drawing together of nations in Eastern Europe under Russian leadership . . .'.

In October Churchill arrived in Moscow, nervous at the prospect of communism expanding through the Balkans as the Red Army swept forward, bent on securing a division of the area into two spheres of influence: British and Russian.[79] The resulting deal did not, however, include Poland which was not yet under Russian occupation – the Red Army had halted on the eastern bank of the Vistula in August. The reasons why were plain: the western allies had proved unable to bring the London Poles and the Russians to the same table in a common spirit of compromise. And it was now all too evident – hence Churchill's Moscow visit – that the Russians could redraw much of the map of postwar Europe unilaterally. This was the time Carr decided to embark upon his *History of Soviet Russia*. The ultimate explanation for this decision could be read in his editorial of 6 November 1944:

> The Russian armies now pounding at the defences of Budapest and firmly ensconced on East Prussian soil are the instrument and symbol of a great turning-point in history – the emergence of Soviet Russia as the greatest Power on the European continent. The moment is likely to prove as decisive for the future as the establishment of the British command of the seas at Trafalgar or as the downfall of French predominance at Waterloo and at Sedan.

But he did not believe that Moscow would embark on an expansionist course. 'Russia, like Great Britain, has no aggressive or expansive designs in Europe. What she wants on her western frontier is security', he wrote. How far Russia might go to achieve it was a question unasked. And Carr also did not believe that Stalin would seek to extend communism:

> It is feared or suggested that Russia's newly won status in Europe will be used to propagate 'communism'. It is true that the Russian revolution has exercised a lasting influence on social and economic thought; that the influence was enhanced by – if indeed it was not mainly due to – the failure of the western countries and of

---

[79] The most detailed account is now to be found in M. Gilbert, *Road to Victory: Winston S. Churchill 1941–1945*, London 1986, pp. 992–3.

the United States, by the application of 'orthodox' economic policies, to avert the scourge of the great depression. It is true that Russia's amazing achievements in the present war, and the background of industrial efficiency and self-sacrificing devotion which can alone explain them, have enormously raised Russian prestige in the eyes of Europe and the world. It is also true that British and American prestige in Europe, both absolutely and in relation to that of Russia, will in the future largely depend on the success of Britain and the United States respectively in framing social and economic policies which will create full employment, productive efficiency, and rising standards of living. But it is certainly not true that Russia is at present using her influence on other countries to promote 'communism' or anything like it; nor is there any reason to suppose that her attitude in this respect will change.[80]

By the time the allied leaders met at the Black Sea resort of Yalta in February 1945, the disposition of Russian forces was such that the west had no real hope of rescuing the Poles from their clutches, even had the will existed. In an editorial on the conference Carr displayed his total intolerance of the London Poles and dismissed out of hand their warnings that the supposed reorganization of the government in Warsaw to include representatives from those in exile was a mere fig-leaf. There is little sign of Barrington-Ward's qualifying clauses set up at regular stages downstream to slow down the smooth eloquence of his prose. And the leader is worth quoting in extenso because it reveals unadorned Carr's basic attitude to the Polish government-in-exile, its claims and its legitimacy, acquired since his first encounter with the Polish problem in 1919.

First there was the agreement at Yalta on the Curzon line as the new Soviet–Polish frontier. The existing line had little legitimacy, Carr argued, drawing on his own memories. The proposed Curzon line had been worked out as the fairest division of territory based on ethnic realities, but the powers at Paris had failed to implement that line and the Poles had occupied regions originally attributed to others. Before 1939 these territories, according to Polish census figures, placed the number of Poles at less than 2.5 million out of a total population of 11 million. 'It was widely held then,' he asserted, 'and it is equally true now, that an extension of the Polish frontier to the east of the Curzon line could only be a source of grave weakness to Poland.' But this advice was not heeded. He continued to demolish the bases for protest:

> In the summer of 1919 the Poles expelled the Ukrainian authorities by force of arms from East Galicia – an action against which the Supreme Council helplessly protested. Even proposals from the Supreme Council for an autonomous regime in East Galicia were rejected by the Poles. Yet the archives of the League of Nations in the period between the wars contain much evidence of the discontent of the Ukrainian majority in East Galicia with Polish rule and of the repressive measures which the Polish authorities were driven to adopt in order to maintain it. In 1920

---

[80] 'Russia, Britain, and Europe', *The Times*, 6 November 1944.

PILSUDSKI marched against Russia. After many changes of fortune the war ended in a
sweeping Polish victory over an exhausted Russia and in the conclusion of the
treaty of Riga, fixing the frontier which remained in being till 1939. That the
Russian signatories at the time prudently made a virtue of necessity could not alter
the nature of the concessions to which they had been compelled to subscribe. A subsidiary episode was the seizure of Vilna from the Lithuanians, which provoked
strong protests and long but fruitless discussions at Geneva. By 1923 it was plain that
there was no military force in eastern Europe strong enough to contest these Polish
acquisitions, and the allied countries accepted the fait accompli by recognizing
the frontiers thus established.

Even therefore if it were true that the decision of the Crimea conference to
endorse the Curzon line was simply the reflection of superior military force, a
protest against it on that ground would come with no great conviction from apolo-
gists for the frontiers recognized in 1923.[81]

Carr thus drew the conclusion that the acquisition of those territories had
'as little foundation in justice as in political wisdom'. Then came the issue of
reorganizing the Polish administration. Here, too, it was not hard for him to
dismantle the claims made to legitimacy. He questioned whether the Polish
government-in-exile had 'an exclusive title to speak for the people of Poland'
and 'a *liberum veto* on any move towards a settlement of Polish affairs'. 'The
legal credentials of this Government', he added, twisting the knife in the
wound, 'are certainly not beyond challenge if it were relevant to examine
them: the obscure and tenuous thread of continuity leads back at best
to a constitution deriving from a quasi-Fascist *coup d'État.*' Moreover the
removal of Mikolajczyk, head of the Peasant Party, as prime minister of the
government-in-exile raised further questions in his mind:

> The representative quality of the provisional Government now functioning in
> Warsaw is admittedly defective. But what can be said of the representative quality of
> M. ARCISZEWSKI and his colleagues? Is it seriously suggested that the proceedings in
> Polish circles in London which led to the replacement of M. MIKOLAJCZYK by the
> Government of M. ARCISZEWSKI reflected the will of the mass of the Polish people, or
> indeed had any relation to it whatever?[82]

All this was, of course, perfectly true. What was questionable was his facile
assumption that 'what MARSHAL STALIN desires to see in Warsaw is not a puppet
Government acting under Russian orders, but a friendly Government which,
fully conscious of the supreme importance of Russo–Polish concord, will
frame its own independent policies in that context.'[83]

Fighting a constant battle at *The Times* to impress his controversial views
on the leader columns against a sympathetic but over-cautious editor eventually took its toll. In the summer of 1943 Carr had peremptorily rejected

---

[81] 'Poland', ibid., 27 February 1945.
[82] Ibid.
[83] Ibid.

the idea of writing a work of history when proposed by Daniel Macmillan, Harold's brother, who had taken over the business during the war. Penguin, however, offered him the chance of writing a book on foreign policy, which very much appealed.[84] But Barrington-Ward was having none of it (he would not be able to bowdlerize the result as he could on *The Times*, while the book would doubtless be seen as the true views lying behind the more cautious leaders). Just as the Foreign Office became an intellectual strait-jacket by the mid-thirties, so too did *The Times* now start to make Carr feel cramped rather than liberated. By the beginning of 1944 he was tiring of the struggle and actively looking for an academic post more worthy of his undoubted achievements and abilities. On 1 March he went down to Cambridge, dined at Sidney Sussex College (courtesy of the young historian David Thomson), saw Trevelyan, Master of Trinity, and put in an application for the Chair in European History. He was to be disappointed. On 19 March Butterfield's appointment to the Chair was announced. More disappoint-ment followed: the next day he heard that Llewellyn Woodward had got the Montague Burton Chair in International Relations at Oxford.

Sleepless nights followed at the flat in London (partly because of an air raid) but also at Honeypots. He was clearly depressed, took more and more time away from the office and, on 30 March, went up to town to talk to Barrington-Ward about his future at Printing House Square. Carr very much wanted to drop all the administrative load that the assistant editor customar-ily carried, which would cut down his duties by half, enabling him to come in just two or three days a week. Barrington-Ward noted in his diary:

> He feels the need for reading, thinking and taking in after some years of putting out. I readily agreed and said I felt that the Chairman would be ready to treat this as leave on full-pay, though I couldn't commit him. Carr raised again the question of my recent refusal to let him write a Penguin on foreign policy . . . (About which I am quite unrepentant: he cannot help to run policy on the paper and lay down policy independently elsewhere; pointless and probably embarrassing.)[85]

Still restless and dissatisfied, Carr vented his frustration in a memorandum suggesting a complete reorganization of the office, which – like much that he wrote at that time – caused rather more offence than he had anticipated. It was, on the whole, constructive criticism and designed to relieve the editor of burdens which the head of an organization should normally not have to bear. And there were some delightful touches, such as the recommendation that an editorial private secretary be appointed: 'The post is not hard to fill; a mod-icum of intelligence, a lot of tact, a ready but non-committal pen, a not too shabby old school tie and a bedside telephone manner are the chief requi-sites.' But tactless references to 'the present inefficiency at P.H.S.' and the

---

[84] McLachlan, *In the Chair*, p. 241.
[85] Ibid.

argument that *The Times* must now go out and recruit the best talent for the
postwar period and that if it did not do so 'what will turn up will be another
generation of third- and fourth-rate writers' were badly calculated to win
Barrington-Ward over.[86]

He also foolishly disclosed the depths of his dissatisfaction to Morison
who – now more wary of his former idol and forever conspiratorial – warned
Barrington-Ward that Carr

> does not seem to understand at all all that is involved in the position of *The Times* as
> an impersonal, national organ, closely related to the springs of political power, and,
> in particular, with public opinion. This illustration can be quoted: Carr said that he
> was aware that the Editor thought that it was not impossible that the P.M. would con-
> duct a Coupon Election. Secondly, he said that the Editor believed that this would be
> a wrong thing to do. Carr then made the point that, although this was the Editor's
> view, it would not necessarily be championed in the paper. He expressed no criticism
> of the Editor beyond saying that *The Times* was not a 'fighting' journal. He was aston-
> ished when I [Morison] said that, for my part, I would not denounce a Coupon
> Election unless I felt sure that public opinion was either opposed to it, or so equally
> divided that the opposition of *The Times* would turn the scale.[87]

Barrington-Ward was himself frustrated at being unable to leave Carr to his
own devices, though immensely impressed with his talents: 'I never have any
trouble with his contributions when we have talked them over beforehand. It
is only when he goes off by himself and volunteers some unheralded piece
that the rifts appear, perhaps because he "tries it on" me. But what a superb
leader-writer he is when he stays in the team.'[88]

Carr's reading took two distinct directions. He began surveying books on
the philosophy of history, clearly with an eye to exactly the kind of work he
had rejected so abruptly less than a year before. He also began to think about
a book of a more general type that would follow on from *Conditions of Peace*,
but not quite so directly related to policy that it would disturb Barrington-
Ward. His mind was ruminating on the problem of creating a collectivist
postwar order that would meet the demands evident since 1929, including
economic welfare and a strong sense of direction or faith that would at the
same time allow for individual freedom. On 31 May Stanley Morison noted:

> Carr is contemplating a book on how much totalitarianism our economic needs will
> compel us to swallow and how it can be made compatible with personal freedom . . .
> I am convinced that economic democracy is possible. He is troubled with
> doubts about the incentive being plainly insufficient. A moral purpose had to be

---

[86] Untitled memorandum of ten pages: *Carr Papers*. The failure to follow his radical proposals
left its mark. 'I fear the poor old Times will sink without a trace,' Carr wrote during the financial crisis at the end of 1966, 'but it was dead anyhow.' Carr to Isaac Deutscher, 24 December
1966: *DA*, 27.

[87] Quoted in McLachlan, *In the Chair*, pp. 237–8.

[88] Ibid., pp. 239–40.

rediscovered. To have any true vitality it must be rooted in religion, and our present-day religion lags behind the needs of the age, cluttered up with intellectual difficulties. Yet a restatement which cleared the difficulties would shatter the [Church] organizations.[89]

The reading occasions no surprise: back to Niebuhr's *Moral Man and Immoral Society*, which had so helped in writing *The Twenty Years' Crisis*; Weber's *Protestant Ethic*; and Spengler. But there was, of course, also a Russian connection with all this. What did the Soviet experience have to tell? Carr took up Berdyaev's *Slavery and Freedom*, and found something of an idea for a book in Richard Heindel's pathbreaking study of *The American Impact on Great Britain*, which analysed the impact of American civilization abroad at the turn of the century. The chapter on 'The Industrial Giant', that looked at the manner in which rapid economic growth in the United States 'Led to a severe British self-analysis which had spiritual as well as technical significance', drew his attention by analogy back to his own early reflections on the impact of the Five Year Plans in Russia on a Europe wracked by Depression.[90] The net result of these musings was to be a collection of lectures delivered at Oxford in March 1946, published shortly afterwards as *The Soviet Impact on the Western World*, to which we will return later.

His partial withdrawal from *The Times* was made easier by the recruitment of the deputy editor of the *Observer* and of the *Economist*, Donald Tyerman, as another assistant editor. At that time Tyerman was a man with views not dissimilar from Barrington-Ward and Carr (in some of its aspects). But this was not the main reason for recruitment. He was an extremely competent administrator of sound common sense rather than the intellectual high flyer, such as the young, blind and right-wing T.E. Utley, whom Carr had examined for the Cambridge History Tripos and whom he had tried more than once to recruit for the paper.

Carr, Barrington-Ward and Tyerman pulled together in respect of a major controversy that broke out in the winter of 1944–45: over the British occupation of Greece. When, on 9 October 1944, Churchill and Stalin struck a secret deal in Moscow which effectively divided the Balkans into British and Soviet spheres of influence, Greece fell to the British sphere. The Greek Communist Party, which masterminded a front organization known as the EAM to further the war effort and its future bid for total power, was thereby left to its own devices without assistance from Moscow (though the Yugoslav Communists not only encouraged insurrectionism but also promised arms). Churchill, privy to the secret communications of the Communists courtesy of Bletchley's code and cipher crackers, was bent on disarming the EAM and securing the rule of the royalist government-in-exile under Papandreou until free elections

[89] Ibid., p. 243.
[90] R. Heindel, *The American Impact on Great Britain 1898–1914: A Study of the United States in World History*, Pennsylvania 1940.

could be held.[91] The EAM were both bent on seizing power and determined to resist any attempt to disarm them while their opponents still bore arms. A collision with British forces occupying Athens was thus inevitable. This occurred on 3 December. Accurate information was hard for *The Times* to obtain; the government was not about to tell them of the intercepts. Instinctively Carr sided with the EAM, initially unaware of the extent to which it was merely a Communist front and indignant at the manner in which an unpopular monarchy (associated with the prewar dictatorship of Metaxas) was apparently being thrust down the throats of the people.

Two days later Carr lunched at the Reform Club as a guest of the economist Nicholas Kaldor, then lecturing at the London School of Economics. There they encountered Tyerman who was lunching as a guest of Leslie from Political and Economic Planning. A 'heated discussion on Greece ensued'. The following day Carr wrote a leader on the crisis. Entitled 'A Tragedy of Errors', it opened with unambiguous regret: 'The disagreeable truth . . . is that British armed forces, originally invoked in the desire to avoid bloodshed, have become involved in a Greek civil war.' Carr went on to ask some awkward questions that the prime minister, for one, was loath to answer. He attacked the notion that there was 'a greater allied interest' in maintaining the royalists in power 'than of any other of the numerous groups or parties in Greek politics'. Neither Greece nor Britain could afford a civil war in which British troops would be 'used, and British lives sacrificed, fighting against Greeks on behalf of a Greek Government which exists only in virtue of military force'. 'Grievous errors' had been committed. Britain should now seek to reconcile the two sides in 'strict neutrality'. 'It is time,' he concluded, 'before it is too late to find a way out of a disastrous predicament whose consequences will be felt quickly in neighbouring countries and beyond.'[92] Churchill was predictably 'enraged' at this attack. On his behalf Jock Colville wrote to the Ministry of Information enclosing the leader and the more cautiously worded column written by the diplomatic correspondent (Iverach McDonald), expressing the prime minister's wish for 'some straight talking' to Barrington-Ward:

> The diplomatic correspondent had undoubtedly taken the trouble to be well informed of the true nature of the events in Greece and no doubt the leading article represents the opinion of Professor Carr.
>
> The leading article was, to say the least, a very unhelpful contribution to the Government in handling the Greek situation.[93]

Carr was not unduly fazed by such criticism. He was unusually impervious

---

[91] Gilbert, *Road to Victory*, chapter 58.
[92] 'A Tragedy of Errors', *The Times*, 7 December 1944.
[93] Colville (Prime Minister's department) to Sendall (Ministry of Information), 11 December 1944: *FO* 371/43709.

to pressure of any kind once his mind was made up. His vision of the future of the west, building a social democracy and engaged in planning economic consumption, made him critical of the conservative aims that Churchill was relentlessly pursuing in states like Greece, even if it meant that this placed him in the same camp as the Communists. That he found himself in such company was a matter of indifference, though clearly not to others. It reflected the streak of idealism within him.

Somewhat shaken by the vehemence of the criticism – not just from *The Times* – and as daunted by the prospect of civil war as its critics, the government edged towards compromise. But Carr gave few marks for its efforts. On 29 December he published another leader, 'Next Steps in Greece', in precisely the same vein as his original piece, despite Papandreou's resignation and the appointment of Archbishop Damaskinos as Regent. Belatedly recognizing the fact that the conflict was 'due in large part to their [the EAM's] belligerent and provocative attitude in the past', he went on to the offensive:

> There is no ground for pride or satisfaction in the knowledge that British troops have been engaged in house-to-house fighting in a working-class suburb of Athens or that further British reinforcements . . . are on their way to Greece . . . Some form of Greek Government could no doubt be established and maintained by British bayonets and machine-guns in this area – but surely at the expense of incurring, both for that Government and for Britain herself, the enmity of the rest of Greece, where E.A.M. now appears to exercise almost unchallenged authority.

Carr's attitude may very well have been influenced by his memories of the allied war of intervention in Russia; the conclusion that Britain would have done better to have kept out of the conflict almost certainly weighed heavily on his mind when writing these leaders, and the fact that he was just embarking upon the writing of his *History of Soviet Russia*, and returning to the scene of 1917–18, undoubtedly reinforced this comparison. As if to underline his conviction that the EAM were the rightful heirs apparent to postwar Greece, he emphasized in moving towards his conclusion that British troops were 'fighting against forces representing what is according to all evidence the largest organized party, or group of parties, in Greece'.

Barrington-Ward had seen this leader in draft and, typically, 'expected him [Carr] to modify it',[94] which he decided not to do. Churchill had had enough. He dictated a letter of protest to Barrington-Ward on that very day; only the urging of others dissuaded him from sending it.[95] The article, the prime minister complained, 'sets the signal for the general attack by the extreme Left-wing forces upon the Archbishop's chances . . . . The harm may be measureless. The dead and wounded can no doubt be counted up later on.' Had

---

[94] Entry in Barrington-Ward's diary, 1 January 1945, as quoted in McDonald, *The History*, p. 120.
[95] Entry, 2 January 1945: J. Colville, *The Fringes of Power: Downing Street Diaries 1939–1955*, London 1985.

The Times 'no responsibility?' Unable to contain his fury any further, Churchill lashed out in the House of Commons on 18 January 1945 with a 'pugnacious' speech. Leaving no doubt about which paper he meant by 'important organs of the press', he accused them of maligning and traducing the government's motives. He particularly resented the 'spirit of gay, reckless, unbridled partisanship' unleashed on those who bore the burdens of power.[96] Of course, the outburst – and the uproar it elicited in the House – was precipitated not by Greece alone, though this had proved the final straw, but also represented, as Barrington-Ward noted, 'a protest against all that has, rightly or wrongly, enraged the Tories in the paper' over the previous three years.[97]

Although sensitive to these accusations, Barrington-Ward none the less asked Carr to frame a balanced retort. What he produced was certainly not that. He welcomed news of an amnesty, but went on to defend the EAM on the grounds that it had feared retribution and that this alone had motivated the conflict which had ensued – a rather one-sided view, it has to be said. He then attacked the prime minister for being over-selective with the evidence to the point of distortion of the truth and launched into an eloquent defence of the role of *The Times*:

> It was indeed difficult to recognize the PRIME MINISTER's charge of 'gay, reckless, unbridled partisanship' in the anxiously weighed, restrained, and on the whole constructive criticism which responsible organs of the Press have brought to bear on this tragic and embittered scene of civil bloodshed in which Britain has become so unhappily involved . . . the unity which the [British] coalition represents has never been, and never should be, construed as inhibiting a right of independent judgements and criticism, particularly on issues which lie altogether beyond the scope of that main purpose; and the criticisms which have been addressed to some aspects of Government policy in Greece are a healthy vindication of the right of democracy to examine fully and frankly how far particular actions and particular policies are likely to contribute to the attainment of the declared national aim. Public confidence in the coalition, consistently upheld in these columns as a necessity now and for as long as national security in the fullest sense demands more than party government, depends upon the assurance that the Press will discharge its natural duty.[98]

At the Foreign Office Permanent Under Secretary Cadogan, who held Carr in some regard, was infuriated: 'I hope someone will tie Barrington-Ward and Ted Carr together and throw them into the Thames', he confided to his diary that evening.[99]

Carr did not cease fulltime work on the paper until the summer of 1946.

---

[96] Quoted in McDonald, *The History*, pp. 121–2.
[97] Entry in Barrington-Ward's diary, 18 January 1945, as quoted in ibid., p. 122.
[98] 'Mr. Churchill on Greece', *The Times*, 19 January 1945.
[99] Entry, 19 January 1945: *The Diaries of Sir Alexander Cadogan 1938–1945*, ed. D. Dilks, London 1971, p. 697. Carr always liked Cadogan and disapproved of publication of the diaries because he felt they trivialized his reputation (in conversation with the author).

Thereafter he continued to write leaders on foreign affairs for several years. The arrival of Tyerman had relieved him of the less interesting and more onerous side to the job and had given him the time to write another book. This was *Nationalism and After*, which appeared in 1945. It was the most fruitful by-product of the seminar he had chaired at Chatham House in the latter half of the thirties, a logical extension of his ideas concerning the role of the nation-state in a world where self-defence was impracticable for most. It also stemmed from his concern for the future position of Britain and western Europe, sandwiched between the United States and the Soviet Union, the powers that actually won the war. Unlike many of his riskier predictions, Carr's anticipation of the process of west European unification has proved astonishingly accurate. If international organizations were to be the solution chosen for the re-establishment of world order, his preference was for regional units rather than global structures:

> The history of the League of Nations, beginning with the insertion in the Covenant of the original Monroe Doctrine reservation, bears witness to the persistent attempts to escape from a theoretical and ineffective universalism into a practical and workable regionalism. A world organization may be a necessary convenience as well as a valuable symbol. But the intermediate unit is more likely to be the operative factor in the transmission from nationalism to internationalism.[100]

He saw these units as established for economic planning as well as defence. Here the elision between regional organization and spheres of influence of the great powers is cleverly concealed by sweet reasonableness. Europe alone could not stand independently between Britain and Russia. 'There are already signs of such an association between Russia and the nations of eastern Europe'![101] This was, of course, a polite euphemism for domination. A natural corollary would be the establishment of British hegemony over western Europe: 'the establishment of more intimate links, couched in terms appropriate to the western tradition [by which he meant less repressive than the Russian equivalent], between Britain and the nations of western Europe'.[102] This was nothing less than the carve-up of the map that Carr had been pressing for throughout the war, but packaged to suit a world in which the old internationalist idealism he had so vehemently rejected had reappeared in new form.

It is not this aspect of the work that is the most enduring, however, but the prelude which discusses the origins and development of the nation-state, 'The Climax of Nationalism', which he traces from the break-up of medieval Christendom to the Second World War, a worthy complement to *The Twenty Years' Crisis*. Ernest Gellner, whose work on nationalism has become a leading

---

[100] Carr, *Nationalism and After*, London 1945, p. 45.
[101] Ibid., p. 73.
[102] Ibid.

authority, confessed on re-reading *Nationalism and After* that he had forgotten, when he wrote, just how much he had absorbed from Carr without proper acknowledgment. A student of politics, philosophy and economics in postwar Oxford, he was very impressed by the fact that 'it was clearly about the real world. I wasn't at all used to that.' The economic theory he was served up was largely deductive and rested on assumptions that seemed unreal; the philosophy, which he subjected to withering criticism in print a decade later, was stranded on an island of irrelevance; and the

> fact that politics were also on the menu did not help matters much: it was, in fact, announced about that time that the subject was due to die pretty soon. As a matter of fact the same was also claimed for philosophy, but its death was somehow supposed to be specially glorious, a kind of Viking's funeral, and the illumination which this particular decease engendered, conferred special and remarkable benefits on mankind.

In stark contrast, Carr's mind

> clearly was not guilty of that near-total insensitivity to the diversity of historical situations and context, which otherwise seemed to prevail in the academic world . . . here was a man dealing with a phenomenon, nationalism, which I knew to be real and important, and dealing with it in a manner which was intelligible, and which related it to major changes in society.[103]

---

[103] Gellner to the author.

5

The Prophet Outcast

The study of the Slavic world had always been something of an orphan in Britain. In 1909 a committee on oriental studies was responsible for setting up a school within London University specializing in the Orient. But of 'Russia and Russian the national ignorance was almost complete . . .'.[1] There were, of course, odd teaching posts in the language. Cambridge University, for instance, had in 1904 become the beneficiary of a private endowment enhanced by the Worshipful Company of Fishmongers, who effectively paid for a lectureship in Russian. What changed matters initially was the First World War. Prime Minister Asquith was prompted to set up a committee to enquire into the position of modern languages in the educational system. It reported a widespread prejudice against modern languages throughout a system dominated by classics and mathematics. The committee therefore recommended the establishment of a 'London School of European Languages', taking German, Italian, Russian and Spanish as the priorities. They were to be studied in their historical, political and cultural contexts. The rationale was that 'The systematic study of one or two countries, with their history, economics, & etc., as well as their languages, would be an excellent preparation for a career in the Foreign Office and Diplomatic Service.'[2]

The School was unfortunately never established, although the committee did succeed in altering the place of living languages in the national curriculum. Russian, however, never acquired the status of the west European languages. The only glimmer of light shone from King's College, London University, where there was a small nucleus of specialists on eastern Europe. They now acquired a governing body of their own, at least half composed of representatives from government departments – Foreign Office, War Office and Board of Trade – in return for a government grant. Bernard Pares, a former journalist with extensive experience of Russia who had proffered Carr

---

[1] *Report of the Committee to Enquire into the Position of Modern Languages in the Educational System of Great Britain*, London 1918: *Command 9036*.
[2] Ibid.

a helping hand at the end of the twenties, was installed as the first Professor of Russian Language, Literature and History. But the very events that made the creation of the School of Slavonic and East European Studies an urgent necessity, namely the Russian revolution, which had caught everyone unawares, complicated the fulfilment of the larger part of its mission. The Bolsheviks put paid to any hope of close contacts; the School was thus in respect of Russia almost stillborn. A troubling sign of the times came in 1935–36 when proposals to create a hostel for British and American students in Moscow fell victim to the onset of the regime of terror at the hands of Stalin. Pares subsequently resigned from his Chair and no candidate of British nationality was deemed suitable to replace him, thus further weakening an already vulnerable structure and underlining the woeful lack of development of the field since 1918. Thereafter, administration of the School fell into the inadequate hands of the Canadian Professor of Polish Literature and History, William Rose.

It took World War II and the evident importance of the Soviet contribution to the defeat of Hitler to galvanize the more energetic into action to change this feeble state of affairs. In October 1943 the only dynamic factor in the equation, Dorothy Galton, the effective administrator as secretary of the School, launched an initiative to fill the Russian Chair and simultaneously transform the School into a research centre in Russian studies.[3] And at the Foreign Office, Geoffrey Wilson had returned from the embassy in Moscow to the Northern Department appalled at the level of ignorance of things Russian, not least the language, in official circles. In February 1944 he persuaded Sargent, now Deputy Under Secretary, to set in motion the formation of a committee on Russian studies.

The thoughts behind the proposal very much reflected the common spirit of the time, namely that 'The Foreign Office had a particular interest in this country [Russia] because (a) British post-war security would be largely based on the 20 years' Treaty of Alliance with Russia, and (b) British post-war economy required that trade between Great Britain and Russia should be increased in every way possible.' Contacts between British and Russian peoples would have to be 'close, friendly and co-operative and not merely limited to officials and businessmen'. All this 'required widespread knowledge of all aspects of Russian life and activities', which had 'never been extensive or widespread, and 25 years of isolation since the last war had destroyed most sources of knowledge and made it very difficult for new ones to develop spontaneously now that we wanted them'. The Foreign Office felt, therefore, that it ought to give a lead in trying to build up some system for recreating knowledge about Russia in Great Britain.[4]

---

[3] *Rockefeller Foundation archives*: RF RG 2 1943 401. University of London, School of Slavonic Studies, f 1756.
[4] Minute by G. Wilson, 25 February 1944: *FO* 371/43375.

Yet from the outset it was understood – at least within the Office – that the role of the committee was merely to encourage others to develop the field. An overlapping decision was then reached by Foreign Secretary Anthony Eden on 31 May 1944 to establish a commission under the Foreign Office 'to enquire into means of improving the existing agencies for the study of Oriental, Slavonic and East European Studies in this country'.[5] This commission – under the chairmanship of Lord Scarborough – came into being on 15 December 1944. But it worked at a snail's pace and did not issue its report until nearly three years later.[6] Because the Russian studies committee was already in existence, the decision was taken that the Scarborough commission would defer to the Russian studies committee in matters Russian. Unfortunately the committee itself moved painfully slowly and was obviously encumbered by the fact that there was no evident financial backing for whatever recommendations came forth. The Treasury turned down the offer to participate – perhaps suspecting that this might imply future funding – and its leading light, Keynes, who had Russian interests, not least because he had a Russian wife, declined on the grounds that he was too busy.[7] Thus it was left to private initiative to set the ball rolling. Perhaps one symptom of the problems in this regard was the high degree of suspicion with which the Federation of British Industry treated the invitation to attend the committee.

Thus the initiative taken by Dorothy Galton was by no means superseded by the activities of government, but it also meant that if she were going to get things moving she would have to turn elsewhere to find funding. And in her scheme of things the right man to take Pares's vacant Chair was none other than Carr, whose views on the subject of Russian studies in Britain were robust, to say the least. The 'serious study of Soviet history and institutions has been almost entirely neglected in Great Britain', he argued; one of the major reasons for this was the 'rather faint-hearted and cowardly dislike of becoming involved in controversial issues which almost inevitably expose one sooner or later either to the charge of being a blimp or to the imputation of fellow travelling. As long as we are afraid of studying Soviet affairs for fear of being thought Red, we shan't get far', he concluded decisively.[8]

Impressed with him, Galton sought to link Carr's future appointment with an appeal for money directed to the Rockefeller Foundation in the United States. The officials at the Foundation were well informed about the inadequacies of Russian studies in Britain, which were not dissimilar to the problems in their own country. There, one of the prime movers had been Professor Geroid Robinson from Columbia University, the leading historian of the Russian peasantry and, since 1942, head of the Russian (analytical)

[5] Ibid.
[6] Foreign Office, *Report of the Interdepartmental Commission of Enquiry on Oriental, Slavonic East European and African Studies*, London 1947.
[7] Letter of 5 February 1944 from J. Barlow to O. Sargent: *FO* 371/43375.
[8] Carr, 'Problems of Writing Modern Russian History', *Listener*, vol. xl, no. 1028, 7 October 1948, p. 52.

section of the Organization of Strategic Services (OSS), the wartime intelligence apparatus. It was he who laid out the case for the funding of institutes
of Russian (read Soviet) studies at various universities. Those initially marked
out for funding included Columbia, Cornell (later ruled out after a leading
Russianist was recruited by Columbia) and Harvard (where Karpovich,
Leontiev and Fainsod were already in place). Robinson stressed forcefully that
funding was essential 'to meet the country's urgent needs'.[9] 'The *power* of
Russia will make it indispensable that a certain number of Americans shall
have a special understanding of that country', he successfully argued.[10] Other
moves were also afoot to create a School of International Affairs and Regional
Studies at Columbia; funding was sought and obtained from the Naval School
of Military Government and Administration and the Rockefeller Foundation.
Rockefeller were thus major players in this pioneering project in the United
States. Galton had certainly chosen the right source for likely assistance.

The School of Slavonic Studies was in a good position to move ahead of
possible rivals. At Oxford, Professor of Russian Konovalov was active but working alone; Slavonic history had suffered when Humphrey Sumner left to take
a Chair at Edinburgh. Christopher Hill, a former student of the School, was
a Fellow of Balliol College, Oxford and was currently in the Foreign Office
Research Department, but he was chiefly interested in seventeenth century
English history. Dimitrii Obolensky was working at Trinity College,
Cambridge, but there was no Chair in Russian there. Max Beloff had worked
at Chatham House on a study of Anglo–Soviet relations from 1929 to 1941,
but he was now back teaching at Manchester and appeared to be returning to
American history.[11] The only possible rival came from the 'energetic and
ambitious' Elizabeth Hill, who had escaped the revolution as a teenager,
turned herself into a teacher of Russian at the School, then transferred to
Cambridge as a lecturer very much specializing in training potential diplomats and members of the armed forces in the language, and was now bent on
securing a department, including a Chair for herself, from the University
Grants Committee at Cambridge.

Dorothy Galton talked Rose into the idea that Carr was the most promising
solution to their problems. On 1 November 1944 Rose broached the matter
with him. He appeared interested but made it clear that he 'would not, however, be likely to accept the Chair unless he could become Head of a
Department capable of conducting research work'.[12] On 6 and 14 November
meetings were held between Galton, Rose and John Marshall of the

[9] Proposals dated 27 November 1944: *RFA* 200 S. Columbia University Russian Institute 1944.
     RG 1.1, Series 200, box 321. fldr. 3819.
[10] Ibid.
[11] This then led Beloff to write a history of Soviet foreign policy in several volumes. For Beloff's
     recollections of this period: M. Beloff, 'The Dangers of Prophecy', *Cross Current*, supplement
     to *History Today*, September 1992.
[12] Entry, 1 November 1944, Carr *Diary*; 'Memorandum for the Principal', 15 November 1944:
     RFA: RF RG 2 1944 401. University of London, School of Slavonic and East European
     Studies, F 1872.

Rockefeller Foundation. Marshall thought it possible that Rockefeller could help promote Russian studies at London University. Rose said he had a likely candidate for the Chair and named Carr's conditions, adding that he would also favour funding for a Readership for Maurice Dobb, who came up to London from Cambridge one day a week to lecture to students.[13] Philip Mosely was a Russianist with links to the Rockefeller Foundation serving as political adviser to the US delegation on the European Advisory Commission in London. After consulting him, Marshall telegraphed David Stevens, Rockefeller's Director of Humanities: 'would you consider grant to school where comparable those to Harvard Cornell and on same conditions Mosely concurs might be key to highly desirable strengthening of work in Russian studies here hesitate to let negotiations proceed without you cabled advice.'[14] Stevens replied: 'November sixteenth request glad you and Mosely can develop project of this type.'[15] What Marshall had in mind was a working grant for the School to enable appointments to be made in fields such as Russian history. 'This matter,' he wrote, 'has been carefully canvassed with *Mosely* and with others involved.' He sought Stevens's assurance 'that the idea was feasible, because the whole thing must proceed for the present on an "as if" basis; knowing that there is some possibility of such a grant, the University will proceed to approach the man in question. If he is willing to accept the appointment, with the stipulation of avoiding duplication with Harvard and Cornell, J[ohn] M[arshall] will proceed to recommend, with the hope of early action. This move is favorably regarded by everyone, including *Geoffrey Wilson* [a member of the School's Council] with whom JHW [Joseph Willits, Director of Social Sciences at Rockefeller] discussed the situation of the School.'[16]

Dorothy Galton pressed her views without qualification. 'If Professor Carr were appointed to a Chair at the School, it is obvious that this would have far-reaching effects both upon the School itself and upon the future of Russian studies,' Galton wrote, adding for good measure: 'If the School should miss this opportunity of doing distinguished service to the cause of Russian studies, it may well in due course find itself superseded by some other institution with greater vision . . .'.[17] This turned out to be a prophetic pronouncement, for not everyone shared Galton's enthusiasm. She herself largely shared Carr's view of the relationship with Moscow: 'it is necessary and desirable to preserve and develop further the best possible relations between this country and the U.S.S.R.',[18] though for professional rather than political reasons: hostility between London and Moscow in the interwar period had hindered interest in and development of the Russian area. This, however, was decidedly not the view of the redoubtable Elizabeth Hill, a member of the School's

---

[13] Ibid.
[14] Marshall to Stevens, 16 November 1944: ibid.
[15] Stevens to Marshall, 17 November 1944: ibid.
[16] Marshall to Stevens, 21 November 1944: ibid.
[17] Dorothy Galton, 'Memorandum on the Russian Department', 28 December 1944: ibid.
[18] Ibid.

Council. And at a meeting of the Council on 13 December 'it was apparent that there were some doubts as to the suitability of Professor Carr to hold a Chair of Russian History, and also considerable misgivings as to the desirability of instituting a Professorship mainly for research in Russian studies.'[19] Carr's pro-Soviet proselytism in *The Times* was enough to convince Hill that he was a Communist, or as good as one and, having fled the Bolsheviks and lost the family fortune in the process, she was not about to aid and abet the promotion of people with Communist sympathies in academic life; quite the reverse.[20] And she was not alone in this. As the Communist *Modern Quarterly* noted several years later on the basis of inside information: 'As long ago as 1947, the head of one school in the University of London refused to support a candidate of outstanding reputation for a post for which he was eminently qualified on the ground that he would not be a party to "any further infiltration of Communists into university posts".'[21]

Stevens, ignorant of what had occurred, and given to understand that academic appointments in London were made as informally as in the United States, then telegraphed Marshall in London: 'Desire Edward Hallet Carr to consider six months here for conferences and planning materials.'[22] Marshall had to alert him to the problems ahead: 'Stevens Carr now in situation where discussion of visit would be damaging Mosely and I hesitate to broach matter unless urgent for reasons unknown to us further put Foundation in awkward position Visit clearly desirable later if current developments materialize Shall take no action unless further instructed.'[23] By mid-March not only had no progress been made, but the entire process had been badly set back. As Marshall explained in a memo on negotiations:

> While in Paris, I received a somewhat troubled cable from Miss Galton saying that negotiations were going badly and asking if I would not meet with the School's Directing Committee on my return to explain The Foundation's interest. On my return, I found that things had indeed been going badly. Rose, it seems, had presented the whole matter most ineptly to the Directing Committee, allowing them to gain the impression that any grant from The Foundation was contingent on the appointment of Carr. This appointment The Committee then opposed ostensibly on the grounds that it violated University procedure in appointment which required the advertisement of a post, etc., but actually I think because Rose's presentation had led them to feel that Carr's appointment was being forced through to get a Foundation grant. In the meantime, fortunately, Rose had left ona mission to the near East so that Miss Galton could take charge.[24]

[19] Ibid.
[20] Telephone conversation with Dame Elizabeth Hill, 27 January 1989.
[21] '"The Modern Quarterly" and Academic Freedom', *Modern Quarterly*, 4, vol. 5, Autumn 1950, p. 358.
[22] Stevens to Marshall, 2 January 1945: *RFA*: RF RG 2 GC 1945 401, University of London, F 2061.
[23] Marshall to Rockefeller Foundation, 3 January 1945: ibid.
[24] Marshall, 'Negotiations with the School of Slavonic and East European Studies of the University of London', 15 March 1945: ibid.

She drafted a paper on the situation for the principal of the University, Harold Claughton, who regretted that the matter had not been put in the proper terms by Rose to the committee. Marshall went to see Claughton to reinforce the point: it was a serious scholar they wanted; selection was up to the School. Marshall was now more optimistic. Several key people were in favour of Carr's appointment, including Wilson, director of the School of Oriental and African Studies R.L. Turner and Humphry Sumner, a member of the School's Council: 'there was a good probability that when Carr's appointment had been dealt with, the University would wish to ask The Foundation for assistance of the type discussed.'[25]

Carr, too, was optimistic. In June he wrote to Evans to warn him of the possible appointment, without, of course, being too explicit:

During the past two or three weeks [sic!], I have been sounded about a job which would fit in with my own work and be in some respects more – in others, less – attractive than the Wilson chair. There are financial as well as other hurdles to be got over, so that I have no idea whether it would materialize even if I came to the conclusion I wanted it. But if it did materialize, the date mentioned to me as potentially suitable was January 1 next [1947]. If I was in fact moving from A[berystwyth] to another job, there would be obvious advantages in synchronizing both the change itself and the announcement, so that I am unwilling to take any step until I know more of this. It is hardly likely that there could in the most favourable event be any decisions before next month. But it seems to me that if I were to announce my intention any time before Oct[ober] 1 that would be quite reasonable notice; anyhow I should prefer to leave the matter alone just for the moment.[26]

But his optimism was misplaced. Marshall saw Galton in July during her tour of Slavonic departments in US universities. He reported: 'the failure of the London School of Slavonic and East European Studies to make an appropriate appointment to the Chair of Russian History makes Miss Galton doubt that any grant for the development of Slavonic studies in Great Britain to the London School should be considered.'[27] He had learnt more of what had occurred by the end of the year. His appointment was definitely ruled out 'ostensibly under somewhat ridiculous grounds that Carr is no scholar, but actually Miss Galton suspects on grounds more personal'. This was, he noted, to the 'great detriment' of the School.[28]

Two factors were responsible, neither of which was alluded to by Marshall. First, Carr's image as the advocate of a pro-Soviet line had by no means been diminished by his recent leaders in *The Times*; second, the breakdown of his marriage.

---

25 Ibid.
26 Carr to Evans, 3 June 1946: College archives, Aberystwyth: R/DES/IP/1 (8).
27 Marshall's record of an interview with Galton, 13 July 1945: *RFA*: RF RG 2 GC 1945 401, University of London, F 2061.
28 Marshall, 'London School of Slavonic and East European Studies', 27 November 1945: ibid.

No peace conference was ever called to settle the aftermath of war. The allied summit at Potsdam in August 1945 had dealt with the issue of Germany, but not decisively; moreover the status of the other Axis belligerents had yet to be finally settled. The London Foreign Ministers Conference which had convened to deal with southeastern Europe had broken up in disagreement early in October 1945. Carr's conclusion was that this was due to inconsistency in the application of individual spheres of influence. His leader, 'A Failure to Retrieve', began with the reassuring (to the Foreign Office) acknowledgement that 'in the latter stages the main obstacle to a last-minute compromise which might have saved the conference was the intransigence of Mr MOLOTOV, who appeared to be bound by instructions from Moscow to demand the reversal of an agreement previously accepted by him. But,' Carr went on, and this is where he cut across the thrust of British policy, 'the breakdown was evidently due to more deeply rooted differences whose origins and character will require to be carefully examined and pondered.' He had understood that hitherto the great powers were aiming at a settlement in which 'each of the Great Powers takes primary responsibility for the security of certain regions'. In Romania and Bulgaria the Russians had established governments 'which are democratic in the Russian rather than in the English-speaking connotation of the term and whose friendship for Russia is one of their main qualifications'. He continued:

> it would be idle to deny that other great nations, both in the remoter and in the recent past, have pursued the same policy in regions of the world which they deemed vital to their security. During the past few weeks, however, the English-speaking Powers have adopted an attitude towards Balkan affairs which seemed to imply the contrary view that any of the three Powers may claim a right of intervention even in regions especially affecting the security of one of the others; and the clash of these opposing views, each of which can be formidably sustained by argument, underlay all the difficulties of the Foreign Ministers in their discussion of Balkan affairs . . . it is certain that no compromise can be reached, and that no settlement will be possible, if it becomes the habit of the Great Powers at one and the same time to claim special zones of influence for themselves and to contest similar claims by their peers.[29]

In 'After the Setback', published on the following day, he went still further, arguing for the recognition of the Communist-dominated regimes in Romania and Bulgaria by the British and American Governments and doing so in terms which were almost calculated to irritate Whitehall: 'the Russians are entitled to point out that democracy on the western pattern has been tried and failed in these countries in the past; or alternatively that the British and American Governments have not shrunk in the past from recognizing Governments which were not merely imperfectly democratic, but openly

---

[29] 'A Failure to Retrieve', *The Times*, 3 October 1945.

Fascist in character.'[30] He believed that the Cold War arose essentially from the failure of the west to respect the understandings on spheres of influence that Churchill had concluded with Stalin.

The head of the Foreign Office News Department, William Ridsdale, whose contacts with Carr when the latter was in charge of foreign publicity cannot have been easy, wrote to Sargent, now Permanent Under Secretary and himself somewhat depressed and fatalistic about Britain's future standing in the world:

> So far as public opinion is concerned in Great Britain in particular and through-out the world in general, the position we have taken up in regard to the deadlock in the Council of Foreign Ministers could hardly be stronger; and it is possible that the Russians, when they have done a little stock-taking, will be impressed by the critical and suspicious tone adopted towards them in newspapers, e.g. the *News Chronicle*, hitherto prepared to put a most favourable gloss on all their actions and arguments.
>
> The one weak patch in our position are the leader columns of *The Times*, where Professor Carr, with persistence and impartiality, continues to sabotage the policy of the Labour Government and of its predecessors on all matters where Russia and her Eastern Bloc are concerned.

Ridsdale attached the leader and one of the following day which were, he noted, 'considerably worse when they were written than as they appeared when printed, as certain passages were amended after the Diplomatic Correspondent [Iverach McDonald] had fought strenuously for their amendment (with partial success)'. He went on to recall that overseas they considered *The Times* semi-official and that therefore the leaders would have the effect of causing the Russians to believe that 'if they keep up the pressure, we shall give way; and serve at the same time to bemuse the minds of other foreigners who are sympathetic to and grateful for our stand, but are doubtful whether we shall hold our ground'. Carr, he added, 'is dogmatic and over-bearing in his views which he has imposed, to our despite, on his Editor at various critical moments during the last few years'.[31]

Naturally Carr did not welcome Churchill's 'iron curtain' speech at Fulton, Missouri, in March 1946. On the contrary, although carefully modulated, his leader on 6 March emphasized elements which Churchill left unsaid and which contained within them more than a mild rebuke: that the forthcoming east–west settlement 'must take account both of the effective interests and of the effective power of both parties. So far as Britain is concerned, favourable results will not be achieved by a policy of words unaccompanied by action, and still less by reliance on American support as a substitute for a balanced and carefully weighed British policy.' And he objected strongly to the Manichean division of the world into Communists and democrats: 'while

---

[30] 'After the Setback', ibid., 4 October 1945.
[31] Ridsdale to Sargent, 4 October 1945: *FO* 371/50921.

western democracy and Communism are in many respects opposed, they
have much to learn from each other – Communism in the working of political institutions and in the establishment of individual rights, western
democracy in the development of economic planning and of social aims and
incentives.' The ultimate issue, he wrote,

> will be determined neither by clashes of eloquence nor by clashes of arms, but by
> the success of the great nations in dealing with the problems of social organization
> in the broadest sense which the war has left behind it. Vast areas of the world
> which are committed neither to western democracy nor to Communism will watch
> the practical achievements of both, and pass judgement on the results.[32]

In September 1940 he had told an interviewer: 'You probably know that I
am not an unreserved admirer of everything that has been done in Soviet
Russia.'[33] But back then the USSR had yet to undertake, let alone pass, the
supreme Hegelian test for the stamina of any society: war. The scepticism
expressed in 1940 as to whether Russia had anything to teach the west had
since been eradicated by Soviet victory in war. For some time now Carr had
come to believe that its part in the peace settlement 'may be as great in the
realm of ideas as in that of power'.[34] The ideas behind the 1946 Oxford
University Carpenter lectures, later published as *The Soviet Impact on the
Western World*, had thus been in gestation for some years; they reached back to
his musings during the height of the Great Depression in his writings on
Russian industrialization. Published as a book, it was, as he later admitted,
'hastily written, one-sided (it didn't profess to be anything else), and contained some exaggerations. But it made a lot of valid points.'[35] Here Carr
reiterated his philosophy: the 'age of individualism' was 'now drawing to its
close',[36] a new age of 'totalitarianism' lay ahead.[37] The writing is as ingenious
as his leaders in *The Times*. One never entirely knows whether he agrees with
statements he makes in describing Soviet developments:

> The impact of the Soviet Union has fallen on a western world where much of the
> framework of individualism was already in decay . . . it thus fell on well-prepared
> ground; the men of every nation who helped to spread communist ideas in the
> west were not as a rule venal 'fifth columnists' (though these no doubt existed),
> but men who sincerely saw in those ideas a cure for the evils of their own
> country.[38]

The bold and somewhat frightening predictions Carr made for the new

---

[32] 'Mr. Churchill's Speech', *The Times*, 6 March 1946.
[33] Interview with C. Brooks: *Listener*, 30 September 1940.
[34] Review of H. Laski, *Reflections on the Revolution of our Times*, in *Listener*, 16 September 1943.
[35] *Autobiographical sketch.*
[36] Carr, *The Soviet Impact on the Western World*, London 1946, p. 112.
[37] Ibid., p. 114.
[38] Ibid., p. 115.

collectivist order were moderated by a plea for 'a compromise, a half-way house, a synthesis between conflicting ways of life'.[39] He was reflecting the dilemma of the British left: caught between the Communist monolith and the US capitalist giant, seeking a third way but with Britain lacking the means to secure an alternative route. Britain had, he insisted, to search for 'new forms of social and economic action in which what is valid in individualist and democratic tradition can be applied to the problems of mass civilization'.[40] The very argument now offered that the west had something to learn from the Soviet experience was anathema to Elizabeth Hill; this proved sufficient to deprive him of the Chair. What completely destroyed Carr's chances of any alternative position and, indeed, his existing standing, was his errant private life.

Universities still have statutes providing for dismissal in the event of moral turpitude. In this period, any involvement in what were then considered morally unorthodox activities could lead to the termination of academic tenure, although homosexual activities in certain ancient foundations appear to have remained untouched. The end of the war brought to a head a crisis in Ted's relations with Anne. The marriage had been under strain since Anne had recovered from sarcoma, an experience which, according to her closest friend Winnie Elkin, left Carr in 'a state of acute distress'.[41] Once again he could not cope with the emotional sea-sickness that resulted. After her recovery they had drifted apart, not least because the illness had changed Anne considerably. Winnie claimed the experience seemed to intensify Anne's peculiarities. Indeed, in her view the break-up of the marriage 'was largely the backwash of this illness'.[42] Ted's son John – then at boarding-school – was barely in his teens and it may well have been this reason as much as lack of opportunity that kept the marriage together.

It was certainly not that Carr was indifferent to a pretty face. At Aberystwyth he had encountered a colleague, Daryll Forde, Gregynog Professor of Geography and Anthropology, who had pinioned Ted to the wall with boring conversation at college receptions. He, however, had a sexually attractive and very feminine wife, Joyce (née Stock), born of an expatriate family in Constantinople in December 1903. She had moved to Britain on the outbreak of the First World War and later trained as a librarian at University College, London, where Daryll Forde was a research student. He had obtained a Commonwealth Fellowship at the University of California at Berkeley and it was there that they had married, in 1930. Joyce was much taken with the Carrs when she met them in Aberystwyth. At this stage, the only outward sign of Ted's interest was a laconic note in his diary for 5 June 1940 concerning a visit to Joyce, who lived in a house along Marine Parade, on one of his regular trips to the university during the war. Contact was renewed only in late

[39] Ibid., p. 116.
[40] Ibid.
[41] Winnie Elkin to the author, 22 January 1984.
[42] Ibid.

November 1944 when Daryll and Joyce met Ted for lunch. Daryll, who had served briefly from 1941 to 1943 as deputy head of the US section of the Foreign Office Research Department, then headed by Toynbee and based in Oxford, had just been elected to a Chair at London University. At lunch there was, quite naturally, 'great excitement over his London appointment', though it would not take effect until the following academic year (October 1945).[43]

By that time, however, Joyce's marriage had fallen apart. Living alone in Oxford, Daryll had fallen in love with Evelyn Singer, the younger sister of an old friend. Carr's diary gives a clue as to the subsequent sequence of events. On 30 January 1945 he had dinner with Joyce at Aberystwyth. On his next visit he lunched with her and the children (Martin and Tom, then still of school age). The future still seemed uncertain, but it was apparently clear to him that Anne no longer held anything for him; the marriage had gone cold. Where Anne was a dominating personality and difficult to be sweet to, Joyce was apparently much softer and very much the homemaker; and whereas Anne was older than Ted, Joyce was over ten years younger. The death of his father on 15–16 June made the decision easier to take, since parental disapproval still mattered. He saw Joyce again a little over a week later for both tea and supper in London on 24 June and again, this time in Aberystwyth, on 2 July. Joyce, of course, had her faults, but she was not vindictive. She did not wish to see Daryll's career, now crowned with success, damaged by suing for divorce on the grounds of adultery; yet Daryll wanted to re-marry. Once Ted's interest in her became apparent, and once they had agreed to settle down together, Ted was persuaded to act as co-respondent in the Fordes' forthcoming divorce proceedings.[44] The assumption he must have made was that his own career was safe in a way that Daryll's was not; and that decision was taken when he was still optimistic about the School of Slavonic Studies. Yet Ted was also a realist in personal affairs and surely knew he was running a dangerous risk. One also suspects that this act of self-sacrifice was not merely unalloyed altruism but that it was also calculated to secure Joyce's affections.

The moment therefore came to break the news to Anne. They had been moving towards a separation, but Anne had no idea anyone else was involved. Following his previous encounter with Joyce, Ted had written to Anne on 4 July letting her know his decision to sell Honeypots. She resisted. Finally, evidently to force the break, on 2 September he screwed up sufficient courage for a 'difficult talk' in which he 'disclosed J.'s identity'.[45] However, he chose the worst conceivable time: Anne's daughter Philippa was due to go in for a very serious operation that very day. His extraordinary insensitivity left the family stunned. More importantly, it left Anne deeply embittered. Ted thus emerges from this episode as both knight errant (for Joyce) and callous

---

[43] Entry, 22 November 1944: *Carr Diary*.
[44] Interview with Tom Forde.
[45] Entry, 2 September 1945: *Carr Diary*.

husband (to Anne). He could put up with months, indeed, years of tension and frustration but then, as in his treatment of 'the woman', having steeled himself to separate he was characteristically ruthless in following through. The damage was done.

In April 1946, with Daryll's divorce proceedings under way, he confided the news to Evans to alert him of possible trouble. On 3 June he wrote a follow-up letter; and with his usual skill at composition put to useful purpose, he ensured that it made absolutely no sense to anyone not otherwise apprised of the subject under discussion:

> I have asked myself several times whether I was right to tell you what I did in April. It seemed to me then, and still seems, that I ought to do so. But my motives were purely personal: we have always been on such close personal terms and you have always showed me such unfailing kindness and sympathy that I could not lay a mine which might one day explode under your feet without warning you well in advance. Officially, on the other hand, I had nothing, and still have nothing, to tell you: I have no official cognizance of any action taken or contemplated, and I suspect that these things may even move more slowly than I expected when I first spoke. The tiny handful of people who know the personal situation will not talk [Ted had forgotten about Anne] and those to whom you have mentioned it in Aberystwyth are equally safe. For the moment, therefore, the situation is intact.[46]

Not for long, however.

At the School of Slavonic Studies Dorothy Galton now tried another tactic. This was to separate out the directorship of the School from the Chair of Russian. It would be more difficult to argue that Carr was unsuitable on grounds of scholarship if the position in question seemed administrative and Carr had a fine reputation at the Foreign Office as an administrator. She contacted Marshall the very day Carr wrote to Evans, expressing her anxiety to 'keep him [Carr] going for the time being' until she could sort out the appointment of the directorship, for which she now believed he 'may be the successful candidate after all – that is, if any action is taken. But the main difficulty is MONEY, as usual, and I am cudgelling my brains just now to see how we can find some to keep him going for the time being.'[47] Marshall replied a few days later: 'Is there anything I could do? Carr is, of course, most highly regarded here and if he is in need of assistance for some specific job, I feel reasonably sure that all concerned would be glad to explore the possibility of Foundation assistance . . . if you could tip us off as to what Carr's situation was, we might even be able to take some initiative.'[48] Galton's plan was to 'suggest Ted as Director of the School in general and of research in particular'. This would then enable Rockefeller to come forward with funding as originally

---

[46] Carr to Evans, 3 June 1946: College archives, Aberystwyth.
[47] Galton to Marshall, 3 June 1946: *RFA*: RF RG 2 GC 1946 401, University of London, SSS, F 2310.
[48] Marshall to Galton, 7 June 1946: ibid.

intended.[49] A memorandum for the University was drafted which recommended him as 'certainly outstanding. Here is a man who knows what wants doing and would set himself to do it – from the bottom upwards.'[50] However, at some time between the last week in June and the first few days of July, Galton canvassed opinion and concluded 'I do not now think that Carr has any chance at all . . . . The University is very opposed, and now I know some private details about him I must admit that I am not able to support his candidature very strongly against opposition.'[51] Anne had got to senior members of the University and vividly portrayed his involvement with the wife of another senior member. The Commonwealth Fund Professor of American History, Hugh Bellot, one of nature's administrators rather than its researchers, came out forcefully against Carr.[52] Not a word could be said in his defence, of course, for fear of compromising Daryll Forde. It was a tragedy with Anne, the embittered wife, in the role of Nemesis.

A last-ditch effort to salvage the situation was made by Galton, despite her personal misgivings; the future of the School was after all at stake. Towards the end of September she 'found those most nearly concerned with the matter [were] still of the opinion that Carr is the only possible candidate', but she did not think the Council would give unanimous approval. 'He has unfortunately got himself into some personal tangle just at this moment, which makes things a bit more difficult than ever. But,' she continued, 'I know he is the right man, and I shall be bitterly disappointed if we don't get his appointment through. I saw him only yesterday, and I feel that he has a grasp of the situation and of what wants doing in it that no one else has.'[53] A month later the selection committee had been established and there had been two inconclusive meetings. They had reduced their list to seven candidates. Carr was one of the seven.[54] By the beginning of November there were two lists: one of those qualified as scholars of standing, the other of younger men qualified as administrators. Only Carr and Wren, who taught at Oxford, were on the first list; half of the selection committee were completely opposed to Carr and it was doubtful whether Wren would accept anyway. Geoffrey Wilson was on the second list.[55] The committee was deadlocked. By early January no decision had yet been released. Wilson wrote to Marshall: 'The general atmosphere is pretty anti-Russian and I am suspected of being far too sympathetic [!]. Also, the University authorities want somebody "safe" and from that point of view too it appears that I would not be considered an asset.' The two favourites

---

[49] Galton to Marshall, 14 June 1946: ibid.
[50] Memorandum enclosed in Galton to Marshall, 14 June 1946: ibid.
[51] Galton to Marshall, 4 July 1946: ibid.
[52] Bellot (1890–1969) was then a member of the senate of the University and soon rose to become successively a member of the court (1948–53), chairman of the academic council (1948–51) and chancellor of the University (1951–53). The source is the late Hugh Seton-Watson: interview, February 1984.
[53] Galton to Marshall, 27 September 1946: *RFA*, loc. cit.
[54] Galton to Marshall, 29 October 1946: ibid.
[55] Marshall's record of a meeting with Galton, 4 November 1946: ibid.

were a philologist and George Bolsover, formerly a teacher of Russian history at Manchester University, who had served in the Moscow embassy during and immediately after the war; no great scholar but a very 'safe' choice.[56] Wilson did not mention his name in the letter but said that he was someone he knew, 'who knows a lot about Russia and dislikes it all and who, if it is safety they want, is exactly their man'.[57] Indeed, that is precisely what Bolsover proved to be, and by July 1948 Galton was expressing her deep misgivings to Stevens at Rockefeller about the impact Bolsover was making on the School: 'Without letting this become a detailed account of what goes wrong,' Stevens 'found it due to Bolsover's close attention to government interests.'[58]

It is unlikely that Carr would have failed so disastrously purely on the grounds of morality. And it was the drastic deterioration in the political climate with the onset of the Cold War that also explained in large part why, though strongly recommended and without question the leading academic authority on the subject in the English-speaking world, he was not appointed to the Montague Burton Chair of International Relations at Oxford in 1948. As Christopher Hill recalls:

> Such matters are difficult to document, but the story is that his [Carr's] name was considered (with others) by the electing board, which decided that none of them was worthy of election. The electors asked one of their number to stand down, whom they then elected to the Chair. It is no reflection on the Professor [Agnes Headlam-Morley, daughter of Carr's one-time superior] to say this seemed to many a surprising decision, which could hardly be justified on purely academic grounds. It is not an edifying story.[59]

Hill was, of course, being diplomatic.

This was the unpropitious atmosphere in which Carr attempted to write a history of Soviet Russia. Of course, when he had embarked on the project the atmosphere had been very different. On 16 August 1943 Daniel Macmillan, dealing with authors while his brother Harold worked in government, had written to suggest he write another book.[60] Carr had expressed no interest.[61] A year later, however, and something had crystallized in his mind. When Daniel wrote, Stalin's forces had already succeeded in driving the Germans from Stalingrad and had then launched the first successful counter-offensive at Kursk. Thereafter a Soviet victory seemed not only possible but highly probable, particularly if the allies in the west invaded through northern France as they did in the summer of 1944. To Carr the dramatic success of the Soviet war effort, in stark contrast to the humiliating setbacks of 1914–17,

---

[56] See the obituary by Dorothy Galton, *Independent*, 30 April 1990.

[57] G. Wilson to Marshall, 8 January 1947: *RFA*: RF RG 2 GC 1947 401, University of London, SSS, F 2569.

[58] Stevens interview, 15 July 1948: ibid., RF RG 2 GC 1948, University of London, SSS, F 2835.

[59] Obituary in the *Balliol College Annual Record*, 1983, p. 21.

[60] Daniel Macmillan to Carr, 16 August 1943: Macmillan's company archives.

[61] Carr to Daniel Macmillan, 23 August 1943: ibid.

underscored the achievements of planned industrialization. It was in the autumn of 1944, with the Red Army poised on the eastern banks of the Vistula outside Warsaw, that he conceived the idea of writing a history of Soviet Russia. On 17 October he broached the Russian project with Daniel Macmillan, who made an offer over lunch at the Garrick that November. But it was not until over a year later, at around the time that moves were afoot to enlist him into the Russian Chair at the School of Slavonic Studies, that Carr finally settled on a contract with Harold Macmillan, who had returned to head the firm after the Conservatives lost the general election in the summer of 1945. It must have seemed then that everything was coming together in a most satisfactory way.

What he envisaged was a 'large scale study of the Soviet Union since the death of Lenin'. The contract signed was for *A History of Soviet Russia since the Revolution*.[62] Most of the reasoning behind his project will no doubt by now sound familiar, but it is worth quoting all the same:

> It seems to me that capitalism of the old-fashioned kind, what Marx called bour-geois capitalism, was doomed to break down partly because it had itself evolved away from a free-for-all, competitive system of individuals and small units into a highly rigid system of large-scale monopoly enterprises, and partly because of the increasing organization and strength of the workers who were bound to revolt against the privileged classes of the old order, so that bourgeois capitalism was in the nature of things likely to be succeeded by a new order containing both ele-ments of planned economy and elements of socialism in the sense of a more equitable distribution of this world's goods. It seems to me that the conditions for that breakdown or transformation of capitalism had matured, at any rate over most of Europe, when the first world war broke out; after that war capitalism in the old sense never came back and there was an uneasy interregnum in which capi-talism and socialism, national planning and socialist planning, jostled one another without really finding any working compromise.
>
> That was the bad period between the two world wars. The only country in a position to attempt a thorough-going experiment in socialism and planned econ-omy was Russia; and in Russia the revolution had been so easily successful for a negative rather than a positive reason, not because the workers were strong and advanced but because capitalism was weak and backward. The socialist experiment had to be tried out in a country whose citizens had no experience or training in democracy and whose primitive economic development inevitably condemned it for some time to come to the lowest standard of living in Europe. That is the tragedy of the Russian revolution and the tragedy of socialism. Lenin, I think, rec-ognized the nature of the problem when he complained, as he did once or twice towards the end of his life, of the cultural and economic backwardness of the country. It is the successes and failures of the Bolsheviks in grappling with this car-dinal problem, and the expedients they adopted in the attempt to grapple with it, which make up the history of the Russian revolution and its sequel – a history

---

[62] Harold Macmillan to Carr, 11 December 1945: ibid.

which I find not only exciting in itself, but full both of lessons and of warnings for the rest of the world.[63]

It was naturally expected that it would be a major work and one that could take the reader up to the present day. By 1948, however, he had cut back on his original expectations – 'I hope to go as far as the Stalin constitution of 1935, or perhaps even to the beginning of the second world war, though that might mean more than one five-year plan for myself', he told radio listeners.[64] But no one, least of all the author, ever expected it would grow into fourteen dense volumes that would take the best part of thirty years to complete, and that it would go no further than 1929. Indeed, his report to the Woodrow Wilson Chair Advisory Board a year later confidently spoke of the work as 'a major call on my time and energies for the next three years'.[65] He had no idea that the impact of Housman's fascination with arcane detail would increase strongly with the years and draw him inexorably down innumerable obscure, untrodden paths.

By then he had plunged with enormous enthusiasm into early reading. The first few months from October 1944 were spent in rapt attention 'reading Lenin' every other day when not writing leaders for *The Times*. By early the following year he had graduated to Trotsky – he had always admired Trotsky's history of the revolution; it was amongst the many works he had reviewed in the thirties. He was thus no novice to the field, though of 'neither a Marxist nor a Russian background'. Aside from work on the nineteenth century, he had been reviewing on Russia, including Soviet Russia, since 1929, and at the Foreign Office he had been well acquainted with the established techniques for analysing the Soviet press to understand Soviet policy. He regularly turned to others for advice; and this was always a characteristic of his work. In return his helpers witnessed a remarkable intellect in action.

At the outset it still 'seemed natural (though no doubt foolish) to hope that the co-operation uneasily established during the war would be continued and further developed after the victory'. But it was not to be. Carr had originally planned to visit Moscow in the spring of 1946 'if conditions permit'.[66] They did not; he tried again in 1947 but international conditions were fast deteriorating. He had difficulty enough gaining a visa to visit Soviet-occupied Vienna while en route to Prague, where he delivered lectures on economic planning in April 1947; this was less than a year before the Communists seized power in Czechoslovakia at Soviet bidding.

The Vienna visit left a baleful effect on the British political mission. Carr lectured at the Institut für Kunst und Wissenschaft in April 1947 on 'Britain's

---

[63] 'Problems of Writing Modern Russian History: E.H. Carr on his forthcoming "History of the Soviet Union"': Talk on the BBC, 3 October 1948, printed in the *Listener*, 7 October 1948.
[64] Ibid.
[65] Report, 16 November 1945: College archives, Aberystwyth: R/DES/IP/3.
[66] Ibid.

place in a changing world'. The lecture was characteristically undiplomatic and significant not only for references to 'United States capitalistic imperialism' but also, as the British political representative noted, for 'Carr's apparent acceptance of the idea that Great Britain was now a second rate power', which 'had caused a painful impression among Austrians in the audience'. He stayed with the pro-Soviet Smollett, whom he had known in London, and 'seems to have moved chiefly in Communist or fellow-travelling circles', as the British representative disapprovingly recorded.[67]

Carr rationalized his failure to reach Moscow: even 'if you did get there you wouldn't . . . find available in the libraries a lot of the original sources for, say, the first ten years of the revolution.' He therefore had to be content with libraries in the west. By October 1948 he still did not 'yet know exactly how difficult it is to get adequate sources for the 1930s', though he fully expected that this would 'obviously' be 'much more difficult than for the 1920s'. In his view 'up to 1923 – and rather less confidently up to 1928 – you have as good a chance of discovering what significant things happened, and why they happened, and why they were significant, in Russia as in any other country.' For the earliest period, 1917–23, which he was initially not going to cover at all, he considered there might even be a 'better chance'. The reason was that 'Not many disputes went underground in this early period; the student is far more likely to be bothered by the superabundance of material than by the lack of it.' This did not mean

> that even in that early period there aren't still an awful lot of things you would like to know which aren't in the records both about what actually happened and the motives which made people, whether individually or collectively, behave as they did behave. But that sort of condundrum continually confronts the historian whatever country he is studying and whatever material he is using. The real job of the historian is never simply to ask questions and look up the answers in the book, but to find the answers which aren't in the book; and that requires understanding and imagination quite as much as access to facts.[68]

He was thus hamstrung by Stalinist conditions in Moscow; he had lost the chance of an ideal leading position in London University from which he could build up the academic study of the Soviet Union as well as pay for his research needs (in large part due to his inability to accept what Stalin meant for relations with the west); and then, to crown it all, the secure position that he had held at Aberystwyth collapsed beneath him. The divorce gossip had penetrated to the Welsh coastline and reached the willing ears of Lord David Davies, who immediately mobilized the legions of nonconformist outrage for the final attack. To forestall further bad publicity Carr went down to Aberystwyth on 2 December 1946 and, after talking matters over with Evans,

---

[67] UK political representative (Vienna) to Dean (Foreign Office), 16 April 1947: *FO* 371/64085.
[68] Carr, 'Problems of Writing Modern Russian History'.

two days later he wrote a letter of resignation. On 5 February 1947 he wrote
again, asking that the resignation take effect as from 30 June, and added: 'the
ideas under discussion at the School of Slavonic Studies have, as I rather
anticipated, fallen through altogether; there is nothing to be done with that
institution – it's dead from the waist up.'[69]

It was an unmitigated disaster. Moreover Anne would not divorce him and
before long this became a bone of contention in the new relationship. He had
moved in with Joyce; her children were in Daryll's custody. He had left the staff
of *The Times* in July 1946, when the issue of the directorship of the School was
still in balance. He continued to write the occasional piece and now began to do
leaders of an academic nature for the *Times Literary Supplement*, edited (since
1945) by his friend Morison. He was still invited to appear on the BBC Third
Programme. But he was embarking on a new life at the age of fifty-four, when
most are looking forward to a peaceful retirement; he had no salary or grants
to fund his research; he had a dual duty to maintain both Anne and Joyce; and
he was fully committed to write a history of Soviet Russia at a time when international relations between east and west had so deteriorated that access to
sources was severely circumscribed. For all his defects – and Anne could say
much on that score, and was loudly doing so to anyone willing to listen – lack
of courage was certainly not one of them.

Increasingly Carr found himself in internal exile, at odds with the establishment, cut off from a secure source of income, living entirely by his pen. But
his reputation among many was still high. Even those who disagreed strongly
with him, such as former colleague and future Permanent Under Secretary at
the Foreign Office William Strang, continued to lunch or dine with him for
an exchange of views. And once engaged in his *History of Soviet Russia* he did,
as always, rely on the assistance of others more specialized in particular areas
of his fleeting interest. He researched primarily in the Reading Room of the
British Museum, the London Library, Marx House (effectively the library of
the British Communist Party), the LSE Library, Chatham House (where he
was in charge of research on Russia) and the Foreign Office Research
Department Library. Jane Degras (née Tabrisky) who, as a young Communist,
had once helped him with his biography of Marx, was now editing documents on Soviet foreign policy and the Comintern at Chatham House and
proved a helper in these new circumstances, even though her views had mellowed since her youth. Another source of assistance was Andrew Rothstein,
son of the Bolshevik Theodore Rothstein. Rothstein, who had grown up in
Britain during his father's exile, was an untenured lecturer in Russian history
at the School of Slavonic Studies until he was cleared out by Bolsover in 1950
in an attempt to purge the School of undesirable influences. He was invaluable to Carr in lending him rare collections of published documents
unavailable elsewhere in western Europe; he also offered critical comments

[69] Carr to Evans, 5 February 1947: College archives, Aberystwyth R/DES/IP/I (8).

on early drafts, particularly attacking 'rash or vulnerable phrases, sometimes inserted in a moment of irritation'.[70] He did not, however, exert any real influence over the final product.

The material assistance thus offered was not insignificant. But relief from spiritual and intellectual isolation came increasingly from an entirely unexpected source: Isaac Deutscher. The Deutschers did not come into Carr's life until 1947 by which time he was settled with Joyce, with whom he appeared entirely happy. She was pleasant company, with a good sense of humour, less well educated but further to the left than Anne (though only as far as the *New Statesman*), and much more the homemaker. They had set up house at 5 Heath Drive in Hampstead in the first week of August 1946. Within a year, however, they packed their bags for the countryside. There was nothing to keep them in London once the jobs fell through and at Orchard House, a picturesque property near the village of Appleford in Abingdon, they had more room and, during the years of food rationing, they could provide for their own food from the kitchen garden, orchard and henhouse; they were also conveniently close to Oxford.

Carr had first met Isaac Deutscher soon after the war but a relationship did not develop until later. Deutscher, a Jew, had been expelled from the Polish Communist Party for 'Trotskyism' in 1932, which meant simply that he had questioned the Party line from a leftist position. He remained a militant Marxist, however. He worked for a while as a journalist until publication of his views became impossible. In April 1939, fearing Poland would fall either to Hitler or to Stalin, he fled to Britain. There he eventually found work at the *Economist*, a journal for which he had some respect. On arrival his English was extremely weak, but with the aid of an edition of Macaulay, the *Shorter Oxford English Dictionary*, Talmudic self-discipline, a prodigious capacity for memorizing words and a sharp brain, he polished his prose to the point where – except for occasional quaint archaisms – he, like Joseph Conrad half a century earlier, could more than match the fiery eloquence of the best native speaker. Like Morison, Deutscher was largely self-educated. It was easy to see what drew Carr towards him. He was a revolutionary by outlook, an outstanding intellect and a pugnacious polemicist who could easily wound less armoured minds. Carr found him not only fascinating but also endearing. He was in so many ways like the colourful romantic exiles or that 'energumen' Bakunin.

The relationship began early in 1947. Deutscher was then living with the pretty and charming Tamara Lebenhaft, whom he was soon to marry. Having grown up in a Jewish intellectual family in Łódź, she had arrived in England via Belgium after the fall of France and learned her English from Isaac, using Carr's leaders in *The Times*. The two of them were working all hours on a biography of Stalin.[71] Deutscher's name later became inextricably associated with

---

[70] Carr to Rothstein, 5 January 1949: Rothstein correspondence.
[71] The best, but all too brief, description of Tamara Deutscher can be found in an obituary by Daniel Singer in the *Independent*, 10 August 1990.

biography, yet biography was 'not his favourite form of history writing'. It was, however, seen as the best means by which he could reach the public.[72] By chance Carr had just completed Stalin's obituary for *The Times* on 14 January, in anticipation of the dictator's demise. He came to tea on 23 March – the Deutschers were then living at Haverstock Hill – and, unusually, he noted in his diary how much he had enjoyed the occasion. Six months later – 22 September – it was dinner. Thereafter these enjoyable occasions, enlivened by the Deutschers' ample vodka supply, became increasingly frequent, as Ted's attachment to Isaac became increasingly evident. To some extent the relationship that developed was one-sided. Isaac and Tamara greatly respected him as a scholar, they loved his writings on the romantic exiles, but inevitably held deep reservations about his ruthless realpolitik; they stood much closer to Carr the utopian than Carr the realist. As Poles, albeit Jewish Poles, they reacted against his cool indifference towards the grim fate of the former rulers of eastern Europe with deep misgivings. On one occasion when they were discussing the Polish question and the issue of the government-in-exile came up, Joyce abruptly suggested that they – the government-in-exile – should all be sent to some far away place 'with an awful climate'. At this, Tamara recalled, 'even Ted winced.'[73] But both Deutschers assumed that she was unwittingly echoing her master's voice.

Carr was always unconditional in his loyalties. Since Soviet victory at war, Deutscher had suppressed his instinctive dislike of Stalin and his regime and, for a time at any rate, drew closer to the pro-Soviet and statist world view of Carr the ex-diplomat. In December Carr arranged for *The Times* to publish two of Isaac's articles on 'Soviet Diplomacy'. Here Isaac argued that Soviet foreign policy was driven not merely by Marxist–Leninist postulates but also by the tactical exigencies of day to day diplomacy (it has to be remembered that at a time of growing alarm about Soviet intentions, the obvious needed restating).[74] On 24 July 1948, after tea at the Deutschers, he took home sample chapters of the Stalin manuscript. His enthusiasm was unbounded. Always given to understatement in pronouncing on the work of others, the fact that he described these chapters as 'brilliant' and that he had read them with the 'greatest pleasure' was praise indeed.[75] On 7 October he began handing over his own drafts for criticism.

A curious emotional bond now began to form. But the relationship between the two was asymmetrical in other ways. To Deutscher, Carr was characteristically English, not merely in appearance but also in cast of mind: empiricist to the core. He was, despite everything, of the establishment; whereas Deutscher was not only quite at home with theory and brilliantly but

[72] Interview with Scheinman. I have the script from Tamara Deutscher.
[73] Tamara Deutscher to the author, 8 December 1984.
[74] 'Soviet Diplomacy: I. Principles and Practice since the Revolution', *The Times*, 17 December 1947; and 'Soviet Diplomacy: II. Spheres of Influence since the War', ibid., 18 December 1947.
[75] Carr to Deutscher, 27 July 1948: *Deutscher archive*, vol. 12.

awkwardly out of place in polite English society, he was also a committed Marxist. He could not but judge everyone intellectually in terms of their proximity or distance from Marxism; and Carr was never, ever, a Marxist. 'He is, on the whole, inclined to learn and take notice of criticism,' Deutscher wrote some years later, with lofty condescension though considerable perspicacity; 'but it is very difficult or perhaps impossible for him to get out of his skin, theoretically and ideologically. He is steeped in English empiricism and rationalism, his mind is very far from what to him are abstract dialectical speculations, and so he cannot really break down the barrier between his own way of thinking and Marxism.'[76] The reader may judge whether this ultimately proved a strength or a weakness.

By the end of 1947 work on the *History of Soviet Russia*, which had been held up by 'a troublesome house-moving', was going ahead 'at full pressure'. One result of this was that 'the material has changed shape as I worked on it.'

> My original notion was an introductory volume to cover up to Lenin's death. I now find that there is so much more available material for the earlier period, material which nobody has yet worked over, than I suspected; and my present idea is that the period up to 1924 will occupy two volumes. This is not entirely an expansion of scope as some of the subjects which I had intended to leave over altogether for a later period will now be treated in the earlier period with a corresponding saving of space later on. All this is admittedly somewhat vague, but the result for the present purpose is that instead of having nearly finished one volume, what I have in hand is far more like the half of two volumes, and it looks as if I should come nearer to delivering two volumes at the end of the year than one at the end of the present year.[77]

In fact he ended up delivering only one volume early in January 1949. As he had foreseen in that same letter to Macmillan: 'The thing that frightens me most is that the more I work on it, the more material I find; the subject has hitherto been almost completely neglected by any serious writer in this country.' Indeed, that might stand as the epitaph for the entire opus. What drove him on, however, was the determination 'to produce something that will really stand for some years to come'.[78]

The lack of materials in Britain was a severe handicap, an obvious legacy from the hostile attitude to the revolution: 'we just assumed that the Bolsheviks were stupid or incomprehensible or obnoxious people who disturbed our traditional and well established ways of thinking and acting, and that to take them seriously and treat their documents as worth collecting or their ideas worth studying was too uncomfortable.'[79] The United States, and

---

[76] Deutscher to Brandler, 3 January 1955: *Unabhängige Kommunisten: Der Briefwechsel zwischen Heinrich Brandler und Isaac Deutscher 1949 bis 1967*, ed. H. Weber, Berlin 1981, doc. 58.
[77] Carr to Daniel Macmillan, 30 October 1947: Macmilllan's company archives.
[78] Ibid.
[79] Carr, 'Problems of Writing Modern Russian History', p. 518.

not least former President Herbert Hoover, was more far-sighted. The interest in Carr from across the Atlantic was almost exclusively due to *The Twenty
Years' Crisis* which served as a *vade mecum* for those concerned that, as the new
world power, the United States conduct its policies along 'realist' lines.

The Institute for Advanced Study in Princeton was not only home to Albert
Einstein and Robert Oppenheimer but also had a School of Humanistic
Studies and a School of Economics and Politics. It was to the latter that
Edward Mead Earle had sought to bring Carr since the spring of 1946. From
Oxford, Llewellyn Woodward had recommended him as 'good with firm con-
ceit and dogmatic views. Social relations indifferent but academic sound.'[80]
Earle wanted Carr to join a regular seminar that met each week to focus on
'power problems' which were, on his view, 'so shockingly abused and misun-
derstood by American scholars and publicists'. This was not to be an exclusive
arrangement. He was also offered a course of lectures at Columbia
University's new School of International Affairs and its seminar on war and
peace. He was also encouraged to seek further commitments elsewhere in the
country.[81] Unable to free himself with duties in Aberystwyth due in October,
Carr asked to postpone the visit. When, of course, matters fell apart in Wales,
he gladly accepted. The visit not only provided financial reward of no inconsiderable size but also the opportunity to use the best libraries.

Thus it was that on 2 January 1948 he set sail on the *Empress of Canada* for
Nova Scotia (he hated flying) for the first of several expeditions for research
materials, subsidising the expenses by conducting a lecture tour taking in the
institutions he needed to visit. The trip took him to Denver, Colorado, where
he lectured on the moral foundations of foreign policy on 12 January (a
rather dull performance); to the orchards of Palo Alto, California, where he
visited the magnificent collection of Soviet sources at the Hoover Institution
on War and Revolution; and from there across the bay to Berkeley, where he
was shown around by a young graduate student, R.W. Tucker, then working
under the formidable Hans Kelsen.

The Twenty Years' Crisis had now, with the emergence of the United States in
a world role, become something of a bible for those who saw the crucial
importance of the factor of power in international relations: not only to
Tucker, but the entire generation of realists – Robert Osgood, Kenneth Waltz
and others. En route through Los Angeles and heading for the Grand
Canyon, Carr took time off to write 'On the Pacific Coast', an article which
The Times published on his return. What surprised him about the west coast
was not its 'phenomenal record of progress' and the current 'wave of prosperity', but an 'undercurrent of anxiety' similar to that found in the east. In
his opinion only on the surface were these anxieties attributable to 'the Reds',
because the Russians were really in no position to threaten the Americans.

---

[80] This supporting reference was elicited by Earle in April 1946: Archives, Institute for
Advanced Study, Princeton, Carr file: HS – (E/P) 1947–48.
[81] Earle to Carr, 9 May 1946: ibid.

'The questioner is soon driven to the conclusion that fear of Russia, so far as concerns the west coast, is far more psychological than military,' he wrote. 'Dislike and fear of Russia is closely bound up with a domestic *malaise* of which there are many other symptoms as well . . . Hatred of Russia and anxieties for the future of the capitalist order in the United States are two facets of the same phenomenon.'[82]

From Colorado, now thoroughly disturbed at what was going on around him, he continued on to the University of Chicago, before reaching Princeton for three months writing, lecturing and researching, with occasional trips to Boston and New York: a precious three months from February through to April 1948. The Cold War had yet to reach its height. But the early signs were ominous enough. On later visits the atmosphere had noticeably chilled; by then he was, to say the least, not entirely welcome at some ports of call.

Volume one of the *History of Soviet Russia* at last appeared in 1950. He had worked on it 'in a rather unsystematic way' because he 'had not decided up to quite a late stage exactly how much' he 'could get into it'.[83] Intended as a mere prelude to the main work, which would deal with the construction of Soviet Russia rather than the revolution that gave birth to the new regime, it was originally to have been entitled *Lenin*, and then, on subsequent reflection, *The Legacy of Lenin*, the first chapter of which would be called 'The Man and the Instrument'.[84] And it is in his characterization of Lenin that the work is perhaps best known, because although he saw the revolution as basically spontaneous in generation and working-class in origin, it was Lenin who had the brilliance to seize the moment. Carr clearly admired his 'immense learning, his analytical skill, his outstanding intellectual power in the marshalling of fact and argument . . .'.[85] This was not an uncritical assessment. 'The combination of a fundamental simplicity of thought and character with fanaticism in opinion and ruthlessness in action is,' he wrote, 'strongly reminiscent of Robespierre.'[86]

The Bolshevik Revolution was the title suggested by the publisher, in order to avoid confusion with biography. Volume one opened with the caveat that the work was originally intended as 'a long introductory chapter, in which I should have analysed the structure of Soviet society as it was established before Lenin's final withdrawal from the scene in the spring of 1923 – a moment which approximately coincided with the foundation of the Union of Soviet Socialist Republics. But,' he noted, 'this framework proved on examination almost ludicrously inadequate to the magnitude of Lenin's achievement and of its influence on the future.'[87] The result thus 'retains

[82] 'On the Pacific Coast – Dislike of Russia and Concern for Capitalism', *The Times*, 17 February 1948. This was followed by 'American Hopes and Fears' in two parts: 15 and 16 June 1948.
[83] Carr to Rothstein, 5 January 1949.
[84] Carr to Harold Macmillan, 20 April 1950: Macmillan's company archives.
[85] Carr, *The Bolshevik Revolution 1917–1923*, London 1950, vol. 1, p. 23.
[86] Ibid.
[87] Ibid., p. v.

something of its character as the introductory stage of a larger enterprise', purporting to contain 'not an exhaustive record of the events of the period to which it relates, but an analysis of those events which moulded the main lines of further development'.[88] It was for this reason that the reader would find 'no consecutive narrative of the civil war'. His interest was thus in the order that grew out of the destruction, rather than the process of destruction itself. His focus was very much on Lenin, 'a great revolutionary – perhaps the greatest of all time'[89] but he saw Lenin as state-builder rather than revolutionary.

As far back as the mid-thirties, when he reviewed Chamberlin's classic account of the Russian revolution for the *Sunday Times,* Carr had formed the opinion that the revolution was essentially spontaneous. This was in reaction to the conspiratorial view prevalent when he had dealt with the issue at the Foreign Office in 1917 and resulted from reading both Trotsky and Chamberlin: 'It was not, as nearly every foreigner believed at the time, the work of a band of fanatics or agitators inciting the mob to violence. Again and again it was the masses who drove their hesitating and temporizing leaders further and further down the path of revolution.'[90] The revolution thus developed from fundamental causes which completely undermined not only the old regime but also the provisional government that succeeded it; hence his controversial conclusion that 'the Bolsheviks succeeded to a vacant throne.'[91]

This radical interpretation brutally pushed aside existing historiography, largely composed of emigré reflections on the unfulfilled potential of bourgeois democracy in the Russia of 1917 and, indeed, on the idea that the Tsarist regime itself could well have continued with minor constitutional modifications but for the Bolshevik plot. It reflected Trotsky's description of the revolution as mass action and undermined Soviet orthodoxy on the critical role of the Bolsheviks in the entire process, while sustaining Lenin as the hero of the piece. But that historiography was lamentably weak, blatantly self-serving on both sides of the divide. In one sense, therefore, Carr was pushing at an open door. With the exception of Chamberlin, his was the first scholarly account of the Soviet period of Russian history written in any language and drawing from documents and according to standards applied to the study of other countries. This was no accident. Most in the west had assumed the revolution was an unpleasant historical accident and that the order which grew out of it would sooner or later be swept aside by the forces of mainstream history. World War II made that seem unlikely. The reading public was therefore ready for a work such as this and it was welcomed as a 'relief from crusading popular literature of both anti- and pro-Soviet varieties'.[92]

Read with detachment – and it has proved impossible for some ever to do

---

[88] Ibid., pp. v–vi.
[89] Ibid., p. 25.
[90] *Sunday Times,* 6 October 1935.
[91] Carr, *The Bolshevik Revolution,* p. 25.
[92] Barrington Moore Jr. in *American Political Science Review,* vol. xlv, September 1951, no. 3, pp. 885–9.

so – it is hard not to admire the smooth elegance of the prose, the vividness of some of the descriptions, the confident sweep of the judgements (even when one disagrees with them), and the lucidity of the narrative. The text of this and later volumes also made way for some superbly barbed projectiles anticipating liberal criticism of the revolutionaries. Were the Bolsheviks really so very different from ourselves? Were they any more utopian than Adam Smith in talking of the withering away of the state?

> The liberal doctrine of the harmony of interests did not suggest the nature of men would change, but that their natural egoism would be found in suitable conditions to serve the interests of society. This is the political doctrine of the dying away of the state; and Adam Smith has not escaped in recent years the charge of utopianism commonly levelled at Marx and Engels and Lenin. Both doctrines assume that the state will be superfluous in so far as, given the appropriate economic organization of society, human beings will find it natural to work together with one another for the common good. It is the context in which human nature displays itself rather than human nature itself which will be changed. In this sense both doctrines are consistent with belief in an economic order determining a superstructure of political ideology and behaviour.[93]

It was Carr the utopian who conceived the idea that the experience of Soviet Russia could hold lessons for the west – a view which he ultimately dropped – but it was very much the realist who researched and wrote most of this history. Carr's cool account of the unscrupulous way in which Lenin exploited the liberal doctrine of national self-determination underlines that this was a formidable historian with few illusions. Not surprisingly that stark realism evoked a mixed response from readers. Those convinced Russia could have come up with some alternative to the Bolsheviks were faced with some harsh judgements; on the Mensheviks, for example: 'The failure of Menshevism, a failure marked both by tragedy and by futility, was a result of its alienation from Russian conditions. The Russian social and political order provided none of the soil in which a bourgeois-democratic regime could flourish.'[94] And, having alienated ex-Menshevik emigrés, social democrats and liberals, he went on with equal facility to upset devoted Communists: 'The tragic dilemma of the Russian revolution, which neither Mensheviks nor Bolsheviks could wholly resolve, rested on an error of prognostication in the original Marxist scheme.'[95] None the less he stood four-square with Marxists of all affiliations in describing this as a 'proletarian revolution'[96] and this alone was sufficient to outrage liberals, conservatives and probably, also, democratic socialists in the west.

The most formidable attack from the right came some years later from the

---

[93] Carr, *The Bolshevik Revolution*, p. 249.
[94] Ibid., p. 41.
[95] Ibid., p. 43.
[96] Ibid., p. 44.

American ex-Communist Bertram Wolfe, who had completed a colourful and fascinating study of *The Three Who Made the Revolution*, was now chief of the ideological advisory staff of the Voice of America and who – as Carr always asserted – had a love–hate relationship with Lenin, whom he had known and worshipped in his youth. Carr had, in his preface, announced that the historian needed 'an imaginative understanding of the outlook and purpose of his dramatis personae'. 'But,' Wolfe retorted,'we find only one persona in his pages': Lenin. 'Throughout . . . we get Lenin's side of every serious controversy, and only that side. His doctrines and modes of reasoning are so expounded that it is frequently difficult to tell whether Carr is merely paraphrasing them without subscribing to them, or advancing opinions he holds in common with Lenin, or working out a more "reasonable" statement and defense of Lenin's views and acts than Lenin himself had thought of.' Thus the opposing sides in the Russian social democratic movement and the factional disputes within the post-revolutionary regime were given short shrift.

Wolfe had other strong objections. 'There is doctrine, but no clash of ideologies or faiths; famine, but no hunger; revolution, but no bloodshed. Titanic social transformations are ascertained in documents bereft of conflicts, tears, or exultations.'[97] This was partly a difference in temperament; in part it was also deliberate. Carr's personality, as we have seen earlier, was such as to compress emotion deeply within and to avoid at all costs any outward public expression of it. Even descriptions of the beloved romantic exiles were overlain with ironical detachment. More importantly, perhaps, Carr was also consciously seeking to lower the temperature of debate in an atmosphere of growing hysteria about Russia. He sought to present the order that emerged from the revolution in the manner of historians writing centuries hence. Of course, this rested on the assumption that the new order would not only survive, but thrive; an assumption that may seem threadbare from the perspective of today.

A further criticism which emerged was that he paid too much attention to forms of government that bore little relation to their substance. This was partly his addiction to documentation (unsurprising, perhaps, in a former government official) but partly also the standard approach to history since the nineteenth century, a time when constitutional and political history dominated almost to the exclusion of anything else. And this was a defect which Carr came to acknowledge later, not least because of the incessant criticism of it by the Deutschers. 'An air of unreality clung to the earliest, as well as to more recent, Soviet constitutions. They made little impact on the society for which they were devised, and were moulded by it in ways far removed from the intentions and professions of those who drafted them. Writing today,' this being thirty years later, 'I should shape my first volume very differently, giving less prominence to the formal constitutional arrangements of the new

---

[97] B. Wolfe, 'The Persuasiveness of Power', *Problems of Communism*, IV, no. 2, March–April 1955, a review of the first three volumes), pp. 43–8.

regime, and more to the geographical, social and economic environment in which it operated.'[98]

There was another, and no less important, element to all this. After graduating at Trinity he was indisputably of the elite. Entry into the Foreign Office had reinforced two facets of his personality and outlook. First, it cut short the sense that there could be a multitude of possible outcomes to any situation; once an event had occurred, whether it was good or bad, the diplomat accepted it and moved on – 'it is as difficult for the historian as for the statesman not to respect the fait accompli', he once wrote.[99] Second, it underscored his identification with rulers rather than ruled; certainly writing leaders at *The Times* did nothing to counteract this tendency. He thus saw society from the top down. And in writing the *History* Carr subconsciously transposed his early identification with the ruling class in Britain to the ruling caste in Soviet Russia. The result was a history narrowed in scope, but with the inestimable advantage of analysing and documenting the regime's activities in its own terms; certainly no Soviet historian successfully did so, and no post-Soviet historians are likely to do so. It was thus a unique exercise that no one else in the west would, or in the east could, undertake; how worthwhile that undertaking was, is up to each reader to judge.

Carr the historian undoubtedly developed with the *History*. The second volume, which appeared a year later, dealt with the emergence of the Soviet economy. Here a new tone is struck. Although by no means trained in economics, he had picked up a good deal of knowledge over the years: from his early career in the Contraband Department through to leader-writing on *The Times*. From the outset in volume two he firmly impressed upon the reader that 'The war of 1914 quickly revealed the inadequacy and the impotence of the Russian national economy in conditions of modern warfare . . . . At the end of 1916,' he added, 'it was clear that Russia's main industrial effort was exhausted.'[100] He spoke here with some authority. He had, after all, been monitoring the Russian economy through to the revolution. He was, of course, intimately associated with the decisions to tighten the stranglehold around the new regime. It may have been this that alerted him to a critical feature of the entire evolution of Soviet Russia in the period under examination: that a great deal of what happened, most notably on the economic front, was due less to doctrine, as evidently he along with everyone else had always supposed, than to force of circumstance, the conditions themselves. It first appears to strike his attention with respect to the establishment by Lenin of a state monopoly of foreign trade, which came into force within six months of the seizure of power. This was, he discovered, due less to dogma than 'certain specific conditions',[101] not least the allied blockade which he himself had

---

[98]   *Foundations of a Planned Economy 1926–1929*, London 1978, vol. 3, III, p. viii.

[99]   Review of H. Friedjung, *The Struggle for Supremacy in Germany 1859–1866*, in *Sunday Times*, 22 July 1935.

[100] Carr, *The Bolshevik Revolution*, vol. 2, London 1952, p. 25.

[101] Ibid., p. 126.

rigorously enforced since the Soviet compromise peace with the Germans at Brest-Litovsk in March 1918.

The case of nationalization of the banks and cancellation of foreign debts aside, elsewhere too he found 'the financial conceptions of the Bolshevik leaders were fluid and uninformed . . .'.[102] The collapse of the currency was also found to be due to circumstances rather than policy, and where he came to consider the origins of economic planning in this period Carr points to the role of the German war economy as model. It is almost as though he was going out of his way to make it all seem so normal, so unoriginal, so mundane. If that was his purpose, he succeeded and succeeds still in sounding convincing. What he also conveys is that the simple certainties that drove Lenin and the Bolsheviks into power were replaced rapidly on achieving it by a series of unexpected crises that challenged their ability to do anything other than improvise solutions. This in fact constitutes the lasting originality of Carr's interpretation. There is a texture to the description of these processes that he uniquely uncovers and presents to his readers in calm, limpid prose.

Volume two not least for this very reason elicited much greater praise than its predecessor. The third volume, covering the evolution of Moscow's foreign relations until 1923, appeared early in 1953. It is indisputably a masterpiece in conception and detail: self-evidently the work of Carr the untrammelled realist; if anything over-eager to jettison Lenin's utopian aspirations in his portrayal of the harsh reaction to the failed international revolution, of which the October revolution was intended merely as prelude. Here he breaks with the orthodoxy of both sides – in making it abundantly clear that from the outset Lenin was determined on spreading the revolution throughout Europe (a favourite topic of the anti-Communist camp) but also, as in the discussion of the decree on peace issued in 1917, in emphasizing the 'Wilsonian' tone of Soviet diplomacy at that time and the interest in peace (which harmonized with the Moscow line). And whereas anyone pro-Soviet would have gone out of their way to avoid even mentioning the secret understandings established by the Bolsheviks with the German Government in 1921–22 for military cooperation (notably against Poland), Carr not only dwells upon it at length but throughout the following volumes seems to take a perverse delight in unearthing ever greater detail on this, the seamiest side of Soviet realpolitik. Carr always dismissed the idea that any differences of interest could arise between the diplomats at the Commissariat of Foreign Affairs and the revolutionaries at the Communist International which Lenin set up, a fiction Moscow tried to maintain to the very extinction of the Soviet Union. 'It was,' he noted, 'theoretically possible to ask whether, in any given issue of policy, priority should be given – or, in retrospect, whether it had been given – to Soviet national interest or to the international interest of world revolution; and this could, in the heat of political controversy, be depicted as

---

[102] Ibid., p. 139. Similarly (p. 146): 'The civil war broke with the financial and fiscal policies of the Soviet Government still in the main indeterminate and unformulated.'

a choice between principle and expediency. But, since it was difficult, at any period now in question, to diagnose any fundamental incompatibility between the two interests, the question remained largely unreal, or reduced itself to a question of tactics.'[103]

With few exceptions, even the harshest of the most knowledgeable critics stood back in awe at the temerity of someone daring to paint on such a vast and challenging canvas. The results might be uneven; the perspective might have appeared distorted to the liberal eye; but the infectious confidence of the sweeping judgements, quite apart from the sheer scale and wealth of detail of the enterprise, impressed even the most sceptical reader. And it was for that very reason that Carr was increasingly regarded as dangerous by the self-appointed guardians of liberal thought. Had the work been as bad as some would now like to maintain, no one would ever have bothered to challenge and seek to destroy his considerable reputation.

He had first visited the United States in the late thirties, when the Great Depression made a dramatic come-back. To all appearances at that moment this was not an economic system that could boast of much success. His rejection of the capitalist model of development (inevitably) ensured that he would never reconsider the United States in more favourable terms on later visits, though he could not but be impressed by the immensity of its power, for good or evil. To him the United States was the 'capitalist luxus'.[104] His ambivalence towards it was certainly reciprocated. His second research trip was made at the end of 1950, when the Cold War had reached its height. In June Communist North Korea had, with Stalin's sanction and Soviet military planning, invaded the South. The intervention of the United States and its allies was so effective that it enabled the invasion of North Korea. But this then precipitated the intervention of Communist China. That autumn Washington rumbled with rumours of nuclear war.

The only force that drove Carr across the Atlantic was the need to use American libraries. The Johns Hopkins University, situated on a rather unpromising wind-swept hillock in Baltimore, Maryland, had invited him to deliver six Albert Shaw Lectures on Diplomatic History. The fee would more than cover the expenses of research in the Library of Congress and New York Public Library (which contained one of the best collections of Soviet newspapers in the west). He and Joyce thus embarked on the *Empress of France* – packed with eager tourists – on 20 December 1950. Joyce basically acted as a research assistant on these excursions, typing and taking copies as well as keeping house. Work on the lectures began almost as soon as they set sail. The ship tied up at Montreal eight days later and they took the train down the northeast corridor to Baltimore, where they arrived at the end of the month.

During the course of the subsequent three months Carr delivered six neatly crafted lectures published by the University in 1952 as *German-Soviet Relations*

---

[103] Carr, *The Bolshevik Revolution 1917–1923*, vol. 3, London 1953, p. 20.
[104] Carr to Isaac and Tamara Deutscher, 2 April 1951: *DA*, vol. 13.

between the Two World Wars, 1919–1939 – a panoramic survey of relations between the two great powers from Versailles to the outbreak of World War II which became a fundamental text for diplomatic historians for years to come. It was written largely on the basis of documents from the German Foreign Ministry captured by the allies at the end of the war and thus appeared startlingly original; and where those documents contained important lacunae, his own experience at the Foreign Office enabled him to fill in the gaps – both through direct knowledge and inspired guesswork. Here, once more, Carr the realist was in the ascendant, so much so that he even anticipated the future fourth division of Poland in secret discussions between the Germans and the Russians back in 1921–22 (and was told off by Deutscher for doing so). But he 'took these lectures in a fairly light-hearted way (I did not want to publish them at all, but it was in the terms of the grant) and merely regarded them as a sort of first draft' for volume three of *The Bolshevik Revolution*.[105]

The lectures may have been 'light-hearted' – a typical exaggeration – but the prevalent mood in the United States was emphatically the opposite. 'Having been fairly careful not to stick out our necks,' he wrote to Isaac Deutscher,

> we did not get badly bitten; but the atmosphere in academic circles is anything but comfortable, and the conversation was very apt to flow in different channels according to who was present. It is often difficult to be sure, when American intellectuals are talking to Englishmen, whether they are agreeing for the sake of politeness or whether they are making reservations; in some cases, one has the impression that they have ceased to have an opinion of their own because this may be dangerous. As usual, it sometimes happens that those whose orthodoxy is unimpeachable talk much more radically than those who might be shot at. The *New Statesman* is widely read among intellectuals because it says something different, though if it were an American paper nobody would dare be seen reading it.[106]

When hopes for the continuation of postwar collaboration proved mistaken in 1945–46, he tended to give Moscow the benefit of the doubt and this created tension with the Foreign Office. But his reserve with regard to the Americans was shared by many in Britain and not just the left. He clearly articulated the dilemma that many found Britain to be in as the Cold War set in: sandwiched between a power committed to unfettered capitalism and a power equally committed to dictatorship and communism: 'if acceptance by Europe of an economic system based on that of the Soviet Union is unattractive,' he wrote in a leader on 'Peace, Trade, Output' on 26 October 1946,

> many of its political manifestations acutely distasteful – the prospects offered by unqualified adherence to the American system also appear to many bleak. The nineteen thirties provided a convincing demonstration, which has not been

---

[105] Carr to Deutscher, 15 November 1951: ibid.
[106] Ibid., 2 April 1951: ibid.

forgotten in many parts of Europe, that policies of non-discrimination and the
removal of restrictions on trade in themselves furnish no barrier against economic
distress and may even hasten its contagious spread from one country to another.

What he appealed for was a British initiative towards the rest of Europe pointing to 'a middle way between the Soviet and American extremes'. The
problem was that Britain had diminishing resources. To some this suggested
a different alternative: cut back on commitments and return to the home
islands. Toynbee favoured Carr's 'middle way' but wished to combine it with
a retreat to British shores. In a discussion with Toynbee on the radio on 1
November 1946, after he had given four talks on British foreign policy, Carr
rejected the suggestion that Britain 'liquidate without too many qualms our
political commitments and economic outposts in other continents . . .'. This
was, he believed, unrealistic: 'The trouble about politics and economics is that
if you run away from them they are apt to run after you – especially if you
occupy, as Britain does, a conspicuous and coveted and vulnerable position.'[107] Carr was no isolationist.

The middle way was predicated upon the assumption that Britain not
commit itself to either Washington or Moscow. 'Either of these Great Powers
will strangle us without the slightest compunction, without even noticing that
they are doing it, if we put ourselves at their mercy. And it follows that we
cannot afford to quarrel with either one of them in such a way as to make us
dependent on the other.'[108] However, the hope of any middle way soon evap-
orated as tension grew in relations with Moscow. In retrospect Carr claimed
that by the middle of 1946 all this had become apparent; but as we have seen,
the truth dawned sometime later, certainly not before 1947. None the less he
is almost certainly accurate in recalling that 'I was very much disillusioned.'[109]
And with the loss of eastern Europe a fait accompli, those differences he had
with Whitehall temporarily tended to narrow. In a series of articles on 'Russian
Reconstruction' published in *The Times* at the end of December 1946 he
argued that the Russians were not pursuing a policy of strength, nor a policy of
isolation, but 'a policy shot through and through with mistrust and anxiety –
mistrust inspired by the traditional deep-rooted belief in the hostile designs of
the capitalist world, anxiety reinforced by the difficulties of the food situation
and of industrial reconstruction'. Domestic and foreign factors were reacting
on one another, but he was still optimistic: 'other things being equal, it is a fair
guess that international mistrust will tend to subside as domestic policy sails
into smoother waters.'[110] Yet the Chancery of the embassy in Moscow acknowledged that the articles 'accord pretty closely with our general line', so much so

---

[107] 'The Virtue of the Middle Way', *Listener*, 14 November 1946, p. 679.
[108] Ibid.
[109] Writing to Donald McLachlan in 1969: McLachlan, *In the Chair*, p. 247.
[110] 'Russian Reconstruction: I. Obstacles to Agricultural Revival', *The Times*, 30 December
       1947; and 'Russian Reconstrucion: II. Man-Power for Industrial Recovery', *The Times*, 31
       December 1947.

that allied missions attributed the articles to the penmanship of the embassy itself.[111]

But this was a very brief reconciliation. When the Americans offered Marshall aid in June 1947 and Carr expressed the hope the Russians would accept and the postwar division would not become permanent,[112] he stood closer to the Labour left than Foreign Secretary Ernest Bevin, who hoped to use US aid to detach the east European states from the Soviet grip. One suspects that resistance to the idea that war with the east was on the horizon and that Britain would have to succumb to US predominance was as much a product of Carr's own nationalism as it was an ideological preference for a socialist solution to the outstanding social and economic problems of the time. He had, after all, grown up at a time of unalloyed British imperial supremacy. It was very hard, indeed, for him and his generation to accept British subordination to another leading power.

Carr was, for instance, quick to see the significance of Communist Yugoslavia's breach with Moscow in the summer of 1948 and saw some hope that this might augur a break from the increasingly ideological nature of the east–west conflict, a view strongly shared with the left-wing Labour member of parliament Aneurin Bevan: 'It is this identification of Communist ideology with Soviet power, pointed by the looser, but none the less patent, defence of western democratic ideas and capitalist practices with the power of the United States, which makes the present international conjuncture so dark and menacing,' Carr wrote:

> That the two strongest Powers in the world should today have become the centres of groups of nations formed on the basis not of the old-fashioned alliances of power politics, but of contending views on the way in which society should be organized, enhances the dangers of conflict in a way which no contemporary observer can ignore. It would be a striking reversal of existing trends if Yugoslavia succeeded in vindicating for herself either a position of independent authority within the Soviet alliance or a right to stand alone outside it.[113]

The US Government, perhaps for this very reason, took an unduly lengthy period of time to grasp the advantages this opportunity might offer, but eventually did so in 1949–50. By that time, however, Carr the utopian was reluctantly but inexorably giving way to Carr the realist; the Russians had seized power in Czechoslovakia, hitherto unhappily poised precariously between east and west, now imprisoned in the Soviet bloc; and then Stalin launched a blockade of West Berlin.

Although Carr never altered his view that the western powers began the problem by denying Russia its sphere of influence, he now gloomily accepted

---

[111] Chancery (Moscow) to Northern Department (Foreign Office), 24 January 1947: *FO* 371/66289.

[112] 'Europe's Opportunity', *The Times*, 19 June 1947.

[113] 'Spectre of Communism', ibid., 2 July 1948.

that worse might lie ahead: 'a weak or undefended country on the confines of present Russian defences would be pretty quickly absorbed into the Russian orbit.' And in an eerily prophetic comment, he added: 'This would probably happen, say, to South Korea . . . if American troops were withdrawn.' He continued: 'Similarly, on the ideological front, if a structure is rickety and likely to fall at a push (as seemed at one moment to be the case in France and Italy), Moscow might assist the local communist party to give that push. But where a structure is solid, the Russians are not likely to expend any great effort, or incur serious risk, in attempting to disturb it.'[114]

This bleak assessment, produced for Morison at *The Times*, did not, however, throw him firmly into the pro-American camp. On the contrary, he continued to believe that the Americans had placed Britain in a more disadvantageous position than it would have been in had the British struck out on their own or in closer collaboration with the rest of western Europe, to the exclusion of the United States:

> The acceptance of the American loan with the conditions attached to it in 1946 was the turning point at which Britain ceased to control her own economic destinies. It is still arguable that the conditions should have been rejected and the consequences of rejection faced. The results of acceptance were perhaps psychological even more than practical. But the practical results should not be ignored. Though the conditions were never fully enforced, the fiasco of sterling convertibility in the summer of 1947 was extremely costly; and American objections to a western European economic union continued well into 1947 – by which time the practical difficulties of its realization had enormously increased.

Carr's main concern was, however, the psychological impact:

> The American loan opened the way to a silent infiltration of American influence into almost every walk of British public life. It is today almost impossible to imagine the appointment to any important public post (including posts in the armed forces and in the civil service as well as in industry) of anyone not persona grata in corresponding American circles. To be pro-American pays handsome dividends: to be known as anti-American is a bar to promotion to a responsible position in any walk of life. Worst of all, British dependence on the United States is now taken for granted in quite broad sections of the population and had [sic] bred a widespread sense of hopelessness and incapacity to help ourselves, so that American help and American patronage which were intended to provide a stimulus to increased productivity in Britain are in danger of producing the opposite result.

But what was the alternative? Britain had succumbed to US diktat in economic negotiations because Britain was 'no longer a first class power'. It could not sustain itself in any future war. Neutrality was no option, however:

---

[114] Memorandum, untitled, dated 10 August 1948. In the author's possession.

'whatever chance there was of remaining neutral seems to have been abandoned when American bombers were allowed to base themselves on Britain for "cold war" operations [July 1948]; it would be extraordinarily difficult to withdraw this permission if a shooting war started hereafter.' Britain had no choice in war but to stand with the United States and would be 'virtually wiped out' for the simple reason that 'the fate of an immobile air-craft carrier, even an unsinkable one, in a prolonged modern air battle would probably be unenviable.'

Carr's logic marched resolutely on. If Britain could not break free, if war with Russia broke out and Britain would likely as not perish, then Britain 'can have only one major objective of foreign policy at the present time: to stop war breaking out'. 'It is not a matter of great moment to any appreciable number of English people who wins the next war: their sole interest is that war should not occur. Every decision of policy should be tested by one question and one alone: does it increase or diminish the likelihood of war?' The thought inevitably occurred to him that this sounded very much like the Carr who advocated appeasement in the thirties. 'Needless to say,' he added, with no great conviction, 'this is not identical with the issue of firmness v. "appeasement": either may be at any given moment the best way of avoiding war. But peace at any price must be the foundation of British policy.' Here, however, his logic faltered: how could Britain adopt a firm policy and withstand US policy given its relative weakness? The thrust of his conclusions was that the British should largely leave foreign policy to its fate, since they could affect it little or not at all, and that they should instead focus on economic reconstruction:

> It may be that the question whether war breaks out between Russia and America affects us far more than the question whether we can increase the productivity of labour or improve the organization of industry or the distribution of consumer goods. But the point is that we can hardly do anything about the first question and a great deal about the second.

And with reference to the second question, he argued that 'our principal target' should be 'to make ourselves independent of American aid'. As far as foreign policy was concerned, Britain could hope to play only a moderating influence on both sides: 'our superior diplomatic experience gives us an advantage here if we choose to exercise it.'[115]

Even after the outbreak of the war in Korea in June 1950 Carr continued to find dependence on the United States uncongenial, though by then the power of the fait accompli had finally wrought its effects on his thinking. Some in the establishment saw Carr as a menace in the propaganda war then waged with the east. 'Carr has proved himself so often a very dangerous

---

[115] Ibid.

seller of opinion, and very often prejudiced opinions of only local or temporary significance at that, – in the disguise of facts and apparently purely
academic or final historical judgements', wrote the editor of the *Listener's
Digest*, seeking to avoid publishing Carr's broadcasts on 'The New Society'.[116]
Yet, for every individual trying to hold him back, Carr invariably found support elsewhere. And his views had evolved, certainly in matters of foreign
policy, towards a more orthodox stance on the dangers from Stalin's Russia.
In a memorandum for Lord Beaverbrook on 15 May 1952 he argued:

> In Europe Russia, in Asia China, will attack no position held by American (or
> British or French) forces, but will infiltrate (not necessarily by military action) any
> position not so held.
>
> In Europe, there is equilibrium so long as American forces remain and
> American aid flows to the western countries. Once these were withdrawn or seri-
> ously curtailed, the existing governments of western Europe would collapse
> overnight and pass, probably through some intermediate stage, into communism:
> this would be achieved without the movement of a single Russian soldier. We are
> thus in the fearful dilemma of being dependent for our security on American
> fears of Russia (which American industry and American labour have fortunately
> a strong interest in maintaining); we have to pretend that the danger from Russia
> is military (which, except in a remote sense, it is not); and we are then caught up
> in an inevitable American demand that western Europe should rearm to help bear
> the burden of defence.
>
> Western rearmament is valueless (so long as the Americans remain in Europe,
> it is superfluous; if they go, it is worthless by itself); and it seriously damages and
> weakens the economies of the countries concerned (Great Britain most of all). We
> are in a vicious circle: we need American help, but have to purchase it by policies
> ultimately damaging to the purposes for which it is given.[117]

Although still strongly anti-American, he was now less disposed to take the
Russians at their word. Carr the realist was increasingly to the fore; the illusions
of the forties had receded into the past. In a review of the *Survey of International
Affairs 1949–50*, edited by Peter Calvocoressi and published by Chatham House
in 1953, he commented that during the period surveyed, the 'main scene of
the world drama had shifted from Europe to Asia'. He continued:

> This shift of scene . . . may be attributed to the firm attitude of the United States
> and the western Powers, especially during the Berlin blockade, which served
> notice on the Soviet Union that any further attempt to extend Soviet power and
> influence westwards in Europe would be fraught with immediate danger: this
> seems undoubtedly to have been one of the factors impelling Moscow to seek an
> outlet, and safer opportunities for further expansion, to the east rather than to the
> west.[118]

---

[116] Roger Cary to O.T.M (BBC), March 1952: 'E.H. Carr's Talks', 2: *BBC.*
[117] Memorandum for Lord Beaverbrook, 15 May 1952. In the author's possession.
[118] 'Shifting Scene', *Times Literary Supplement*, 19 June 1953.

6

In from the Cold: Balliol

'The fact that I was working against a cold war background of western political opinion ... inevitably meant that my work was regarded by my critics as an apologia for Soviet policies', Carr recalled.[1] None of this made finding regular employment at a university any easier. By 1948 he was unemployed and largely unemployable. He was clearly only too aware of the analogy with his own position when he wrote:

> Would a teacher of international relations in a British university who became known for the skill and effectiveness with which he analysed and demolished the arguments invoked by the western Powers in the ideological dual with Moscow really improve his chances of promotion?
>
> The fact that some such question could in the 1930s have been confidently answered in the affirmative, but would have to be answered negatively today, shows the distance that we have travelled in the past twenty years, and the peculiar difficulties attending the academic study of international relations at the present time.[2]

He took this very real obstacle to his own career remarkably philosophically. By others he was seen as committed to the Soviet Union. He saw himself trapped between alternatives from which he refused to choose. In response to a fiercely anti-Communist review that appeared in the Chatham House journal *International Affairs*, he wrote: 'I think the Journal should on the whole steer clear of the Coates [fellow travellers] and Rothsteins [Communist Party members] on the one side and the C.G.s [the initials of the anti-Communist reviewer] on the other: I find myself continually fighting this battle on both fronts. Unfortunately Ch[atham] House doesn't run to party members, so I'm deprived of my "middle" position and left to occupy a flank.'[3]

By the summer he and Joyce had moved, as we have seen, from Heath

---

1. *Autobiographical sketch.*
2. 'Academic Questions', *Times Literary Supplement*, 16 April 1954.
3. Carr to Cleeve, 10 August 1949: RIIA archives, Carr membership file.

Drive, Hampstead, to Orchard House, Appleford, Abingdon, just outside Oxford. It unfortunately meant that he was now a long way from Isaac Deutscher. They were both isolated intellectually and politically and therefore clung together for mutual moral support. But they managed to maintain a regular correspondence and exchanged drafts for comment. 'I read Ruth Fischer [memoirs of the former German Communist] while surrounded by dust and displaced furniture,' Carr wrote to Deutscher on 6 March 1949, 'and have written something which is rather incoherent and much too long. But please have a look at it before I attempt to cut and dress it, and see whether I have been too unfair. You know I generally overstate in my first drafts.'[4] Similarly he sent the drafts of the first instalments of his history to Deutscher for criticism. 'I have received the proofs,' he wrote in late July, 'and now send the rest for your kind attention (I am glad you noted that your previous criticisms had led to some improvement!).'[5] But apart from the special relationship with Deutscher, the horizon was bleak and this inevitably undermined any lingering tolerance of work unalterably hostile to the Russian revolution. Carr was unforgiving of those who joined the propaganda battle in the Cold War on the side of the west.

One of these was the talented young Hugh Seton-Watson. They had first met in 1937 at an international conference of the International Student Service. In 1939 Seton-Watson, Hannah Arendt and Martin Wight had also been shortlisted for the lectureship that Routh had given up and which, incidentally, the young Max Beloff had had his eyes on as well. Jobs in academia at that time were very rare, so it was not so unusual to have such a distinguished shortlist. Carr had chosen Seton-Watson. But the war had supervened and, Seton-Watson recalled, 'deprived me of what would have been the wonderful experience and discipleship of three years' work under his leadership'.[6]

This thought remained with Seton-Watson for many years. With the war drawing to a close, however, Carr had sought to bring him onto *The Times*, and it was on behalf of the paper that Seton-Watson went out to eastern Europe to cover developments.[7] He described this as the beginning of 'an invaluable lesson in the process of learning, thinking and putting my thoughts in to clear language'. Up to that point he was of typical liberal and pro-Soviet inclinations, like so many who felt enormous respect for those who held the line at Stalingrad and were inclined to give Stalin the benefit of the doubt. A few months witnessing growing Communist repression in eastern Europe was enough to change all that, and Seton-Watson returned irrevocably hostile to the new dictatorships that the Soviet Government had installed. Typically he

---

[4] Carr to Isaac Deutscher, 6 March 1949: *DA*, 12.

[5] Ibid., 27 July 1949: ibid.

[6] Seton-Watson to Betty Behrens, 11 November 1982. Much of this was also repeated in an interview with the author on 10 February 1984.

[7] H. Seton-Watson, 'Reflections of a Learner', *Government and Opposition*, vol. 15, no. 3/4, pp. 512–27.

never felt any need to change his attitude to his former mentor, of whom he continued to speak very warmly. Despite their differences, 'nothing could diminish my admiration for his continuing, enormously impressive oeuvre', he freely acknowledged.[8]

Carr, however, became increasingly hostile to one he wrongly saw as having changed his colours to fit the changing times. Seton-Watson was, in Carr's words, an 'emotional mountebank'.[9] Seton-Watson's subsequent meteoric rise in the academic firmament at such an early age, and his use of that position – he succeeded to the Chair at the School of Slavonic Studies which Carr had been denied – and of his undoubted talents (including Carr's way with words) to propagate the anti-Communist cause, alienated him from his mentor completely.

Carr bore his isolation with Olympian disdain and scorned vindictiveness. In defeat he customarily picked himself up, dusted himself off and set about his next destination. In one notable instance, however, he did lash out at some-one who for him epitomized all that was going wrong with Soviet studies in the Cold War climate, and this was Leonard Schapiro. Born of Russian Jewish parents in Glasgow, Schapiro had spent his early childhood in Riga and Petrograd before returning to Britain in 1920. Educated at St. Paul's and University College, London, he had worked as a barrister until the war, when he joined the BBC's monitoring service before ending up in military intelligence (MI14), covering the Russian front. After the war he had worked for the Allied Control Commission in Germany on Soviet military capabilities. He then returned to the Bar but began looking for an academic slot in which he might pursue his new interests. His overt hostility to communism blended well with the drift into Cold War. It was Dr Violet Conolly from the Foreign Office Research Department who offered to help. Conolly was a friend of Schapiro's wife Isabel de Madariaga.

Carr chaired the very successful Soviet and East European Studies sub-committee at Chatham House which had commissioned, edited and published (through Oxford University Press) a series of excellent studies on the Soviet Union, including that of Max Beloff – another of Carr's young admirers, a lecturer in Namier's History Department at Manchester – who had been invalided out of war service and set to work on a history of Soviet foreign policy from 1929 to 1941.[10] Conolly represented the Foreign Office on the sub-committee. Other members included Bolsover and Jane Degras, now in her post-Communist incarnation.

Carr had hitherto dominated the sub-committee and its projects reflected his outlook. A challenge now arose. Knowing Carr's views only too well, but equally determined to make good use of the sub-committee for policy

---

[8] Seton-Watson to Betty Behrens.
[9] Carr to Isaac Deutscher, undated but sometime in 1953: *DA*, 14.
[10] For Beloff's recollections: 'The Dangers of Prophecy', *History Today*, September 1992.

purposes and simultaneously help a deserving colleague, Conolly recommended (evidently after informal consultation) that a study of the show-trials of the prewar period be undertaken. The proposal was 'that this should be an analysis of the legal techniques employed in the trials of "National Deviationists", "Menshevists", "Shaty" [Shakhty] (mining experts), and various Trotskyist groups; implications of the prosecuting technique both in regard to Soviet relations to Great Britain, France, E.S.A. [should evidently be USA] etc., and to class and colonial warfare'. She saw this as 'not only of basic importance itself but essential to an understanding of the approach of the Soviet Government in the post-war period to the new Communist Deviators (real or hypothetical) in Yugoslavia, or other countries where opposition to the Kremlin line may occur'.[11]

The fact that an unusual, if not unique, combination of legal skills and knowledge of Russia would be required to undertake such a study was of course not accidental. It precisely matched Schapiro's qualifications. Conolly asked the research secretary Margaret Cleeve to contact Schapiro and invite him to discuss the proposal. This was duly done on 20 October 1948, and as a result of that meeting Schapiro was asked to submit a note to the sub-committee outlining what might be done. Schapiro did so on 20 November, followed by a letter of 4 January 1949 cutting back his proposal from 1922–45 to the period 1928–38.[12] But when faced with Schapiro's project – *Opposition in the Soviet State* – Carr immediately voiced objections and came into direct collision with Conolly. This was 20 January 1949.[13] A week later he met Conolly again, along with Bolsover.[14] A compromise was reached. Schapiro would work on an earlier period first. They would withhold judgement until the results had appeared.

A letter was accordingly despatched to Schapiro on 8 February informing him that the *Opposition within the Russian Communist Party* (Carr's subtle but revealing shift of the topic) had been agreed upon as the subject for study. 'For this purpose they suggest that the period 1917–23 should be examined and that you should let the Sub-Committee have a report on the results obtained in a period of 6–12 months . . .'. Schapiro fought back, expressing himself 'unable to agree that the period 1917–23 would be suitable as a preliminary study' because 'this period of opposition is mainly of academic interest, and a study of it does not seem to me likely to throw much light on the most interesting aspects of the succeeding years, the struggles of which have a distinct bearing on contemporary problems.'[15] He was much more interested in the period after 1923 leading up to the show-trials. The sub-committee (essentially Carr) was not to be moved, however, and Schapiro was obliged to concede.

---

[11] Cleeve to Schapiro, 20 October 1948: *Schapiro Collection*, Hoover Institution Archive, box 4.
[12] Schapiro to Cleeve, 4 January 1949: ibid.
[13] Entry, 20 January 1949: *Carr Diary*.
[14] Entry, 27 January 1949: ibid.
[15] Schapiro to Cleeve, 16 February 1949: *Schapiro Collection*, box 4.

As it was, Schapiro completely reversed himself on the importance of 1917–23, which could not have enhanced his credibility with the sub-committee; but it did at least mean that he could embark on the more detailed research with some enthusiasm. After more than a year's work, he offered the manuscript to Isaiah Berlin. The Berlins and the Schapiros had been friends in Riga. The story is that when they were still children, Berlin had telephoned Schapiro and announced: 'this is the little Berlin speaking, our parents say that we ought to be friends.'[16] Schapiro was two years older than Berlin and from 1916 to 1918 they saw much of one another, Schapiro being a good deal more learned than his younger friend and inducting him into modern Russian art.[17] The Berlins had left for Britain before the Schapiros; both boys had gone to St. Paul's.

Berlin was cautiously enthusiastic about Schapiro's manuscript; he had no detailed knowledge of the subject but he was about as well informed as any Russianist who took an interest in the period. The work was, he wrote, 'a gen-uine addition of knowledge; and one which I have not seen remotely recorded anywhere else, since all other meticulous and scholarly work on 1917 is done either from a self-justifying (Miliukovo-Kerenskian) point of view, or, at best, from Trotskyist or Leninist anti-Stalin zeal'.[18] Lurking at the back of Berlin's mind was surely the fact that Carr's first volume was about to appear. The ambivalence Berlin had always felt towards him had by now intensified with the onset of the Cold War.

From 1941 Isaiah Berlin had worked as a reporter on US public opinion at the British embassy in Washington. From there he had volunteered for Moscow, in mid-September 1945. The Cold War had yet to begin and Russian intellectuals were still able to associate with foreigners more freely than hith-erto, though when Berlin arrived at the embassy they seemed shocked when he suggested that he would call on the leading lights of the intelligentsia. He enthusiastically visited writer Boris Pasternak – who had 'some curious licence to see foreigners during the late Stalin years'[19] – and the poet Anna Akhmatova (who had been driven into internal exile during the war) and talked for hours; at last the Soviet regime appeared to have relaxed its iron grip. Berlin finally left Moscow in January 1946.

Almost from that moment began the persecution of the literary intelli-gentsia at the hands of Andrei Zhdanov. Stalin in particular was infuriated that Akhmatova had received a member of the British embassy: 'I see that our nun now receives foreign spies', he is reputed to have snapped.[20] Akhmatova, who attributed some of her misfortunes entirely to Berlin's visit,[21] was let off fairly lightly; others were less fortunate. Berlin's close identification with the

---

[16] I am most grateful to Isabel de Madariaga for this and other information on Schapiro.
[17] Berlin to the author, 29 November 1995.
[18] Berlin to Schapiro, 12 August 1950: *Schapiro Collection*, box 4.
[19] Berlin to the author, 29 November 1995.
[20] Interview with Berlin, *New York Review of Books*, 28 May 1992.
[21] Berlin to the author, 29 November 1995.

Russian intelligentsia heightened his awareness of Carr's role in apparently legitimizing such a repressive system; a role all the more significant because of Carr's unusual gifts, which clearly still held their fascination for Berlin even as he was repelled by the work on which they were being so successfully deployed. 'How differently Carr's coming oeuvre will read!', he wrote to Schapiro on 12 August 1950, 'and what a nuisance it will be to look at the reviews which praise him for exact and unbending scholarship.'[22] By then, of course, the Cold War was reaching its zenith. Less than two months before, with Soviet planning and assistance, the Communists of North Korea had invaded the South; and that summer fears were rife that a similar fate awaited western Europe from the Red Army in the eastern zone of Germany.

Thus Berlin's commitment to the success of Schapiro's enterprise soon became a touchstone for battles with Carr's 'errant' intellect. It was this as well as his well-entrenched affection for Schapiro which caused Berlin to devote much detailed attention to improving the manuscript (unbeknown to Carr). At this stage the impetuous Schapiro was in a hurry and wanted only minor suggestions, leaving the larger issues to be dealt with after Chatham House had pronounced that November. But Berlin simply could not resist making some general comments. The manuscript lacked coherence: 'there is not enough connection between the chapters'; and there were no character sketches or profiles of the main actors: 'it will never be done except by learned and earnest vulgarians like [Bertram] Wolfe who is a typical Eastside ex-communist and not intelligent, or fastidious enough, nor as privy to the atmosphere as ever you or I . . .'.[23] Finally, after working on Berlin's recommended changes page by page for the best part of a month, Schapiro delivered the 140,000 word draft to Chatham House on 19 September 1950, suggesting this be published as a complete book.

The fat now hit the fire. The sub-committee was due to meet with Schapiro in attendance, appropriately some may think, on 7 November. On the second, however, Carr succumbed to (partly diplomatic) lumbago and, although soon better, four days later he wrote to Miss Cleeve claiming to be 'immobilized', though he was actually immersed in the final corrections to his history. Unable or, more likely, unwilling to attend the meeting, he sent a note of his comments. In fact he had not looked at the manuscript since 26 September and even then gave it only cursory attention. He began, diplomatically, with the assurance that he was 'very much impressed by the immense industry and general ability' evident in the work – a typical Carr pronouncement more important for what it left unsaid than for what it actually said. He went on more forthrightly to suggest that Schapiro would 'write a better proportioned book if he confines it to opposition *in* the party'. Moreover, and this had more justification, he argued that Schapiro should carry on at least until 1928,

---

[22] Berlin to Schapiro: *Schapiro Collection*, box 4.
[23] Ibid.

'where there is a definite pause with the final consolidation of Stalin's dicta-torship'. This would, he wrote, help Schapiro get the perspective right on the earlier period (change his mind?) and enable the writing of 'a book which does not merely contain a lot of facts and references, but forms a real whole and can be read'. His general conclusion was that it 'would be . . . a pity to spoil it by a lop-sided and premature publication'.[24]

This was not what Schapiro wanted to hear. In a letter to Miss Cleeve on 19 November 1950 and at a further meeting of the sub-committee (with the director general of Chatham House in attendance) on 28 November, he defended his refusal to make these changes. There it was agreed that Schapiro could have his way with respect to both the subject matter and the period. Berlin then offered further detailed suggestions for improvements on the final chapter which he had not hitherto commented upon, once again ranging from issues of interpretation to stylistic infelicities. Carr once again emerged in an aside. Commenting on Schapiro's treatment of the Workers' Opposition of 1920–21, Berlin wrote:

I think you have a slight tendency to idealize these people because they protested: but e.g. demands for physical labour for all party members are so childish and Doukhoborish and Tolstoyan that you almost induce sympathy for Lenin's 'real-ism' by contrast – did the Work. Opp. have something serious to offer beyond their purity of heart? If not you must avoid falling quite so sweetly into E.H. Carr's grandmother wolf's open jaws.[25]

It is hard to see Schapiro as Little Red Riding Hood, but he seemed to find the jaws irresistible. In October 1951 the revised manuscript was delivered to Chatham House. The temperature had risen still further. Schapiro drew a line of battle by expressing his profound disagreements with Carr when he reviewed *The Bolshevik Revolution* in the press. Carr reported to the Research Board on 14 December. Conolly had read the entire manuscript. At her sug-gestion Carr focused on chapter four (which dealt with the Brest-Litovsk debates of early 1918 over peace with Germany). Conolly concluded that Schapiro had amassed for the first time a great deal of material useful to stu-dents of the subject. Bolsover approved chapters one to three and, subject to some rearrangement, agreed with Conolly. From both there appeared to be no great enthusiasm, though they might have been carefully taking a mini-malist position to avoid showing excessive favour. Carr was predictably damning about chapter four and, in essence, accused Schapiro of wilfully pro-ducing a distorted record of events, what amounted to an indictment of Lenin by a practised barrister in the court of history.[26] Carr was particularly

---

[24] 'Copy of a letter to Miss Cleeve from E.H. Carr dated 6 November 1950', 7 November 1950: *Schapiro Collection*, box 4.
[25] Berlin to Schapiro, 21 December 1950: ibid.
[26] 'Research Board', 1948–52: RIIA archives.

incensed that 'There is nothing here of the historian whose business it is to explain why people act and think in the way they do.'

> Whether the Bolsheviks were right or wrong does not, from my point of view, matter. But it is the elementary duty of the historian when discussing a controversial subject to explain why people acted as they did. Nobody unfamiliar with the subject would really discover from this chapter what happened at Brest Litovsk, or what the Bolsheviks were trying – rightly or wrongly – to do.[27]

He then went for the jugular:

> On page 179 there is the suggestion that the Bolsheviks could perfectly well have continued or re-started the war against the Germans, but that Lenin was unwilling to do so because this would have strengthened anti-Bolshevik elements in Russia. I have never seen these views suggested by any serious writer, though they were no doubt current in the Party politics of the day. They seem to me just as fantastic, and based on just the same kind of embittered prejudice, as the Stalinist misrepresentations of Trotsky's position.[28]

The jaws closed.

On 21 January 1952, the eve of the next meeting of the sub-committee, which was still in deadlock, Cleeve sent Schapiro Carr's comments on the chapter (Conolly had already discussed with Schapiro her suggestions for revision). Emotion rather than reason had taken hold, just as it had during composition of the polemical and more biased aspects of the manuscript. Schapiro replied on the following day. He was rightly chagrined that Carr had mistakenly thought the chapter was a new addition to the manuscript, whereas in fact it had appeared in slightly different form in the original draft Carr had read inattentively over a year before, and he 'strongly resented' the accusations of bias. He considered that this was 'an objective and critical analysis of the part played by Lenin'. Moreover, he added scornfully, now giving even greater hostage to fortune and standing on somewhat uncertain ground methodologically, 'if it be the case that no "serious writer" has ever suggested that one of Lenin's motives for opposing any form of continued resistance to Germany was the fear that it would result in the overthrow of the Bolsheviks, it can only be because this explanation is obvious.' He concluded in resolute defiance: 'I hope that a decision will not now be delayed any longer by belated and unsubstantiated criticism of this nature.'[29]

The next meeting on 22 January 1952, which Carr does not appear to have attended, agreed to refer the manuscript to Sir Reader Bullard for comment.[30] We do not know what happened. But by the time the Research

---

[27] 'OPPOSITION IN THE SOVIET STATE: Comments by Mr. E.H. Carr', *Schapiro Collection*, box 4.
[28] Ibid.
[29] Schapiro to Cleeve, 22 January 1952: ibid.
[30] 'Research Board', 1948–52: RIIA archives.

Board next met – on 19 February – they were back to square one. There Carr 'expressed the opinion that though the MS contained valuable material, much of it not previously available, its presentation was inadequate and that it was not suitable for publication by Chatham House'. In reply Conolly 'said that possibly the subject should never have been accepted, but that despite inadequacies of arrangement she hoped it could be published. She had found the subject matter most interesting.' The others – including Jane Degras – also favoured publication. But, once again, Carr's was the most authoritative voice and, as chairman, he framed the minutes summing up the results of the meeting:

> Criticism was directed not only to the arrangement but also to the fact that though the position of the opposition was set out in detail it was not always clear what they opposed or what they themselves stood for, e.g. the chapter on the Mensheviks. It was also felt that, though Mr. Schapiro had been invited to insert more historical background in his first draft, this was uneven and that it might be better to eliminate some of this in order to produce a more clear-cut picture.[31]

The recommendation was that, subject to satisfactory revision in the light of the above criticisms, it could still be published. 'Inconclusive meeting on Schapiro', Carr noted in his diary, reflecting his wish that a clear refusal had been issued.

Confusion then ensued. With the sub-committee divided, it was impossible to give any guidance for revision that was consensual. Schapiro therefore selected that advice which seemed least in conflict with his own inclinations. None of this was helped by the apparent lack of communication between Cleeve and members of the sub-committee. On 23 May Schapiro thus presented his revised manuscript, rejecting suggestions for rearranging the material chronologically – an issue raised by Degras on 24 March – and protesting against various other suggestions. His objection to chronology was that 'For the most part these parties [in opposition] were not so much opposing a particular Bolshevik policy, but struggling for survival. Therefore a good deal of what they did and thought cannot be interwoven with the story of the development of Bolshevik policy.'[32]

It was Conolly who led him to believe that his selective acceptance of guidance for revision would be acceptable. In a letter of 27 March and on the basis of no authority other than her own, she suggested he 'go ahead with the recommendations you find acceptable and feasible. After all,' she added, wilfully oblivious to the implications of her own advice, 'we all agree that on the substance of the work, you are the best critic and if any of the recommendations can be shown by you to injure the substance (apart from the form), I have no

[31] 'Report of the Soviet Studies Sub-Committee, 19 February 1952, to Research Committee', 12 March 1952: ibid.
[32] Schapiro to Cleeve, 23 May 1952: *Schapiro Collection*, box 4.

doubt that they would be withdrawn.' What this lack of doubt was based on, it is hard to say. She did, however, warn him that in the matter of editorial supervision Chatham House was strict in its procedures, and that Beloff, for one, 'had to cut and revise and alter his drafts very drastically before he got the all-clear. Mrs. Degras,' she added, for good measure, 'was also the go-between in his case.'[33] Cleeve appears to have been equally misinformed. On 28 May she foolishly advised Schapiro that 'the Sub-Committee felt that in dealing with an author of your standing it was enough to point out what in their view were the deficiencies of the work, leaving it to you to resolve them.'[34] She sent the revised manuscript to Chatham House's editorial department to prepare for publication. There, however, the eagle eye of Miss Oliver noticed that it had not been rearranged chronologically as Degras had recommended; she also found it 'confused and disconnected'. This led to a further confrontation; but this time Schapiro refused to concede.[35]

Informed of all this by George Katkov, Fellow of St. Antony's College, Oxford and a wartime friend of Schapiro's, Berlin wrote expressing his indignation and suggesting that he – Berlin – write direct to Oxford University Press extolling the merits of the oeuvre.[36] 'Why do you go on with these horrible Chatham House characters?'[37] At OUP, Geoffrey Cumberlege responded to Schapiro's missive by contacting Chatham House, who made clear that the Press could go ahead and publish under their pre-existing arrangement once the work was 'overhauled'.[38] After further discussion with Berlin and others, Schapiro wrote to Cleeve on 28 September refusing to comply with the suggestions made and asking for a return of copyright on the manuscript.[39] At a meeting of the Board on 14 October it was reported 'that Mr. Schapiro was unable to revise his study to meet the criticisms of members of the Soviet Studies Sub-Committee, and was accordingly informed that his work cannot be accepted for publication under the Institute's auspices in its present form'. The Board also noted that 'Mr. Schapiro has sent a letter criticizing the decision in regard to his study to the Chairman and Vice-Chairman of the Council, Sir Orme Sargent (the former chairman of the Research Committee), and the Director General.'[40]

Indignant at the treatment his friend had received and with his worse suspicions confirmed in conversation with Bolsover, who gave a somewhat biased account of events,[41] Berlin now stepped in to rescue Schapiro's embryonic

[33] Conolly to Schapiro, 27 March 1952: ibid.
[34] Cleeve to Schapiro, 28 May 1952: ibid.
[35] Schapiro to Cleeve, 17 June 1952, as quoted in 'Memorandum', 21 October 1952: ibid.; also Cleeve to Schapiro, 19 June 1952: ibid.
[36] Berlin to Schapiro, no date: ibid.
[37] Berlin to Schapiro, no date: ibid.
[38] Cumberlege to Schapiro, 6 August 1952: ibid.
[39] 'Memorandum', 21 October 1952: ibid.
[40] 'Russian Committee report', 14 October 1952: RIIA archives.
[41] Certainly judging from Berlin's recollections, which do not fit the documentary evidence: Berlin to the author, 29 November 1995.

academic career, expressing the apparently firm conviction (which was surely a product more of emotion than reason) that 'this book is the greatest single contribution to the history of Bolshevism made by anyone in our time . . .'. But whatever he meant by this, it certainly kept Schapiro's drooping spirits up. Berlin immediately resigned from Chatham House. Bolsover tried to persuade London University to publish the manuscript, according to Berlin, who adds that he then wrote to Merle Fainsod at Harvard and asked him to look into publication in the United States.[42]

The Origin of the Communist Autocracy eventually secured publication in 1955 by Bell and Sons with Karl Popper's assistance under the auspices of the London School of Economics. Berlin then backed Schapiro for a temporary teaching post at Yale until he received a lectureship at the London School of Economics, which was seeking to establish Soviet studies in the curriculum, with the combined efforts of Berlin and Seton-Watson. Battle had been joined; battle had evidently been won. It was in large part about the politics of the Cold War and it was most unlikely that in any such conflict Carr could guarantee the ultimate victory.

These were bad years not just for Schapiro; they were also very disappointing for Carr, still in pursuit of an academic post. Living just outside Oxford, he was none the less in an academic exile, broken only by lunching or dining occasionally with colleagues like Balogh, Berlin or Christopher Hill. To one such dinner Hill invited him to meet a 'talkative American named [James] Billington writing on Mikhailovsky'.[43] Together with his friend John Brademas, who was writing on Spanish anarcho-syndicalism, Billington would visit Ted and Joyce for a meal, taking with them a can of ham or some other such luxury sent from the United States. Billington recalls being much impressed by the fact that although he 'was obviously in a very difficult period of his own life . . . nevertheless, he was giving of his own time and substance to two American graduate students who had no particular status and for whom he had no responsibility'.[44]

Carr's hopes were raised by news from Cambridge. King's College, by reputation the most liberal institution in the university, had decided to elect to a senior research fellowship. This might have enabled him to complete the *History of Soviet Russia* in palatial tranquillity. The leading economist at the college, Keynes's close collaborator Richard Kahn, whom Carr had known for several years, was the moving force in his favour. It was he who invited Carr

---

[42] Berlin to the author, 29 November 1995.

[43] Entry, 2 May 1952: *Carr Diary*.

[44] Billington to the author, 28 October 1994. Billington went on to publish *Mikhailovsky and Russian Populism* (Oxford 1958); he became Professor at Princeton in 1964 and later Librarian of Congress. Brademas published *Revolution and Social Revolution: a contribution to the history of the anarcho-syndicalist movement in Spain, 1930–1937* (Oxford 1953; published in a Spanish edition in 1974), and went on to become Majority Whip in Congress and later President of New York University.

down to dine with the Provost, the Vice-Provost and others to be looked over. In those days everything was done informally. The following morning Carr consulted papers in the University Library and then lunched in Kahn's rooms to meet a couple of Fellows and a couple of students. Thereafter he dined again in Hall and took dessert in the combination room where he talked to other Fellows. One of the key figures involved in any decision was the historian and assistant tutor Noel Annan – already influential well beyond his years – who vehemently opposed Carr's election on the grounds that he had supported the appeasement of Hitler and now held open sympathies for the Stalin regime.[45] Thus it was on purely political grounds that Carr received the bad news on 17 March from Kahn that King's had turned him down. But just as Schapiro found support in the face of adversity from Berlin, so too did Carr find support from 'Tommy' Balogh, the economist at Balliol. The college had lost a Fellow in Politics. Balogh rang him on 29 June 1952 to enquire whether he was interested. Since a research fellowship was nowhere on offer, Carr said yes. But he heard nothing more until lunch with Balogh on 17 January 1953. Further discussion took place on 9 May. More discussion ensued but progress was faltering. On 13 May Balogh told him of a hitch – Marcus Dicks, for one, had reservations. Four days later Balogh invited Carr to Sunday to meet Dicks and 'some psychologists'. He was then asked to dine at Balliol on 25 May, where he 'tried to impress the Master' – now Sir David Lindsay Keir. He did not, however, make much of an impression. On 21 June he faced a formal interview. 'Horrible day over Balliol,' he confided to his diary that night; 'Master was disagreeable.'

The Master's attitude mattered: he could veto an election to a fellowship. And the reason why he might do so had nothing to do with politics but with Carr's role as co-respondent in Daryll's divorce proceedings. Soon after the end of the war Balliol had been struck by a wave of 'immorality'. One Fellow had deserted wife and children for another woman and resigned. A second – like Carr – was cited as a co-respondent. A third – the chaplain – had committed adultery with the Master's secretary. The Fellow who led the battle against Carr's election had previously been married by that chaplain; when the chaplain's sin had been uncovered, he had promptly arranged a new marriage ceremony by an untainted vicar. It was, however, possible to reach a compromise 'after [a] stormy meeting', whereby Carr was appointed Tutor in Politics for three years, but without a fellowship, with heavy teaching and no tenure. The Fellow who had won the battle was asked whether having an immoral person as a Tutor but not a Fellow would actually protect the students from his evil ways; he assured the governing body that it would. It was an ignominious gesture to a scholar of international standing, whatever his politics and his mores; though it was many years later compensated for by the offer of an honorary fellowship. The Master showed his continued displeasure by disregarding a request – conveyed to him through economics Fellow Hugh

---

[45] Telephone interview with Lord Annan.

Stretton – from Joyce that Ted be given a ground floor room facing into the college for peace and quiet. Keir instead put him in an upstairs room facing the junction of Beaumont Street and St. Giles.

Carr was, however, determined to make the most of it. On 9 July he wrote to Isaac Deutscher in good spirits: 'The Balliol job is quite fun [work had yet to begin], and there have been fearful rows over the appointment: but everything else seems very difficult. No flats or houses to be had!'[46] Joyce had made a preliminary search of the area early in April and come up with nothing. Another search a few days before writing had proved equally fruitless. And he was rushing to complete volume four of the *History of Soviet Russia*, arguably the best integrated and most persuasive of all: *The Interregnum*. Both he and Joyce were also due to sail for South Africa on a lecture tour in two weeks' time. This had been set up by Charles Manning, a friend of longstanding at LSE, whose approval of apartheid (then in its early stages) was something Carr found impossible to understand.

Joyce and Ted embarked at Rotterdam on 24 July 1953. During the subsequent three weeks on board he prepared his lectures on Soviet foreign policy and politics in general scheduled for Balliol in the Michaelmas term. By the time the boat docked he had completed the lectures and begun on the background to volume five – *Socialism in One Country, 1924–1926*. He and Joyce stayed in windy and dusty Johannesburg at the house of a 'bore' but with the luxury of servants; not that Ted would have noticed much, since Joyce did all the chores at Appleford – he fed the chickens and tended the garden. The first public lectures – on international politics and political thought – were a great success: 'crowded out with people literally sitting at the lecturer's feet', which he modestly put down to the fact that the audience was starved of culture. The load was by no means heavy but, having delivered a further performance – equally 'crowded out' – on the historical foundations of the Russian revolution, he decided thereafter to make the students talk.[47] As a result he gained some direct insight into conditions in South Africa and wrote an article for *The Times* on 'Discrimination in South African Universities'.[48]

They returned home by Comet on 8–9 October via Entebbe, Khartoum, Beirut and Rome. Two days later – a Sunday – Carr dropped into Balliol for lunch. On Monday he began interviewing students to allocate tutorials. Work on volume five none the less continued but it faced severe competition from heavy teaching for a productive man in his early sixties. The Christmas holiday – which he usually loathed – actually came as a much needed break. He not only took to college life after forty years' absence, but he was also keen to find congenial company. It seemed logical to attend the Russian studies seminar that met at St. Antony's College. It was run by David Footman,

---

[46] Carr to Isaac Deutscher, 9 July 1953: *DA*, 14.
[47] Ibid., 25 August 1953: ibid.
[48] 'Discrimination in South African Universities', *The Times*, 3 November 1953.

biographer of Lasalle and a Russianist formerly in the Intelligence Service.
Carr had known him since the late thirties and had lectured for him at the
Military Intelligence School at Worcester in the late 1940s. But he decided to
give the seminar the 'cold shoulder'. His firm opinion was that it 'has a pre-
dominant, though not very clearly defined, "white" flavour'.[49]

Oxford proved an unhappy and exhausting time, though Carr put a brave
face on it. Berlin, still brooding on Carr's unhealthy attachment to the Soviet
model, suggested the two of them run a Modern History Group. Whatever his
motives – he later claimed it was a gesture of support – Anna Kallin, a friend
of Carr's from the BBC, commented that the seminar 'must have been a
harassing experience. As a result of I.B's continuous attacks, E.H.C. retired
into an over-reserved, cold lecture-room climate, though perhaps subconsciously (unless I am being over-subtle) trying to emulate some of I.B.'s glitter
of presentation.'[50] The forces of mutual intellectual attraction and common
interests still bridged the deepening political differences that separated
them – just. The atmosphere was informal; there were at least a dozen or so
participants and the focus was really the history of Russian ideas. In January
1954 Carr tried to lure Isaac Deutscher up to Oxford to address the Group.
When Footman heard of this, he asked Carr for Deutscher's address, having
every intention of inviting him to address the St. Antony's seminar. But
Deutscher received a warning from Carr that 'Probably one of several reasons
for wanting you is to demonstrate their broad mindedness.' 'Living in Oxford,
and working in the University,' he wrote later, 'I am clear that my only course
was to keep aloof from the St. Antony's affair.'[51] Thus in one sense, at least, it
can be said that his isolation was self-inflicted. Several reviews of *The Bolshevik
Revolution*, volume three, had by now appeared. They had been 'early and
prompt if nothing else. A.J.P. Taylor at his most irresponsible, but at bottom
the Manchester Liberal who, if driven to it, will swallow Carlyle in preference
to Marx. I thought I saw that young ass Hugh Seton-Watson in the premature
review in the *Listener*; but the *Manchester Guardian* affair was still more egre-
gious.'[52] By now it was largely a matter of indifference. Only those really close
to him could inflict real and lasting damage, and thereby change his mind.

Balliol had given them a college flat at 2 Rawlinson Road. Joyce was, however, unhappy. Relations with Ted had by now cooled from their initial ardour,
no doubt partly because of the unwelcome – to Joyce – move from Appleford
and the new stresses and strains of the teaching load insensitively imposed
upon him at Balliol. Friends observed that their feelings towards one another
were 'amiable' rather than 'warm'; that they led parallel lives.[53] 'It's very
queer living in a town after the country. Prof. likes it but I find it's much

---

[49] Carr to Deutscher, 22 February 1954: *DA*, 15.
[50] Anna Kallin to C.T., 27 April 1955: E.H. Carr Talks File II, BBC Written Archives Centre.
[51] Carr to Deutscher, 16 March 1954: *DA*, 115.
[52] Ibid., 22 February 1954: ibid.
[53] Professor Lampert to the author, 19 September 1984.

harder work and there are few compensations for Appleford',[54] Joyce wrote to the Deutschers. It was temporary, anyway.

Rightly unsure of his future at Balliol, Carr began looking again instead to where it all began: Cambridge. The chances were greatest at Trinity which took a more detached view of scholarship. The first mooting of the 'Trinity project', as Carr called it, occurred on 18 June 1951, when Carr raised the matter with former Foreign Office official Michael Vyvyan who had, since the late thirties, been the college's Russian historian. A clever but unproductive scholar, he was prepared to lend a hand despite his misgivings about the kind of history Carr wrote. In seeking his election, Vyvyan could count on support from the imperial historian Gallagher and from that larger than life figure, Kitson Clark – 'conservative, Christian, rich' and 'midwife to radical reform' of the History Tripos[55] – who had never read anything Carr had written but knew him to be a famous figure. Carr had not pursued the matter on receiving the invitation to Balliol, but once it was clear that Balliol was a cul de sac, he reactivated the Trinity project. After the examiners' meeting at Corpus Christi (Cambridge) came to an end on 18 June 1954, Gallagher mentioned the Trinity project again, 'and said he would broach it again with Kitson on the latter's return'.[56]

Vyvyan then wrote to Carr on 1 July, enquiring whether he was still interested or was likely to remain at Balliol, expressing regret that Trinity had been unable to take him on at the last attempt. Carr also expressed regret. 'The prospect seemed too remote and uncertain when the invitation arrived from Balliol; which I did not think I ought to refuse. But the Balliol job is, on both sides, something of a stop-gap – I don't want to remain in regular teaching – and the Trinity project is far from dead as far as my side goes.' He added: 'I could reasonably extricate myself from Balliol a year hence – they have a junior fellow just going to the States for a year who would be ripe to take over on his return.'[57] He would none the less have to give some sort of notice early in the Michaelmas term were he to leave in the summer of 1955. And he was especially concerned that discussion of this option within Trinity should not reach Oxford before he had enlightened the authorities at Balliol. But then a setback occurred. On 29 July he received a 'rather putting off letter from Michael Vyvyan'. The correspondence with both Gallagher and Vyvyan nevertheless continued, mostly consisting of bad news. The late autumn of 1954 thus found Carr uncertain about the future and with a maximum of two more years at Balliol, while his magnum opus expanded remorselessly in scope, eating away at whatever time he stole from his heavy teaching and, last but not least, eating the life out of his marriage.

---

[54] Joyce to Tamara Deutscher, 1 January 1954: *DA*, 15.
[55] *The Making of an Historian: The Collected Essays of J.H. Plumb*, London 1988, p. 164.
[56] Entry, 18 June 1954: *Carr Diary*.
[57] Carr to Vyvyan, 3 July 1954. The late Michael Vyvyan kindly gave me a copy of the letter.

Deutscher delivered his paper on 'Trotsky at Alma Ata and the Party Opposition' to the Group in October 1954 and earned Berlin's undying hostility in the process; Deutscher clearly underestimated his own unfortunate capacity for inflaming the sentiment of others by getting carried away in wounding and ad hominem polemic. Blood was drawn and no quarter spared. Given Berlin's views, a clash with Deutscher was inevitable. The spectacle of the two in battle must have been unforgettable. It is, to say the least, unfortunate that none present can yet be found to describe what must have been a memorable occasion.

Deutscher was by nature combative. He had berated Carr in private in an effort to change his views and 'made penetrating criticisms' of his drafts.[58] But Carr seemed largely impervious to such criticism. He, of course, had no idea that Deutscher would ever attack his own work in public. They were allies in the same cause, or so he had blithely assumed. In July he expressed great disappointment that they had 'so few opportunities for meeting', adding that he was 'now submerged in the vast mass of material for vol. 5 (or 5 + 6): round about 1925 it really begins to get interesting and difficult'.[59] But Deutscher did not fully reciprocate Carr's affection and although he deeply respected his work, there was inevitably a keen sense of rivalry not far beneath the surface of close cooperation. A militant by vocation, Isaac Deutscher had been obliged to earn his living in journalism at the *Economist* and through syndicated columns. Tamara encouraged him to become a leading academic historian, but the absence of professional academic credentials effectively barred him from the institutional ivory tower, and even the type of history he chose to write – political biography – and he did a masterful job, was in a sense thrust upon him by the fact that publishers were unlikely to sign a contract with a journalist for serious history such as Carr was writing.[60]

The fourth volume of the *History of Soviet Russia – The Interregnum –* appeared in September 1954. It is even now a gem of a book, successfully interweaving the foreign, domestic political and economic policies of the regime at that critical moment when Lenin passed from the scene and internecine strife broke out in full force within the Bolshevik Party. The emphasis here, as in the three volumes of *The Bolshevik Revolution,* is still very much on the political; the economic playing the subordinate role, though an increasing one. By 1924 the regime had secured international recognition and the last serious attempt – described as 'a fiasco' – at revolution in Germany had failed abysmally. At home the introduction of the New Economic Policy as an emergency measure had made of the peasant 'the arbiter of the Soviet economy'.[61] Trotsky was already dangerously isolated; Stalin was stealthily manoeuvring his way to the top. As Carr points out:

[58] Carr, *The Bolshevik Revolution 1917–1923*, vol. 3, London 1953, p. vii.
[59] Carr to Deutscher, 11 July 1954: *DA*, 15.
[60] I am most grateful to Daniel Singer for setting me straight on these matters.
[61] Carr, *The Interregnum 1923–1924*, London 1954, p. 117.

'Having emerged from the ordeal of Lenin's testament, and having, unperceived, immensely fortified his control over the rank and file of the party through the Lenin enrolment, he now only awaited the moment to show his hand and reveal the full scope of his power and ambitions.'[62]

Isaac Deutscher was asked by the journal *Soviet Studies* to write a review article of the *History of Soviet Russia*, encompassing volumes one to four (*The Interregnum* constituting volume four). What he produced was, he insisted to Carr, somewhat disingenuously, 'in the spirit of amicus Socrates, amicus Plato sed magis amica veritas.' Which, in brief, meant that truth was more important than their friendship. 'I am sure you will take it in this spirit, too', he added in a letter to Carr enclosing the article in draft.[63] He could not have been more wrong. As ever, personal crisis triggered illness. Two days later Carr succumbed. Finally, he decided to send up a distress flare. On 16 November he wrote:

> My first inclination was to say, as I usually do in such cases, 'Publish what you like'. But our relations have a rather special character, and I think that there are some phrases and passages in this article which I should be sorry to see in print over your signature. The personal and polemical note which you have struck in these passages might be suitable if you wanted to express fundamental disapproval of someone's point of view, but seems to me very exaggerated when applied to differences of emphasis, or differences of interpretation on points of detail.[64]

What he did not see was that differences with Deutscher were more fundamental. Some changes appeared in the final draft, but the essence of what he wrote appeared in pristine form under the title 'Mr. E.H. Carr as Historian of the Bolshevik Regime', much to his distress.

'Mr. Carr is a historian primarily of institutions and policies,' Deutscher wrote, with alarming candour; '. . . he is preoccupied primarily with the State, not with the nation and society behind it . . . it might be said that his *History of the Soviet Union* [sic] is primarily a history of the ruling group.' It is here that the onslaught becomes personal, though sharply to the point.

> He tends to see society as the object of policies made and decreed from above. He is inclined to view the State as the maker of society rather than society as the maker of the State . . . . His passion is for statecraft, not for 'subversive' ideas . . . . If he had chosen to epitomize his work in some epigrammatic motto he might have opened his *History* in the Churchillian manner with the following text: 'How Russian Society Collapsed Through the Folly and Ineptitude of its Old Ruling Classes and Through the Utopian Dreams of Bolshevik Revolutionaries, and How These Revolutionaries in The End Saved Russia by Giving up Their Quixotic Delusions and Learning Arduously and Painfully the ABC of Statecraft'.[65]

---

[62] Ibid., p. 366.
[63] Deutscher to Carr, 8 November 1954: *DA*, 15.
[64] Carr to Deutscher, 16 November 1954: ibid.
[65] 'Mr. E.H. Carr as Historian of the Bolshevik Regime', I. Deutscher, *Heretics and Renegades*, second edition, London 1969, pp. 91–110.

Set against such ingenious and merciless mockery, Deutscher's words of praise inevitably sounded somewhat hollow, though undoubtedly no less sincerely intended.

The temptation was to respond in kind. Writing to Deutscher, Carr pointed out that 'you are probably right in thinking that my background predisposes me to overemphasize the statesman at the expense of the revolutionary, but . . . your own background probably makes you lean over just as far in the opposite direction.' He suggested that Deutscher make it clear that he was 'also conscious of approaching this problem with the bias of a particular attitude of mind. We can none of us wholly emancipate ourselves from our own past.'[66]

Deutscher never took this advice. It would, after all, have severely blunted the thrust of his attack. But when he died tragically in August 1967 and Tamara asked Carr to write an introduction to a collection of Isaac's essays that included – perhaps somewhat tactlessly – the offending piece, an opportunity arose to redress the balance which, after initial hesitation, Carr grasped with both hands. He added the words he had over a decade ago asked Isaac to insert.

> He calls me 'a great respecter of policies and a despiser – sometimes – of revolutionary ideas and principles', and speaks of my 'impatience with Utopias, dreams, and revolutionary agitation'. Any such bias I should now strive to correct. But does not Deutscher lean to the other side? Are not his eyes sometimes so firmly fixed on revolutionary Utopias and revolutionary ideas as to overlook the expediencies which so often governed policy – even in the Lenin period?[67]

Yet despite the differences now publicly marked between them, Carr's sense of common purpose with Deutscher reasserted itself in the face of a mutual enemy. The attacks on him continued to grow. Mostly they were taken in good humour – at least outwardly – but there were clear traces of bitterness in the acidic asides they prompted. Deutscher wrote suggesting he review *Heretics and Renegades*, which was a collection of essays about those who had turned from communism to anti-communism. He replied: 'H. Seton-Watson would be the appropriate reviewer!'[68] The *Times Literary Supplement* then refused to send Carr the book on the ground that it was about him – which proved a source of wry amusement all round and he managed to persuade them that it was not.[69] When Bertram Wolfe attacked him in *Commentary* that March for 'unavowed apologetics',[70] he expressed reluctance to engage in controversy. 'I think,' he concluded, 'one can only hope that the violence of these attacks may end by discrediting him.'[71] And Joyce was in Paris with the boys when on 19 April 1955

---

[66] Carr to Deutscher, 16 November 1954.
[67] Deutscher, *Heretics and Renegades*, pp. 3–4.
[68] Carr to Deutscher, 11 January 1955: *DA*, 16.
[69] Ibid., 19 April 1955: ibid.
[70] B. Wolfe, 'Professor Carr's "Wave of the Future"', *Commentary*, March 1955, p. 190.
[71] Carr to Deutscher, 24 April 1955: *DA*, 16.

Carr alerted Deutscher to the fact that 'we are jointly attacked in a book by Shapiro [sic] which is really a shocking piece of Wolfery – made all the worse by the fact that he has done a lot of detailed research on the particular points which interest him.'[72] He told Deutscher that work was 'going quite well, but slowly and with a long way still to go. At the moment, partly prodded by your reproaches that I had omitted the social side of the picture, I am trying to do something about the structure of Soviet society in the early NEP years, the role of the party, the intelligentsia, and so forth. I may ask you to have a look at it sometime.'[73]

Renewed contact with Deutscher raised his spirits, which had been very low that previous winter after the review appeared. He had been depressed about the arrangements at Balliol, and frustrated at the rather humdrum teaching insensitively required of him. Indeed, Joyce had signalled trouble on Boxing Day 1954: 'The Prof is rather tired of teaching,' she wrote to Tamara and Isaac, 'and anything which upsets his routine such as Xmas is disagreeable to him.'[74] The experience at Balliol unfortunately cured Carr of further interest in teaching the young; he was, after all, now 62 years of age. Less than six years later he readily confessed that 'When I was younger, I found stimulation in teaching younger minds, but now it would simply bore me.' The strain was felt again when term resumed; and an added factor was continued uncertainty about prospects at Trinity.

A Cambridge examiners' meeting was scheduled for 11 May. Carr went down a day earlier to collar Kitson Clark, dine in college, and address the college history society. He also saw Vyvyan and the (Communist) economics Fellow Maurice Dobb, and then returned home 'very exhausted'. The path to Trinity had now been cleared, however. All that remained was for an election to take place. And on 23 May he was delighted to hear officially that he had at last succeeded. He had finally been elected to a Senior Research Fellowship (title B) for five years, with a possible renewal for a further two: an unusual honour held by such as Bertrand Russell and Wittgenstein. Isaac was told immediately. 'The advantages are (a) no teaching (b) no retirement age [this in fact had not yet been settled] (c) it's my own place.' Then comes the revealing afterthought: 'House-hunting is going to be a problem for Joyce.'[75] Up to now Joyce had stoically put up with a lot. Uprooted from beloved Appleford for an unsatisfactory life in Oxford, with Ted overworking and increasingly depressed; now a move to Cambridge, leaving friends behind once more and still with no real life of her own except as an adjunct to Ted's great enterprise.

Signs of resistance began to appear. Joyce now handed house-hunting to Ted (which she had cause to regret). On his next visit to Cambridge for an

---

[72] Ibid., 19 April 1955: ibid.
[73] Ibid., 24 April 1955: ibid.
[74] Joyce to Isaac and Tamara Deutscher, 26 December 1954: ibid.
[75] Carr to Deutscher, 24 May 1955: ibid.

examiners' meeting on 17 June, he stayed on for four more days to find accommodation. But only after a further foray on 9 August did he find 6 Prospect Row (next door to the Free Press public house – not that he would ever make use of it), which he promptly bought for a mere £2000 on the following day. It was 'a very small house – formerly two cottages – in a slum area: but its position is central,' he wrote, 'and I think it will suit us quite well.'[76] The move took place on 21 September. There were a few drawbacks, however. His room in Nevile's Court was disappointingly small: 'since I have no teaching obligations any claim on *Lebensraum* in college does not rank very high', he noted with a tinge of regret.[77] But this was a minor, hopefully temporary, inconvenience compared with the enticing prospect of uninterrupted research for the next five to seven years, the limits determined only by his own stamina and longevity.

An unfortunate footnote to an otherwise successful year was the publication of *Notes for a Journal* purportedly by Maxim Litvinov, formerly commissar for foreign affairs of the Soviet Union. This was a forgery produced in Paris by the émigré Bessedovsky. The manuscript had been sent to Wolfe by Harpers and he had, after careful examination of the internal evidence, rejected it. Wolfe's friend, Joseph Freeman, who had been a lover of Ivy Litvinov's, knew the truth of Litvinov's memoirs (they had been burned by him on Litvinov's instructions in 1946) and privately confirmed Wolfe in his initial judgement: 'every page of it is forged', he wrote.[78] Carr, however, knew nothing of this. On 27 March 1953 he received the manuscript from André Deutsch. Shortly afterwards Deutsch wrote warning that Bessedovsky was mixed up in it. That should have been warning enough. But Carr instead set off for Paris to see Bessedovsky, who naturally gave him his word of honour that it was genuine. At the Deutschers' in Coulsdon on 16 June Carr was again warned not to trust Bessedovsky. But he did, with the result that he wrote an introduction authenticating the text only to have Wolfe expose it as a forgery in the *New Leader* in 1955. Thereafter the very mention of the book was enough to make him acutely uncomfortable.

---

[76] Ibid., 1 October 1955: ibid.
[77] Ibid., 3 August 1955: ibid.
[78] J. Freeman, 'Memo on *Notes for a Journal*', 11–15 August 1955: *Bertram Wolfe Papers*, Hoover Institution, Stanford, box 103–10.

7

Return to Trinity

The return to Trinity at the age of sixty-three inaugurated a new and more tranquil period in Carr's career, capped by the honour of election to the British Academy a year later.[1] Here in the fens he found uncomprehending acceptance and respect. 'On all accounts Trinity is far better, and Cambridge is far more tolerant (probably because it cares less) of political idiosyncrasy', he wrote.[2] This was not least because 'Cambridge is infinitely more remote from the world than Oxford', as he noted in a letter to Deutscher.[3] Indeed it was. The history syllabus barely dealt with the world beyond Europe's shores except under the archaic rubric 'Expansion of Europe'; and the social sciences, with the distinguished exception of economics, scarcely figured in the curriculum.

But Cambridge was ideal for Carr's overriding purpose. The absence of distractions meant that he could work without limit and he did so, unremittingly. The *History of Soviet Russia* had in fact taken over his entire life, and that of Joyce as well. By the time the first Christmas in Cambridge arrived he was thus not surprisingly 'tired and depressed'. Part of the problem arose from the fact that Joyce had nothing to do and wanted a normal social life, whereas Ted found all social activities a strain. Before long she was cursing the damned Bolsheviks in terms not dissimilar to those Anne had used towards Herzen and Bakunin. A pattern was repeating itself. He always hated Christmas because libraries closed, unhelpful demands were made on his precious time, work was disrupted; and on this occasion the imminent arrival of Joyce's family made him more misanthropic than usual. Writing to Tamara Deutscher on 27 December, with the worst now behind her, Joyce cheerfully tried to disguise the problem: 'The Prof bears it all very well; luckily Trinity never closes,

---

[1] His nomination was proposed by Charles Webster, Lucy Sutherland, Lewis Namier and G.P. Gooch. His work on Russia was described as 'a remarkable achievement in historical research and analysis': British Academy archives.

[2] To Niuta Kallin (from Balliol), 29 May 1955: E.H. Carr Talks File II, BBC Written Archives Centre.

[3] Carr to Deutscher, 15 May 1955: *DA*, 16.

so after 2 days of rather intensive family life he was able to slink away to his room and all-male lunch.'[4] On the following day he escaped to London, stayed over at the Club, and did not return until the thirtieth.

In London he visited old haunts, checking out new sources. In Cambridge the college librarian was soon endeavouring to obtain what he could on inter-library loan. But British libraries were simply inadequate to Carr's voracious needs. A further spell in the United States was required. Teaching commitments at Balliol had prevented him from crossing the Atlantic on any long term basis. Courtesy of Herbert Marcuse at Brandeis University, he had received an invitation to lecture for an entire semester (October to January); that was in April 1955. Now, with his hands free from outside obligations, he accepted when the invitation was renewed in January 1956, and booked passage for New York in February for 6 September 1956. But this was a second-best: to have to teach in order to subsidise his research, when the teaching not only restricted his movements but also absorbed many of the energies that could be channelled into his history. He therefore played with the idea of seeking funding from the Rockefeller Foundation, which had looked so favourably upon him in the forties. The idea was that he meet with Kenneth Thompson in New York upon arrival and before taking the train up north. But after a rough crossing they docked late on 14 September and Carr missed the meeting. They reached Boston the following day. After a preliminary foray in the Trotsky archives at the Houghton Library in Harvard, he moved on to Brandeis. The plan was to stay on in the area until the late spring of 1957, and for this purpose he had obtained a place from January to April 1957 as visiting scholar at Harvard's Russian Research Center, which had since benefited from the kind of funding from Rockefeller denied to the School of Slavonic Studies, and which was then headed by the far eastern specialist Paul Langer. Langer had not read all his published work, but had 'always been deeply and on the whole favorably impressed' with the *History of Soviet Russia*; it was, in his opinion, 'a work of high and permanent value'.[5]

It was from Harvard soon after arrival that Carr wrote to Thompson explaining the need for money to fund a visit to the Hoover Institution at Stanford and a four to six week stay. Philip Mosely, now Professor of International Relations at Columbia, wrote from the Council on Foreign Relations in enthusiastic support of his application. Although in his opinion Carr was 'not an easy or smooth personality', he had 'a high regard for his scholarship'; Carr was, Mosely explained, 'in the midst of the most important single study of the history of the Soviet regime . . . and even when other scholars disagree with his findings, they will be forced through his efforts to lift the entire work of this field to a higher plain'.[6] Thompson had also written for an

---

[4] Joyce to Tamara Deutscher, 27 December 1955: ibid.
[5] Langer to Thompson, 15 January 1956: *RFA*: RF RG GC, 401, Carr, E.H., f. 376.
[6] Mosely to Thompson, 4 October 1956: ibid.

opinion from Harrison Salisbury at the *New York Times*, even then a veteran Moscow correspondent.[7] Salisbury had a reservation: the Litvinov diary forgery. But he was otherwise very positive. Carr was, he considered, 'one of the half dozen greatest specialists in Soviet affairs and in Soviet–German affairs' and he expressed the 'very greatest respect for his work, particularly for his intricate close study of the early years of the Bolshevik Revolution'.[8]

The teaching load at Brandeis was not heavy: three lectures and one graduate seminar per week. The lectures were no burden and Carr's unflagging energy enabled him to carry on researching the rest of the day. As ever, he expected to continue working after dinner into the evening. Meanwhile the world outside was in turmoil. In an act of late imperial folly Britain, in collusion with France and Israel, bombed and invaded Nasser's Egypt in an abortive attempt to repossess the Suez Canal. In the Soviet Union the new leader, Nikita Khrushchev, had in February roundly denounced Stalin, only to precipitate an explosion of unrest in neighbouring Poland and in Hungary, which ultimately resulted in a full-scale Soviet intervention to crush the Hungarian revolt. Carr made a point of listening to the news on the radio on 31 October 1956 to hear the latest on Suez. But typically he 'Refused to go to [a] discussion on Hungary and Poland with Marcuse' on 5 November.

Thompson tried to draw him back to New York for a seminar on international politics to be addressed by Niebuhr, but Carr was working to a tough schedule that did not allow for distractions, however interesting; he was still one of Niebuhr's 'warm admirers'.[9] It did not appear that the Foundation would oblige with funds for an extended trip to the west coast, so he went alone and spent 'a hurried but fruitful 2 and a half weeks at [the] Hoover', pausing on the way back long enough to lecture at Salt Lake City, collect his luggage in Cambridge, Massachusetts, and then return via Newfoundland on 19 April. At his advanced age, the experience was not one to be repeated. En route he put in for a major grant from Rockefeller, which reads like a wishlist amounting to over five figures in dollars. 'I am in my 65th year and, while I still believe myself capable of my best work, this will not last indefinitely,' he wrote. 'I want in – say – the next five years to carry on my history to 1928 to 1929, when the materials begin to dry up. This means, on the scale on which I am working, about six more volumes including two which are now nearly completed. This is now my main, almost exclusive task.'[10]

The main reason for the request was to fund future visits to the United States which were 'imperative' if the job were to be done properly: 'I do not want to have to come again on the conditions on which I came this time, i.e. to be obliged to deliver a substantial number of lectures in order to finance myself. This exhausts my energies, and partly defeats the purpose for which I

[7] Thompson to Salisbury, 27 November 1956: ibid.
[8] Salisbury to Thompson, 12 December 1956: ibid.
[9] Carr to Thompson, 12 January 1957: ibid., f. 371.
[10] Ibid., 15 April 1957: ibid.

come.' He also sought money for microfilms of sources and periodicals in the United States, which were expensive. In addition, the fellowship at Trinity paid little – £600 a year, supplemented by royalties and past savings. This did not really allow for payment of skilled secretarial help and research assistance. Then there was Joyce:

> As regards travel, I want to bring my wife with me: she not only looks after my material well-being, but seeks out books for me in libraries and does copying and extracting for me, thus very much lightening the load. On this occasion I could not afford to take her with me to the west. Then I would like sometimes to be able to travel pullman instead of always having to cross the ocean on continental tourist, as I have done this time: it does relieve the pressure a little. And next time I come I want to spend some weeks in N.Y. to work in the Public Library, and some time in the Library of Congress; and stays in Washington and N.Y. are both expensive . . .[11]

He was told to submit a formal application later. He was now 'in the awful stage where one has to put in all the minor details one left in the heat of writing to check later, and when one is fed up with the whole thing: my latest nightmare is that it's too long to get into a volume – that's the result of coming to America to collect material'.[12] The United States had, as usual, been 'both stimulating and terrifying'. He had returned home 'glad of a spell of Cambridge – which is neither'.[13] Back at Prospect Row early in May he went into 'strict retirement' to complete the first (economic) volume of *Socialism in One Country* for the press. It turned out to be an 'arduous job'. The manuscript was delivered to Macmillan's on 11 August.

In the preface to *The Interregnum* Carr had already acknowledged that the title intended for this future volume, *The Struggle for Power 1923–1928*, 'seemed too trivial, and inadequate to the fundamental issues involved in the struggle'.[14] The new volume thus shifted the order of priorities. 'Precedence has been given to the narrative of economic developments; for, though the rivalry between party leaders was the most conspicuous, and superficially the most dramatic, feature of these years, the forms which it took were dependent on basic economic issues.'[15] 'The historian who seeks to explain the major developments in the history of the Soviet Union in the nineteen-twenties will,' he asserted, '. . . derive comparatively little help from the study of the characters of the principal leaders and of relations between them.' They formed only a 'minor part' of the story.[16] Even so the pen portraits of those men easily lodge in one's memory: of Trotsky – 'the most European'[17] of the early

---

[11] Ibid.
[12] Carr to Arno Mayer, 12 June 1957: Arno Mayer's personal correspondence.
[13] Carr to Isaac Deutscher, 22 July 1957: *DA*, 16.
[14] Carr, *The Interregnum 1923–1924*, London 1954, p. v.
[15] Carr, *Socialism in One Country 1924–1926*, vol. 1, London 1958, p. v.
[16] Ibid., p. 139.
[17] Ibid., p. 146.

Bolshevik leaders; the hollow figure of Zinoviev – 'None of them inspired so little personal respect';[18] Kamenev, who 'had neither the desire nor the capacity to lead men';[19] Bukharin – the 'tragedy of . . . a weak, amiable and keen-witted man caught up in the turmoil of events too vast for his moral stature';[20] and not least Stalin (of whom, more below) – 'reared in an educational tradition which was not only indifferent to western ways of life and thought, but consciously rejected them'.[21]

Instead Carr focused on the larger context: historical and economic, and the change in attitudes of mind, besides dealing for the first time with the family, church, literature and law since the revolution. Much had therefore changed under the impact of further research and contemplation, and not merely due to persistent criticism from Deutscher. 'The progress of the work,' he noted,

> has produced, as generally happens, a growing sense of the complexity of the issues with which I am dealing. What I take to be the conventional view of Soviet history in the years after the revolution, i.e. that it was the work of determined men – enlightened pioneers on one view, hardened villains on another – who knew exactly what they wanted and where they were going, seems to me wholly misleading. The view commonly expressed that the Bolshevik leaders, or Stalin in particular, were inspired primarily by the desire to perpetuate their rule, is equally inadequate. No doubt every government seeks to retain its authority as long as possible. But the policies pursued were not by any means always those apparently most conducive to the undisturbed exercise of power by those in possession. The situation was so complex, and varied so much from place to place and from group to group of the population, that the task of unravelling the decisive factors in the process has been unusually baffling.[22]

Indeed, this is the very originality of Carr's contribution to our understanding of the period. In this volume he both highlighted but then also contextualized the personalities engaged in the struggle for power. Only the kind of detailed research and analysis he alone was willing to carry out enabled such a fine-grained account to emerge. The entire picture is framed against his presentation in the first chapter of 'The Legacy of History', a *tour d'horizon* of breathtaking confidence and lucidity, tracing the tension between continuity and change in the Russian past. Inspired by de Tocqueville's reflections on the reassertion of continuity after the drama and bloodshed of the French revolution, Carr here outlined the same such forces at work in Russia after 1917. First, he argued, although a revolution inspired by Marxism, it was 'realized in a country with a predominantly peasant population and still

---

[18] Ibid., p. 156.
[19] Ibid., p. 162.
[20] Ibid., p. 173.
[21] Ibid., p. 180.
[22] Ibid., p. vi.

largely pre-capitalist economy'.[23] Second, the victory of the revolution necessarily transformed the insurrectionists into established government. Writing
as the ex-bureaucrat, Carr could not but sense that in 'certain technical
aspects'[24] all governments were alike. Third, the formation of a government
forced the insurrectionists into relations with other states. The dictates of
geography and the needs of the economy ensured that this element of continuity was 'the most rapidly and conspicuously asserted'. Here the parallels
with other revolutions were close. Where Russia parted company lay in the
fact that the ideas that inspired the revolution had been imported.
Restoration in Russia therefore inevitably went hand in hand with the reassertion of 'the Russian national tradition'.[25]

Carr's picture of Stalin had also shifted with the years, but only in emphasis. In reviewing Boris Souverine's life of Stalin in October 1939, he had
argued that 'no verbal analysis can explain the rise of this unattractive and
apparently undistinguished man to a position of absolute personal power
scarcely paralleled in modern history. Stalin possesses a gift for politics –
using the term in no very elevated sense – which amounts to genius; and
genius always eludes definition.'[26] He did not now deny all this but explained
it in terms of vast impersonal forces. Stalin's success came as a result of pursuing aims 'which were dictated by the dynamic force inherent in the
revolution itself'. Indeed, this was how he had come to see the entire process.
It was an approach which very much fitted in with his reluctance to pass
moral judgements on individuals in history and pleased Isaac Deutscher no
more than his previous tendency to see Soviet Russia in almost exclusively statist terms. In this instance, however, Isaac remained silent. But on one
occasion after Deutscher's death, when he was staying at Tamara's and turned
to consult a volume of the *History of Soviet Russia* from her bookshelves on
some point of fact, a sudden silence descended. He had inadvertently opened
a page that touched on Stalin only to find in Isaac's familiar hand: 'Wherever
possible, give Stalin the benefit of the doubt.' 'Oh, so that's how it was', he
retorted.

In some senses the gap between the two had been bridged – *Socialism in One
Country* bore witness to that fact. In another sense the gap had widened. The
Deutscher who wrote the Stalin biography, which stood close to Carr's interpretation, had himself since shifted position in the course of writing his three
volume biography of Trotsky. The man who wrote *Stalin*, which is in some
respects apologetic (certainly in respect of the origins of the Cold War), had
by the late fifties became much more critical. Whatever one's view of his
treatment of the role of these personalities, Carr's book was the first objective
and detailed treatment of the struggle between the factions for supreme

---

[23] Ibid., p. 4.
[24] Ibid., p. 5.
[25] Ibid., p. 8.
[26] 'The Bolshevik Dictator', *Spectator*, 13 October 1939.

power, and an exhaustive account as to how that struggle was, to a large extent, determined by the parallel battle within the economy between the forces of peasant capitalism and state socialism.

Reviews tended to follow a set pattern. Deutscher argued that Carr's premises were still 'essentially conservative'. Wolfe offered praise tempered by warning of the 'exclusive dependence on Bolshevik sources and his own vulnerability to the persuasiveness of concentrated totalist and victorious power'. From Harvard, Merle Fainsod described this volume with something of a backhanded compliment: 'Of its kind it is a distinguished and unique achievement, but there is in it a bloodless quality from which many will recoil. The human dimensions of Soviet history, the agonies and triumphs of its people, will have to find their historian elsewhere.'[27] He liked the second volume of *Socialism in One Country*, however, which appeared in 1959. He found it 'scrupulously fair', a 'work of rare detachment and objectivity' and 'one which penetrates below the surface of official apologetics and polemics to reveal the realities of Soviet power.'[28] These were men who, for all the ideological misgivings, and they ran deep, felt they were, at the very least, dealing with a most unusual and powerful contribution to history. Finally Carr had won the kind of more general recognition from the voices that mattered in the profession. Yet the air of McCarthyism still hung heavily on the United States. Only at exceptional institutions like Columbia University were his works seriously recommended; not least because historians elsewhere were generally not permitted to research and write on the Soviet period, on the flimsy pretext that there were 'no sources'. This was the case in several distinguished institutions, most certainly up to the the Gorbachev era. Carr's *History of Soviet Russia* showed they were wrong; and the power of his example undoubtedly opened the way, intellectually if not institutionally, to the proper study of the Soviet past.

Carr followed Cato's maxim that the wise learn even from fools but fools learn from no one. He farmed his work on Soviet history out to others, just as he had with his previous works. He was never one to overestimate his knowledge, his abilities and, now that he was past retirement age, his energies; this was one, albeit only one, secret of his success. And his competence in the field of numbers was not quite equal to his facility with words. Robert (Bob) Davies was a first class product of the School of Slavonic Studies. Until the invasion of Hungary he was a dedicated Communist and thus identified with Rothstein rather than Deutscher. Temperamentally, too, he shied away from verbal fireworks, preferring the subtleties of quiet and persistent persuasion and solitary research. But his obliging manner and surface softness overlay enormous energy, strong convictions and a sharp mind. The relationship with Carr was almost entirely professional, though Carr always retained a certain affection

---

[27] *New York Herald Tribune Book Review*, 8 February 1959.
[28] Ibid., 21 August 1960.

for the 'young' man. For Davies the loss of faith in the Party was compensated for by Carr's vision of the utility of economic planning, though the applicability of the Soviet economic model had now silently shifted from its value to the west to its utility for the Third World. Davies thus complemented rather than challenged his perspective. Whereas Deutscher had, upon Carr, the influence of the scholar as ideologue, Davies had the influence of the scholar as technocrat; where Deutscher was seized by the power of words, Davies was gripped by the power of numbers. And numbers now mattered, because the major task ahead was the volumes of the *History of Soviet Russia* dealing with the *Foundations of a Planned Economy, 1926–1929*.

Carr was frustrated. In a letter to Deutscher on 18 September 1958 he wrote: 'Not much sign of Stakhanovism, I fear, either on my part or that of the publishers. I've published nothing since 1954, and came back from the U.S. last year with vols 5 and 6 [*Socialism in One Country*, volumes two and three] more than 3/4 finished.'[29] He continued to drive himself on and, as Davies, himself no stranger to hard work, soon discovered, Carr all too easily assumed that others were equally driven. Davies was then a young assistant lecturer at Glasgow University. He had written a pioneering thesis of considerable complexity on the development of the Soviet budgetary system under the draconian supervision of Alexander Baykov, an authoritarian emigré who had laid the foundations for the study of the Soviet economy at Birmingham University in the thirties. Carr's attention was drawn to the thesis on a trip to Birmingham on 15–16 February 1955, where he lectured on Russian history (the outline for chapter one of *Socialism in One Country*). Davies's account of Soviet finance was of use for the economics volume, part two. After obtaining the thesis on loan and having worked through 'with great interest' on 24 June, he wrote to Davies three days later. What he had seen was that Davies had all the statistical agility he himself required to grapple with the intricacies of Soviet economic development. 'The question which worries me most of all,' he wrote, 'and is a constant nightmare when one approaches Soviet economics and finance, is the diversity of statistics . . . .'[30] They met on 4–6 June 1956, when Carr came up to Glasgow.

It was not until the beginning of 1958, however, that Carr decided to offer Davies the chance to collaborate in completing the history. He had counted on asking him in person at a National Association of Soviet and East European Studies conference at Hanover Lodge in London on 7 January, but en route he fell over while on a bus – a cruel reminder of his age – and, fearing a fracture, he decided to return home immediately. Instead he wrote on 12 January:

> The present section 'Socialism in One Country' is in three vols. (1) Introductory
> & Economic – now in the press (2) Political – almost finished (3) Foreign – still to
> be written. That done, I want to go to the next section ('The Approach to

---

[29] Carr to Deutscher, 18 September 1958: *DA*, 18.
[30] Carr to Davies, 27 June 1955: *R.W. Davies Papers*.

Planning' or something of that sort) which will begin where I have now stopped
in the spring of 1926 and go on to ?? some point in 1928 or 1929 – the adoption
of the First 5-Year Plan and the defeat of the Right Opposition? This section will
contain an economic volume, obviously of great importance. Finally, I am beginning to feel the burden, I don't get any younger; and for some parts at any rate of
the economic job I feel not over well-qualified.

It would be possible to imagine collaboration in the form of someone taking
over full responsibility for the economic volume – so that it would really be his, not
mine; or of taking over certain sections of it where I feel weakest (industry,
finance, planning, perhaps trade); or of collaboration and assistance without
responsibility . . . There will have to be fairly close agreement on basic issues. My
impression (I may be wrong) is that we are fairly close in this respect. You are not
a Menshevik or (like Nove apparently) a Bukharinite; you are not a Trotskyite in
the sense of wanting to spend all your time throwing stones at Stalin. You're probably more interested to explain why (quite contrary to original intentions) they
moved into collectivization than to pass moral judgements on it.[31]

There were many assumptions here, as Davies acknowledged, but mostly
correct.

Davies responded positively, although now busy as a full time lecturer at
Birmingham and attempting to transform the thesis into a book, and
suggested a meeting at Easter. Carr was impatient, however, and tried to wrap
it all up by correspondence. Davies took the minimal option of industry,
planning and finance. Carr wanted to take the story to April 1929: an 'obvious
stopping point politically'. 'As regards time-table,' he wrote,

it may seem that I have raised this question prematurely but I felt that you, having
got the finance book off your hands, would be laying new plans, and that now was
the time to strike. My own position is this. I'm now on the last stages of vol. 6
[*Socialism in One Country*, volume two]; and, though these last stages sometimes
last longer than one expects, I feel sure that, barring accidents, I shall be through
by April. Then, however, I have to do the foreign relations volume for 1924–1926.
Some of the material is already collected; and I tend to find that this is more
straightforward, and goes quicker, than the domestic volumes. Still, it would be
utopian to expect to finish before autumn 1959. I shall not therefore get down in
detail to our economic volume (Vol. 8) till the winter of 1959–60.

But – heedless of Davies's new commitments – he pressed his young collaborator to 'blaze a trail in advance'.

It was the afternoon of 2 April 1958 when Davies arrived in Cambridge and
stayed overnight at Trinity. Carr's diary reports: 'Davies came round in [the]
morning and lunched: left on 3.19. Everything tidied up.' But he was cautious.
A follow-up letter on 8 April then raised the potentially explosive issue of
interpretation: 'Should we fail to agree on any point of fact or interpretation,'
he wrote,

---

[31] Carr to Davies, 12 January 1958: ibid.

we should aim at including both views in the text as possible alternatives between which it is impossible to decide with certainty: should, however, one or other of us feel too strongly on the point to allow of this, then, I fear, my view must prevail, but your dissent will be recorded in a separate note. (I frankly think this contingency most unlikely to arise: but we had better make hypothetical provision for it.)[32]

In fact the collaboration proved very harmonious and not because there were no differences in outlook. Writing to Davies about the first draft of a BBC schools broadcast on collectivization of agriculture, Carr suggested some amendments partly to avert complaints from listeners but partly also because he did not want to 'slur over too much what a shocking business it was (like some other industrializations)'. He added:

> The point, the only point, on which I really do disagree with you is in treating 'Stalinism' as a serious and original contribution to theory, and being apparently willing to recognize Stalin as a *thinker*. This seems to me sheer . . . nonsense.[33]

In reply Davies chided him for belittling Stalin's views. This prompted a rejoinder:

> I'm not sure whether you are right in saying that I don't regard Stalin's views as 'important'. It's a vague word. Franklin Roosevelt's speeches on the New Deal were immensely important: even the coining of the phrase like 'quaranteening the aggressor' was important. But you wouldn't say that F.D.R. was a man of any great *intellectual* calibre or originality. He was a statesman who had a genius for picking up the right idea and plugging it at the right moment. Stalin was brought up in the Marxist, not the empiricist, tradition, and therefore expressed himself in theoretical terms. But what he said was politically apt, not intellectually substantial.[34]

The autumn of 1958 found him working on the third – foreign relations – volume of *Socialism in One Country*. 'I find the foreign affairs stuff a sort of relaxation', Carr wrote. 'Somehow it isn't quite serious, and it's amusing to work out how things happened, and who outplayed whom. Soviet–German relations are particularly rewarding from this angle.' The only problem was a superabundance of documentation. 'I have just got a list of the files on Russian affairs from the archives of the Auswärtiges Amt [German Foreign Ministry] in the 1920s – most of them available on microfilm,' he told Tamara Deutscher. 'I shall never be able to read half of them. Too many documents! The writing of history will become impossible till there have been a few good conflagrations to reduce the volume of material.'[35] The Comintern, from that point of view, was less of a problem, 'I confess to finding the curious world of intrigue,

---

[32] Carr to Davies, 8 April 1958: ibid.

[33] Ibid., 31 July 1958: ibid.

[34] Ibid., 9 September 1958: ibid.

[35] Carr to Tamara Deutscher, 2 October 1958: *DA*, 18.

with its mixture of conviction and calculation, rather fascinating,' he wrote to Davies in October 1958, 'but I fully realise that it isn't very important, and I ought to get back to agriculture.'[36] In fact the last volume of *Socialism of One Country* would take until 1963 to complete, but part of the reason for this was that Carr's health collapsed.

On 7 June 1958 he had acquired a new house at 4 Wilberforce Road, a much more salubrious part of Cambridge on the western fringes of the town, and considerably closer to the University Library and the college, for £3356. But it needed extensive refurbishing. Joyce had wanted something larger, any hint of which Ted ridiculed as a *folie de grandeur*. After all, capital tied up in a house could not be productively invested. To Ted the issue was that simple. They moved in the last week of September. 'The practical complications of civilization are horrible,' he wrote, adding revealingly: 'Joyce is continuously swallowed up in these affairs.'[37]

By November galley proofs for volume two of *Socialism in One Country* had arrived, and work on them now punctuated research on the Comintern. Then towards the end of the month Jane Degras arrived for a weekend and Carr felt exhausted. As usual it was the stress of additional social activity that threatened his health. Although he felt he was recovering early in December, on the night of the twelfth to the thirteenth he suddenly fell ill. Joyce wrote to Tamara: 'it looked like 'flu but the doctor was worried and came twice in 2 hours, the second time bringing a specialist.'[38] The symptoms now looked more like those of a stroke. Carr was rushed off to Addenbrooke's hospital and 'it was only when they did a lumbar puncture that they found it was meningitis.'[39] He was rushed by ambulance to a special neuro-surgery unit at the Radcliffe Infirmary at Oxford. 'They immediately bored a small hole in his skull and put in penicillin close to the source of the infection.' And once the critical twenty-four hour period had passed, the doctors were 'astonished' at the 'rapid rate of recovery'.[40] But it was, as Joyce confessed, 'a terrible week'.[41]

Carr took to hospital life well enough, but complained at the mental level of the nurses. As soon as he could, he was dictating a letter to inform Davies of what had happened and, as the letter read, 'assure you that there will be no diminution in his mental capacity!' 'But there is no doubt,' Joyce added, evidently without his knowledge, 'that in view of the virulent attack this bug made, he will have to have a longish rest before he starts work again.' Carr suggested he and Davies meet in Cambridge that Easter (1959) to discuss a rough draft of Davies's plans for his sections of the *Foundations of a Planned Economy*. Joyce also relayed the suggestion 'that in view of this illness he would

[36] Carr to Davies, 19 October 1958: *R.W. Davies Papers*.
[37] Carr to Tamara Deutscher, 2 October 1958: *DA*, 18.
[38] Joyce to Isaac and Tamara Deutscher (from Oxford), 20 December 1958: *DA*, 18.
[39] Joyce to Davies (from Cambridge), 27 December 1958: *R.W. Davies Papers*.
[40] Joyce to Isaac and Tamara Deutscher (from Oxford), 20 December 1958: *DA*, 18.
[41] Joyce to Arno Mayer, 23 December 1958: Arno Mayer's personal correspondence.

like to hand over to you more . . . than you had originally agreed on; if you don't *want* to do more, he wonders if you have any ideas as to roping in somebody else to do some of his work for you both. Any ideas?' Joyce was, of course, seriously concerned lest 'he will try and do too much too soon.'[42]

She was right. By the end of December he had begun reading Boris Pasternak's *Doctor Zhivago*, 'but not enjoying it'.[43] He was already seeing visitors. Christopher Hill called in and, much to Carr's evident surprise, Moley Sargent turned up twice – he was also a patient. But sharing a room with others disturbed Ted's sleep and once a private room became available at Addenbrooke's on 2 January 1959 he was transferred by ambulance to Cambridge. Two days later he made his first attempt to walk and by 22 January he was back home, itching to return to work. An amusing and revealing episode occurred while Carr was in hospital. Thompson wrote from the Rockefeller Foundation to Lord Adrian, Master of Trinity, for a candid evaluation of Carr's history, its 'objectivity and integrity' in particular.[44] This was obviously done under the misapprehension that a Cambridge college was something like a university department and that Adrian would have some idea of what Carr actually did. Of course, he had no idea at all, and he wrote an unenthusiastic reply, the only helpful aspect of which was in pointing out that senior research fellowships at the college were rare (at that time only three were in existence) and previous holders included Bertrand Russell and Ludwig Wittgenstein.[45]

On 20 February Carr wrote to Davies: 'I am convalescent, and begin to be somewhat bored. But the doctors have been so efficient in this case, and so encouraging, that I feel I ought to obey their injunction not to attempt any serious work before the end of March.' And he calculated that 'this affair will have cost me the best part of six months . . .'.[46] There was some good news, however. The application for a grant from Rockefeller, which Joyce had had to put together rapidly while Ted was ill, would no longer be required. Just prior to falling ill he had been angling for a place at 'the think-shop at Palo Alto'.[47] 'I hope very much this may come off,' Joyce wrote, 'as a year in Hoover is quite his idea of heaven, but the foundations don't really like him and it may fall through. He may not be dynamite, but still potentially explosive material . . .'.[48] In the event, on 4 February he was invited to spend the winter in California at the Center for Advanced Study in the Behavioral Sciences at Stanford, 'which provides funds without strings (no teaching, no seminar) and is in close proximity to the Hoover Library, where I can delve

---

[42] Joyce to Davies, 27 December 1958: *R.W. Davies Papers*.
[43] Ibid., 1 January 1959: ibid.
[44] Thompson to Adrian, 30 December 1958: *RFA*: RF RG 2 GC 1958, 401, Carr, E.H., 1 folder.
[45] Adrian to Thompson, 7 January 1959: ibid., 1959, 401, Carr, E.H.
[46] Carr to Davies, 20 February 1959: *R.W. Davies Papers*.
[47] Joyce to Arno Mayer, 23 December 1958: Arno Mayer's personal correspondence.
[48] Ibid.

for vols. 7 and 8 [*Socialism in One Country* volume three, and *Foundations of a Planned Economy* volume one]. We shall probably leave in August.' Meanwhile Joyce arranged a holiday 'for the sea-breeze'[49] in Brighton at the 'Old Ship', where Ted, still barred from working, corrected proofs of *Socialism in One Country*, volume two, and read Hegel, Boswell, Collingwood and E.M. Forster (*A Room with a View*).

The second volume of *Socialism in One Country* came out later that year. It dealt, among other matters, with the mysterious process by which Stalin manoeuvred his way towards supreme power. Here the material unfolds layer after layer, taking in the weakening of democratic practices within the party, the inadequacies of Stalin's opponents, but above all, as in the previous volumes, revealing the degree to which complex circumstances pushed events fowards and set the framework which Stalin appears to have more immediately understood and acted upon than his rivals. 'Trotsky,' Carr tells us, 'failed to the last to understand that the issue of the struggle was determined not by the availability of arguments but by the control and manipulation of the levers of political power. He had no stomach for a fight whose character bewildered and eluded him.'[50] At times he is merciless in his criticism of Trotsky, struck equally by the man's originality and lack of realism. 'As often in Trotsky's writings,' Carr notes with a tone of finality, 'the analysis was exceedingly acute, the positive prescriptions theoretical and unrealistic.'[51]

Not that Carr gave Stalin more than his due. In discussing, for example, the origins of the doctrine of 'socialism in one country', he writes: 'By a flash of originality of a quality so rare in Stalin's career that it has sometimes been described as a accident, Stalin perceived that this was a real and burning issue which called for a new elaboration of doctrine.'[52] It is clear that Trotsky is to be admired for his sheer intellectual force; but Stalin as the political tactician – the intellectual versus the bureaucrat, as in *The Twenty Years' Crisis*. The idea that no revolution was going to break out elsewhere in Europe was something Trotsky simply could not contemplate. Stalin was here making a virtue out of necessity and the patriotic appeal in so doing not least aided him against his main adversary. And in formulating the policies that flowed from 'socialism in one country', Stalin outmanoeuvred his opposition further by borrowing some of their own pet projects – notably planning for industrialization and, later, suppression of the peasantry for capital accumulation through the forced collectivization of agriculture. Carr had already described in volume one the process by which 'the party, by destroying its rivals, had seemed to absorb the state, so the state now absorbed the party into itself.'[53] He now followed this process to the point where 'The concentration of power

---

[49] Ibid.
[50] Carr, *Socialism in One Country*, vol. 2, London 1959, p. 34.
[51] Ibid., pp. 168–9.
[52] Ibid., p. 38.
[53] Carr, *The Bolshevik Revolution*, vol. 1, p. 213.

in the central organization also meant the concentration of power in the hands of one man.'[54] The corollary was a switch in focus for the secret police, once Cheka, now OGPU: 'Security no longer meant the defence of the Soviets against the champions of the ancien regime; it no longer meant, within the Soviets, the defence of Bolshevik revolution against the challenge of dissident parties of the Left; it meant, within the Bolshevik party, the defence of a specific ruling group or order.'[55]

Carr loved the absorption in the detail. But he also greatly enjoyed the realm of grand generalization. The process of writing history inevitably prompted a good deal of contemplation about the metier itself, which had begun when the History was first conceived in 1944, found form in the *New Society* and stayed with him thereafter to his death. He had begun reading Carlyle before leaving Addenbrooke's and had spent most of February 1959 on Gibbon. Two years before, he had mentioned in a letter to Thompson at Cambridge that he would 'like very much to do a series of lectures or short book on History – the problems of causation in history, moral responsibility etc. I nibbled at it in the first chapter of *The New Society* in a way which no longer satisfies me, and I've been provoked by Berlin's *Historical Inevitability*. I think I have something fresh to say about all this, but it means taking 3 or 6 months out from my other work. I'm not committing myself yet.'[56] When Berlin delivered his Inaugural at Oxford, he was tempted to review it. 'But I daren't – oh! I daren't –', he told a friend.[57] What had changed by 1959 was that Kitson Clark and the other historians at Trinity had asked him to deliver the second series of lectures in honour of Trevelyan early in 1961; they wanted to find out what his work was all about and fully expected that he would treat the occasion as an opportunity to talk about the Russian revolution.

Instead Carr took the chance to write about history in general. 'I could not very well refuse such a[n] invitation,' he wrote; 'nor did I want to refuse it, as I have been looking for some time for an opportunity to deliver a broadside on history in general and on some of the nonsense which is talked about it by Popper and others.' A not unimportant motive was to launch a counter-attack on Berlin for his onslaught, *Historical Inevitability*. He had explained to Deutscher that the lectures would be an attempt 'to answer, among other things, the foolish remarks of Popper, Isaiah Berlin, etc. about history in general and revolution in particular'.[58]

This preliminary reading kept him busy until he could resume work on the *History of Soviet Russia* in the last week of March 1959. The rest of the spring and summer was spent researching the Comintern and German diplomatic sources at the Foreign Office library in London. Joyce, meanwhile, had now found time to put their new quarters into proper shape: 'we have been living

---

[54] Carr, *Socialism in One Country*, vol. 2, p. 227.
[55] Ibid., p. 454.
[56] Carr to Thompson, 15 April 1957: *RF* RG2 GC., 1957, 401, Carr, E.H., f. 371.
[57] Carr to Niuta Kallin, 13 July 1958: *BBC*: E.H. Carr Talks II.
[58] Carr to Deutscher, 29 March 1960: *DA*, 19.

in a world of painting, carpentery, curtains and carpets etc. which seems to me infinitely boring', he told Deutscher.[59] His attempt to resume the old schedule was occasionally broken by the onset of fatigue. Nevertheless the American trip went ahead as envisioned. On 10 September he and Joyce set sail for San Francisco. During the month at sea he counted on working without interruptions and distractions, and it was here that he began on the Trevelyan lectures. By the time the ship docked on 11 October he had 'practically completed the first draft'. They took the train to Palo Alto and moved in to 2105 Birch Street, 'a small and undistinguished house in a quiet street off campus . . . something under two miles from Hoover',[60] their home through to the last week in May 1960. The only problem was that it did not lie within walking distance of the Center for Advanced Study, nestled in the foothills above Stanford. So Joyce bought a car and ferried him in each morning and home to tea each afternoon. It was a marvellous place to work. 'Everything is fine here and the conditions are ideal for the job, except that there is really too much material and one does not know where to stop.' Joyce confided to Tamara: Ted 'spends 1 day a week at Hoover – which has a new Director, an economist from Washington and appointed by Mr Hoover himself, so extremely right in his views. Ted says it's a sad place, everyone bitter and frustrated at the lack of money and the dead hand of H[erbert] H[oover] over all. He himself is working terribly hard, too hard, and we haven't left P[alo] A[lto] since we arrived.'[61]

Unfortunately the availability of a microfilm printer – as yet unknown in Britain – also made it only too easy to accumulate material that was not entirely needed, and Carr's extraordinary self-discipline gave way to indulgence. As he confessed in a letter to Deutscher on 29 March 1960: 'What happened in a small way last time has happened this time in a big way, i.e., that coming over here has produced so much material and shown up so many inadequacies that it has set me back in point of time.'[62] Indeed, it had. Writing to Davies early in December 1959 he said that during the two months since his arrival, he had been working entirely on the Comintern, which he hoped to have finished by the end of the year before devoting a long stretch to far eastern matters which he had not yet touched upon at all.[63] He then took on one of the librarians, Olga Gankin, as a research assistant – much to the annoyance of the Hoover Institution when they found out later (this was tantamount to aiding and abetting the enemy) – and as a result his source base expanded into new, uncharted territory. Predictably he was before long 'Depressed by [the] mass of new material', and months more work on it made little significant impact. Time was nearly up on 20 April and he still felt 'a little despondent'. 'Last time I was over here, I collected so much material

---

[59] Carr to Deutscher, 27 June 1959: *DA*, 18.
[60] Carr to Arno Mayer, 29 March 1960: Arno Mayer's personal correspondence.
[61] Joyce to Tamara Deutscher, 1 March 1960: *DA* 19.
[62] Carr to Deutscher, 29 March 1960: ibid.
[63] Carr to Davies, 9 December 1959: *R.W. Davies Papers*.

that I felt when I returned that I was further than ever from finishing the Volume; and this time this has happened in a big way.'[64]

It is precisely at this point that Carr temporarily lost control over the larger perspective of the entire work. He had to place domestic developments in their international context, and it is unfortunate to say the least that his successors in the field all too often fail to do so. But Soviet foreign policy also included the activities of the Comintern and its national sections. As he confessed:

> My purpose is naturally not to write a history of the party [in this case the Polish Communist Party], but of its relations to Comintern, and I am constantly torn between the desire to omit nothing essential and the fear of becoming too much involved in local details. The thing is at best an unsatisfactory compromise, but I have this problem in regard to all the parties.[65]

He did, indeed. The net result, volume three of *Socialism in One Country*, completed in three parts in 1963, contains some brilliant passages – the introductory chapter on the principles of Soviet foreign policy; the description of the Soviet reaction to the Locarno Pact – but it is also padded with weary detail concerning obscure and entirely unsuccessful Communist Parties, all turned out to perfection, though unfortunately at the expense of the general reader.

Carr ended the stay at Stanford on 27 May 1960 and Joyce and he moved on to Boston, where he spent twenty-four hours sleeping off the farewells in Stanford and the night flight. At the Russian Research Center he launched into a further bout of research and that kept him busy for June. As a result he did not arrive back home until 10 July and thereafter wrote continuously through to September. It was as though meningitis had never touched him.

The only break in this gruelling schedule came with a chance to revisit Moscow. He had been unable to get there during the postwar years; since then, no archives of the Soviet period had been opened to foreign scholars; moreover it had been impossible for foreigners to interview former figures such as Molotov. But with the thaw following Khrushchev's denunciation of Stalin, east–west academic contacts were opened at the official level and Carr, Butterfield, Seton-Watson, Bolsover and Webster were invited to Moscow for a conference as guests of the Institute of History, Academy of Sciences. Carr hoped to 'sound out the possibilities of working there later or perhaps of getting books or microfilms. I shall at any rate get some impression of the general atmosphere.'[66]

They flew to Moscow via Amsterdam on 5 September 1960 and stayed at the Hotel Natsional. Carr was already very exhausted. Unwell for a couple of days, he missed some of the meetings and a trip to Leningrad. But on 9

[64] Carr to Davies, 20 April 1959: ibid.
[65] Carr to Davies, 10 May 1960: *DA*, 19.
[66] Carr to Deutscher, 23 August 1960: ibid., 21.

September he was up and about. 'Far too much time was occupied by conferences and social occasions,' he commented, typically, to Davies, 'but I did manage to investigate two libraries.' This he did over three days in the absence of the rest of the delegation:

> The Lenin Library is well organized but one has to cope with a lot of red tape at the start. It has a large public catalogue on which I spent a great deal of time, though I was often surprised at what was not in it . . . . You get a reader's ticket, and if you have academic rank . . . you get a ticket admitting you to Number One Reading Room. This not only gives you greater comfort, but in this room you are apparently sometimes able to get things which are not in the public catalogue (though nobody would admit that there was in fact another catalogue). The trouble about this is that you have to know exactly what to ask for.[67]

Carr also visited the Fundamental Library of the Social Sciences which came under the Academy, but found little of value. The visit to Moscow was thus a useful reconnaissance and, indeed, before long the more vigorous and youthful Davies would be making regular sorties – on a rigorous diet of coffee and aspirin – courtesy of the cultural exchange agreements signed between the British and Soviet Governments. Yet Carr himself scarcely needed more material. He returned home on 13 September somewhat tired. The remainder of the month was spent on foreign relations. Finally on 27 September he got down to redrafting the Trevelyan lectures that he was due to deliver from January to March 1961.

---

[67] Davies to Carr, 20 September 1960: *R. W. Davies Papers*.

8

What is History?

Delivered to a packed lecture-room on Mill Lane, Cambridge, from January to March 1961, Carr's carefully crafted Trevelyan lectures were a highly individual contribution to an age-old debate on the tensions between causation and chance, free will and determinism, the individual and society, and subjectivity and objectivity. They were peppered with vivid quotation, lucid to the point of transparency, as provocative as possible, and especially notable in three distinct respects: the forceful counter-attack against Isaiah Berlin for his condemnation of determinism in the Auguste Comte lecture on 'Historical Inevitability' eight years before; the controversial claim that one finds objectivity through working as if from some point in the future; and, last but not least, the assertion of the relativism of historiography. The first re-opened a latent conflict with Berlin; the second led directly to the opening of a new front by Hugh Trevor-Roper; and the final thrust enraged establishment historians such as Geoffrey Elton, who considered it a wholesale attack on the standards of the profession. Moreover, on a parochial note, they also prompted the reform of the syllabus for the History Tripos at Cambridge.

But was Carr serious? The most striking feature of the lectures is that at least in one critical respect they appear to stand at odds with the nature of the history he had been writing for the past decade and a half: how could he talk about the relativism of history-writing, while writing a history so firmly cast in a thoroughly deterministic framework of the past? And how could he at one and the same time argue that Berlin was wrong about determinism and yet he was himself right about relativism? In fact the lectures reflect something of a dissonance, of unresolved dilemmas, of an internalized debate that had been buzzing through Carr's mind during moments of quiet reflection at the very least since the closing months of the war when he had taken up the practice of history as a profession.

What is History? thus remained a question in his own mind, despite the apparent certainty of some of his answers. In this sense it belongs much more with the *Romantic Exiles* – with the detached, sceptical, but utopian side of Carr's mind – than it does with the *History of Soviet Russia*; or, at the very least, it represents an uneasy synthesis between the two approaches. As he noted in discussing those lectures years later, when forced to choose between the cynics 'who find no sense in anything' and 'Utopians, who make sense of things on the basis of some magnificent unverifiable assumption about the future', he always preferred the latter. It was also closer in style to his earlier works; even more carefree, perhaps; 'frivolous' was a term he liked in this kind of connection. Moreover, he always had a tendency to lurch between his 'needlework' (detailed empricial research and writing) and grand, irresponsible generalizations. *What is History?* most certainly belongs in the latter category, and to say so is by no means to dismiss its value; on the contrary, written in the style of many other, dry as dust works on the nature of history, including those of some of Carr's most vehement critics, it is unlikely that it would have stirred the profession, or continued to stimulate sixth-formers and university students alike.

The sense of the relativism of historiography had been part of him for a very long time. It was, as we have seen, while he was still an undergraduate that the 'rather undistinguished classics don' who specialized in the Persian Wars had first shown Carr that Herodotus' account 'not only contained a lot of pure mythology, but was shaped and moulded by his attitude to the Peloponnesian War, which was going on at the time he wrote'. This was 'a fascinating revelation, and gave me my first understanding of what history was about'.[1] But this revelation, reinforced in the 1940s by reading Collingwood and Croce, stood side by side and in constant tension with the predominantly Rankean, Victorian or, indeed, Marxist sense of history as some kind of science. For Carr always believed in progress. In a letter to the Cambridge economist Joan Robinson he outlined its importance. 'Neither history nor economics can be fitted into a timeless picture. Change,' he emphasized,

> is of the essence. I suppose you must in the end postulate some absolute – which I would call, for want of better words, growth in economics and progress in history. 'Nil growth' economics is surely an absurdity; people who talk about it mean that they want growth of some different kind. Otherwise it becomes as senseless as in history a return to the Middle Ages or to primitive man.[2]

In a leader in the *Times Literary Supplement* on 19 June 1953 Carr aptly portrayed the dilemma for the philosopher of history as one of 'balancing uneasily on the razor edge between the hazards of objective determinism and the bottomless pit of subjective relativity'.[3]

There are indeed even within the *History of Soviet Russia* some traces of Collingwood. There Carr aimed to place his mind 'in sympathetic communion with the minds of the actors in his drama, to reconstruct the

---

[1] *Autobiographical sketch.*
[2] Carr to Robinson, no date.
[3] 'Victorian History', *Times Literary Supplement*, 19 June 1953.

processes of their thought, to penetrate their conclusions and the motives which dictated their action'.[4] He had also emphasized that

> the facts do not, as is sometimes said, 'speak for themselves', or if they do it is the historian who decides which facts shall speak – he cannot give the floor to them all. And the decision of the most conscientious historian – of the historian most conscious of what he is doing – will be determined by a point of view which others may call biased.[5]

This 'uneasy' balance of course tilted decisively in favour of the 'scientific' tradition. And this happened not only from ingrained habit but also in conscious reaction to the high emotionalism and partisanship of the Cold War. By any standards its outbreak was disturbing, particularly to those who valued old-fashioned liberal Victorian virtues. As has often been said, but usually in relation to military conflict, truth is the first casualty of war. This was no less true of the Cold War. In an editorial on 'Truth in History', published on 1 September 1950, he strongly championed the cause of objectivity:

> Objective history does not exist. It was recently pointed out in these pages that the great Ranke, who claimed to expound history 'as it really happened', had some particularly strident axes of his own to grind. Many western writers have emphasized the inescapable influence of the time, place and situation of the historian on his view of history . . . . The real issue lies, however, deeper. The question is not whether objectivity is attained or attainable by historians, but whether the concept of objectivity in history has any meaning. To assert that fallible human beings are too much entangled in circumstances of time and place to attain the absolute truth is not the same thing as to deny the existence of truth: such a denial destroys any possible criterion of judgement, and makes any approach to history as true or as false as any other . . . it is possible to maintain that objective truth exists, but that no historian by himself, or no school of historians by itself, can hope to achieve more than a faint and partial approximation to it.[6]

The height of the Cold War was a time for taking sides; but this he and Deutscher had refused to do, difficult though it was. And it was in reaction to the self-evident threat to the notion of objectivity that Carr had increasingly felt obliged to defend it. In a further leader entitled 'Progress in History' published on 18 July 1952, he used G.P. Gooch's *History and Historians in the Nineteenth Century* as a convenient point of departure. He acknowledged the subjectivity inherent in the process of research and writing, but expressed concern lest this be taken too far:

> The very conviction that 'facts' are neutral, and that progress consists in discovering the facts and learning lessons from them, is the product of a rational-liberal

---

[4] Carr, *The Bolshevik Revolution*, vol. 1, p. v.
[5] 'History without Bias', *Times Literary Supplement*, 30 December 1960.
[6] 'Truth in History', ibid., 1 September 1950.

outlook on the world which cannot be so easily taken for granted today as it was by our more fortunately placed nineteenth-century ancestors.

Nevertheless, while there can be no return for the contemporary historian to this comfortable anchorage in delusively smooth waters, we have travelled far enough along the road of 'history with a purpose', and of a relativistic attitude to the facts, to realize the chasms that yawn on the right and on the left. Even in this country, where the liberal tradition has remained, perhaps, at its strongest, the embarrassments and misunderstandings attendant on the writing of modern German history during the past forty years, or of modern Russian history today, have been serious enough to inspire a certain nostalgia for a world in which it was still possible to exalt the facts above the conclusions to be drawn from them; and these embarrassments have been as nothing in comparison with what has happened in the Soviet Union, where whole series of well-known facts have disappeared from the record, and recent historical documents have been mutilated, in the interests of currently accepted doctrine. In a world in which there is perhaps a greater danger than ever before of historians being rated not according to the wealth of their learning or understanding, but according to the orthodoxy of their opinions, the appeal to the sanctity of facts has not yet exhausted its cogency. The 'liberty to know and to utter above all other liberties' – the famous text from the *Areopagitica* which DR GOOCH invokes at the end of his new preface – has not become less important because the opportunities of its infringement and the difficulties of its attainment are today so much more subtle and complex than historians of the nineteenth century had imagined.[7]

It is this emphasis in 1952 which differs so markedly from the lectures delivered in 1961.

When liberalism appeared under fierce attack from both sides, Carr came out to defend it; but as soon as that threat had diminished, he felt free to attack it and did so with vigour. What had changed by 1961 was that, for all the crises that continued in east–west relations, there had been an improvement in the atmosphere since Stalin, and Carr was always the defiant optimist. Millions had been released from the Gulag and, in Moscow, Alexander Solzhenitsyn was soon to publish the story of a day in the life of an inmate. The superpowers were now discussing a nuclear test-ban. To Carr

the world was a disturbed, even menacing, place. Nevertheless signs had begun to accumulate that we were beginning to emerge from some of our troubles. The world economic crises, widely predicted as a sequel to war, had not occurred. We had quietly dissolved the British Empire, almost without noticing it. The crises of Hungary and Suez had been surmounted, or lived down. De-Stalinization in the USSR, and de-McCarthyization in the USA, were making laudable progress. Germany and Japan had recovered rapidly from the total ruin of 1945, and were making spectacular economic advances. France under De Gaulle was renewing her strength. In the United States the Eisenhower blight was ending; the Kennedy era of hope was about to dawn. Black spots – South Africa, Ireland, Vietnam –

---

[7] 'Progress in History', ibid., 18 July 1952.

could still be kept at arm's length. Stock exchanges round the world were booming.[8]

And, personally, by January 1961, he no longer felt quite as isolated as before, nor so embattled. There seemed less need to stand by traditional values; indeed, those very values might block the path to further progress. In short the Trevelyan lectures would have read very differently had they been written a decade earlier.

In June 1950 Carr had published a leader in the *Times Literary Supplement* that opened hostilities with a firm rebuke to Berlin for intellectual escapism, for praising 'even a degree of indulgence in idle talk, idle curiosity, aimless pursuit of this or that', for advocating scepticism and 'turning a fastidious back on the disturbing and uncongenial realities of contemporary society . . .'.[9] Perhaps taking him at his word and taking a clear stand, Berlin launched an attack on *The Bolshevik Revolution* in the *Sunday Times* on 10 December 1950. The Russian revolution, wrote Berlin, was 'much the greatest and most tragic issue of our time'. In addressing the issue, Carr was 'uniquely well-equipped for his great task' in his scholarship, his powers of assimilating the material, his capacity for limpid exposition. But he had 'a very definite point of view' which was 'a formidable weapon in his practised hands'. 'Mr. Carr', he went on,

> is deeply affected by the contempt for liberalism made fashionable in the last century by Hegel; he sees history as a procession of events ruled by inexorable laws, which only a fool or a madman would try to ignore or resist or deflect; and like Hegel (and Marx) the tone of his writing suggests that there is something childish or quixotic in approving or deploring the consequences of these laws. The proper task of a rational man is to adjust himself to this great pattern; of the historian to make clear the direction pursued by the central stream of history, and of the men and nations triumphantly afloat upon it, without so much as a background glance at unrealized possibilities upon which great hopes and fears had once been focused, still less upon the victims and casualties of the process.

In Berlin's opinion 'Mr. Carr sees history through the eyes of the victors; the losers have for him all but disqualified themselves from bearing witness.' What particularly worried him was its success. It was 'much the most important contribution made to its subject for many years in any language'. 'If Mr. Carr's remaining volumes equal this impressive opening they will constitute the most monumental challenge of our time to that ideal of impartiality and objective truth and even-handed justice in the writing of history which is most deeply embedded in the European liberal tradition.' He was surely exaggerating; the walls of academe did not cave in, the best of the *History of*

---

[8] Draft for an introduction to a projected new version of *What is History?* In the author's possession.

[9] 'The New Scepticism', *Times Literary Supplement*, 9 June 1950.

Soviet Russia was absorbed without the associated belief system, and it was a measure of the stature of the work that this could so easily be done. But Berlin was not satisfied. At that time no one was writing serious history of Soviet Russia; so his fears could not have seemed entirely unreasonable. Perhaps he felt his own judgement swaying under the impact of Carr's persuasive presentation. There was within Berlin a deep-seated ambivalence towards him.

The attack was followed in October 1951 with a review of Carr's collection of essays, *Studies in Revolution*:

> whereas in previous years his attitude toward his subjects – Herzen, Bakunin, and indeed Marx himself – bordered on ironical detachment, and he saw them as so many gifted eccentrics, remarkable, even fascinating, but to a sane, well-balanced Englishman inevitably a trifle comical, the source of amused affection free from bitterness or contempt, he has, with the advancing years, lost this mood. It is as if the tragedy of our time makes him consider such innocent entertainment as being no longer appropriate; for we have reached a crucial parting of the ways, and we must choose our path irrevocably. Mr Carr leaves no doubt about his choice . . . . Mr Carr has never concealed his dislike of liberals and is not averse to casting a protective mantle over extremists, however foolish or misguided he may think them to be . . . .[10]

The next barrage was discharged at the first Auguste Comte Memorial Trust Lecture on 12 May 1953 at the London School of Economics, which Carr attended. It was published a year later. Clearly what worried Berlin most was the feeling deeply held that determinism eliminated the notion of individual responsibility.[11] In writing disapprovingly of the tendency to adopt a position of moral relativism in making judgements about the events of history, his only footnoted example is to 'the impressive and influential writings of Professor E.H. Carr on the history of our time'.[12] And it is no accident, as *Pravda* used to say, that in criticizing the tendency to attribute to abstract entities a life of their own apart from human will, 'agencies and forces at large in the world, which we have but little power to control or deflect',[13] Berlin cites 'collectivism' as one of three examples (the others being war and doom); there was no need to say who was the great apostle of collectivism he had in mind. Similarly, he attacked those who insisted on refraining from moral judgements on historical figures.

> We are also told that as historians it is our task to describe, let us say, the great revolutions of our own time without so much as hinting that certain individuals involved in them not merely caused, but were responsible for, great misery and destruction – using such words according to the standards not merely of the

---

[10] *International Affairs*, October 1951, p. 471.
[11] I. Berlin, *Auguste Comte Memorial Lecture no.1: Historical Inevitability*, London 1954, p. 25.
[12] Ibid., p. 43.
[13] Ibid., p. 72.

twentieth century which is soon over, or of our declining capitalist society but of the human race at all the times and in all the places in which we have known it; and told that we should practise such objectivity out of respect for some imaginary scientific canon which distinguishes between facts and values very sharply, so sharply that it enables us to regard the former as being objective, 'inexorable' and therefore self-justifying, and the latter merely as a subjective gloss upon events – due to the moment, the *milieu*, the individual temperament – and consequently unworthy of serious scholarship, of the great, hard edifice of dispassionate historical construction.[14]

Berlin probably had no idea just how effective the polemical onslaught was; not that it changed Carr's mind in any fundamental respect, but it was deeply wounding all the same, to an extent that became evident only eight years later. It is perhaps worth reminding the lay reader of the extraordinary vulnerability of intellectuals to the written word, especially when it is selected, honed and aimed with the precision that a Carr or a Berlin could achieve. Not that Carr would show this openly; indeed, his review of Berlin's lecture, when published in December 1954, was the perfect model of restraint. On the issue of determinism, he asked:

> is it really so difficult to reconcile the principle of causation in history with the principle of moral responsibility? Most people would be perfectly ready to attribute, say, a sudden increase in crime to such impersonal factors as bad housing or the incidence of a great war (and this is the kind of cause which historians normally seek to establish), without ceasing at the same time to hold the individual criminal to account.

In other words, causation works on more than one level, and at least one of these levels allows for moral responsibility. On the issue of moral judgements, Carr reiterated his belief that this is not the function of the historian, whose obligation was confined to explanation. And he concluded that all these fundamental problems had 'received fresh illumination from Mr. BERLIN's sparkling and trenchant criticism'.[15] Carr had sent a copy of it before publication: the review was indeed so anodyne that Berlin thought it 'perfectly fair and generous, down to the very last word'.[16]

What had happened in the interim was that, as Carr later complained, Berlin's disciples consistently used his lecture as a means of attacking Carr's work. One aim of the Trevelyan lectures was thus to counter-attack, and he did so in terms which caricatured Berlin's actual position:

> In 1954 Sir Isaiah Berlin published his essays on *Historical Inevitability*. He . . . added . . . the argument, not found in Popper, that the 'historicism' of Hegel and Marx is objectionable because, by explaining human actions in causal terms, it

---

[14] Ibid., p. 77.
[15] 'History and Morals', *Times Literary Supplement*, 17 December 1954.
[16] Berlin to Carr, 3 December 1954: *Carr Papers*.

implies a denial of human free will, and encourages historians to evade their supposed obligation . . . to pronounce moral condemnation on the Charlemagnes,
Napoleons, and Stalins of history. Otherwise not much has changed. But Sir Isaiah
Berlin is a deservedly popular and widely-read writer. During the past five or six
years, almost everyone in this country or in the United States who has written an
article about history, or even a serious review of a historical work, has cocked a
knowing snook at Hegel and Marx and determinism, and pointed out the absurdity
of failing to recognize the role of accident in history. It is perhaps unfair to hold Sir
Isaiah responsible for his disciples. Even when he talks nonsense, he earns our
indulgence by talking it in an engaging and attractive way. The disciples repeat the
nonsense, and fail to make it attractive . . . . It is Professor Popper and Sir Isaiah
Berlin who between them have flogged this very dead horse back into a semblance
of life; and some patience will be required to clear up the muddle.[17]

For although the Auguste Comte lecture had quoted Bernard Berenson,
who took the view that patterns of causation could not be traced from the
events of the past in attacking the 'Moloch' of 'historical inevitability', and in
this sense gave hostage to fortune by leaning too much in this direction in the
remainder of the text, Berlin had, in responding to Carr's review of the lecture, insisted: 'I don't dream of denying causes in history; or the need for cool
judgement; only that all causes are "impersonal" and mostly neutral; and that
individuals play little part; or do as they do because they cannot help it;
whereas I think they are among the main causal initiators of change (or its
absence) and responsible accordingly. All I want to do is to say the individual
acts cannot be wholly analysed into impersonal influences: only to the extent
of 90%, say.'[18] And whereas a letter such as this could easily have been lost, it
remained among the very few that Carr thought worth keeping; so there can
be little doubt that, at the time he attacked Berlin, he was consciously exaggerating his opponent's position for effect.

When the lectures were broadcast over the BBC and subsequently also
printed in the *Listener*, both in slightly abbreviated form, they not surprisingly
elicited a letter of protest from Berlin. The letter began and ended on a
waspish tone, smarting at the anonymity of Carr's *TLS* reviews. 'My friend Mr.
E.H. Carr is to be congratulated on casting off the cloak of anonymity which
he has so often worn when castigating his opponents,' he began, claiming he
did not hold that '1) determinism must be false; 2) historians should not look
for causes of human action; 3) it is the positive duty of historians to give
good and bad marks to the principal personages whose acts they discuss.' He
reiterated the positions he gave in his lecture, praised Carr's 'clear, vigorous
and agreeable' prose; and he concluded that Carr's 'short way with the problem of individual freedom and responsibility . . . is a warning to us all of what
may happen to those who, no matter how learned or perspicacious, venture
into regions too distant from their own' and, tongue in cheek, offered his

---

[17] Carr, *What is History?*, London 1961, pp. 91–3.
[18] Berlin to Carr, 3 December 1954.

'sympathy as he gropes his way in the difficult, treacherous and unfamiliar field of philosophy of history'.[19]

Berlin was, of course, not alone in responding to Carr's barbs. But in a letter responding to most of his critics, Carr dedicated the larger space to answering him. On the first point he insisted that 'Over and over again, he seeks to show that determinism is incompatible with the "notion of individual responsibility"... which he emphatically endorses. If these arguments do not lead to the conclusion that "determinism must be false", I do not see where they lead.' On the second point, Carr misses the mark completely. But on the third point he argues: 'Sir Isaiah sharply dissents from the view . . . "that it is foolish to judge Charlemagne or Napoleon or Genghis Khan or Hitler or Stalin for their massacres" and from the view that it is "absurd" or "not our business as historians" to praise "benefactors of humanity". I took this to mean that it *is* wise and sensible and our business as historians to award good or bad marks to outstanding figures of the past.'[20] The real weakness in Carr's position was that he had wilfully misrepresented Berlin as having opposed the notion of causation. This prompted another letter from Berlin, to which Carr chose to reply confidentially. Here there was a tone of contrition, an attempt to make amends without conceding too much but explaining why he had 'probably overstated' his case: 'if I have to stand in a white sheet,' Carr wrote,

> I should like to plead extenuating circumstances . . . . It seems to me that when a writer piles up arguments which point to a particular conclusion, he cannot be altogether surprised if the reader assumes that this is the conclusion which he wanted to draw. If I have erred on this point, I have erred in common with people from whose views I normally dissent. Each volume of my history which has appeared since 1953 has been greeted by reviewers of the type of Schapiro and Footman with the charge, in terms obviously borrowed from you (neither has ever been guilty of an original idea), that I have embraced the false doctrines of determinism and inevitability.[21]

Berlin was still irritated but evidently appreciated Carr's effort at reconciliation and shared with him the amusing tale of having received a postcard from his colleague A.L. Rowse, historian of Elizabethan England and the first Trevelyan lecturer. Plumb tells us Rowse attended subsequent lectures 'tottering down the lecture hall in gown grown bottle-green with age, swathed in an overcoat which he told me had belonged to his father, brown muffler, grim moustache, steel spectacles, to a warm outburst of welcome . . .'.[22] Rowse thoughtfully advised Berlin that in one of the chapters of his own book on *The Use of History* all the problems had 'long ago been satisfactorily settled and that there was really no need for either your or my remarks on the subject'. His

---

[19] *Listener*, 18 May 1961.
[20] Ibid., 1 June 1961.
[21] Carr to Berlin, 27 June 1961.
[22] J. Plumb, *The Making of an Historian*, Hertfordshire 1988, p. 280.

postcard ends characteristically with the words 'Ever troubled to read it [i.e., his book] any of you?' 'My controversy with Isaiah has now been diverted into private correspondence, which is better,' Carr confided to a friend, 'though I don't think he is wholly appeased.'[23]

Although the defence of his position on determinism sounded lame, Berlin successfully scored on the issue of moral judgements. 'I know of no historians,' Berlin wrote, 'who do not in fact, either by commission or by omission, pass moral judgements: after all you yourself identify some forces or persons as progressive, others as futile or troublesomely reactionary – your evaluation of Lenin – in contrast let us say with Dr. Katkov's – cannot be in much doubt.' And Carr's retort 'that the historian must make up his mind whether he thinks Passchendale or Munich or Suez was justified. But he should not, in my view, judge the character of Haig or Chamberlain or Eden, however many lives lost or however much suffering may have resulted from their decisions' is unlikely ever to find widespread assent. 'I suppose I shall have to bear your now admittedly over-stern strictures in stoical silence when your book appears,' Berlin wrote. 'I don't mind a little caricature,' he continued, 'but I don't want to look too foolish.' Could Carr enclose a footnote in the book 'to the effect that in our exchange in the *Listener*, I satisfied you that I do not in fact hold all the views that you thought I did'.[24] But Carr claimed that it was already too late – it was July 1961 – as the publishers would produce the complete version by the end of September.[25] It appeared appeasement had ended. Berlin therefore re-opened hostilities. In reviewing *What is History?* for the *New Statesman* after it appeared in December, Berlin opened a new sector of the front against Carr, in what was now an intermittent series of engagements in a war that had gone on since of the forties.

The review was suitably entitled 'Mr. Carr's Big Battalions'. Berlin had long ago first attacked what he took to be Carr's Hegelianism, though one might as easily have seen him as teleological in the model of Kant. In *What is History?* Carr presented his view of 'history as progress' and in so doing cited with qualified approval Hegel's dictum that 'only those people can come under our notice which form a state' and reasserted his own belief that 'by and large, the historian is concerned with those who, whether victorious or defeated, achieved something. I am not a specialist in the history of cricket', he added, 'but its pages are presumably studded with the names of those who made centuries rather than of those who made ducks and were left out of the side.' For Berlin this was fair game. As far as he was concerned the only goals that Carr saw in history were 'simply whatever in fact will turn out to have occurred. On this view,' Berlin wrote, 'whatever occurs is good because it occurs – we know the stages we have passed through have been the right goals only because they have been realized.' This was, he concluded, 'the source of

---

[23] Carr to Kallin, 19 July 1961: *BBC*: E.H. Carr Talks, File II.
[24] Berlin to Carr, 3 July 1961.
[25] Carr to Berlin, 18 July 1961.

Mr. Carr's entire view of history as the story of the big battalions, and of progress as being whatever those in power will in fact achieve'.[26] This was not entirely unfair, although it failed to acknowledge Carr's significant caveat that 'Pregnant failures are not unknown in history. History recognizes what I may call "delayed achievement": the apparent failures of today may turn out to have made a vital contribution to the achievement of tomorrow – prophets born before their time. Indeed,' he added, perspicaciously, 'one of the advantages of this criterion over the criterion of a supposedly fixed and universal principle is that it may require us to postpone our judgement or qualify it in the light of things that have not yet happened.'[27]

The irony of Berlin's attack lay in the fact that it was originally he – in a BBC broadcast in 1957 – who had claimed that 'that which works best' rather than some abstract universal principle was a criterion of judgement in history. But of course what he was really attacking was less the lecture than the philosophy that lay behind Carr's own *History of Soviet Russia*; and in this respect he was certainly not wide of the mark. Indeed, in Carr's unpublished reply to the review, he chided Berlin: 'I am still puzzled by this winner-and-loser business. When I write my History of Cricket, I shall give space to Sir Jack Hobbs' 200 centuries. And you will call me a worshipper of big scores, and say that I have consigned to the rubbish heap the nice young man who muffed that catch and lost his place in the team. This seems peculiarly English.'[28]

There was no sign so far that Carr had reconsidered any basic position in the light of Berlin's strictures. But Berlin had, in his review, also returned to the issue of accident in history: 'If Churchill had died before 1939 or Stalin before 1924, is it arguable that these "accidents", although not "generalizable", would have been of no interest to anyone save biographers devoid of a sense of history? Surely Mr Carr here overstates his case.' And it is here that Berlin touched on a question that continued to bother Carr, the question of counterfactuals in history which he never resolved to his own satisfaction. Writing to Deutscher in December, Carr commented: 'I will not return now to the question of History. The matter of so-called "accidents" still worries me . . . . Surely Soviet history was affected by the "accidents" that Lenin died at 53 not 73, and Stalin at 73 not 53.'[29] Over a year later the question still lingered:

> The word 'accident' is unfortunate. Lenin's death was not strictly speaking an accident. It had no doubt perfectly definite causes. But these belong to medicine, and not to historical study. But it seems to me difficult to say that these causes, though extraneous to History, did not affect its course. Even if you maintain that in the long run everything would have turned out much the same, there is a short run which is important, and makes a great deal of difference to a great many people.

---

[26] I. Berlin, 'Mr. Carr's Big Battalions', *New Statesman*, 5 January 1962.
[27] Carr, *What is History?*, pp. 128–9.
[28] Carr to Berlin, 9 January 1962.
[29] Carr to Deutscher, 12 December 1960: *DA*, 20.

The same situation exists, in other sciences, which operate in a specific field, but whose results may be affected by extraneous influences. For instance, a doctor might diagnose a slow but incurable disease, which was likely to be fatal within a year or so. Nobody would suppose that this diagnosis would be invalidated if the patient was killed next day in a car smash. Of course, if History (or the field of any other science) were nothing but a succession of extraneous 'accidents', it could not be a serious study at all. But it is in fact subject to sufficient regularities to make it a serious study, though these regularities are from time to time interrupted or upset by extraneous elements. I do not find this very difficult, and no other approach seems to me convincing. The thesis that these 'accidents' either do not matter or cancel one another out still does not satisfy me.[30]

The distance between Carr and Berlin in respect to their views of history was thus in some respects not as great as the public polemic would suggest; it was with respect to their political beliefs that the distance was undeniable and unlikely ever to be bridged.

Berlin was followed in his attack, indeed even in his words, by the Regius Professor of Modern History at Oxford, Hugh Trevor-Roper. Trevor-Roper, having written little to his own credit before academic elevation, had previously launched high profile assaults on figures like Arnold Toynbee and A.J.P. Taylor with some success. In this instance it took the form of an article in *Encounter* published in May 1962 entitled 'E.H. Carr's Success Story'. The focus was on Carr's definition of objectivity. A historian is objective, Carr had written, first because 'he has the capacity to rise above the limited vision of his own situation in society and in history' by recognizing the degree to which he is a part of that situation; second, because 'he has the capacity to project his vision into the future in such a way as to give him a more profound and more lasting insight into the past than can be attained by those historians whose outlook is entirely bounded by their own immediate situation.' Thus, he concluded, the 'historian of the past can make an approach towards objectivity only as he approaches towards the understanding of the future'.[31]

The first statement will not come as a great shock to most historians who have thought deeply about themselves and society. But the second statement takes us nowhere, since the prediction of the future is inevitably entirely subjective and unlikely to be widely shared by other historians of opposing systems of belief. In no sense can this be called objectivity. And this, the weakest point in his entire exposition, was seized upon with some relish by Trevor-Roper. To Carr, he wrote, objectivity does not mean being uncommitted, 'but the exact opposite, being committed to that side which is going to win: to the big battalions'. In other words Carr's vision of the future was of those who succeeded, those who proved more powerful, like the Soviet Union. But Trevor-Roper revealed his own weak spot when he ventured several words too far. A recognized authority on early modern England, he assumed that because he

[30] Carr to Deutscher, 17 December 1963: *DA*, 24.
[31] Carr, *What is History?*, p. 123.

lived in the twentieth century he knew something of its history; but that scarcely qualifies anyone to pronounce on the accuracy of Carr's *History of Soviet Russia*. And one suspects that he may not have gone much beyond the first volume of the *Bolshevik Revolution* or, at least, the early reviews of it, in stating that 'No historian since the crudest ages of clerical bigotry has treated evidence with such dogmatic ruthlessness as this.'[32] One wonders how a specialist on early modern England is actually in a position to judge. It was undoubtedly to Carr's advantage to have his more articulate opponents tumble completely overboard in their urge to sink him and all his works.

The third major critic did not emerge into print until much later, but certainly not for want of indignation. The historian of Tudor England and later Professor of Modern History at Cambridge Geoffrey Elton, something of a rebel himself in earlier days, published *The Practice of History* in 1967. A true positivist, to the point of dogmatism, Elton took particular objection to those who thought 'that history is what historians write, not what happened', to 'the extreme relativism – of which Mr Carr is only a recent and by no means an extreme exponent'. He also considered it 'pernicious nonsense' that men could not eliminate themselves from the search for the truth; for him facts were clearly independent of the observer.[33] And he disliked Carr's search for a purpose in history.[34] In a sense this highlighted an important difference between them: for Carr, history was a process, interpretation of which could yield information; for Elton, history was a profession, whose duty it was to uncover existing facts. What appears to have driven Elton's attack is the belief that students might have their submission to the discipline of historical method subverted by Carr's somewhat whimsical and irresponsible view of history; certainly his focus on the 'practice of history' suggests as much. The manner in which he treats Carr's polemic and in reaction emphasizes the less glamorous aspects of the profession in turn prompted a counter-attack, in this instance from the Cambridge historian of eighteenth century France, Betty Behrens, who caricatured Elton for whom the 'purpose of history is the development of expertise' rather than 'the purpose of expertise' being 'the elucidation of history'.[35]

A somewhat unexpected voice echoing Elton was that of Isaac Deutscher, who published, anonymously as was then still the custom, a review of *What is History?* in the *Times Literary Supplement* in November 1961. Deutscher as a Marxist was as uncomfortable with the relativistic side of Carr's thinking as Elton: certain historical facts, he insisted, existed as historically significant events quite apart from the choice of the historian – indeed, their very existence called into being the historian's attention. In fact Carr was totally

---

[32] H. Trevor-Roper, 'E.H. Carr's Success Story', *Encounter*, May 1962, vol. XVIII, no.5, pp. 69–77.

[33] G. Elton, *The Practice of History*, London 1967, pp. 56–8. For a critical analysis of this and Elton's later work on the subject, turn to Q. Skinner, 'Sir Geoffrey Elton and the Practice of History', *Transactions of the Royal Historical Society*, 6th Series, vol. 7, 1997, pp. 301–16.

[34] Elton, *Practice of History*, pp. 39–40.

[35] Betty Behrens's notes.

inconsistent on this point. In an interview in 1978 he spoke of the revolution of 1917 as 'so dramatic and so sweeping in its consequences that it imposes itself on every historian as a turning-point in history';[36] this may be merely a rhetorical flourish, but it suggests a rather different view of the relationship between the historian and his 'facts' than that given in the Trevelyan lectures.[37] But what is perhaps more interesting about the review is Deutscher's characterization of Carr, who clearly fascinated him because he was so difficult to categorize. In one respect his attempt to do so rings true: 'Much though Mr. Carr has absorbed from the Marxist conception of history, he does not identify himself with it and maintains a certain reserve towards it; and in spite of his explicit criticisms of the British tradition, especially of its empiricist strand, he is of it, even if not quite in it.' But in another respect he appears wide of the mark: when scratched, he suggested, Carr turned out to be 75% liberal, 'the most unorthodox, radical, and open-minded British liberal of his generation'.[38] Such a definition stretches the term liberal rather more than it really allows; in a fundamental sense his ideology defied such convenient description, the language of current political philosophy being rather too limited for that.

In outlining so idiosyncratic a view of the nature of history it was hard to find anyone of note who entirely agreed with him, though there could be few who did not find something of value in Carr's Trevelyan lectures. A fellow anti-establishment figure like A.J.P. Taylor was delighted by the richness of the polemic – worthy of his own pen – but was none the less as troubled by the 'big battalions' as Trevor-Roper and Berlin:

> History, he insists, is movement. This is well said. But then he goes on to assert that the movement is all in one direction: upwards. Individuals, classes, nations may suffer; for the mass of mankind the march of events is set fair. Since things are getting better all the time, it follows that whatever produces these things should be welcomed by the historians.[39]

Taylor always found Carr's notion of progress an unshared act of faith. But in other respects, he found it very difficult to be consistent. He had begun by condemning Carr's *History of Soviet Russia* and ended up by praising it to the skies. In retrospect and in reaction to the first of several unpleasant posthumous assaults on Carr's reputation, Taylor claimed: 'I venerated him and I am proud to record that Ted Carr and I were bound together by ties of great mutual affection.'[40]

Carr certainly enjoyed Taylor's company, but he could not take him

---

[36] 'The Left Today: An Interview', *From Napoleon to Stalin And Other Essays*, London 1980, p. 264.
[37] Witness the following: 'The historian will strive to disentangle the different strands, and to sort out the casual from the significant. But his standard of significance can emerge only from the process of analysis . . .': *The October Revolution: Before and After*, London 1969, p. 165.
[38] 'Between Past and Future', *Times Literary Supplement*, 17 November 1961.
[39] A.J.P. Taylor, *Politicians, Socialism and Historians*, London 1980, p. 54.
[40] *London Review of Books*, 30 December 1982.

seriously. Taylor lacked the stabilizing core of beliefs that he held to be essential to the best historical work; however sparkling, indeed at times brilliant, he
could never be profound. Carr had reviewed Taylor's most substantial early
work, *The Struggle for Mastery in Europe, 1848–1918*, in the *Times Literary
Supplement* in November 1954. This raised the differences between them. To
the forefront was Carr's sceptical appreciation of the value of diplomatic history. Reviewing *Documents on British Foreign Policy, 1919–1939* (edited by Rohan
Butler and Sir Llewellyn Woodward) only a week or so before, Carr had
observed in the documents published 'the eclipse of diplomacy and of diplomatic history. The historian who seeks to tell the tragic story of the 1930s,' he
had continued, 'will have to reach levels far beneath those plumbed in the
official documents. The diplomatic historian, who appeared to be so trust-
worthy and revealing a guide to the origins of the First World War, can tell us
hardly any of the things that matter about the second.' This was no cause for
congratulation. At least

> diplomacy in its heyday did on the whole stand for the supremacy of reason: even
> its tricks and its lies were rational deceits. The vision of the world which we now
> have to face is rather a Kafka-like nightmare of forces impenetrable to rational
> persuasion and in part even inaccessible to rational understanding. Hitlerism,
> Stalinism, McCarthyism, anti-Semitism, racialism – we have names for some of
> these forces. Every rational person appears to speak loudly in condemnation of
> them: yet they sweep countries and continents, and threaten once more to engulf
> the world. These reflections are not a counsel of despair and are not intended to
> suggest that reason has no longer weapons to use in self-defence. But they spring
> from the vivid impression left by these documents of the helplessness and irrele-
> vance of the old diplomacy and the old diplomatic history, confronted with forces
> which they were not equipped by tradition and training to understand.

This theme reappears later in review. Discussing Richard Ullman's *Britain
and the Russian Civil War,*[41] he noted:

> History seen, thanks to the documents, through the eyes of these [Foreign Office
> clerks] and of a number of minor figures, tends to become personalized in a way
> we had begun to think of as old-fashioned. We are tempted, almost invited, to
> think of decisions taken in Paris about Russia [1919] as the product of a personal
> dual between Lloyd George and Churchill; and this impression may well be
> enhanced when we are allowed to see the still unpublished correspondence
> between the two statesmen. The documents, these documents at any rate, not only
> give no indication of the deeper forces at work which produced these confusions
> and these compromises, they positively obscure them: and these are the factors
> with which the historian is ultimately most concerned – the clash between the illu-
> sion of omnipotence commonly nourished by the victors in a great war and the
> reluctance of war-weary populations to engage in fresh elections, the clash
> between traditional British views of European monarchy or the British Empire and

---

[41] R. Ullman, *Britain and the Russian Civil War*, London 1968.

a new social outlook which Lloyd George, alone of the British delegates, dimly apprehended, the clash between underlying reactions to the Russian Revolution.[42]

One should therefore not be surprised that Taylor was not let off lightly, even though he was writing of the previous century, for he had conceived of a history of diplomacy in Europe totally divorced from the impact of economics and domestic politics. Apart from a promising introduction, his reliance on diplomatic documents prevented him from looking to the societies that conceived them (a criticism equally valid with respect to his *Origins of the Second World War*) and, therefore, at the fundamental forces in action pushing towards catastrophe: World War I. He had, in addition, ignored the expansion of the European powers beyond the shores of the continent. This undermined Taylor's treatment of the balance of power in Europe: 'If we examine the essence of the balance of power in this period, did it not in fact consist in the carefully balanced competitive expansion of Europe into other continents?' It was the ending of the scope for further expansion that 'brought this halcyon period to its inevitable *dénouement*'.

More fundamentally, Carr and Taylor also differed in respect to the issue of 'progress'. Taylor came close to associating himself with the view that most of history was a chapter of accidents:

> Mr. Taylor is so eager not to be taken for a Hegelian or a Marxist – or, *si parva licet* . . . , for a Spengler or a Toynbee – and to disclaim belief in determining causes or scientifically demonstrable trends, that he sometimes comes perilously near to the old Liberal view picturesquely propounded by Augustine Birrell, who once wrote that 'the fields of history should be kept for ever unenclosed, and a free breathing-space for a pallid population well-nigh stifled with the fumes of philosphy,' or by H.A.L. Fisher, who held that there is no pattern in history at all, but merely an accidental concatenation of unrelated events.

To Carr this explained why Taylor never reached the summit of achievement:

> If Mr. Taylor would shed his distaste for ideas, recognize that history would not be worth writing or reading if it had no meaning, and cease to give so many hostages to the assumption that the important explanations in history are to be found in the conscious purposes and foresights of the *dramatis personae*, he would stand in the front rank of living historians.[43]

Only those Carr considered hostile and in the top rank were deemed worthy of attack. He had taken a swipe at Herbert Butterfield, Master of Peterhouse and Professor of Modern History, but at no one else in Cambridge, largely no doubt because he considered them a 'not very distinguished historical community'.[44]

---

[42] 'Lloyd George, Churchill, and the Russian Revolution', Carr, *From Napoleon to Stalin*, p. 31.

[43] 'European Diplomatic History', *Times Literary Supplement*, 26 November 1954.

[44] Carr to Deutscher, 16 November 1965: *DA*, 26.

Since Carr had returned to Cambridge, he and Butterfield had seen 'quite a bit' of one another, usually over a lengthy meal with both wives present. Carr obviously found him interesting. There was also a curious congruity in their views. Although Butterfield took a 'christian' view of history, he also took a rather deterministic position and was as Machiavellian in his attitude to international relations as Carr; indeed, in his view Carr 'seemed more a disciple of *Realpolitik* than he really was'. He had shared Carr's position on appeasement, though fiercely objecting to the pro-Soviet position he took at *The Times*. And when Carr was preparing his lectures it seemed only natural to contact Butterfield for help on a few points – the location of Butterfield's comment that 'the only absolute in history is change' and the source of the remark that Namier had taken the mind out of history (Taylor).[45] But they were not on first name terms and there was certainly no trace of any affection in using Butterfield's *The Whig Interpretation of History* to illustrate the degree to which the historian transposed current beliefs into his interpretation of the past. Here Carr mocked Butterfield much as he had mocked Berlin, both in some fundamental sense outsiders, but both now pillars of the establishment. The book was remarkable, he jibed, 'not least because, though it denounced the Whig Interpretation over some 130 pages, it did not . . . name a single Whig except Fox, who was no historian, or a single historian save Acton, who was no Whig'. What was deemed wrong with that interpretation of history was that it 'studies the past with reference to the present'; it was, wrote Butterfield with a certain sanctimoniousness, 'the source of all sins and sophistries in history . . . . It is the essence of what we mean by the word "unhistorical".'

Carr, who saw this not as a sin but as an inevitable part of the process of writing history, now delighted in demonstrating that Butterfield himself had been as much a culprit in this as anyone. The years passed, Carr pointed out, and Butterfield published another book called *The Englishman and His History* in which he spoke enthusiastically of the 'marriage between the present and the past'. The fashion for iconclasm ended with the war; the Butterfield that wrote provocatively before the conflict wrote conservatively after the outbreak of hostilities. Not surprisingly this annoyed Butterfield, though not perhaps as much as Carr's other jibes had infuriated Berlin. And when Ved Mehta interviewed all the participants in the British debates on the nature of history – including Carr – Butterfield took the opportunity to voice his objections and to point out that the second book was in fact based on a lecture given in 1938 rather than in the middle of the war. But when asked by Carr, Butterfield was unable to come up with the text of the lecture.

Carr responded by letter. 'The climate in 1938 was already very different from that of 1930,' he wrote; 'and, if you made the jump earlier than some of us, all honour to you.' He confessed to finding 'the evolution of opinion

---

[45] Carr to Butterfield, 2 February 1960. For the source of the remark about Namier: 'Accident Prone, or What Happened Next': Taylor, *Politicians, Socialism and Historians*, p. 9.

under the influence of the social environment a fascinating topic. What puzzles me', he added, 'is that this study should be felt as something derogatory to the individual. On the contrary, it seems to me to be an essential part of the individual's make-up.'[46] He had perhaps forgotten the way in which Isaac Deutscher's review of his own work in these *ad hominem* terms in 1955 had upset him so much.

One of the reasons why Butterfield was a target, other than the fact that he had coveniently exposed himself in a manner that delivered him into Carr's hands as a convenient example, was that, although well-regarded, Carr had never been made to feel welcome in the history faculty of which Butterfield was a leading luminary; and Butterfield had been given the Chair that Carr had been denied over a decade ago. This sense of alienation doubtless sharpened his critical focus with respect to the notorious parochialism of that community. In this respect his admission to Trinity as a fellow was an unusually generous exception to the rule. Perhaps even more than Butterfield, the Cambridge History Tripos presented a very easy target. Carr knew it well enough; he had been an external examiner for nearly two decades. Quoting Acton – the Regius Professor at Cambridge at the end of the nineteenth century – on the importance of 'universal' as against purely national histories, he asked where Cambridge now stood in the implementation of this ideal. To treat the history of the English-speaking world as the centrepiece of universal history was, he suggested, 'an unhappy distortion of perspective. It is the duty of a university to correct such popular distortions' and the school of modern history at Cambridge fell short 'in the discharge of this duty'. 'Lectures are, I am told, delivered in this university on the history of Russia and Persia and China – but not by members of the faculty of history . . . . What may well be regarded in the future as the greatest historical work produced in Cambridge during the past decade has been written entirely outside the history department and without any assistance from it: I refer to Dr Needham's *Science and Civilization in China*. This is a sobering thought.'[47]

The Trevelyan lectures ended in March 1961. In May proposals were mooted for syllabus reform and, after general discussion at a faculty meeting in November, a motion was duly put forward by Kitson Clark and seconded by Carr which asked the faculty board to set up a committee to review the Tripos. An unofficial group which included Needham and Carr then presented proposals for change to the board. But not until 1966, and after reducing the proposals of that group to a compromise more acceptable to doubters, were some of these ideas presented and debated in the senate. The debate was heated. Carr spoke not long after Elton, who attacked the proposals on the grounds that they would dilute the curriculum, leaving students with a more superficial knowledge of the subject, and little more. But, coming from those

---

[46] Carr to Butterfield, 8 January 1963.
[47] Carr, *What is History?*, p. 151.

who taught English or medieval history – the areas most likely to lose out –
such criticisms certainly did not sound entirely disinterested.

'The historian's standard of significance,' Carr declared, echoing the lectures, 'whether consciously or unconsciously, has of necessity some reference
to the present.' History could not stand still as an academic subject. The existing syllabus was 'mainly a pre–1914 affair. It assumes,' he continued, 'that
western Europe, and Great Britain in particular, is the power-house of history.'
The situation was 'absurd'. 'All we ask of the Cambridge historian is to recognize that there are countries which today lie outside the purview of history as
interpreted by the History Faculty in Cambridge, that some of these countries
have long and complicated histories which it is important to know about, and
that it is up to us as historians to promote and encourage the study of them.'
And as to claims that students would complete a degree without knowing this
or that, the changes would increase the optional element and this would be no
bad thing: 'History has become so vast a subject that nobody can pretend to
study more than a fraction of it. It is a dangerous dogmatism on our part to
seek to impose on the student a rigid choice of what parts of it he should think
important and worthy of study.'[48] The reformers won a partial victory.
American studies entered the curriculum as a field in its own right. More
modernists were appointed. Eventually an appointment in Russian history
was made, with Carr's letter of support: that of the young Norman Stone.[49]

Carr remained preoccupied with the nature of history. Normally he did
everything to avoid open-ended discussions on questions of fundamental
belief. History was an exception. This was, after all, the man who wrote both
the deterministic *History of Soviet Russia* and the story of tragic and futile
Romantic Exiles who, none the less, in his book 'have their place in history'.[50]
What is History? had not entirely satisfied him, and he continued to collect odd
items – mostly exchanges by letter with colleagues in which fundamental
issues of method arose – with a view to another excursion into this field. They
never added up to a complete entity, but some of the exchanges are worthy of
attention. The first is an answer to a review article published in the *Historical
Journal* in 1965 by Betty Behrens (of whom, more below). Her piece was entitled '"Straight History" and "History in Depth"'. Here she exposed some
confusions and inconsistencies in French writing on the revolution of 1789. In
reply, Carr wrote 'Revolutions and Their Historians', which for some reason
was never published. The Carr writing here is less the Carr of *What is History?*
than the Carr of the *History of Soviet Russia*: the specialist, not the sceptical and

---

[48] 18 January 1966: *Cambridge University Reporter*, 2 February 1966, p. 1020.

[49] For Stone's subsequent evaluation of his former referee's work: 'Grim Eminence', *London
Review of Books*, 20 January–2 February 1983. In February 1973 Carr wrote with respect to
Stone: 'I feel some guilty responsibility for him, because years ago I mistakenly supported
him for a university lectureship when the other candidates seemed even worse. He has now
been dropped (this time I backed, I hope, the right candidate [John Barber]), but keeps a
college job at Jesus – the most reactionary of the colleges.' – Carr to Tamara Deutscher, 19
February 1973.

[50] Carr, *The Romantic Exiles*, p. 241.

mocking critic. On the other hand, there is once again a curious divorce between his reflections on the nature of the subject and the manner in which he practised his profession. He writes on these occasions as though he were Keith Thomas, though his *History of Soviet Russia* does not normally read as though it were Keith Thomas writing. The way he wrote, despite the nod in Deutscher's direction, the rearrangement of the order of volumes and the recruitment of Davies, is very much as a classical historian of politics and diplomacy; even in dealing with the Comintern and member parties little or no attention was ever paid to the socio-economic conditions of the countries concerned. None the less the sense that this was not quite how it should be done evidently buzzed in his ear from time to time.

'Straight history' was to Carr's mind impossible; narrative was 'moulded around presuppositions'. The opposite to 'history in depth' was 'surely super-ficial history'. 'Wickham Steed's quip about digging deep and coming up muddy is countered by (of all people) Maeterlinck's remark (I quote from memory) that perfect clarity often betokens "*une certaine lassitude des idées*". Let us by all means stir up enough mud to compel professors to rewrite their books and lectures. Better deep and muddy than clean and shallow.' He went on:

> Put crudely, the function of the specialist is to knock holes in current generaliza-tions and compel the generalizer to think again. If therefore (to quote Dr Kitson Clark) history is being 'torn to pieces by the experts' or (to quote Miss Behrens) 'history as we used to know it is ceasing to exist', this is a perfectly normal process and a matter for congratulation: it is incidentally the process which Miss Behrens is helping to further by her article. And the generalizers inevitably lag behind the specialists. History is a difficult subject, and becomes still more difficult as knowl-edge increases. It is not unique in this respect.

The second 'and more serious dilemma' was the tension between the politi-cal and the socio-economic. Behrens identified 'straight history' with political history and 'history in depth' with the study of social and economic causes of political events. To Carr this seemed 'mysterious' since economic events in themselves constituted history. 'The notion that political events are history in some sense in which economic events are not, that history *tout court* means political history, and that economic history is somehow subsidiary to it, is unconscionably slow in dying.' But he was more worried about the identifi-cation of history in depth with social and economic history. This seemed to him too sectarian. 'A number of valid explanations can be found for any his-torical situation or event. Any historian worthy of the name will consciously or unconsciously sort out these multiple explanations, establish some order of precedence between them, and decide that some are profounder than others – or perhaps that one is the profoundest of all.' Reflecting his own, par-tially completed, conversion he argued for the primacy of the socio-economic in the hierarchy of explanation but phrased it, as ever, in a tone of detach-ment:

In the present century more and more historians have come to look to social and economic conditions for their profounder explanations . . . . It appears to reflect the current realization that our destinies are more deeply involved in social and economic issues than had hitherto been supposed, and that these issues form, so to speak, a backbone both of history and of contemporary politics.[51]

The sixties were very much the age of social science as well as of the revival of Marxism among the intelligentsia. The idea that history should become a mine for extensive exploitation by social scientists, and the corresponding notion, for historians, that social scientific methods could yield more from historical data, were soon seized upon by the young (and by faddish American scholars), for whom novelty itself is sometimes an automatic and uncritical recommendation for acceptance. Carr in many ways identified with the youth of the day – from a vantage-point of great detachment, it has to be said – favouring the new informality of dress and the notion of admitting women to Trinity, but he was never really responsive to intellectual fashion. Thus he distanced himself openly from Cambridge which was, he averred, 'extraordinarily reactionary when it comes to the study of modern history'.[52]

On the other hand, whatever new that emerged was subjected to critical scrutiny for its broader political as well as purely scholarly merits. From the new left and the position of a social historian, though not yet firmly established at a university, Gareth Stedman Jones wrote in June 1968 concerning a forthcoming discussion on the utility of structuralism for historians. Carr was not terribly enthusiastic. 'Structuralism was, of course, an invention of the linguists, but I am told that they now regard it as "old hat", and that the fashionable theories are those of Chomsky.' He confessed to understanding nothing of this, 'but when the *New Left Review* recently resuscitated the Jakobsen manifesto of 1928, I could make very little of it and thought that it might have been allowed to rest in the library morgue. Lévi-Strauss obviously found the analogy suggestive and for aught I know may have got something valuable from it for anthropology. What worries me is its application to history.' He continued:

Plainly enough, every structure has to be examined not only in its own right, but in relation to other structures. These include other contemporary structures and structures which historically preceded and followed it. Both approaches are clearly necessary, but structuralism appears to put the major emphasis on the former. It seems to me that the former approach is conservative in the sense that it examines a static condition, and the latter radical in the sense that it opens ? on change. However much LS [Lévi-Strauss] may quote Marx for his purpose, (there are no precedents for this) I suspect that structuralism is the fashionable philosophy of a conservative period which does not particularly attract me to it.[53]

---

[51] 'Revolutions and Their Historians', 1965. In the author's possession.
[52] Gerald Freund's record of a meeting with Carr, 26 October 1967: *RFA*: RF RG 2 GC, 1967, 401, University of Cambridge.
[53] Carr to Stedman Jones, 18 June 1968.

The third item which throws light on Carr's thinking on history at this time is an exchange with 'Munia' Postan, Professor of Economic History at Cambridge since 1938, a highly intelligent and eccentric Russian Jewish emigré whose date of birth and memories of the revolution had a tendency to shift with the telling. He had been drafted to work at the Ministry of Economic Warfare in World War II and it was here that he had first met Carr. He was a natural outsider and Carr appreciated his ability to cut directly to the point. Postan in turn also held him in high regard. Sir Keith Hancock remembered Postan telling him that 'Carr and [Joseph] Needham towered over the heads of the rank and file of the Historical Faculty in Cambridge.'[54] They differed profoundly politically, but then so did Carr and Namier. During the war they had shared a healthy respect for Soviet power. At the Ministry Postan 'not only formed an optimistic view of Russia's capacity to withstand the German invasion, but also took the initiative in organizing the economic assistance to Russia'.[55]

Both also took Marx seriously, though from rather different perspectives. In December 1970 Postan sent Carr a collection of essays. The two essays, 'Function and Dialectic' and 'Facts and Relevance', prompted him to write more than a letter of thanks. In discussing 'Function and Dialectic', Carr reiterated his belief in history as a fundamentally radical discipline. But he now reinforced it with the unfashionable view that the social sciences were fundamentally conservative:

> We live in a society which thinks of change chiefly as change for the worse, dreads it and prefers the 'horizontal' view which calls only for minor adjustments. But . . . History is preoccupied with fundamental processes of change. If you are allergic to these processes, you abandon history and take cover in the social sciences. Today anthropology, sociology etc. flourish. History is sick. But then our society, too, is sick. (Of course, 'taking cover' also goes on within the social sciences – economists in economics, philosophers in logic and linguistics, literary critics in the analysis of stylistic techniques, historians themselves in methodology.)

Here there was a measure of agreement, but Postan favoured greater specialization in history. This worried Carr. He himself always favoured a universal approach, just as he always favoured big themes over small subjects.

> We deride the old-fashioned historians who wrote straight 'political' history and ignored the other sectors of society. Do you really want historians to isolate economic history, legal history, military history, demographic history, cultural history etc. etc. in water-tight compartments, sticking firmly to their chosen branch and refusing to examine any interconnections between them?

---

[54] Hancock to Betty Behrens, 30 July 1983.
[55] M. Postan, *Fact and Relevance: Essays on Historical Method*, Cambridge 1971, p. 178.

He was also disturbed at the suggestion that the historian turn to social science for his 'theory'. 'Like you,' he wrote,

> I recognize that many present-day historians are dead because they have no theory. But the theory which they lack is a theory of history, not one delivered from outside. I do not need to tell you what the historian must learn from the economic, demographic, military etc. etc. specialist. But the economist, demographer etc. etc. will also die unless he works within a broader historical pattern which only the 'general' historian can provide. The trouble is . . . that historical theories are by their nature theories of change, and that we live in a society which wants or reluctantly accepts only subsidiary or 'specialized' changes in a stabilized historical equilibrium. Hence the flight from history into 'sectoral specialization'. We both see that it is happening. The difference is that you justify and even glorify it, while I deplore it as a sympom of our current malaise. That's all that divides us – but I'm afraid it's quite a lot!'[56]

The fourth item is the response to an article in the *Cambridge Review* of March 1974, 'The Role of History' by Quentin Skinner, an admirer of Carr's and at that time fully immersed in the writing of his *Foundations of Modern Political Thought*. Here Skinner rejected the total history of Braudel as 'the most discredited form of inductivism in smart sociological disguise'; he found Keith Thomas's 'parochial as well as imperialist' assertion of the death of political history and the centrality of social history equally unacceptable. Skinner accepted the premiss 'that the role of history ought to be that of helping to supply the theories and the materials of the social sciences', but he was essentially writing in defence of political history. Given the interest of social science in problems of revolution in the Third World and its accompanying nationalism, the sort of history needed to explain the process would have to be 'the sort of political history which it is becoming fashionable to dismiss'. He also made the more usual arguments in favour of political history: to understand the reasons for great power behaviour, the nature and development of existing institutions and the ideas that underlie them.[57]

Carr responded that he always found Skinner's ideas 'stimulating' but occasionally found himself questioning the conclusions. Social history as a special branch of history, he thought, had been invented by J.R. Green and 'died with Trevelyan'. He confessed unfamiliarity with the *Annales* and no knowledge of Thomas's article in the *Times Literary Supplement* that had prompted Skinner's piece. But, as ever, when confronted with the choice of two sides in the debate about political history and social history, although first and foremost a masterful practitioner of the former he was a sterling advocate of the latter. Thus he agreed with Thomas and others that social history was pivotal: 'You cannot write intelligently about the struggle between Stalin, Trotsky and Bukharin without some understanding of the structure of Russian peasant society, or

---

[56] Carr to Postan, 31 December 1970.
[57] Q. Skinner, 'The Role of History', *Cambridge Review*, March 1974, pp. 102–3.

about the ideas of Locke without knowing quite a lot about the society in which they became influential. Social history is the bedrock. To study the bedrock alone is not enough, and becomes tedious; perhaps this is what has happened to *Annales*. But you can't dispense with it.' He then attacked Skinner's acceptance of the role of history as a data supply for the theories of social science:

Of course, sciences draw on one another. But it would be odd to say that the role of chemistry is to supply material to the biologist or the engineer. History and the other social sciences have the same object-matter – the behaviour of men in society. The specific difference of history, which leads to other differences, is that it studies past behaviour. The historian can learn from the way in which the sociologist or economist handles his problems in the present. The sociologist or economist should recognise (though some of them don't) that the situations confronting them are not static, and that they learn something from the historian of the way in which these situations have evolved out of the past and will evolve into the future (and never exactly in the same way). As I said in *What is History?* I want to see history more sociological, and sociology more historical. But the specific function of history is to understand the past, or – better, perhaps – the interacting unity and diversity which link past and present. That seems to me good enough for the working historian.

He ended, typically, as he began, with a backhanded and gently patronizing compliment:

Perhaps it is my crude English empiricism which makes me think that the best way to discover what history is about is to write it. I wish you would; and if it is to be the history of ideas, keep a firm grip on the social-historical foundations. I'm sure we should all benefit enormously; and I expect that you would no longer want to define your work in terms of another discipline or to invoke the cliché which ends your present essay. But I shall continue to read you – even if you won't write history![58]

A further item he set aside was a letter to Christopher Andrew in 1978. It was written following a discussion of Andrew's article on British Intelligence and the Zinoviev Letter (reputed to have lost the Labour Party the general election in November 1924). The issue turned upon the provenance of the Letter, which was a fake transmission from the head of the Comintern in Moscow to the British Communist Party containing instructions on subversion. Carr, who had been in the Foreign Office at the time, though not in the relevant department, certainly regarded it as a forgery. Andrew insisted that if it were, then this would imply that the Permanent Under Secretary and others in government had deliberately concealed this fact in order to blacken

---

[58] Carr to Quentin Skinner, 22 May 1974. This was, of course, written before the appearance of Skinner's *Foundations of Modern Political Thought*. As Professor Skinner has reminded the author, Carr never really thought that anything other than books counted in respect of publications; and in fact the letter just predates the publication of Skinner's magnum opus.

the Russians. Carr and Andrew met to discuss their differences, a discussion Carr found 'extraordinarily interesting'. He always enjoyed returning to this period of his own past but also found his and Andrew's differences of outlook a stimulus to further thinking. It is for this reason that he kept his copy of the letter he sent following their conversation. He ruled out conspiracy. 'What is in question here is not a deliberate conspiracy between organizations, but an unconscious consensus of demand, inflamed by the Campbell case and the hope of getting rid of the Labour government.' He continued:

> Behind our differences lies, I suspect, a difference of view on that famous crux, the role of the individual in history. I'm not really concerned to assess the political judgement of Levin or Chalfont or Mrs Thatcher, but only to analyse the group interests and attitudes which mould their thinking. The same goes for [Eyre] Crowe and [Maurice] Hankey. Since I knew them both (and I don't know the trio I've just mentioned), I'm curious about the way their minds worked, very differently, but to the same end; but this isn't all that important for the historian. Ramsay's [Macdonald] wobbling was the result not so much of his personal character (significant only in so far as it fitted him for the leadership) as of the basic dilemma of the whole group represented by the Labour Party.[59]

Unfortunately none of these thoughts was eventually reincorporated into a sequel to *What is History?*, though this was clearly their ultimate destination.[60] To those who now adopt post-modernist views of history, there is an easy temptation to dismiss the various debates centred on *What is History?* as somewhat old-fashioned. Yet it was Carr, after all, who highlighted the fallacy much favoured by Elton that the 'facts' of history exist entirely independently of the historian and this is surely the serious and most significant edge to the post-modernist onslaught.[61] But Carr saw too much relativism as a slippery slope. Throughout the second half of his life he was preoccupied with the relationship between the thinking of intellectuals and the ideology of government, of power. As a resolutely independent thinker himself he sought freedom in self-consciously distancing himself from received opinion. The entire process whereby intellectuals who believe themselves free from authority end up rationalizing the interests of higher powers fascinated him, puzzled him and ultimately eluded him. In this sense he would have found himself amused rather than threatened by post-modernists. He could recognize a clever parlour-game when he saw one, but might well have concluded that it would ultimately end in

---

[59] Carr to Andrew, 4 August 1978.

[60] For those interested in seeing how this might have been done, turn to the introduction of the 1986 edition of *What is History?*, edited by Carr's former collaborator R.W. Davies. It was in the late seventies that Carr spoke to the author about writing another book on the nature of history, but he shelved that project in favour of the history of the Communist International.

[61] For a sober appreciation which, however, rather loosely goes on to describe Carr's view of the Soviet Union as 'Stalinist', see R. Evans, *In Defence of History*, London 1997. Yet Carr haunts the text, however much the author tries to exorcize his pervasive presence. If this biography serves any purpose at all, it is to show that such crude categorization does not really capture the complexities of Carr's views on anything.

intellectual paralysis through denying the possibility of writing genuine history and might, in this sense, ultimately be a reactionary force – for all its claims to radicalism – because it is less subversive than nihilistic in its message.

In his brief notes towards a new version of *What is History?*, written in the late seventies, Carr pointed out that 'We may put our hopes on ultimate resistance of masses to indoctrination' but then went on to ask: 'which side are the intellectuals on?' The psychologists 'have destroyed objective science of psychology,' he noted, adding that 'Historians are on the way to destroy history.' To Carr, who was ironically accused of *la trahison des clercs*, intellectuals could not be trusted to preserve their independence from political power. Only disciplined awareness of that danger would keep them on the intellectual straight and narrow. When asked to prepare a broadcast in June 1957 on the theme of 'Thinking about politics', he replied: 'My theme would be that such thinking goes on normally on two levels; that the discussion of abstract theories for the shop window reflects discussions of highly concrete issues which go on mainly behind; and that our growing consciousness of this division is an important and perhaps disquieting aspect of modern politics.'[62] These views were never further elaborated. The very idea that intellectuals might be the unwitting servants of powerful interests has always offended and unnerved them, whatever politics they aspire to; particularly if they believe themselves on the left but unwittingly further the needs of the right.[63]

In a sense *What is History?* marked the high water mark of Carr's career. He had regained a fame equal to that which he had known during World War II, and which ran well beyond his profession. It is ironical that Macmillans in the United States refused to publish the lectures on the grounds that they would not sell! Arno Mayer at Princeton asked his publisher, Knopf, to consider the manuscript. Knopf were 'simply delighted at this prospect' and hurried to sign a contract.[64] Even a conservative historian such as C. Van Woodward could recommend it as 'a little masterpiece of polemics by a master of the art and a veteran of many wars. I enjoyed every round of it . . .'.[65] Angus Cameron, himself formerly a victim of McCarthyism in the publishing business, thus took Carr on board. *What is History?* very soon sold 31,000 copies in the United States alone and remains his best-seller there today. 'That's a lot of influence on a lot of historians as well as a lot of plain civilians', Cameron noted with some satisfaction.[66] Indeed, the book has to this date sold nearly one quarter of a million copies.

---

[62] Carr to Gregory (producer, BBC Talks Department), 28 June 1957: *BBC* E.H. Carr Talks II.

[63] When the *Guardian* published, posthumously, Carr's embryonic introduction to a new *What is History?*, it cut out the sentences referring to intellectuals and their lack of independence of thought: a striking confirmation of Carr's worst fears, all the more striking for the behaviour of a centre left publication which he once read. See *Guardian*, 7 February 1983.

[64] Cameron to Mayer, 8 June 1960: Arno Mayer's personal correspondence.

[65] Comment dated 11 October 1961: *Knopf Papers*: 736.2 (Harry Ransome Center Archive, University of Texas, Austin), eds Cameron Angus, 1960–70: Carr, E.H.

[66] Angus Cameron to Carr, 23 February 1968: ibid.: 736.1.

9

'Splendid Isolation'?

Many envied Carr his notoriety, the luxury of his fellowship at Trinity – the college now moved to make him a Life Fellow – and the prestige attached to, though doubtless not the labour entailed in, the massive work he had undertaken. They could not know that this was attained at an exorbitant price. His private life once again fell into disarray; though those similarly absorbed to the exclusion of all else could probably have guessed as much. Joyce had given Ted a stable and secure home since his break-up with Anne. He, in turn, wittingly or unwittingly, had sacrificed his academic post to make possible the divorce between her and Daryll. Those who saw them together believed that the relationship was a good one, but they severely underestimated the tensions that were pulling the two apart. There were sharp differences in personality, such as Joyce's judgementalism which, as one can easily see from *The Twenty Years' Crisis* and the disputes with Berlin, were anathema to Ted in private as much as public life. Moreover the disruptive effect of moving from Appleford into Oxford and then on to Cambridge, given that Joyce had no life outside the home, created enormous problems; emotionally it was most disturbing and, as Ted became more and more engaged in his *History of Soviet Russia* to the exclusion of everything else, their minimal social life became lesser still. He did not want people over to the house, and this therefore meant that, in the give and take of normal socializing, they would rarely be invited to the homes of others – which suited him down to the ground. His encroaching old age made him, like anyone, less flexible than ever, not least because of a growing anxiety lest he fail to complete the work before his death and his overriding concern to make it as comprehensive as he could; which meant shooting off to the United States to find more material, expecting Joyce to come with him to make house and drive him to and from work. It was, indeed, a totally egocentric existence. The problem was that Joyce had adapted to this way of life, and therefore rebellion – when it came – proved something of a surprise, and later a shock.

Looking back, though the tensions were always there to some degree, it was the death of Anne on 15 June 1961 that triggered the first real explosions. Ted had not seen her in all the years since their separation in 1946; moreover he had seen little of his children since that time. He had genuinely loved her, though he had found himself incapable of living with her any longer. Her death threw him into confusion, deep reflection, and led inevitably to emotional withdrawal from Joyce. Anne had refused a divorce. Joyce had had to change her name to create the appearance of a respectable marriage. Now that Anne had died, Joyce naturally wanted the marriage formalized. Not the most sensitive of men, Ted did not see the point of it. This issue became a litmus for the state of the relationship. Other grievances that had accumulated over the years were now added to the list. They had no social life worthy of the name:[1] for Ted, going into college each day and lunching there, plus dinner on Sunday, was quite sufficient for his needs. Joyce had no employment and therefore too much free time. He never helped around the home; he was mean with money, he never provided an adequate housekeeping allowance and insisted on their living in minimal accommodation (he preferred a flat to a house, and a small house to a large one).

After the death of Anne, Ted – unaccountably from Joyce's viewpoint – developed a deep affection for his grand-daughter Elizabeth, who was now reaching puberty, and before long he began to feel much closer to his son John. The separation from Anne had badly damaged his relations with his children. John was the first to make up, after a year or so; yet he and Ted had had little in common, and whereas Ted shared a natural anti-establishment sentiment with his ebullient step-daughter Rachel, who had disappointed him years before by rejecting the idea of postgraduate study and an academic career, John did not have an intellectual turn of mind. He was as shrewd as his father but was the practical down-to-earth engineer, not a man of ideas, with little interest in his father's strange pursuits. There were also strong political differences. Whereas Ted read the *Daily Telegraph* – along with Maurice Dobb and the friend of Gramsci, Piero Sraffa – on the grounds that a capitalist paper could not afford to get the facts wrong, John read it out of ideological conviction. Whereas Ted retired from conversation, John had grown – in marriage to Betty – to enjoy the social round. Whereas Ted had not been near a church since his father's funeral, John and Betty were active parishioners. Whereas John and Betty liked nothing better than a holiday abroad, Ted frowned on such frivolity. And nothing could be further from his son and daughter-in-law's values than his rather 'modern' attitude to marriage. In fact, John at this stage had little idea who his father really was, not least because in later life Ted kept relatives, friends and colleagues in separate and sealed compartments: God forbid that they should meet one another.

It was the sense of emotional desertion that hurt Joyce the most. Yet she had always insisted on time spent with her own children who, as a result of the

---

1 By October 1963, Carr was confessing to Deutscher that he refused invitations to every party because he really could not be bothered with them: Carr to Deutscher, 14 October 1963: *DA*, 22.

divorce, were given to the custody of Daryll. What she could not see was that his was a response to the lack in their relationship. In his words, her love for him had become almost completely maternal, even to the point of scolding. It must have seemed to him that 'the woman' had re-emerged in another form. When Ted felt distressed, he retreated into himself. When Joyce felt distressed, she exploded in rage. The more she exploded, the further Ted retreated. Finally, early in 1962 he ran off briefly to the peace and quiet of his sister's at Effingham in Surrey – while Joyce bombarded a somewhat startled but patient John over the phone with tales of Ted's personal habits – and only returned when he and Joyce had re-negotiated an understanding as to how they were to continue to live together, in the course of which he made various promises that, in the end, he was unable or unwilling to keep. The 'Ike' was perhaps the only person Ted could safely confide in; her death in a tragic car accident later, in May 1966, thus came as a heavy blow to such an isolated and tortured soul.

With the relationship patched up, he saw an opportunity to make amends when they saw the Butterfields after their stay at the Villa Serbelloni, a magnificent outpost of the Rockefeller Foundation newly acquired on Lake Como, run by the same John Marshall who had so enthusiastically championed Carr's cause in 1944–46. The arrangement was – as it is still – that a scholar would be invited along with his or her spouse for no more than three months, to read and write in peace and quiet and not inconsiderable luxury – excellent food and wine – provided at no cost to the recipient. The Butterfields were, not suprisingly, full of enthusiasm. Carr accordingly applied to the Foundation.[2] Yet the chairman of the programme committee at Villa Serbelloni, John Maier, had his doubts. There were no questions about Carr's scholarship. But rumours of his citation as a co-respondent in the Fordes' divorce had since been magnified into the notoriety of a veritable Casanova and fears had arisen that he might start bedding the wives of other visiting scholars. 'One understands,' Maier wrote to Butterfield, '. . . – and this is a somewhat delicate point – that he has at times been beset by an astonishing number and variety of difficulties in his personal relationships. Ordinarily this would be of little concern to us, and we would not feel it proper to interfere with the internal affairs of a sovereign individual. However, since problems of this nature may possibly result in unpleasant situations at the Villa – I believe that you have had personal experience of a similar case – it does seem appropriate to give consideration to this issue.'[3] Had Carr known, he would certainly have been amused.

Butterfield was both reassuring and generous in recommending him. It was lucky he had no idea of the trouble brewing at Wilberforce Road. But his comments give one a clear idea of the view taken by those around him in Cambridge.

---

[2] Carr to Freund, 13 June 1962: *RFA*: RF RG 3.2, 900, RF Villa – Scholars (Carr), 1962–63, 506.
[3] Maier to Butterfield, 22 June 1962: ibid.

I personally have seen quite a bit of him and my wife and I always like having him here with his wife, though our contacts have never lasted longer than a lengthy meal-time, and I have never had to get to grips with Mr. Carr in matters of business. I have never heard him mentioned as a difficult person in this University, and personally I think it would have to be admitted that, in general, he and his wife are quiet and polite people, easy in ordinary social intercourse. I think the fact that he was asked to do the second course of Trevelyan Lectures shows that he is highly thought of here, and both in lectures and society he quite certainly showed a good deal of charm.

Butterfield discounted reports that Carr was a difficult person

because, for a number of years, he held a Professorship in Aberystwyth, and if I may speak confidentially, I think he was too liberal-minded for that University and that region, where I have always felt that the influence of nonconformity had led to a censoriousness of a local-minded sort, which I find myself disliking very much. The Chair that he held was one which had a national aspect as well as a local aspect, and if Carr tended to neglect the local side I have half-sympathy, though not total sympathy, with his attitude. I gather that he crowned his unpopularity there by running off with the wife of one of the professors, but this led to what seems to me an unusually nice and happy marriage, and even on this side I always felt that perhaps he had been hardly judged.

He did air his reservations, however, and pointed to the fact that 'he can be fairly bitter as well as uncomprehending in respect of the people whom he attacks in reviews . . .'.[4] At the Foundation Gerald Freund, an assistant director, who had become acquainted with Carr at Balliol, added, for balance: 'I also know some of the reasons for these quirks of personality, which include discriminatory and unfair treatment by institutions and individuals who feared or disliked him and at several crucial turns used their power to besmirch his scholarship and cut him off from research assistance.'[5]

Carr was successful. Reinforcing support came from the Center at Stanford where he had recently spent a year. And on 20 July 1962 Rockefeller sent him an invitation, which he accepted. By this time he was putting the finishing touches to the third, foreign relations volume, of *Socialism in One Country*. The delay in completion was not least due to the massive increase in scope compared to previous volumes, to the attempt to cover the evolution of Soviet foreign policy across the globe and the activities of the Comintern as well as diplomacy. 'I am struggling with the fag end of Volume VII,' he told Davies, 'and China is giving me a great deal of difficulty. Like most other things of this period, the more one looks into it the more dissatisfied one becomes with what has been previously written. There is a great deal of material which nobody has seriously bothered to use.' But this potentially infinite search for

---

[4] Butterfield to Maier, 22 June 1962: ibid.
[5] Minute, 27 June 1962: ibid.

completeness ultimately led to a loss of clear perspective, as the various components appeared increasingly redundant to the overall narrative. 'It is terribly long and detailed,' he confessed to Deutscher, 'but I hope that it is so arranged that people can find what they want in it. Nobody will want to read it all, but I hope that I have not put much in which will be of interest to nobody. It is difficult, when one has taken pains to amass information, to decide to leave it out.' 'Nobody has done all this before, and nobody will do it again for quite a long time, so that it seemed worth while to be fairly thorough', he told his publishers.

He and Joyce arrived at Bellagio on 8 February 1963. He occupied himself initially with a thousand pages of the galley proofs to volume seven; but most of the time was taken up reading microfilm on the moves towards the collectivization of agriculture for the *Foundations of a Planned Economy, 1926–29*, on which he was collaborating with Davies. On arrival they discovered there was no microfilm machine, but Marshall arranged for one to be borrowed from Kodak in Milan. From the villa Carr wrote enthusiastically: 'Here we are in a large palace in a vast park with a retinue of servants.' But there was a serious drawback. 'Joyce is, I fear, bored, and has, so far as I know, written to nobody in Cambridge except our char. I've returned the proofs of vol. 7 (which is a terrible morass of detail), and am back among the peasants.'[6] Back in Cambridge in early April, he told Davies that the expedition had been 'a great success from the point of view of work done'. That cautious phrasing barely concealed difficulties on another front, with Joyce. Bellagio is beautiful, but unless a visiting scholar is willing to forgo work occasionally and accompany his or her partner on outings, there is absolutely nothing for the spouse to do to occupy the mind, particularly in bad weather. And Ted was there to work, not take hikes in the mountains around the lake. It should therefore occasion no surprise to learn that this was the last such trip that Joyce took with him.

When Freund dropped in on the two of them on 4 May there were traces of the tensions that had been resurfacing, but only knowledge of their intimate problems would have alerted their visitor. The unhappiness emerged indirectly in unkind remarks about others. Freund reported:

> Carr, who looked surprisingly well and agile for his 70-plus years, is at the moment in the midst of 1,000 pages of page proof comprising the next two volumes [volume seven was due to appear in two parts] of his history of Soviet Russia; these are scheduled for publication late this year or early in 1964. He and his wife had a profitable time at the Villa Serbelloni. They were full of praise for the hospitality offered by the Marshalls. Both Carrs, but especially Joyce, are always prepared to be snide and critical of other people; and on this occasion they did not hesitate to be unpleasant about Mr. and Mrs. *Zbigniew Brzezinski.*

Carr in fact grudgingly acknowledged Brzezinski's 'brash gifts'; it was his

---

[6] Carr to Betty Behrens, 28 February 1963.

politics that prompted the criticism. 'Very likely Brzezinski can be something of a "pain in the neck",' Freund added, 'and of course he and Carr approach the same field in very different ways. Moreover, Brzezinski may have, as reported, said that next to *Isaac Deutscher* and *Rudolf Schlesinger*, Carr is "the most dangerous" scholar in the U.K. . . .'.[7] He also learned that Joyce 'may or may not' accompany her husband on another expedition to the United States planned for 1964.

Carr had asked for, and received from, the Rockefeller Foundation substantial funds to finance a visit to work on the Trotsky papers at Harvard and then a further stint at the Hoover in California. At the beginning of October he spoke of them both making the projected visit to the United States.[8] Three weeks later he was asking for advice about accommodation at Harvard and more funds on the grounds that 'I am not any longer as indifferent to amenities as I was when I was younger, and need some degree of comfort if I am to get on with my work effectively.'[9] But that was most probably under pressure from Joyce. His indifference to creature comforts lasted to the very end. But appeasing Joyce in such matters did not get him very far. They had been quarrelling about all the old grievances, none of which had since been resolved to Joyce's satisfaction. The only improvement now was that she was busy with an antique shop that she had acquired and this had certainly filled a space in part of her life. But it also meant that going away for extended periods was a problem and this had undoubtedly aggravated her mood at Bellagio; it also meant that the workload at home now seemed more burdensome when it was not properly shared. On 7 November she took a stand and announced that she did not want to go with him to the United States[10] which, apart from anything else, made a stay at Stanford totally impracticable, for without a car and driver there was no way he could make it to and from the campus. Thereafter Carr retreated into silence on all matters in contention.

He could put his feelings on paper, however. From this it emerges that what he objected to most was Joyce's assumption of moral superiority:

> one cannot live with someone who has so acute a sense of one's moral shortcomings and is always passing judgement on them. This is what I cannot stand: I'm always being scolded or condemned for something or other. If I say I want to go to America, and hope that she will come, she does not explain in a friendly way why she doesn't want to come: she at once replies resentfully that it's selfish, thoughtless and inconsistent of me to want to drag her away, and that this is typical of me. Always the moral condemnation, always the assumption of her right to pass judgement. This applies to things great and small; I see no hope of changing it so long as her belief in my moral inferiority remains unshaken.

---

7 Minute by Freund, 4 May 1963: *RFA*: RF RG 1.2, 401, S, University of Cambridge, Carr, 1962–64, f. 583.
8 Carr to Freund, 1 October 1963: ibid.
9 Ibid., 22 October 1963: ibid.
10 Joyce to Betty Behrens, 4 February 1964.

And just as she resented his renewed contact with family, so he too felt that 'she has often made me feel that she was holding me at arm's length, and that she put the boys [Martin and Tom Forde] in front of me.'[11]

Over the Christmas holidays Joyce contracted a severe throat infection and this evidently did nothing for her temper. Finally, on 16 January 1964 he decided he could take no more and went off to college to sleep overnight while he made preparations: 'The situation has become untenable; I could neither sleep nor eat, and she was more and more trying to goad me into discussions of the future or more recriminations about the past. Of course, she resents my going, and this will be added to the list of my sins. Sometimes I feel that I must be very weak and cowardly, and that I ought to have been strong enough to stick it out. But I haven't been.'[12] From the college he checked with the doctor that Joyce would be capable of looking after herself, wrote affectionately to her expressing a 'desire to avoid a complete break and said we must work out a compromise', about which he would write 'later', and announced that he was off to stay with his sister in Effingham for a few days, suggesting she stay with friends. But Joyce would not move and her reply 'was delivered in college within an hour of receipt'. 'It was curt, hostile in tone, and full of half-concealed resentments. It did, however, contain the vital fact that she did not wish to see me and that the house would be empty from 3 to 4.30.' There he found all his clothes laid out to pack. 'On the material side, she was always perfect – when she wanted to be.'[13]

After a few days away from home he did not want to see her again 'for a long time – not till I've established my own independence'. After a further week or so with John at Reading and then the 'Ike' at Effingham, he went on to the United States as scheduled. By the time he reached Harvard, he had made a decision. He wrote to Joyce saying that he proposed to apply for rooms in college and in order to avert a scandal or breach 'unless she makes it', he would explain that domestic circumstances had changed because of her work. He insisted upon having this 'retreat of my own'; but he was also 'ready to come to the house as much as she wishes'. He also said ' – which I believe to be true – that it will be a relief to her not to have me on her hands all the time'. He was hoping for the best. 'If she is friendly it can go very well indeed: if she is bloody, it will be very painful and difficult.'[14] But these hopes were unrealized. Joyce was in no mood for compromise. She wrote to a friend:

> We are dealing with a fairly ordinary woman with normal loves and desires for the companionship of her children, for some social life and a possibly exaggerated love of objects – and a most unusual man, who seems not only not to feel these needs for himself, but who would deny them to the woman. I have tried for 20 years to submerge and submit myself as far as possible to his way of life, and to

---

[11] Carr to Betty Behrens, 23 March 1964: ibid.
[12] Ibid., 17 January 1964: ibid.
[13] Ibid., 24 January 1964: ibid.
[14] Ibid., 2 February 1964: ibid.

teach myself to live with his character . . . . Anne used to rage at him and cry 'Why can't you change?' But even 15 years ago *I* could see this was impossible.

Joyce felt that she had to some extent succeeded in giving him the living conditions he required. 'He could not have done the great work he *has* done since 1945 if I had wholly failed.' She resented his renewed affection for his own family and his saying that Joyce came between them. She felt 'excluded'. Yet she found it impossible to say that she 'loved' him; instead the most she could offer was that she was 'fond' of him 'and extremely anxious for his well-being', and this was clearly at the root of the problem. Her feelings were, as expressed though surely not deep within, more maternal than amorous. That they were in reality much stronger is evidenced by the passionate resentment that built up when she felt rejected and which prompted her to behave 'in a bloody and bitchy way'. 'I can't all of a sudden bear the indifference and egocentricity and even callousness and I punish him.'[15] Yet she still expected him to come back to her and her suggestion was that he merely take a larger room in college with a divan, so that he could retreat only for the occasional night away. He decided to delay his return to England by a few days, evidently in the hope that time would help repair differences. Arno Mayer had asked that he stay on in Princeton to meet students after his forthcoming seminar at the Institute for Advanced Study. He had previously been reluctant. Now he was willing.[16]

But Joyce could not hold back when she most needed to do so. She wrote demanding that Ted reply specifically to all her complaints. 'It was restrained in language,' he noted. 'But the resentments were all there; no word of regret on her side or hint that she might have behaved badly; only pleas and reproaches about my unreasonable behaviour.' Secluded at John Winthrop House, Harvard, he 'reflected continuously on this situation – to the exclusion of almost everything else. I'm clear that, after this third experience, I cannot again return to where we were.' The problem was, as ever, his long-standing inability to cope with violent emotion. 'I do very much need affection. But at my age I need a gentle, equable, above all reliable affection, not one which, however real and deep, is liable to burst out into violent abuse and cruel, wounding denunciation.' He insisted upon pursuing his plans of 'taking refuge' in college.

Once I have my base and haven of refuge there, I'm quite ready to keep up the warmest relations with J., and spend quite a lot of time at No. 4, because then I shall feel secure in having a line of retreat in case of further disaster: I shall no longer be, so to speak, at her mercy if she does break loose again. If she accepts this, there need be no kind of an open break. If she doesn't, a break and every kind of unpleasantness seems inevitable.

---

15 Joyce to Betty Behrens, 4 February 1964: ibid.
16 Carr to Arno Mayer, 7 February 1964 (from John Winthrop House at Harvard): Arno Mayer's personal correspondence.

It was 'a matter of self-preservation to extricate myself from this emotional maelstrom. Perhaps I am cowardly (of the many epithets hurled at me in the last 3 years this is the one which comes nearest to the mark); but I simply cannot stand up to this any more.' Joyce thus faced what amounted to an ulti-matum. He fully expected she would find a decision difficult because, in his words, 'she wants incompatible things.'[17] He then wrote to Arno Mayer. 'There is a subject which I feel I shall have to mention – if only to explain my rather low condition: and it is perhaps less painful to mention it in writing than in speech. My relations with Joyce have struck a very bad patch; and I'm extremely distressed and depressed about it. If we spend much time together alone, I shall probably talk about it – though I know that this really does no good.'[18]

Joyce's silence then left him in an uncertain state. His mood raced up and down. 'Sometimes I'm calm, sometimes angry, sometimes it all seems almost intolerably painful.'[19] He became 'terribly depressed as well as perplexed' at being unable to resolve the situation.[20] Typically, perhaps, this was not as others saw him, so adept was he at concealing his emotions. He gave an inter-view to the student newspaper *The Harvard Crimson*, published on 15 February, which none the less showed all the fight had been punched out of him. 'Visiting E.H.Carr,' noted the student journalist David Gordon, '. . . was like stepping onto a very white, very soft cloud and drifting off into a sky of milk. As he lay back on his sofa and slowly fingered his white hair, Carr talked about the past, present, future and himself with a simple, contented smile and an almost unbelievable optimism.' Not knowing him, Gordon had no means of gauging the nuances. But it is apparent from the subtext of the interview that, although seemingly at peace with the world, he was in an uncharacter-istically defensive mood. When asked what he hoped to prove by his *History of Soviet Russia*, he claimed he was not trying 'to prove anything' but merely hoped to 'throw some light on what motivates the Russians'. Three years later he was far more explicit about what he was doing, as he had been in the forties.

He was equally vague about his role as a historian, evidently much to Gordon's irritation. All he would commit himself to was to say that he avoided 'writing history for the historians' and liked to assume 'I'm writing for intel-ligent people who want to understand something about their past. You can't understand the present unless you've some sort of experience and know how things are apt to work.' And as to *What is History?*, he almost dismissed it by saying 'I just felt like reflecting on what one does when one writes history.' When pressed on whether there was indeed progress at work in history, he

---

[17] Carr to Betty Behrens, 16 February 1964.
[18] Carr to Arno Mayer, 18 February 1964 (also from John Winthrop House): Arno Mayer's per-sonal correspondence.
[19] Carr to Betty Behrens, 6 March 1964.
[20] Ibid., 23 March 1964.

gently insisted on his faith in the future, his 'confidence that the world has a direction. I'm not saying, of course, that every move in the game is a step forward, but I would look to the more promising aspects of modern society.'

He was not taken with Erich Fromm's talk of 'alienated' man (a theme soon taken up by Carr's friend Marcuse): 'People have more education now, and more culture. There is a breaking down of old class barriers. There are more opportunities now, and people are making more of their opportunities. And these are people who once had nothing at all.' He was not daunted by 'teenage rowdyism' nor tribal conflict in Africa. 'You have to remember that the African countries are just starting on the road we've already travelled. That's no reason to condemn them. I dare say there may be a bloody mess on the way, but one has to expect that.' When pressed on the current state of his host country, all he would say was that he sensed that the Americans had lost their feeling of omnipotence in the previous decade; he had not paid much attention to affairs on this trip: 'I came over only to look at your archives, and I haven't seen very much else. There's no real hurry, is there?' Having arrived with great expectation of meeting and writing about a genuine firebrand, Gordon found himself faced with an apparently serene old man whose progressivist philosophy made him all too comfortable with the world as it had become.

The visit to Princeton in late February in the company of Arno Mayer and his family thus offered 'a most pleasant interlude' which enabled Carr 'to release a little the tension' under which he had been living recently.[21] He returned by sea on the Holland-Amerika line due at Southampton on 10 April. His son John met him and put him up for the weekend – 'there I shall enjoy the uncomplicated and unblaming affection which I crave' – before departing via Oxford on the bus back to Cambridge.[22] Here he was temporarily accommodated in Kitson Clark's rooms, while Kitson was away in Australasia. But he still hoped to avoid an open breach. Writing towards the end of his stay at Harvard, he had reiterated the hope that if he stayed in college during the week and saw Joyce only at weekends, 'her irritations and resentments will not all be concentrated so much on me. Also that, if I dispense with the study and remove my books, she can perhaps re-arrange the house to allow for [domestic] service.'[23] But then Joyce never wanted a servant living in – 'I value my freedom and privacy enormously and really hate the thought of a resident maid, poor wage slave waiting on 2 other human brings' – and believed that Ted had no idea what such an arrangement would cost: 'You must remember that he has no experience of the world today.'[24]

---

[21] Carr to Arno Mayer, 4 March 1964: Arno Mayer's personal correspondence. 'I've always felt warmly grateful to you for what you did for me at Princeton 2 years ago when I was about at my lowest ebb,' he wrote in 1966: Carr to Mayer, 18 May 1966: ibid.

[22] Carr to Betty Behrens, 23 March 1964.

[23] Ibid.

[24] Joyce to Betty Behrens, 4 February 1964.

Throughout the crisis both Joyce and Ted made use of mutual friends as go-between. One was Catherine Betty Abigail Behrens. Betty, as she preferred to be called in the latter phase of her life, was sixty years of age in 1964. Born into the upper middle class – her father, whom she adored, had been a senior civil servant at the Treasury – she was a graduate of Lady Margaret Hall, Oxford. She spent one year on a Commonwealth Fellowship at Radcliffe College (Harvard's counterpart for women) and, with the generous support of the diplomatic historian and Regius Professor Harold Temperley, she came to Cambridge University, initially as a lecturer at Newnham. She was appointed a university lecturer in October 1938 and initially specialized in English history of the seventeenth century; later she shifted to eighteenth century France. She cut an unusually fashionable figure, swathed in furs, with her own private income, and accustomed to servants of one kind or another. Known by ageing male dons as 'the glamour girl of Newnham', to her undergraduates she was an inspired, if ferocious and intimidating super-visor. Carr's step-daughter Rachel, who was one of Betty's early charges, recalls: 'She insisted on clarity of thought and of expression and we were lashed unmercifully for any lapse from her high standards. Quite apart from her quality as a tutor her elegant appearance contrasted markedly with that of many of the fellows . . . and increased our wish to meet with her approval.' She also had the kind of mind that Carr liked: it cut through nonsense straight to the substance of the matter. Not that this quality made her popular with those who were careless of what they said and wrote. The term 'second-rate' fell all too readily from her lips and she could be cruel to those who failed to meet her high standards, standards which she herself had difficulty attaining and sustaining; and she could be wildly wrong in her judgement of others. But she could also be exhilarating company; she was extraordinarily well-read (annotating every text that she read, including works of fiction, with her comments); and she had wells of emotion that had yet to be fully drawn upon.

The war interrupted her career and ruined a close relationship with Butterfield. In 1942, much against his wishes, she secured permission to work in government service for the duration of hostilities, writing an official history at the Ministry of Shipping, a work eventually published in 1955 under the uninspiring title *Merchant Shipping and the Demands of War*. What inspired the move to London was her deep infatuation with 'Munia' Postan. The move did not, however, secure the relationship she so desperately sought, and this unrequited love remained an obsession for the rest of her life.

The war over, she returned to Cambridge, where she published next to nothing. When *Merchant Shipping*, though a model of its kind, finally appeared in print it emerged 'dead-born from the press'. Her limitless energies were therefore sucked into the supervision of students and the social whirl; her emotions focused instead on her beloved cat, Pandy. She had created a form of self-sufficiency which to outsiders seemed somewhat daunting and only added to her formidable image. In 1958, deeply disappointed with the indifferent response to her first book and determined to produce something that would make an impact, she succeeded in cutting her teaching by persuading the college to move her to an 'unofficial' fellowship, so that she could focus on research and writing. By the time relations with Carr reached a turning-point, she was fully immersed in a ruthless assault on Marxist interpretations of the origins of the French revolution and had set about writing her own history of the *ancien régime*, with which she momentarily soared into the academic stratosphere when it was published in 1967. Typically incautious was a careless, caustic and costly aside written in her preface. She duly thanked the university and delivered a backhanded and venemous tribute to 'Newnham College (whose way of proceeding have made certain aspects of the Ancien Régime intelligible which otherwise might have not been so)'.[25] When her fellowship came up for renewal that same year, her chief adversary on the fellowship carefully left on the table outside the room a copy of her book opened at precisely this page of the preface. Resentful at her limited teaching and inflamed at her rhetorical flourish at the expense of the college, her not so tolerant colleagues duly plunged in the knife and voted her out.

It is not clear precisely when Betty and Joyce first became acquainted; the earliest reference in Ted's diary is an entry in February 1958. With Joyce she shared a love of social life and a love of precious objects; Betty was addicted to such luxuries and had more of an income to collect them than Joyce, who instead had to be content with buying and selling them. With Ted, Betty found enormous pleasure in such famous company, some intellectual fencing, flattering attention and no small inspiration on historical matters. She had attended the Trevelyan lectures. As one of her former students who was there with her recalls: 'she was tremendously enthusiastic. The broad sweep, the acerbic humour and the almost flamboyant self-confidence were very appealing and she revelled in every minute of it.' This was not least because she was so very critical of the History Faculty, very few of whom had bothered to attend. She regarded her colleagues as far too narrowly focused and she openly welcomed the fact that Carr had thrown down the gauntlet to her fellow historians. From Bellagio in February 1963 he had written to Betty 'to say how much I miss you – and the habit of arguing with you about this and that'.[26] With Betty he could conduct conversation on a completely different plane from Joyce and his letters to her illustrate as much. As the crisis broke in January 1964 he kept her up to date on his feelings, Joyce's reactions and his future plans, and his letters began to show rather more affection than one might expect in a purely platonic relationship. He ended one letter with a characteristically indirect hint that his intentions towards her were not as innocent as they had hitherto been: 'I had better stop meandering now, or

---

[25] B. Behrens, *The Ancien Régime*, London 1967, p. 7.
[26] Carr to Betty Behrens, 28 February 1963.

you will suspect me of being an epistolatory philanderer like poor old Asquith – if that's all it amounted to: my own un-English mind, like Lewy's [Polish Fellow in Philosophy and a dining companion at Trinity], found that part rather baffling . . . . Betty dear, I think of you much and often, and long to see you again.'[27] It may not be altogether unfair to suggest that the thought of substituting Betty for Joyce may have crossed his mind, at some level of consciousness. Her letters to him, with their witty recourse to the eighteenth century and the *philosophes,* cheered him up at Harvard and he was now signing off 'Love, Ted'.

Betty attempted to explain the position of one side to the other and then point to some rational solutions on the material questions such as housekeeping; which meant following her own example, and hiring live-in help. Other than that, there was little to offer: 'At 60 you are not going to change, nor is Ted at 71.'[28] In truth, Betty felt more at home in the world of rationality than that of emotion and the role of go-between was not one she felt comfortable with. All she could suggest was that Joyce propose some 'constructive' solution. Instead, Joyce's response to Ted's ultimatum was to send him packing. After the separation, living in college, he continued to see a great deal of Betty. But their conversations – usually arguments at various levels of ferocity, which he was often not in a positive enough state to cope with – were largely on historical issues. 'How vehement you were on Sunday!', he wrote in late August. 'When you had finished with me, I wanted to find a hole in the ground and crawl into it. Perhaps it was partly because I was in a thoroughly despondent frame of mind when I rang up, and somehow had not expected to be shot out of the cannon's month like that.'[29] The curious thing was that for two people who spent so much time in intense discussion, they really had no views in common, other than a professional interest. Betty was strongly opposed to revolutions, though something of a rebel herself. To him revolutions were essentially positive, the Russian revolution not least. The end justified the means. Being a liberal – of a rather conservative variety – Betty rejected revolution on the grounds that it created untold suffering. To him suffering was a necessary consequence of the historical process, of progress:

> I feel it's useless to continue the argument on the moral plane: things that seem plain and obvious to me aren't at all so to you; and, because you simply don't see the same things that I see, you think me wicked and immoral. I shall not try to convince you. But I'll set down for the record, as unprovocatively as I can, where I stand, and leave it at that.
>
> During my lifetime the state to which I belong has engaged in two major wars and, in the process, has inflicted a large amount of suffering, including many deaths, on a large number of people. Since I was not a pacifist, I must be assumed

---

[27] Carr to Betty Behrens, 17 January 1964.
[28] Betty Behrens to Joyce, 28 February 1964.
[29] Carr to Betty Behrens, 28 August 1964.

to have approved or endorsed this infliction of suffering: I did so on the ground that, though this was an evil, the alternative was a still greater evil. This doctrine of 'the lesser evil' must, I think, be accepted by everyone who is not a pacifist and an anarchist. Refuse to accept it and you become a Tolstoyan.

Once this doctrine is accepted, the argument can proceed on two different lines:

(1) In order to justify your action as a 'lesser evil', you must believe in the goodness of your end. Our bombing was justified, and Hitler's bombing condemned, not because ours inflicted less suffering, but because our end was good and his bad. The criterion, in this argument, resides not in means, but in ends. You could, for example, say that the British conquest of India was justified (and the suffering a 'lesser evil') because the end was good, and Frederick's and Catherine's partition of Poland condemned because the end was bad, though the means employed was much the same in both cases.

(2) In order to justify your action as a 'lesser evil', you must show that the suffering inflicted does not exceed the necessary minimum and is reasonably proportionate to the end in view. Thus, one might approve most of what the allies did in the war, and yet condemn the bombing of Dresden or Hiroshima on the ground that the suffering involved was out of all proportion to the end sought or achieved. Similarly, one might say that Stalin would have been justified in imposing reasonable restraint on kulaks who defied government orders, but not in shipping off car-loads of them to the Arctic circle where most of them were likely to perish. The danger of this argument (though I think it sound and indisputable) is the temptation to treat one's own 'excesses' as unfortunate, but incidental, and the 'excesses' of the other side as basic and destructive of their whole case. This temptation must be resisted: otherwise one falls into the Phariseeism of palliating one's own sins and blackening the other chap's.

All this seems to me, not very original, but plain and sensible and not in the least wicked or immoral. That's all.[30]

The letter is not untypical. A further instance is worth quoting, this time from mid-December, written from the welcome peace and quiet at John's home in Reading, always an escape from 'that nightmare world' that Joyce represented and which he had not yet obliterated from his consciousness. Carr was there for a full month, because Trinity was going to turn off the heating over the Christmas holiday (which infuriated him as 'petty meanness'). He fascinated Betty. She was forever exploring his mind. He, in turn, relished the attention and harboured ulterior motives which had not yet emerged into daylight. On this occasion she had accused him of liking Namier because he was a Polish Jew, of being unresponsive to a long celebrated novel about the last years under the Hapsburgs that she had recommended – Joseph Roth's *Radetzkymarsch*, published in Berlin in 1932 – of only liking books by a certain 'kind of people' and for misusing the word decent.[31] Since he could not pretend to be too busy to answer, he responded as follows:

---

[30] Ibid.
[31] ibid., 9 December 1964.

(1) I like Namier's mind, though I disagree with most of his opinions, because it applies a sharp cutting edge to a lot of woolly thinking. (Come to think of it, I suppose that is why I like yours.) To say that I like him because he is a Polish Jew makes about as much sense as to say that you like Roth because he is a Viennese Jew.

I confess that the C19 Hapsburgs (I know little of the earlier ones) don't attract me – not for the reasons you suggest (the Russian C19 aristocrats who ate more, were infinitely more extravagant, and had far brighter lights, fascinate me – they were tough and vital in their way), but because they present an extreme combination of complacency and ineffectiveness; in the end they make a sort of cult of their own decay. When Chekhov shows up the Russian gentry at the turn of the century doing just this, he seasons it with a subtle irony which makes it aesthetically acceptable; Roth doesn't do this. It's fair to add, though you refuse to believe it, that German is much harder for me to read than English, French or Russian and that the subject has to grip me quite strongly to make me persevere. I might have done better with Roth if he [had] been translated.

. . . Enough about books. But I protest against your assumption that I only like to read about a certain 'kind of people'. My three favourite novelists are Jane Austen, Dickens and Dostoevsky; the only three great English C20 writers are Shaw, Wells (?), and Lawrence. You can no doubt draw psychological and sociological conclusions from my reading. But you must use more probing tools than you have at present.

In writing to her he had mentioned how pleasant it was to find emotional relaxation in Reading, 'almost an emotional vacuum'. It was, he said, 'natural to take an interest in the goings-on of one's offspring and in the development of the young . . . . Perhaps this increases the older one gets. Anyhow it is a decent and comfortable feeling and it was particularly mad of Joyce (and cruel, if one thinks of her as responsible) to make that her target.' Betty attacked him for being inconsistent. He replied:

(2) You slap me down very smartly for misusing the word 'decent'. It's a vague word (I wasn't writing ex cathedra!), and perhaps I was unconsciously defending myself against Joyce. But I don't think I agree that interest in one's offspring is no more 'decent' than wanting 3 meals a day. For me the real and lasting achievement of liberalism is the assertion that only human beings are ends in themselves, and that one's attitude to other human beings is therefore more important than (indeed on a different plane from) one's attitude to things. I've always taken you for a liberal. You certainly use it as a stick to beat socialists and Russians; but are you prepared to assert it equally against conservatives? Or has nostalgia for the ancien régime, and an almost pathological detestation of the bourgeoisie, swamped your liberalism? Have you aligned yourself, in your scheme of human values, with the 5% (a generous estimate) of the human race for which frugality can be a matter of moral choice? These questions have been seriously worrying me since I read your letter.[32]

---

[32] Carr to Betty Behrens, 16 December 1964.

By the summer of 1965 relations between the two had blossomed into something much more than intellectual chit-chat, though Betty was still wary of his blandishments and he thought she talked too much, which she did. Deutscher thus found him – after nearly a year's silence – 'so fit, full of energy and ideas – in excellent form all round'.[33] In August Ted was once again staying in Reading and writing to Betty. 'You asked me what I should be doing here,' he wrote,

> and here I am sitting in the garden and thinking about you and writing to you. By way of occasional interruption I instruct [grandson] David on the finer points of cricket or reassure Elizabeth that her shorts are becoming . . . . I feel in the relaxed condition of being unable to take anything very seriously, except that I love you and want you and need you, and would like you to love me and need me a little. Meanwhile I'm in a state of suspended animation till I see you again on Saturday afternoon, by which time you will have undergone your 'perm'. I note that, in this transitory world, permanent = lasting for 3 months.[34]

A sad counterpoint to his new infatuation was Joyce's letter to Tamara saying that she had had 'a hard two years' and was 'busy trying to learn to live a new life'.[35]

Early in November the college, having agreed to re-house Carr because his existing rooms in Angel Court were wholly inadequate, began renovating a set of much larger rooms in the first set of the majestic Nevile's Court, flanked by the Wren Library to one side and the Tudor dining-hall to the other. Carr returned to Reading while adjustments were under way but they were not done until April and he had another few uncomfortable months in minimal quarters in college. In Reading he was not only temporarily without a home, he was also emotionally restless. 'Dear love, you know perfectly well what I think and feel and want (though you sometimes profess not to understand me), and it would be boring of me to say it all again. I think of you very much and childishly count the time till Wednesday morning.'[36] Much as he looked forward to the new set of rooms, he heartily disliked bachelor life in college. 'I hate living alone,' he wrote, 'even in college, and find it demoralizing and debilitating, but seem to have no alternative at present.'[37] On 12 December when he wrote to Freund to explain that he had left Joyce – 'a tragic break in our relations which has now become total and permanent' – he repeated himself almost word for word.[38] And in a letter to the Deutschers he similarly lamented: 'I have so many meals nowadays in institutions and restaurants.'[39] Living thus also disagreed with him in other ways. 'Even when he lived in

33 Isaac Deutscher to Tamara Deutscher, 11 July 1965: *DA*, 25.
34 Carr to Betty Behrens, 11 August 1965.
35 Joyce to Tamara Deutscher, 28 September 1965: *DA*, 26.
36 Carr to Betty Behrens, 6 November 1965.
37 Carr to Mayer, 21 May 1966: Arno Mayer's personal correspondence.
38 Carr to Freund, 12 December 1965: *RFA*: RF RG 2 GC, 1965, 401, University of Cambridge.
39 Carr to Isaac Deutscher, 23 June 1966: *DA*, 27.

Trinity,' Betty Behrens wrote years later, '. . . he became so miserable that he made himself continually ill with minor complaints . . .'.[40] 'My darling, my sweet love,' he wrote on 16 December:

> Writing to you is just a way of lightening the darkness – the sort of blankness which descended on me when you had driven away the other night and I realized that I wouldn't see [you] again for nearly a week . . . as soon as Xmas was over, we should really undertake some serious thinking about our future. (I would suggest that we should go away for the purpose, but dare not risk being turned down.) I find increasingly that this 'bits and pieces' existence, in which we can never be continuously together for more than an hour or so, imposes an unbearable strain – on me. I doubt whether it's really so good for you. But this may be wishful thinking on my part, since I desperately want to feel that there is something (other than a little intellectual prodding) that I can do for you: otherwise I am overcome by the feeling that I am just exploiting you or by the fear of becoming a burden on you. Anyhow I'm sure the time has come to think things out in a bit more detail. I've always recognized the many reasons for not being too impatient about this: but I don't really want to go through another winter in this way if it can be helped . . . I'll ring tomorrow morning (probably before you receive this letter) just for the joy of hearing you. But telephone conversations are the very epitome of 'bits and pieces'.

In February 1966 he was still complaining about 'the (for me) unsatisfactoriness of the way we live now'. As soon as she had left the night before, he began to think of all the things he wanted to say to her. The letter is of interest as a form of apologia, a belated response to Betty's incessant agitation against his rejection of the liberal world view. At these moments he would retreat under cover only to re-emerge with an uncompromising reassertion of his fundamental beliefs:

> My mind *does* move slowly in things I find difficult, especially in politics. Though I know better than most people that history-writing does involve some sort of political commitment, I don't really want to be involved in this all the time; and I was relieved, when I came back to Cambridge, to find it so much less political than Oxford. This is, I'm sure, because I find it so much harder than you to be self-assured and self-contained in my political views, and so much less able to see things in nice clear lines of black and white.

After describing his gradual deconversion from liberalism from one war to the next, he added:

> As the [Second World] war went on, and especially as we approached the end, it seemed more and more clear that liberalism no longer worked. (Winston helped here by proving that hatred of the Nazis didn't mean *per se* a liberal outlook.) I began to see that the Russian Revolution occupied the same place in the modern

---

[40] Betty Behrens to Sir Martin Roth, 21 March 1981. She kept copies of most letters of any importance that she wrote, including this one.

world as the French Revolution, and that, in spite of its horrors and of the hostility it provoked among most civilized people, it had brought into the world a lot of new concepts and new ways of looking at, and organizing, society. I wanted to study this, and discover what these new ways were and how they worked; and this is what I'm still doing. Yes, I suppose I've rather by-passed the horrors and brutalities and persecutions. But then I'm a historian, not a politician; and is the serious historian of the French Revolution primarily concerned with denunciations of the guillotine or the noyades de Nantes? Don't look at me disapprovingly. I'm not saying that these atrocities aren't awful. But are they the things on which one ought to concentrate if one wants to get at the ultimate significance of the revolutions? Is the number of people killed on the roads the most important factor in considering the significance of motor transport for our civilization? In India, where liberalism is professed and to some extent practised, millions of people would starve without American charity. In China, where liberalism is rejected, people somehow get fed. Which is the more cruel and oppressive regime?

I could go on and on, but should only make you angry. You often seem to have the answers to questions which I find difficult and obscure. But don't you achieve this facility by excluding large areas of the world from your consciousness? I can't quite do this. Some degree of uniformity is implicit in the idea of justice; and judgements on these profound issues do require some general world picture if they are to be fair and convincing.

We shall go on arguing about these things. But I'm not in the least afraid of that. You are ultimately a fair minded person, and I'm really not intolerant or dogmatic.[41]

In April Carr's living conditions at Trinity improved drastically with his move to a spacious and elegant suite in Nevile's Court, doubtless decorated on Betty's sage advice.[42] But she wavered to the last. One particular letter shows very clearly that there was still work to be done to establish a balance between them:

Naturally I've gone on thinking about (what else?) us. Did you happen to see in the *Sunday Times* a review – not a very good one – of a book about G.B.S.? The book had dealt with Shaw's childhood with a drunken father and a mother so absorbed by the struggle to remain genteel that she had no time for the children. The key sentence of the review went something like this: 'Like all those who have suffered emotional deprivation in childhood, Shaw rejected emotional life and took refuge in a cult of the intellect, a cult of art, and a cult of self'. A bit crude and muddled, but not without current application (except that nobody could accuse you of 'cult of self'). You suffered from emotional deprivation in childhood, and have tried to suppress any emotional relation (except with a cat). I suffered from a surfeit of the wrong kind of emotion, and have failed to establish a balanced emotional relation in which I could give as well as take (by 'give' I mean emotionally, not just intellectually). We had to meet, so to speak, somewhere in the middle; and it's reasonably clear by now that we have

---

[41] Carr to Betty Behrens, 19 February 1966.
[42] Carr to Davies, 13 April 1966: *R.W. Davies Papers*. This was also the letter in which Carr asked Davies to drop the brick industry.

done so. You have travelled quite a way. When we are together you make me feel
(which for a long time you didn't) that I am wanted and needed (emotionally,
not just intellectually), and that I'm no longer alone and useless. When we are
apart, you still tend to relapse. After we returned from Oxford, you didn't write
for three days and then sent a letter of which 4/5 was devoted to the mirror
('cult of art') and most of the rest to Christianity and Marxism ('cult of the intellect'), and not a word of emotion. Can you wonder if I was a bit dispirited? My
darling love, till you learn to write love-letters (you'll come to it soon!), I shall
always be miserable when we are are separated. After all, what's the good of
being an intellectual if one's inarticulate on paper about things that matter?
Nothing in this implies that I reject, or dislike, or disapprove of, mirrors. But
first things first. If the brute is hungry, feed him; and he will then be in a better
state to appreciate the mirror.[43]

What is surprising is that, given her knowledge of the worst of his last marriage, Betty should choose to undergo the same herself. But Joyce, who had
by now lost all of two stone in grief and bitterness, made accusations against
Ted 'which were ludicrously untrue, and', as Betty later recalled, 'caused me
in consequence, though unfortunately and foolishly, to disbelieve the other
things she said which, as I have learned, were only too true'. What she preferred was a continued friendship. But, as she confessed later, 'he is . . .
capable of a high degree of sensitivity and has a passionate longing to be
loved. This moves everyone to whom he displays it; and combined as it is with
his intellectual distinction and his proverbial indifference to most people, it
is very flattering to the chosen few. I know this not only from observation but
from my personal experience before I married him.'[44] Finally he gave her an
ultimatum. Enlisting the advice of her closest friend Margaret (Peggy) Denny,
who suggested she take the plunge, Betty finally agreed to marry. By mid-
September 1966 the matter was finally settled. She went off on a trip abroad
and he returned to Reading once more, this time to break the good news.

Ted's relations with John and Betty had grown much closer since the crisis
with Joyce. Rachel – 'the Child' – always retained a special affection in his
heart but she was very much her mother's daughter and her father's attachment to Joyce had alienated her greatly. Moreover she was wrapped up in her
considerable family, her remaining energies concentrated in voluntary social
work, a practical affirmation of a deep commitment to social reform in contrast to her stepfather's purely abstract attachment to the 'new society'.
Reading was thus the secure retreat when emotional problems became over-
whelming. 'The news of our intention [to marry] was well, even warmly,
received. Betty was obviously quite genuinely pleased, and John sagely
remarked that it seemed very sensible. Really you ought to get on well with
John,' he wrote, 'he is almost as matter of fact and rational as you are.'[45] Right

---

[43] Carr to Betty Behrens, 26 July 1966.
[44] Betty Behrens to Dr Meyer, no date.
[45] Carr to Betty Behrens, 22 September 1966.

to the very last Betty wavered. A few days before she took the plunge, she invited herself to lunch with one of her former students. 'We had our usual non-stop analysis of the iniquities of the world', she recalls. 'Over the second cup of coffee there was a pause, and then Betty said: "Tell me, if, at the advanced age of 63, and for the first time, I were to contract matrimony, would you think that to be extremely foolish?"'

To Carr, at least, marriage on 10 December 1966 came as an enormous relief from loneliness. 'I need not say how relieved and elated I am that the rather miserable life I have led during the past three years has come to an end. Splendid isolation is not my ideal of happiness', he told Isaac and Tamara Deutscher.[46]

---

[46] Carr to Tamara Deutscher, 24 December 1966: *DA*, 27.

10

Completing the Work

From Cambridge early in 1967 Carr reported that he was now 'happy and at peace with the world'. But the emotional disturbances of the previous two years certainly slowed his normally high rate of progress towards completion of the *History of Soviet Russia*.[1] And he was not entirely happy about the *Socialism in One Country* volume that had appeared in 1964: it had without question grown to the point where no one was likely to read it through from beginning to end; it had become more a work of reference than a monograph, as he himself acknowledged more than once in confidence to friends and colleagues. It is as though the vast impersonal forces he portrayed had themselves taken over.

At its best, however, was the broad sweep of the introductory chapter on 'Principles of Foreign Policy', which still gives the most authoritative survey of the bases of Moscow's international relations for the period. Carr's basic message is encapsulated in the following sentence: 'Of the two complementary factors in the dual policy of the Soviet regime – the encouragement of world revolution and the pursuit of national security – which had been in potential conflict ever since the days of the Brest-Litovsk treaty, the second seemed to have established a clear claim to priority.' The volume thus treated the process of transition from utopian visions to hard reality in foreign policy that paralleled the painful adjustment to the idea of building socialism in one country at home instead of waiting on the final crisis of capitalism abroad.

Carr was invariably at his best discussing international relations. But it was not the all too familiar world of diplomacy that captured his keenest interest. The machinations of the great powers in the 1920s were only too familiar; it was, instead, the byzantine intricacies of the Comintern which presented a genuine challenge. The foreign policy of the Soviet Union of which this formed the most interesting part was, however, to him merely a sideshow – albeit a necessary one – to the main drama played out in the villages and cities

---

[1] He claimed that having a collaborator 'inevitably makes things slower'. Carr to Mayer, 8 February 1966: Arno Mayer's personal correspondence. But this was by no means the only reason.

of Russia. The introduction of the New Economic Policy in 1921 had gradually led to the enrichment of a portion of the peasantry, for whom capitalism was becoming a way of life. In a country with a predominantly peasant population that ran on democratic lines, this would mean a regime committed to the capitalist path of development. But the regime was not only not democratic, it was committed to the opposite principle, and although it had allowed capitalism to grow in the countryside in order to facilitate production, its long term aim was to socialize agriculture along with the rest of industry. Russian industry was only now reaching prewar levels of production, however. It had fallen way behind the west in terms of technology as well as growth of output. Without a revolution in Berlin and German assistance to the development of the Soviet economy, Russia would have to squeeze capital from the wages of the worker and the profits of the peasant. The option finally chosen was to import the capital goods necessary to re-equip and modernize Russian industry. To pay for those imports, the regime would export grain, and in order to be able to depress industrial wages and keep the worker at the bench, the regime would have to guarantee cheap supplies of food from the countryside. To collect the grain it would have to seize it from the peasant, since it could not afford to pay for it at the market price. And all this was to be achieved at a time when world market prices for grain on the Chicago exchange dropped catastrophically from the spring of 1929 as a result of overproduction. The scene was thus set for a major confrontation between the Bolsheviks and the peasant, between town and country.

In the division of labour between Carr and Davies, Carr took agriculture, labour and trade; Davies took industry, planning and finance. But Carr found the burden weighing heavily upon him as age took its toll on the number of hours a day he could work. 'Even though Bob Davies is taking over a part of the economic section,' he informed Freund, 'I have still so much material to cope with that I badly feel the need of further assistance if I am to get through it in any reasonable time – or, indeed, at all. I have for some time been looking around for research assistance, but have hitherto been deterred by the two difficulties of finding a suitable person and of financing it.'[2] That assistance proved impossible to obtain.

Work on agriculture had proceeded apace since the early sixties. Carr was on top of the subject by January 1963 when he presented the Raleigh Lecture on History at the British Academy, a superb distillation of his extensive knowledge of the Russian countryside and the dilemmas of development. Agriculture, he affirmed, was 'the crucial problem of the Russian revolution'. He took the view more firmly than he had done in *The Bolshevik Revolution* that, had the October revolution not occurred when it did, the countryside would have overturned the old order sooner or later. It was often said that the Stolypin reforms interrupted by the war could have stabilized the old order by granting land to the peasant as it had done in France after the revolution:

---

[2] Carr to Freund, 18 August 1964: *RFA*: RF RG 1.2, 401, S, University of Cambridge, Carr, 1962–64, f. 583.

What would have happened if this idyllic picture had not been rudely disturbed by the impact of war and revolution? This is one of the popular might-have-beens of recent history. Writers who apply Western criteria to Russian conditions are inclined to assume that, given two or three decades of peace, a class of Russian peasant proprietors would have developed the tradition of efficient conservatism commonly attributed to the peasant proprietor of western Europe. Writers more familiar with Russian history tend to argue that, in default of an industrial expansion infinitely more rapid and more far-reaching than would have been either practicable or tolerable, the pressure from the mass of peasants threatened with hunger, servitude, or expulsion by the advance of Stolypin's vigorous and prosperous small proprietors would quickly have produced an explosion as brutal and as anarchic as anything that occurred in the revolution of 1917.[3]

He also took the view that the assault on the peasantry by the Bolsheviks during the civil war to seize grain and livestock was a result of 'need, not dogma'.[4] And although recognizing that 'the form which industrialization took in the Soviet period was dictated by the revolutionary character and ideology of the regime . . .',[5] his conclusion was that the decision to collectivize agriculture finally taken in the autumn of 1929 bore 'all the marks not of a premeditated stroke of policy, but of an adventure inspired by panic, a desperate throw when every alternative seemed to have failed, a resort to shock tactics to win an essential objective which had resisted every other type of assault'.[6] He also argued that a major miscalculation – the belief that the majority of peasants would support the move – 'turned what was planned as a police operation into a civil war of the Government against a large sector of the peasantry'.[7] And he openly acknowledged 'the awful cruelties and brutalities' that attended the execution of Russia's revolution from above from 1929.[8]

The issue of the price paid in human suffering for the revolution and the subsequent repression, including that endured under the forced collectivization of agriculture, had always led to vigorous argument with Betty, not least because she was habitually so judgemental. 'The truth is,' he wrote to her from Reading just prior to their marriage in 1966, 'there's no moderation about me. Either I do my fine needlework which is so minute that only specialists, and not all of them, will read it; or I indulge in these wild generalizations which make you angry.'[9] Those generalizations exposed that strong sense of injustice, revealing the romantic streak that Namier had always seen within him,[10] that invisible link with the *Romantic Exiles* as well as the

---

[3] 'The Russian Revolution and the Peasant', *The Raleigh Lecture on History*, British Academy, London 1963, p. 78.
[4] Ibid., p. 83.
[5] Ibid., p. 84.
[6] Ibid., p. 90.
[7] Ibid.
[8] Ibid., p. 93.
[9] Carr to Betty Behrens, 22 September 1966.

distant radical liberalism of the Edwardian era. They serve as a useful reminder as to why he became so engrossed in his *History of Soviet Russia* in the first place. Referring back to an argument he had had with Betty's friend Margaret (Peggy) Denny, he wrote:

> It irks me when those who have always had, and enjoy, material abundance belittle the demand for material security from those who have never known it, and are so ready to condemn sins committed in the struggle to attain it. Perhaps our ancestors in the cause of the same struggle may sometimes have been tempted to cut Gordian knots by ruthless means. (Of course, these were passing aberrations; but this is what the Russians are already saying of Stalin's sins, and will say more effectively in 200 or 300 years' time.) Nor do I think that the achievements of the Russian revolution are purely material. A country whose population 50 years ago was 80% illiterate or semi-literate peasants now has as high a population of educated people as any other country, is in the forefront of many branches of knowledge, and invents, builds and operates as complex and sophisticated machines as the most advanced countries. And what do you do with the 50-million white-collar population whose fathers and grandfathers were peasants and great grandfathers serfs? Do you wipe them off on the ground that they still lack some of our advantages and refinements, and say that all this ought not to have happened? I cannot. I will state as many facts as I can as fairly as I can, and will condemn individuals when necessary. But I will not 'draw up an indictment' against a whole historical process: this seems to me morally as well as historically unsound. Probably this sounds priggish, and I don't like to talk like this.

He also enclosed a note, replying to the charges Betty made against Isaac Deutscher for being inconsistent. Betty had, he wrote, called Deutscher inconsistent 'because he praises Lenin for taking steps which, on his own admission, led, and were likely to lead, to evil consequences'.

> It seems to me that statesmen are often praised for taking such steps, on the grounds (a) that the consequences of not taking them would have been even worse (b) that the short-term evil would be outweighed by the long-term good to be expected. (Anarchists and pacifists *may*, of course, deny the possibility of (b).)
>
> On a rather trivial plane, [Prime Minister Harold] Wilson is praised for imposing the credit squeeze precisely on these grounds, though nobody doubts that the short-term consequences will be bad.
>
> On a weightier plane, English statesmen are often praised for going to war with Germany in 1914;
>
> for fighting the war to the bitter end, instead of making a compromise peace in 1916;
>
> for going to war with Germany in 1939. But nobody doubted the fearful consequences of these decisions.
>
> Where Isaac differs from you is (1) in being sympathetic to what Lenin wanted to

---

[10] 'You are probably right to call me a utopian,' he wrote to Betty. 'Namier, whose rather crass egocentricity did not make him unperceptive, called me a Romantic (this at a time when I was generally regarded as a hardened cynic).' Carr to Betty Behrens, 6 March 1964.

achieve (2) in believing that, thanks to his action, much of this is being, or will eventually be, achieved. You may think I[saac] wrong, but cannot call him inconsistent.[11]

He had already proposed Deutscher as the next Trevelyan lecturer. What Deutscher offered was what Trinity historians had asked for and failed to obtain in 1961 – an extended and illuminating discourse on the significance of the October revolution, *The Unfinished Revolution*. Carr hoped that 'these lectures will give an impetus which is badly needed to the hitherto neglected treatment of Russian history here.'[12] By the time Deutscher arrived in Cambridge to deliver the first lecture, Carr and Betty Behrens were married. Joyce not unnaturally felt wretched. She wrote despairingly to Tamara Deutscher on 28 January: 'I feel frustrated and miserable that I cannot come to Isaac's Trevelyan lectures. But you will know that Ted has married again – the woman who was my closest friend and go-between at the time of our separation . . . I cannot pretend that I am not extremely unhappy – both Ted and Betty Behrens knew how much I hoped he would return to me.'[13] In fact she had become so vehement and bitter in her attacks on him and his family that Betty Behrens had had no reason to believe that their relationship was salvageable.

The lectures were a tremendous success – the room was packed with enthusiastic students starved of information on the Soviet Union thanks to the slow pace of syllabus reform in Cambridge – but it proved Deutscher's last publication. He had first shown symptoms of heart trouble in 1953. Since then the enormous strain of working for the *Economist* (which paid little in those days) and other periodicals as a freelance journalist, uncertain where his income was coming from and what it would amount to, had taken a severe toll; moreover the decision by Sussex University not to appoint him to a Chair in History, prompted by Isaiah Berlin's suggestion that he was worthy only of a Chair in Marxism,[14] had come as an unhappy blow, particularly in view of the fact that it was politically motivated. It meant there was no end in sight to short-term commitments and therefore little time to work on the biography of Lenin, which he saw as the crowning-point of his life's work. On 19 August

---

[11] Carr to Betty Behrens, 22 September 1966.

[12] Carr to Isaac Deutscher, 7 July 1965: *DA*, 25.

[13] Joyce to Tamara Deutscher, 28 January 1967: *DA*, 28.

[14] Sir Isaiah Berlin in conversation with the author, 1983. The situation was as follows. Tariq Ali published a review of Carr's *Twilight of Comintern* and in it referred to Berlin's blocking Deutscher's appointment at Sussex (*Literary Review*, March 1983). The author had, meanwhile, written to Berlin to elicit comments on his relations with Carr. Berlin instead insisted on a visit and then attempted to clear the air about the Sussex affair, emphasizing that he had not actually voted against Deutscher's appointment as Professor of History, merely suggested that he was not qualified for the job.
   The publication of Michael Ignatieff's biography of Berlin now makes it clear that Berlin was not telling the truth. Ignatieff quotes a letter from Berlin dated 4 April 1963 to the Vice-Chancellor, in which he threatened that Deutscher was 'the only man whose presence in the same academic community as myself I should find morally intolerable'. It was thus evident that the appointment of Deutscher would precipitate Berlin's resignation from the University's academic advisory committee. See M. Ignatieff, *Isaiah Berlin: A Life*, London 1998, p. 235.

he quite suddenly collapsed and died from a heart attack while at a conference in Rome. 'Everything crumbled around me,' Tamara Deutscher wrote.
'I am full of anger at what happened – this is certainly my most futile rebellion.'[15]

Carr was badly shaken by the news; Isaac Deutscher was a man for whom he
felt a unique affection as well as deep respect. 'You know how warmly and
deeply I felt about him, but I find the expression of these things in print very
difficult', he confided to Tamara, when she asked him to write a preface for
Russia after Stalin.[16] He succumbed eventually and wrote a preface for *Heretics
and Renegades* instead in 1968.[17] Carr also composed a brief tribute in the
Cambridge Review and dedicated to Deutscher his collection of essays, *The
October Revolution: Before and After*. In an extremely restrained appreciation
Carr expressed admiration for his 'scholarship and balanced judgement' and
identification with his 'belief in progress and an optimism about the future
destinies of the human race which would not have seemed singular in
nineteenth-century England, but which sometimes exposed him to derisory
comment in the more cynical and guilt-laden western world of today. No
charge was more frequently made against his journalistic writings than that of
excessive optimism.'[18] His sudden death was an enormous loss and it would
doubtless have plunged Carr into unrelieved gloom had he not now found
meaning in a new relationship.

The marriage was still healthy, though not entirely harmonious. It began to
occur to Betty that Joyce might not have been exaggerating. Ted's conception
of love and marriage collided with Betty's. 'Actions,' he would say, 'don't
matter, only states of mind.' This was a rather convenient philosophy because
it meant no obligations – which he always hated – and no need to express gratitude for kindnesses from one's partner. The absence of a normal sense of
obligation became brutally apparent when, within weeks of the marriage,
Betty got the car stuck in a rut in a car park off Mill Lane. The Automobile
Association had to be called. But instead of waiting with her – it was 10.30 at
night – Ted went off to his rooms at Trinity and left her to deal with it. His
lack of interest in the lighter side of life, particularly his dislike of social life,
also became a major irritant. With his congenital inability to put himself into
the shoes of others, he had clearly convinced himself that Betty's frantic
social life before she married him was a substitute for the intimate relationship she lacked with any one man.

The marriage worked well while he continued to live in Nevile's Court, she
out at Barton; an arrangement which continued until an annexe was built, for
which he paid £20,000, so that he could have his own study and the servants,

---

[15] Reply to Betty and Ted's letter of condolences, 5 September 1967.
[16] Carr to Tamara Deutscher, 31 January 1968: *DA*, 29.
[17] Tamara Deutscher to Carr, 1 February 1968, and Carr to Tamara Deutscher, 7 February
1968: *DA*, 29.
[18] 'Isaac Deutscher: In Memoriam', *The October Revolution: Before and After*, London 1969, pp.
177–8.

a Portuguese couple, could be accommodated in their own wing. In the meantime the newly weds lived apart and occasionally had to communicate by letter, which was no bad thing because the weekly separation kept the relationship both fresh and stable. Differences had arisen, however. At this stage both possessed a considerable amount of capital: Betty had about £100,000 (excluding the value of Dales Barn before its extension); Ted had £150,000 but gave one-third to Joyce (in addition to the house) who had nothing, and it was from the remaining £100,000 that he paid for the extension.[19] At parties to which Betty initially succeeded in dragging him along he quickly became bored, particularly with people who had nothing of interest to say and to cut them off he would lapse into a stony silence. At this Betty would get angry and an argument would follow. He would then work to placate her but he sounded condescending and was really no more given to compromise with respect to his preferences and behaviour than was she. Social life was only one bone of contention. Betty also favoured taking regular vacations abroad, which did not interest him at all. He did, during the early years, agree on a holiday to Germany so that Betty – of Jewish extraction – could overcome her hatred of Germans. But, as she complained, he stayed within the walls of the hotel for the entire six weeks, avoided all contact with other guests and worked all the time. Moreover, she was now much more interested than before in the physical intimacy she had denied herself for so long, but he, while regarding sex – this now precluded full intercourse – as basic to life, did not have the appetite.

'On this particular question of "having fun",' he wrote,' – whether this means going to parties, or having sex or going on Mediterranean cruises – I'm fully aware that this is a fair and reasonable activity, and think it's probably a defect or shortcoming in me that I've never had enough of it. But I think that "having fun" must be peripheral to a life which has some other centre, and can't be central in itself; and I think that in your case party-going, though your enjoyment of it is fair and reasonable enough, serves objectively as an antidote for the loneliness of living alone . . . . And because of my social defects, I do not really have access to this party-going antidote – or rather it doesn't work in my case.'

He underestimated the importance of this fundamental difference in temperament. Betty invariably found people interesting; so did he, but in small measure and only for ironic observation, not full-blooded interaction. He was also defensive on the issue of physical affection. 'Was I 'sweet' to Anne and Joyce? Anne was a difficult person to be sweet to: this was possibly one of the sources of trouble. I certainly wanted and tried to be sweet to Joyce. But, after the initial period, the only love she had left for me was of the maternal kind, which seeks to confer, but not receive, benefits, to organize and scold and punish; the only kind of sweetness she wanted, or could bear, was the

---

[19] Betty Behrens to John Carr, 21 July 1982.

sweetness of the submissive child.' The problem with Betty was exacerbated by the familiar complaint that, when faced with emotional difficulties, he found it next to impossible to talk about them. 'I've told you that I talk more slowly, and with more limitations than I think and write', he acknowledged. This must have been an unexpected drawback for Betty, since he had confided to her at length during the breakdown in the relationship with Joyce. It was not so much that he could not talk about such problems as that he could not talk about them directly to the other party. At this, the earliest, stage in the marriage it was possible for both to look upon these as minor irritants.

By the time they married, work on the *History of Soviet Russia* had at last reached the point where the end was in sight. When Carr began the work he had thought to proceed to the mid-thirties, but there were no reliable sources available past 1929 with the exile of Trotsky and the establishment of Stalin's personal dictatorship. The story would thus end as the forced collectivization of agriculture was about to begin. In Paris an emigré, Moshe (Misha) Lewin, had been writing his *doctorat d'état* on *The Peasants and Soviet Power*. There he had been recruited to join the growing team established at Birmingham's Centre of Russian and East European Studies. Lewin had been born a Jew in Vilnius, the original capital of Lithuania which had been forcibly annexed by Poland in 1920. When Poland was forcibly divided by Germany and the USSR in 1939, Vilnius was returned to Lithuania only to fall to the Red Army in the summer of 1940. Lewin was thus both eye-witness to, and participant in, the sovietization of Lithuania, including the forced collectivization of agriculture. Since that time he had become a Zionist and left the Soviet Union in order to participate in the construction of the new state of Israel but, having become disillusioned with Israel's role in the attack on Egypt alongside Britain and France in 1956, he returned to his past as a scholar in Paris.

Lewin's own dramatic experiences thus gave his work a particularly vivid aspect. He had acquired a certain detachment but sustained a commitment to the socialist cause, marking out a position as pro-Lenin and anti-Stalin. To Carr he thus represented something of the same curious pedigree as Deutscher and this undoubtedly influenced him into taking a favourable attitude towards his work. But whereas Deutscher was as much a fatalist with respect to history as Carr, Lewin took another tack entirely, and it was here that Carr and he parted company though, as far as Carr was concerned, within a broad range of agreement. Writing to Lewin to thank him for a copy of his thesis, he expressed admiration for the 'thoroughness and detail' of the text. But he disliked the counterfactual nature of Lewin's argumentation and felt that he was being too indulgent towards the peasant. It is fair to say that Carr had little sympathy for the peasant. His views emerge most clearly in a letter to Davies of 10 October 1966. Chiding Davies gently for not letting him have his little epigram about 'the peasant as the spoilt child of NEP and the problem child of Planning', he wrote:

NEP was designed primarily to benefit the peasant. The standard of benefit was miserably low; and it is true that other people also benefited from NEP. But from 1921 to 1927 people in Moscow did tread softly for fear of antagonizing the peasant; and this is perhaps what being a spoilt child implies. It would have been unthinkable that any other sector could have been invited, even by an industrial Bukharin, to enrich themselves. The trouble is that western historical writing is infected nowadays by a conscious or unconscious anti-Marxist fanaticism. Marx did not like peasants, therefore peasants have a halo. The peasant is always right. I notice that you carefully cut out any phrase or epithet of mine which seems to reflect in any way on the peasant, though you do not show the same squeamishness about other sectors (except of course Narkomfin experts!). I expect some of them will creep back, as I cannot quite take this picture of the peasant as a blend of hero, saint and martyr. I should like to say that the peasant is the spoilt child of western historians. But I had better keep that for my review of Lewin when his book appears.[20]

In a further letter of 25 October he replied to Davies's assertion that the peasants withheld grain from the towns because of shortages and the high prices of industrial goods:

Some peasants certainly held up some grain on these grounds: that can be documented: but how many, and how much? Can we generalize this? I am inclined to prefer a less simplified and less rational picture. I fancy that most peasants who had substantial surpluses hung on to them (a) as an insurance against future needs (think what they had gone through) (b) as a speculation on higher prices next year or the year after (their constant experience since 1914) (c) from sheer miserliness and reluctance to part with their most precious possession, the same compulsive urge which made the traditional French peasant stuff his mattress with bank notes, and makes people in India and elsewhere hoard gold. I suspect that these motives, or a mixture of them, were far more general and more potent than any calculation about availability of industrial goods; and I am not at all convinced that an abundant supply of such goods would have brought out the grain. The trouble arises from applying the rational categories of economic man to a primitive society used largely to a natural economy. The Russian village was a different world from that of the economists.[21]

And it seemed to him that when Lewin said that a historical process was not inevitable, he was 'either uttering a rather meaningless platitude' or else committing himself to 'some view of a desirable and practicable alternative, which in turn involves certain presuppositions'. Unless this were spelt out, he did not see that it helped much towards a conclusion. He doubted whether Lewin wished to 'argue that the Bolsheviks should have dispensed with collectivization altogether, or merely that they should have carried it out more slowly and more mildly (as for instance they might have done if Lenin and not Stalin had been in charge)'. This then led to various subsidiary questions.

---

[20] Carr to Davies, 10 October 1966: *R. W. Davies Papers.*
[21] Ibid., 25 October 1966: ibid.

Did Lewin mean that 'planned industrialization, including the development of heavy industry, could have been carried out, perhaps a little more slowly, but still effectively, without measures of forced collectivization?' Or did he mean that 'the development of heavy industry should have been indefinitely postponed?' Or did he mean that 'planned industrialization should have been dropped altogether, and market forces allowed to dominate the situation, in the hope that some new Stolypin, or an influx of foreign capital, would have reorganized agriculture on lines of individual ownership?' As to Lewin's indulgence towards the peasant, he was no less severe:

> You draw much more of a black-and-white picture than I do. The peasant comes out in your narrative as the innocent child (dare I say the spoilt child?), starved and beaten by the wicked stepmother. My picture is different. The peasants were a primitive, cunning, ignorant and brutish lot. (How, given the historical past, could they have been anything else?) The original design of the regime – to educate the peasant, to mechanize and modernize and organize agriculture – was perfectly sensible and enlightened. It did, however, ignore the smallness of the numbers and the low quality of those capable of carrying out such [a] policy, and the almost total lack of resources; also it must be said that the Bolsheviks as a whole had no understanding of the peasant. In short their plan was Utopian; and, when they came up against peasant stupidity and peasant obstinacy, they quickly became exasperated, and began to employ violent measures on the supposition that peasant resistance to anything so sensible must be inspired by wickedness. This produced a terrible tragedy. But it seems to me that the tragedy eludes you, if you treat it simply as a question of innocent victims and brutal exploiters.
>
> My other point is simply that, by constantly insisting on the inefficiency of the government, you create the one-sided impression of an eagerness to discredit them in every possible way. All governments faced by complicated problems are inefficient. Think of the efforts of the British government to cope with the economic crisis between 1930 and 1932. It seems to me that some at any rate of the Bolsheviks had a pretty clear conception of what the problem was; but it was an insoluble problem and the violent methods which they adopted made it in some respects worse. The question whether they could have solved it in any other way goes back to the questions which I raised in the beginning.[22]

Having stated his differences, Carr characteristically expressed the hope that they would meet some day to continue the argument. But he regarded Lewin's book as 'extremely good';[23] and he did not dish out compliments like this very often.

Differences of approach may have separated him from Lewin, but both saw the revolution in positive terms. This was not, of course, the case with others, as one is reminded when reading the record of the Harvard conference held early April 1967. This was a gathering of the great and the good in the profession – including Berlin, Merle Fainsod and George Kennan – and hosted

[22] Carr to Lewin, 24 January 1967.
[23] Carr to Tamara Deutscher, 8 July 1969: DA, 30.

by Richard Pipes at the Russian Research Center. Pipes was scarcely one of Carr's ardent admirers, but he had, only the year before, acknowledged in a review of *Socialism in One Country* that there was 'no history of Soviet foreign policy in the 1920s that can remotely compare with Carr's treatment as far as factual coverage is concerned'. He was, wrote Pipes, 'a one-man encyclopaedia'.[24] It would therefore have been inconceivable to hold such an occasion without inviting him. Carr did not think much of the conference. 'He was particularly critical of a paper given by *George Kennan* in which he propounded the thesis that the Czarist regime was really not that bad, that both more liberal policies and industrialization would have taken place without a revolution.'[25] He always considered Kennan a moralist rather than a historian – a typical Carr contradistinction, though one borrowed originally from Namier. But he respected him and thus kept silent during the proceedings rather than attack someone who shared his belief in the need for détente with Moscow. Bertram Wolfe was another matter entirely, and he took evident pleasure in accusing Wolfe of being incapable of being objective about Lenin.

In turn Carr presented 'A Historical Turning-Point: Marx, Lenin, Stalin'.[26] Here in uncompromising terms he restated his view that 'the most significant of all the achievements of the Russian Revolution' was the 'success of the Soviet campaign for industrialization, which in 30 years, starting from a semi-literate population of primitive peasants, raised the USSR to the position of the second industrial country in the world and the leader in some of the most advanced technological developments'. He was ready to acknowledge that it 'would be wrong to minimize or condone the sufferings and the horrors inflicted on large sections of the Russian people in the process of transformation. This was a historical tragedy, which has not yet been outlived, or lived down.' He nevertheless lent his support to the balance-sheet approach to historical progress, a practice he generally avoided but was now having to come to terms with as he reached the last volumes of the history: 'however the reckoning is made, it would be idle to deny that the sum of human well-being and human opportunity is immeasurably greater in Russia today than it was fifty years ago.' The problem with this is that the same might have been true had some other elite ruled Russia for the previous half century. He was on more solid ground asserting that it was this achievement that had 'most impressed the rest of the world' and had 'inspired in industrially underdeveloped countries the ambition to imitate it'.

This may seem far-fetched to those who did not live through that period, but it was something of a commonplace at the time, and not just on the left. At a meeting of the US National Security Council in January 1956 the fiercely anti-Communist Secretary of State John Foster Dulles said 'the United States

---

[24] *American Historical Review*, vol. 72, October 1966, p. 246.
[25] Freund's record of a meeting with Carr, 26 October 1967: *RFA*: RF RG 2 GC 1967, University of Cambridge.
[26] R. Pipes (ed.), *Revolutionary Russia*, Cambridge, Mass., 1968, pp. 282–94.

had very largely failed to appreciate the impact on the underdeveloped areas of the world of the phenomenon of Russia's rapid industrialization. This transformation of Russia from an agrarian to a modern industrial state was an historical event of absolutely first class importance.' All the underdeveloped countries saw were 'the results of Russia's industrialization and all they want is for the Russians to show them how they too can achieve it'.[27] Carr himself could not have put it better.

He was under pressure from Betty Behrens to take her travelling. He conceded her a few days in Paris together at the end of September 1967; but resisted other such distractions. Perhaps a way could be found to combine work on the next volumes with trips abroad? While in the United States he had talked to Kenneth Thompson at the Rockefeller Foundation and proposed another stay at Bellagio, perhaps the coming winter; he also raised the idea of a trip to Asia, which Betty was most interested to see, presumably with work on the foreign relations volume of *Foundations of a Planned Economy* in mind – China would occupy a major portion of the text. By the summer, plans had been switched to March 1968 for Bellagio and the projected Asian trip somehow never materialized; Freund was now chairman of the programme committee, so at least there was no problem in securing an invitation to the villa.

Asia was then at the centre of everyone's attention: Gunnar Myrdal's massive study of the problem of development in India, the *Asian Dilemma*, had just appeared; China was in the throes of the misnamed Cultural Revolution; and the war in Vietnam was reaching its peak. A further distraction were the student revolts of 1968. Isaiah Berlin returned from Columbia University in May, where the students had struck out against the university administration as an extension of their protests against the war in Vietnam. In turn the New York police force made the most of an opportunity to beat them up. On return Berlin wrote to Carr referring ironically to 'Marcuse's "Red Guards"', though admitting that the authorities had acted with little sense. It was obvious where Carr's sympathies would lie, as was also the case with the *événements* in France; yet these sympathies were inevitably suffused with grim presentiments about their likely outcome. 'We are at present absorbed in the French affair [the demonstrations that eventually brought down De Gaulle]. The French do not have a very good image here,' Carr wrote, 'and attempts to demonstrate in favour of the French students have come to very little. What has happened in France is only too clear. The Unions are coming to an agreement with the Government which will give the Police a free hand with the students. The trouble about student power is that, when it comes to the crunch, there is so little of it.'[28]

Unrest in western Europe and the United States was mirrored in Warsaw

---

[27] 273rd Meeting of the National Security Council, 18 January 1956: *Eisenhower Archives* (Abilene, Kansas).

[28] Carr to Mayer, 28 May 1968: Arno Mayer's personal correspondence.

and Prague. The causes had little in common with the anti-Vietnam rebellion
in the west. Soviet hegemony over east-central Europe lay like a deadweight
on society. On the one hand Moscow seemed a success story to those such as
Carr who believed it had blazed a trail that others, in less developed countries,
might follow. Indeed, this appeared not entirely implausible at the time when
the world was still reeling from the unexpected success of the launch of the
world's first artificial satellite from Soviet soil, and Yuri Gagarin's spectacular
spaceflight two years later: the Americans overtaken at the highest levels of
technology. Moreover by early 1967, deeply embroiled in the disastrous war in
Vietnam and in grave danger of being beaten by Moscow in the accelerated
arms race, the US Government had abruptly opened a dialogue with the
Russians on the limitation of strategic nuclear weapons and defences. We
were still in an era when the apparent magnitude of Soviet economic achievements overshadowed the structural flaws that were ultimately to topple the
entire system.

But while the Soviet Union appeared to be progressing in one dimension,
in others it had visibly taken a cruel step back. The trial of writers Sinyavsky
and Daniel in 1965 were the first dark cloud on the horizon: the anti-Stalinist
'thaw' that had begun in 1956 was clearly over with the removal of Nikita
Khrushchev from power in October 1964. In bed at home on 21 August 1968
at 5am Carr listened to a Russian language broadcast from London reporting
the Soviet-led invasion of Czechoslovakia. The invasion dashed widespread
hopes for 'socialism with a human face', which Czech Communist Party secretary Alexander Dubček had proclaimed as his regime's ideal. Betty was
down in London and she was not unnaturally indignant and wanted to know
what Carr thought. He wrote:

About the événements I've a lot of different reactions: –
(1) About the Russians. It's depressing to find that there's so little left that's revolutionary – at any rate in their foreign policy. [The era of support for revolutions
in Africa, Latin America and southern Asia had yet to arrive.] They've just become
a Great Power, and behave like one. Since you don't like revolutionaries, and I
don't like Great Powers (since we ceased to be one), we may converge on this
point. What I find sinister is that, for the first time, the military seem to have been
the decisive factor. They obviously had the whole thing sewn up and thoroughly
well prepared, and were itching to go. The party people on the other hand obviously weren't prepared at all, and have bungled their part of the job: their name
will be mud.
(2) About the Czechs. Except that my emotional involvement is much weaker, I
don't suppose my feelings differ much from yours. The Czechs are a most unfortunate and unhappy people, poised at a crucial geographical point between west
and east, between Germans and Slavs, and apparently doomed to be a bone of
contention between them.
(3) As you say, 2 wrongs don't make a right. But I think it's wrong not to consider
how these things will look to a lot of Asians, Africans, and negroes in the U.S., who
will say something like this: 'When a small white nation gets pushed around, you
and your governments raise loud cries of indignation. But millions of non-whites

have been, and are being, pushed around – some still more brutally and with greater loss of life. Some individual whites make ineffectual protest. But of your governments, some condone these operations, others actively support them or just look the other way. Not one of them has protested or denounced these things – at the U.N. or elsewhere.' Perhaps the young people on K[ing's] P[arade] [Cambridge] who a fortnight ago waved placards about Vietnam, and last week about Biafra, and yesterday about the Czechs, deserve more respect than Mr. George Ball or our official spokesmen.

I share all three of the above reactions, and find it extraordinarily difficult to fit them together into a coherent judgement. It's nearly 40 years since I first became preoccupied with these problems of international relations and morality, and only for a short period in the middle did they ever look simple and clear-cut.

The reference to *The Twenty Years' Crisis* is a rare retrospective. Since the early fifties Carr had ceased to write about current international relations and it was certainly true that he had not openly discussed the issue of morality in that context since the late thirties. He distanced himself from the *Crisis* in reviewing Hans Morgenthau's *American Foreign Policy* in May 1952. The 'almost universally accepted doctrines of the Wilsonian epoch' that 'the problems of the world could be solved by the application of a few well-conceived rules or principles, such as non-aggression, self-determination and the sanctity of treaties' led to a reaction which placed power back at the centre of international relations. This reaction was, Carr noted, 'at first altogether healthy'.[29] The implication was, clearly, that it was no longer so. But he never amplified upon this. His reticence was further evident when Kenneth Thompson, a specialist in the field in his own right, attempted to lure him back into the fray in the late fifties with the offer of money from the Rockefeller Foundation. Carr politely replied that he was too preoccupied with his *History of Soviet Russia* to oblige. Because he turned down the offer, Thompson turned instead to Butterfield who, courtesy of Rockefeller, ran a seminar at Peterhouse from 1958 for the better part of a decade. It included the two rising stars in Britain, Martin Wight and Hedley Bull, and resulted in a novel collection of essays, very much in the British tradition, under the staid and unpromising title *Diplomatic Investigations*.

It was surely rather odd to hold a seminar on international relations in Cambridge without inviting the world's leading authority who lived within a mile of the college; but then Butterfield was in some ways hard to understand and, despite his own marital infidelities, sided with Joyce after the split, refusing to have anything to do with Carr again. On a visit to Cambridge in October 1967 Freund had asked Carr about the seminar. Carr responded that Butterfield had at no time asked if he wanted to take part and that he had no idea who attended or what went on.[30] Since he first wrote on international relations, an enormous amount had been published, most especially in the United States,

---

[29] *Listener*, 15 May 1952.
[30] Freund's record.

matching Washington's ascent to world power. Dazzled by the growth of economics, ignorant of diplomatic history, and ambitious to stamp their mark on a
rising subject, professors of political science – to some extent aped by British
counterparts – elaborated theoretical models which bore little or no relation to
reality and presented them to a baffled reading public with claims to the status
of science.

Back in the forties in a note written for the Council of Aberystwyth on the
teaching of international politics Carr had defined what he meant by 'this difficult subject' and what was required to teach it. The view very much reflected
his personal experience of diplomacy and the stance since taken by the policy-
oriented schools of study in the United States:

> If I were asked to define what international politics meant as an academic disci-
> pline, I should be inclined to call it the application of political philosophy to
> international relations which had hitherto been studied mainly as a part of history
> and not as a province of political science.
>
> International politics in this sense is, however, pre-eminently a living subject
> and does not lend itself to study exclusively from books and documents.[31]

In the late fifties, when his young friend Arno Mayer took an assistant professorship in history at Harvard, having taught international relations at
Brandeis, Carr took the view that he was 'increasingly sceptical of
'International Relations' as a separate subject. By all means,' he wrote, 'let the
historian specialize in international history if he wants to: but don't let him
imagine that he is something different from a historian.'[32]

Carr's approach thus placed him at great remove from the mania for theoretical models in the United States. That trend was under attack from
Harvard. Professor Stanley Hoffmann, who led the charge, made considerable use of *The Twenty Years' Crisis* in support of his position lambasting these
sterile intellectual voices. Carr read the article in *Daedalus* with great pleasure
and wrote, inter alia, to set Hoffmann right on a few points of detail. He concluded the letter with a comment which left little doubt about his views on the
debate, spiced with a more provocative thought:

> Whatever my share in starting this business [the field of international relations
> theory], I do not know that I am particularly proud of it. I suspect that we tried to
> conjure into existence an international society and a science of international
> relations. We failed. No international society exists, but an open club without
> substantive rules. No science of international relations exists. The study of inter-
> national relations in English speaking countries is simply a study of the best way to
> run the world from positions of strength. The study of international relations in

---

[31] 'Note by Professor E.H. Carr on the teaching of International Politics', 1 June 1943: College
archives, Aberystwyth, R/DES/IP/1 (8).
[32] Carr to Arno Mayer, 15 March 1959: Arno Mayer's personal correspondence.

African and Asian Universities, if it ever got going, would be a study of the exploitation of the weaker by the stronger.[33]

Carr's last point unquestionably overestimated the degree of 'realism' in the study of international relations in most universities; unfortunately a great deal bore little relation to any reality, even that dictated by state interests. His assessment of the weakness of the field was more to the mark. In a letter to the young Sheila Bruce (later Fitzpatrick), he was even more vehement on the subject. She was applying for a job in international relations and had asked Carr to act as referee on the strength of their acquaintance and his familiarity with her study of Commissar of Enlightenment Lunacharsky. He in turn expressed neither surprise nor objection that she should seek to teach in a field apparently so distant from her own. 'I have long thought that International Relations is a rag-bag into which one is entitled to put anything one pleases. Charles Manning's attempt [at LSE] to turn it into some sort of organized self-contained subject was a fiasco.'[34] Thus wrote the sometime external examiner for Manning's department.

Carr was in so many respects extraordinarily consistent in his beliefs, whether in respect of world politics or the Soviet Union, that it is perhaps all too easy to fall into the trap of assuming that nothing changed over time. Yet the publication of the first two parts of *Foundations of a Planned Economy 1926–1929* points to such shifts in his thinking. In many ways this was the ultimate destination of the *History of Soviet Russia*, the reason why he had twenty five years before embarked on the entire enterprise. How had the Russians under Stalin reorganized their economy and society, and what lessons were there for the west? Hitherto those writing about the period had focused almost exclusively on the political dimension, whether from the left (Isaac Deutscher) or the right (Leonard Schapiro). During the early fifties Carr had begun with the assumption that the politics was primary, but then switched to the belief – under the impact of further criticism, research and reflection – that the functioning of the economy and the dynamics set in motion were in fact fundamental. Without this sea-change it is unlikely he would ever have set about the economy in such a methodical manner and taken on the services of Davies from Birmingham. The two volumes published in 1969 presented the most meticulous and detailed account of the way in which the Soviet leadership set about the reconstruction of Soviet industry, trade, finance and agriculture, in a form that remained substantially in place until Yeltsin. 'I'm afraid I get more detailed and more long-winded as I go on', he confided to Tamara Deutscher in a characteristic moment of self-deprecation.[35] A deep

---

[33] Carr to Hoffman, 30 September 1977.
[34] Carr to Bruce, 4 November 1977.
[35] Carr to Tamara Deutscher, 18 December 1969.

sense of achievement was none the less there; it was merely not for open display.

Following the theme developed in *Socialism in One Country* and his British Academy Lecture of 1963, the emerging collision between the regime and the peasantry now took centre stage. Rapid industrialization was required because the external world was deemed irrevocably hostile and the countryside no less untrustworthy. Only by this means could the regime defend itself against western levels of defence technology. But only through extracting a surplus from the recalcitrant peasantry was rapid industrialization possible. The assumption was that this could be done with the support of the poorer peasants. The dilemma was outlined thus:

> In pre-1914 Russia industrialization, though extensively financed by foreign investment, already led to severe indirect pressure on the peasant. The prices of the agricultural products which he had to sell were geared to the world market; the prices of the industrial goods which he bought were inflated by a high protective tariff. In the Soviet economy, which could not count on an influx of foreign capital, the attempt to build up a modern heavy industry would involve a programme of large-scale capital investment, maintained over a period of years without any substantial rise in the production of industrial consumer goods. The peasantry, which constituted the vast majority of the population, would be required to supply increasing quantities of agricultural products to the growing towns and industries. If, however, increased taxation, and rising prices, or acute shortages, of industrial consumer goods, imposed too great a strain on the peasant, he would reduce instead of increasing his deliveries of agricultural products, hoard his surpluses, reduce his sowings for the market, and retreat into self-sufficiency. On this delicate issue relations between the regime and the peasantry were to turn.[36]

As he discovered in researching the economics volume of *The Bolshevik Revolution*, an experience reinforced in the writing of *Socialism in One Country*, Carr (along with Davies) came face to face with the fact that it was the circumstances in which the regime found itself, the logic outlined above, which had dictated the eventual outcome, rather than the ideological proclivities of the leadership *tout court* as the likes of Schapiro insisted. By the summer of 1929, therefore, with no sense that near civil war and famine were in the offing but with the logic of events pressing them on, Stalin decided on the 'liquidation of the kulaks [rich peasants] as a class'.[37]

The situation with regard to the pace of industrialization appears no different. When Carr had embarked on his *History of Soviet Russia*, it was in large part to see what could be learnt from Soviet planning. Here, however, in *Foundations of a Planned Economy*, he reiterated the conclusion drawn in *Socialism in One Country*: the system that came into being was thus not adopted

---

[36] Carr and Davies, *Foundations of a Planned Economy 1926–1929*, vol. 1, part 1, London 1969, p. 26.
[37] Ibid., p. 263.

purely as the result of ideological dictates in search of an ideal and rational solution to the problem of economic development. On the contrary, it was an improvisational response to a succession of crises, both internal and external. Carr and Davies quote Stalin on 19 November 1928 asking, rhetorically, whether they could not proceed more slowly?

> Speaking abstractly, and independently of the environment abroad and at home, we could of course do the job at a slower rate. But the point is that, first, it is wrong to reason independently of the environment abroad and at home, and secondly, if one thinks in terms of the environment in which we are placed, then it must be recognized that this environment compels us to adopt a rapid rate of growth for our industry.[38]

Writing in the section on finance, Carr and Davies conclude: 'The problem of the later nineteen twenties was not, therefore, so much to design an efficient system of financial planning as to bring the existing system into line with the policy of rapid industrialization.'[39] The entire process that Carr describes from the time of War Communism and culminating in 1929 is thus one where the main actors, not least Stalin, appear to be turning in the wind, a wind driven by meteorogical forces far beyond their own control; but Stalin, of course, being the one least committed on point of principle, was more successful at tacking to the wind than any of the others.

It is here that Carr's account far transcends what we hitherto understood of the mainsprings behind the entire process that transformed Russia into the leviathan that defeated the Germans on the eastern front and which held the balance of power in Europe for decades thereafter. But whereas he believed he had, after years of intensive effort, now fully grasped the economic dimension of the Soviet regime, the question as to what kind of society had been created in the process was not so easy to answer.

The paper given at Harvard on the anniversary of the revolution was the first attempt for many years to sum up his findings. It was a section of the *Foundations of a Planned Economy 1926–1929*, volume two, entitled 'The New Soviet Society', which finally grappled with these thorny issues at greater length. What exactly was this new society? Certain issues were as clear as before, and here he marked himself out resolutely from most admirers of the Soviet Union: 'The dictatorship of the proletariat . . . was a political myth.'[40] If it was not the dictatorship of the proletariat, was it nevertheless socialism that had been established? His answer was, yes and no:

> The Soviet industrial revolution firmly rejected the bourgeois pattern of industrial revolution, and was based on the conception of central planning in the collective interests of society. In this sense its socialist credentials were impeccable, and the

---

[38] Ibid., p. 327.
[39] Ibid., vol. 1, part 2, London, 1969, p. 719.
[40] Carr and Davies, *Foundations of a Planned Economy 1926–1929*, vol. 2, London 1971, p. 442.

scepticism of the opposition was unjustified. But, in the sense in which socialism was identified with the aims or achievements of the proletariat, and proclaimed social equality as the goal, it could not be called socialist . . . . What Marx and Lenin meant by a proletarian revolution, and what the Russian revolution failed to achieve, was a process of human emancipation which would abolish exploitation, not a revolution which would expose the masses to new forms of inequality and new forms of bureaucratic organization and oppression.[41]

At the apex of the process stood 'a politically oriented and organized ruling group, whose core consisted of a small circle of party leaders by whom major decisions of policy were taken'.[42] And above them towered Stalin. Here Carr goes one step further than he had been willing to go when writing *Socialism in One Country*, for he now wrote that 'Stalin's personality, combined with the primitive and cruel traditions of Russian bureaucracy, imparted to the revolution from above a particularly brutal quality, which has sometimes obscured the fundamental historical problems involved.'[43] Stalin also broke the link with the revolution: 'It was no longer quite clear in what sense the regime stood for revolution at all.'[44] He continued: 'In action, Stalin exploited the worker as mercilessly and as contemptuously as he exploited the peasant. He drove into opposition, crushed, and finally exterminated the old party leaders of the school of Lenin . . . . The purges had more of the aspect of a "white" than of a "red" terror; their principal author stood out in the guise of a counter-revolutionary monster.' These assertions and references to Stalin's 'cruel and capricious personal dictatorship'[45] are very much at odds with the strange silence with which he dealt with these matters in the 1940s and 1950s. In one sense this was not so strange: he was always writing against the current, attempting to balance himself between the pressures exerted from both camps, the camp he lived in and the camp he wrote about; he was now, with Brezhnev's gradual rehabilitation of Stalin and the growth of détente between east and west, willing to acknowledge the camp in the east as part Gulag. As soon as opinion in the west swung back to its former position in the mid-to-late seventies and began feverishly excoriating the Soviet regime once again, Carr's own views swung in the opposite direction and he began speaking out for the east against the west as he did in the early days of the Cold War.

The constant struggle to retain his balance, to sustain a form of objectivity artificially by distancing himself from current and prevailing opinion east and west, arose again in a lecture he gave to students in Cambridge in late April 1972. He had come to Trinity in retirement. He was never officially a lecturer of the university. Moreover Herbert Butterfield and others had kept him at arms' length from the History Faculty (with mixed success), though he was

---

[41] Ibid., pp. 443–4.
[42] Ibid., p. 444.
[43] Ibid., p. 448.
[44] Ibid., p. 448.
[45] Ibid., p. 451.

occasionally asked to lecture at the Faculty of Economics and Politics. Students thus rarely saw him, let alone had a chance to speak to him. Carr had taken on a small succession of graduates since his return to Cambridge, most recently John Barber, sent by Plumb from Christ's. One such was Jonathan Frankel, who had the singular experience of being supervised both by Betty Behrens (as an undergraduate) and Carr (as a graduate). Moses Finley, the American classicist, had recommended him to Carr. Finley, by virtue of his ostracism from the United States during the McCarthy era and his equally distant relationship with the History Faculty, had found common ground with Carr soon after the latter's arrival. Although Frankel was primarily interested in Jewish history, these interests did intersect with Carr's past involvement in nineteenth century Russian radicalism; so he was taken on with the kind of open generosity he later showed others equally bereft of expertise in the History Faculty. The fact that Frankel was closer to Betty Behrens in his negative view of Lenin and the revolution seemingly made no difference. Carr, as a supervisor, always took the back seat and avoided direct interference in the work under way. The only moment when a chill draught entered the room was on the occasion when Frankel had the temerity to remark that it was extraordinary how similar Communist Russia was to Tsarist Russia despite all the vast and terrible upheavals. Carr 'made no attempt to hide his irritation and snapped back that, on the contrary, the extent of the change was extraordinary and it was that fact which mattered'. The hitherto unsuspecting Frankel suddenly realized 'that there was a core of very passionately held beliefs underneath the matter-of-fact exterior'.[46]

Not that, at his advanced age, Carr could have borne long abstract conversations with highly energetic young students; but on occasion Carr found himself both flattered by and interested in the adulatory enthusiasm of the young. 'Like you,' he wrote to Tamara Deutscher, 'I prefer the company of the young. But I've been conscious for a long time of many things I cannot share with them – pleasure in crowds and noise and unlimited talk . . .'.[47] None the less he accepted the offer to lecture. All that remains of it are his unpublished and fragmentary notes for the occasion, but what they have to tell us is sufficient. 'Need not dwell on [the] darker side . . .,' he wrote:

Coercion of the peasants, leading to mass deportations and famine costing millions of lives.

Terrible political purges and of the concentration camps where millions were condemned to forced labour.

Rigid suppression of dissentient opinion.

Though the worst of all this lies in the past, there are still forms of oppression and destruction of liberty which we have not learned to tolerate in the west.

---

[46] Frankel to the author, 19 October 1994.
[47] Carr to Tamara Deutscher, 2 December 1973.

   He would not dwell on this because he took the view that suffering was part of the natural order, the price of progress (it is here that he and Betty Behrens disagreed the most). 'Human achievement involved in suffering', he noted, evidently meaning the reverse. 'It was a Victorian illusion – noble illusion, perhaps, but one which impoverished Victorian literature – that it is possible to obliterate tragedy from [the] pages of life – or history.' And as to the balance-sheet approach of historical achievements, very much evident in both the Harvard lecture (1967) and the *Foundations of a Planned Economy* – 'seldom . . . has so monstrous a price been paid for so monumental an achievement'[48] – he now insisted that the metaphor was 'unreal' because the 'beneficiaries [are] not the same as those who paid the costs'. Moreover, for the historian in search of an objective vantage-point to view the onward march of events he seemed to imply that natural human emotions got in the way; he dealt with this through the operation of a form of self-censorship in the endless search for balance:

> In this overheated, emotional atmosphere
> Swimming against current
> Swept away or over-react
> Try to keep afloat and keep balance

What the historian had to do, as Carr had explained in the Trevelyan lectures a decade earlier, was to identify with the imaginary historian of Russia a century or so ahead. 'Why histories of revolutions cannot be written too soon: Carlyle,' he noted. 'Rash decision of 25 years ago [to embark on the history],' he reflected; 'Rashness of youth.' This is followed by the disturbing comment: 'Attitudes to Hitler and Stalin. More than that, [the] historian needs long-term perspective which abstracts from [the] emotions of the moment. He makes moral judgements, but long-term.' What he meant by this is clear. When he spoke to Ved Mehta over a decade before, he had stressed that he did not 'think there are such things as bad people. To us, Hitler, at the moment, seems a bad man, but will they think Hitler a bad man in a hundred years' time or will they think the German *society* of the thirties bad?'[49]

   Carr consistently refused to cast moral judgements on figures in history; those that did so were 'moralists not historians'. But what of Hitler and the Holocaust? His residual sympathies for Nazi Germany sat uncomfortably with his explicit rejection of anything smacking of anti-semitism. Unlike others of his background and generation in the Foreign Office, he had if anything a clear preference for the company of Jewish intellectuals, whether famous writers like Stefan Zweig or distinguished historians like Lewis Namier and Munia Postan; not least his old favourite Isaac (and later Tamara) Deutscher. And he had, after all, married Betty Behrens. Moreover,

---

[48] Carr and Davies, *Foundations of a Planned Economy 1926–1929*, vol. 2, p. 451.
[49] V. Mehta, *Fly and the Fly-Bottle: Encounters with British Intellectuals*, London 1963, p. 153.

it was at this same lecture that he stated bluntly: '[The] Historian of [the] future will record the magnificent achievements of [the] Israeli state over 25 years . . .'. One can imagine what his *History of Israel* might have been! But there still lingered the thought that Hitler achieved something in lifting Germany out of the Great Depression and restoring its national pride.[50]

In an important sense, therefore, he was attached to a Darwinian view of history. Indeed, one might be forgiven for suspecting that, had he not achieved notoriety as a historian of the Soviet regime, his view of history might otherwise have identified him as a conservative. Most certainly his history of the English industrial revolution would have shocked liberal and socialist critics by its cold and matter of fact treatment of the bloody balance-sheet. His was an incurable optimism, a steadfast belief in 'progress'. This was a Kantian or Hegelian, rather than a Marxist, cast to his conception of the historical process; a feature largely obscured by the fact that he wrote of a regime born of revolution and published utopian tracts during one brief phase in his long career. Indeed his latter-day attachment to socialism seemed at one remove, an affiliation of the head rather than the heart. If we turn away from 'immediate discontents', he noted, 'and try to look at C20 from [a] long-term perspective of a C21 historian, [I] don't think the total picture will be one of decay and disaster. Disasters and decay there have been, and are. But will these dominate the picture?

> Difficulty in believing that all the positive things that are happening will go for nothing.
>
> Technical advances and material life: vast improvement in health; extension of education at all levels and in all countries (shortcomings, but what advance has not had its drawbacks); advance in psychology – knowledge of ourselves; increasing awareness of the world (superficial stuff); rise to social and political consciousness of primitive peoples all over the world.
>
> To the historian of the future C20 will appear as a remarkable century – [a] century of remarkable achievement as well as of calamities; and well in the middle of this picture will stand R[ussian]. r[evolution]. of 1917 which has been the starting-point of so much, and for good and for evil has dominated the century.

By all accounts the lecture made a great impression. By the beginning of May he had seen only about half the number of students who wanted to come and talk:

> most of them quite intelligent, but the usual mixture. One wanted to judge everything in terms of Marxist doctrine, another in terms of liberal democracy. But the question which interested them most was how far Stalin just inherited from Lenin: this apparently came from the lectures of John Barber which had been pro-Lenin

---

[50] On one occasion the author recalls Carr's objection to his use of the term 'chauvinist', with respect to the Nazi Party. 'Nationalist', he insisted.

and anti-Stalin: one of them had also heard [Richard] Geary [also his research student, a Junior Research Fellow at Emmanuel College] on the German revolution.[51]

The resurgent interest of the young was gratifying. The sense of intellectual
isolation he had long endured was by now nothing like as total as it had once
been, though the death of Isaac Deutscher still left him strangely incomplete.

Having completed and in 1971 published the second, domestic politics and
society volume of *Foundations*, Carr now faced the enormous task of writing the
final volume, detailing the Soviet Union's foreign relations up to the end of
1929. He usually found the sections of the opus on international relations
much the easiest to research and write, not least because of his Foreign Office
experience. But in writing this section of *Socialism in One Country* he had been
overwhelmed by the vast amount of data he had gathered concerning the
activities of the Comintern and member parties. The prospect of reliving this
experience into his ninth decade had impelled him to seek the collaboration
of Ivan Avakumovič from the University of British Columbia, who agreed to
carry out much of the detailed work involved. He and Avakumovič had met to
compare findings and set plans in the summer of 1969. Carr subsequently
approached Freund for more funds in order to visit California again in 1971 to
work on the next volume and to back the collaboration with Avakumovič.
This threw Rockefeller into something of a dilemma. Carr had dipped into
their pockets rather frequently in recent years. Freund wrote, somewhat sar-
donically: 'the man has remarkably bedevilled our earlier, unhappy prognoses
of his longevity . . .'.[52] He had succeeded in securing another visit to the villa
with Betty Behrens in the spring of 1970. But further funding proved impossible. The all-powerful Internal Revenue Service now objected to its grants to
individuals. Down to the end of March 1970 Avakumovič had written enthusiastically of their work, but then silence descended and Carr announced in the
preface to volume two of *Foundations* in June 1971 that for 'personal reasons'
Avakumovič would be unable to continue.

This was depressing news. In February he had written to Davies that he
would have difficulty tackling this volume alone. 'On the other hand a
research student who reads Russian, but knows little or nothing of the subject,
is of no use to me, as he does not know what to look for.' What was required
was 'someone with a knowledge of Russian who has at least some knowledge
of Comintern and Profintern affairs, and would be sensible and level-headed
about them, and this is extremely difficult to find'.[53] Had Davies any ideas?
Davies talked it over with Moshe Lewin, who suggested a talented and
dynamic young American called Stephen Cohen.[54] Born on 25 November

---

[51] Carr to Tamara Deutscher, 1 May 1972.
[52] Comment by Freund to Thompson, 14 November 1969: *RFA: RF RG2 GC1969 401 Carr, E.H.*
[53] Carr to Davies, 11 February 1971: *R.W. Davies Papers.*
[54] Davies to Carr, 26 February 1971: ibid.

1938 in Indianapolis, reared in Owensboro, Kentucky, Cohen had studied at Indiana University under Robert C. Tucker,[55] before going on to complete his doctorate at Columbia in 1969. Cohen had taken the position of Assistant Professor in the Politics Department at Princeton, where Tucker now held a Chair. Here he was working to complete a biography of Bukharin. Nothing came of the suggestion that he be taken on as an assistant and, for the time being, Carr gave up the idea of finding an overall collaborator; instead he began toying with the idea of getting help on particular episodes. He particularly wanted 'someone on the General Strike and its sequel, but it would have to be someone who was prepared to tackle the Russian sources, and was more interested in the Russian reactions than in anything else'.[56]

Davies then came up with the name of a young Israeli research student supervised by Richard Kindersley at St. Antony's College, Oxford, now one of the key centres of Russian studies in Britain.[57] Kindersley was well-meaning but knew little of Soviet foreign policy during the period in question. He had therefore urged Gabriel Gorodetsky to visit Carr. But Gorodetsky was nervous about wasting the time of so eminent a scholar. Carr took the initiative: 'I should be most interested in anything which you were able to dig up. I need hardly say that I would gratefully acknowledge, in whatever form you thought suitable, any help I had from you.'[58] The problem was that Gorodetsky was more interested in British diplomatic reactions to Soviet behaviour than in Soviet reactions to events in Britain. And as an extremely thorough – Carr saw this as a typically Israeli trait – and single-minded student, he was unlikely to switch course mid-stream, however tempting the offer of collaboration. They finally met that November. Carr took to him and came away with some hope of cooperation if he could persuade Gorodetsky that diplomatic relations were 'really of secondary importance and interest'.[59] In February 1972 he took the bit between his teeth and wrote in anticipation of their next meeting: 'I am very anxious to explore whether we can establish any plan of collaboration – on any terms which you would like.'[60]

This was an unusual proposal. His experience of full-scale collaboration had been both limited and mixed. The ideal model was Davies; yet even here Carr sometimes chafed at the need to restrain himself from rewriting everything. *The History of Soviet Russia* had become such a personal possession that, at the very least subconsciously, there was a deep need to cast it entirely in his own words. But he required someone to reduce the vast amount of research

---

[55] Tucker, author of a multi-volume biography of Stalin, elicited this comment from Carr: 'I met him many years ago and read one of his earlier books. My impression is that he is a clever man, but that his interest in psychology misleads him in seeking personal explanations of historical events, and this makes the ultimate result disappointing.' Carr to Tamara Deutscher, 29 November 1977.

[56] Carr to Davies, 4 May 1971: *R.W. Davies Papers.*

[57] Davies to Carr, 7 June 1971: ibid.

[58] Carr to Gorodetsky, 16 June 1971.

[59] Carr to Davies, 7 December 1971: *R.W. Davies Papers.*

[60] Carr to Gorodetsky, 8 February 1972.

ahead. And Gorodetsky was not only ploughing the same field – albeit only one corner of it – but he was also well-equipped with languages (German and Russian) and, not unimportantly, although at St. Antony's, he was 'not in the least a St. Antony's type',[61] by which he meant hostile to the revolution like David Footman and George Katkov. It was not long, however, before it became evident that Gorodetsky's focus was not only 'diplomatic' rather than 'revolutionary' but that, as Carr noted in a letter on 18 April 1972, 'whereas I have looked at it all from the Soviet angle as an item in Soviet policy, you looked at it almost exclusively from the British angle.'[62] He had drawn the disappointing conclusion that both the pace and direction of Gorodetsky's research did not meet his own demanding and pressing requirements, except perhaps at the margin. Gorodetsky later completed and published a successful thesis; Carr read and generously commented on his work while looking elsewhere for assistance on Comintern matters.

It was certainly no accident that within a week of writing he contacted Tamara Deutscher, casually but purposefully mentioning that he would be in town for lunch and to check references in the reading room of the British Museum. It would be 'delightful' to see her; 'Would it be convenient if I called on you on the way back – say about 3.30 just for an hour.'[63] He followed this up in May with an apparently inconsequential letter, saying how nice it was to talk the other day. 'Write some time soon.'[64] Now this would not be worthy of note from anyone else; but from Carr this was highly unusual – everything he did was to the purpose. Completing the *History of Soviet Russia* overrode all else. Tamara Deutscher did write, but in distress at a savage attack on Isaac written by Labedz that appeared in *Encounter*, the anti-Communist journal.[65] Carr was philosophical, weary from his own unpleasant experiences, evidently of Macaulay's opinion that 'the place of books in the public estimation is fixed, not by what is written about them, but by what is written in them; and that an author whose works are likely to live is very unwise if he stoops to wrangle with detractors whose works are certain to die.' He wrote to Tamara:

> Disgusting, yes. But can one descend into this arena, and notice this sort of stuff? Dignity apart, it doesn't pay [to respond by letter to the editor]: the writer or the editor has the last word, and will reply to any comment with a fresh spurt of spite. Anyone who has figured publicly in a controversial field like this will get this kind of attack, and neither Trotsky nor Isaac is likely to be immune. Look after yourself and don't worry about this – it is really of no consequence.[66]

---

[61] Carr to Tamara Deutscher, 7 March 1972.

[62] Carr to Gorodetsky, 18 April 1972.

[63] Carr to Tamara Deutscher, 24 April 1972.

[64] Ibid., 1 May 1972.

[65] Labedz had first attacked Deutscher in *Survey* in April 1962. For comment, see Tariq Ali, 'For E.H. Carr', *Literary Review*, March 1983.

[66] Carr to Tamara Deutscher, 30 May 1972. Labedz launched a similarly vicious attack on Carr, also after the subject's death: 'A History in the Making', *Times Literary Supplement*, 10 June 1983.

By October he could conceal his purpose no longer. The opportunity came when Tamara wrote suggesting she visit Cambridge. Betty Behrens was delighted – the rarity of a social event in which the old man would actually have a substantial interest.[67] The reason for the visit was to ask Carr to inspect two entries for the Isaac Deutscher memorial prize. He was not exactly at home with the kind of literature on offer. These were the days when the *New Left Review* – in some ways still under Deutscher's influence – was engaged in fierce debates about Althusser's interpretation of Marx, battles over the validity of the continental European as against the Anglo-Saxon Marxist traditions. Carr rated those in the continental camp more highly on intellectual content, but the native variant higher on clarity of exposition. 'I'm very much an amateur Marxist,' he wrote, 'and soon get out of my depth. Also I have a hidden preference for the English idiom, in which I grew up, over the German–American. Unexpectedly – since I don't give [Ralph] Miliband a very high intellectual rating – I find myself on his side.' But his attention was not fully engaged. He was 'brooding on another question' on which he needed her help. He would write again in a few days.[68] On the eighteenth he outlined his predicament:

As you know I'm working on what should be the last volume of the history, dealing with international relations for the period 1926–29. I've done quite a bit, but it seems to grow in my hands. The amount of material which I ought to consult is enormous, and I sometimes get oppressed – and depressed – with the idea that I shall never be able to finish.

Then came the offer:

Will you help me? I won't attempt to define exactly what I need – whatever you can give me – searching for material in the B.M., in the LSE (where it can be borrowed), perhaps in the University Library here, which has a few things, making drafts, looking over my drafts and criticizing and correcting them. It would be a relief to have someone to consult, and feel I was not working entirely alone.

Then came the flattery: 'Nobody could do this for me except you.' To buttress his case he argued: 'I know that you found work at the BBC boring – I hope this might be a little less so. I know that you also found it tiring – with me you could at least be able to work as much or little as you wanted, and when you wanted; there would be no time-table. I know that I can no longer work long hours, or very fast, myself.'[69] This was, of course, a very relative matter. When asked how many hours he used to work in his younger days, his reply was 'all the time'; and the speed with which he could work in various languages and turn out an immaculate text in the first draft was still remarkable.

---

67 Betty Behrens to Tamara Deutscher, 2 October 1972, plus enclosure from Carr.
68 Carr to Tamara Deutscher, 16 October 1972.
69 Ibid. Deutscher, 18 October 1972.

But then, Tamara Deutscher had to be persuaded. He suggested she delay answering until she came down to lunch at the end of the month. 'Anyhow don't answer, No. I'm sure if we talk, any difficulties or hesitations you feel can be cleared up. I don't know exactly how we can work together, but I'm sure we can. We shall have to make some financial arrangement, but that is the least of the problems. It's time and energy that are short, not funds; I think Trinity will surely help out on this.' He added, in a separate note, that the plan had been discussed at length with Betty who, only too aware how frustrated he had become, was 'in complete agreement' and that 'this will be an occasion for us to see one another often, which will please me very much.'[70]

Within days he received a reply. He opened the letter in trepidation but was 'delighted and relieved' at the good news.[71] Tamara characteristically insisted she knew little of the subject; but this was false modesty. She had an array of languages – Russian, Polish, German, French and Italian. She had worked for Isaac on the Stalin biography and the Trotsky volumes that followed. And anyway, to Carr her relative ignorance was of no importance: 'it isn't knowledge of facts which matters – there are more than anyone can cope with – but the feel for the right facts to know. We may disagree on this or that, but our approach is sufficiently similar to make us at one on that point.'[72] But Tamara soon got cold feet and they agreed on three months merely as a trial run. She did not want to take on the responsibility of being co-author. He was reassuring:

> I don't mind writing up the stuff and putting on the final polish – this comes easily to me . . . . What I can no longer do is turn over the whole mass of materials and sources; and this you do admirably . . . . *Please, Tamara dear, don't worry* . . . . Perhaps I shouldn't say this; but, apart from all the other things you can do for me, I do feel the need of some kind of – how to put it? – prop or partnership. For many, many years I've worked entirely alone. In Oxford, they knew what I was doing, and disapproved. In Cambridge, they approve, and even admire, but have no idea what I'm doing. I used not to mind this at all. But nowadays I do sometimes have an irksome sense of isolation. With you I can have the assurance that, though we may sometimes differ on particular points, we talk the same language. If you understood the importance of this, you would perhaps have fewer qualms. And DONT WORRY.[73]

A close and fruitful collaboration followed from the autumn of 1972 which was to last to his death, a decade later. It was above all a working relationship but, as Carr seemed to indicate in the note that he sent after the original invitation, he also – at first no doubt only subconsciously – sought a companionship otherwise absent from his life. The hours spent in the natural

---

[70] Carr to Tamara Deutscher, 18 Ocober 1972.
[71] Ibid., 22 October 1972.
[72] Ibid.
[73] Ibid., 16 November 1972.

chaos at Tamara's in Hampstead became a release. Here he could relax and be accepted for himself without being judged. However much the intellectual sparks continued to draw him to Betty Behrens, and she was delightful company when in a positive frame of mind, there were stronger forces at work pulling the marriage apart: political and intellectual as well as emotional. A mere hint of trouble appears at this stage. Betty, he told Tamara, 'will not be much interested in detailed discussions of our work. Betty has a hidden – or not so hidden – conviction that revolutions are wrong, and should not have been allowed to happen, so that she is more concerned for those who tried to prevent them from happening than those who tried to make them happen, and sometimes mildly reproves me for excessive interest in revolutionaries. Fair enough!'[74]

Tamara was puzzled. He explained:

> She is unreservedly in favour of my having you to work with me – she even suggested it, long after I had begun to think about it – because she genuinely wants me to finish the job and to do it well. But basically she hates the Russian revolution and only wants to discuss it in terms of condemnation. She was immensely impressed by Isaac's biography of T[rotsky], and at that time was a little inclined to idealize T[rotsky] as the enemy of Stalin. Since then, our growing troubles, trade unions, New Left and all that, her attitude has shifted – not her admiration for Isaac, but her toleration of Trotsky. If his name comes up nowadays, she will point out that he was as bad as/worse than the rest in advocating violence and defending the terror. She likes and admires you personally, but I should be chary of getting her involved with you in any discussion of what we are doing – sparks might fly![75]

Apart from what appeared to be minor intellectual differences over revolutions, the marriage gave every outward impression of stability, happiness even. But two events, which occurred within a year of one another, precipitated a crisis. First, the rennovation of Dales Barn was completed and Carr moved in on 1 June 1970.[76] Second, Betty Behrens retired from her university lectureship in 1971 and now had neither a university nor a college post with which to keep herself occupied. Retirement threw her back onto her own resources and exposed an empty shell where a rich inner life should have been. She had always suffered from minor bouts of depression – which she referred to euphemistically as her *Nachgrübeling* [literally, moody contemplation][77] – and these grew in intensity and extent upon her retirement. Moreover the dramatic and humiliating deprivation of the Newnham fellowship after over thirty years of devoted service was scarcely compensated for by a fellowship at Clare Hall, which, while an extremely congenial new graduate college open to academic visitors from all over the world, unfortunately

---

[74] Ibid., 22 October 1972.
[75] Ibid., 20 November 1972.
[76] Ibid., 13 May 1970.
[77] Betty Behrens to Tamara Deutscher, 3 April 1970: *DA* 31.

offered no room nor sufficient substitute for the intense satisfaction she had always drawn from heavy teaching. While she was immersed in teaching, she would wistfully muse about the time lost to research. But once the teaching ended, a *grand ennui* opened up before her. She told Frankel and his wife Edith that she regarded her career as a productive historian as at an end.[78] Carr never accepted this and in November 1968, after the great success of the *Ancien Régime*, he had tried 'to steer her to doing something about the Prussia of Frederick the Great, which has been too long neglected by western writers, and tendentiously handled by the Germans'.[79] The idea appealed; but somehow she could not put her mind to the task.

The state of the nation made matters worse. Betty Behrens was very much attached to material things in the form of *objets d'art*: she was also only too aware of the fact that she largely lived off the interest from her investments. It does not take a genius to see that this made her extremely sensitive to threats to the existing order emanating from below. The early 1970s saw the advent of a Conservative Government under Edward Heath, growing inflation and widespread industrial unrest. The coal-miners struck early in 1972 and the government declared a state of emergency. A wage and price freeze followed as union after union struck for higher wages. The postwar consensus had begun to crumble as the British economy slipped more steeply into secular decline. As a historian of the *ancien régime* it must have seemed alarmingly familar. Returning from a couple of days at Tamara's in Hampstead in mid-January 1973 Ted was surprised to be met with smiles. This lasted until 10pm.

> Then, having read Heath, she [Betty] launched into a long spiel about prices, the impossibility of dealing with the unions, the danger of revolution and so on, and tried to drag me into an argument. (We had had a long and futile discussion on Sunday). I said as nicely as I could 'Don't let's start a political discussion at this time of night'. This provoked an outburst of rage. After 2 or 3 minutes she felt a bit ashamed and calmed down, but for the rest of the evening continued to be bitter about my unwillingness to talk politics.

He concluded that something had to be done about these violent swings of mood and toyed with the idea of persuading her to see their G.P. about it.[80] But Betty would not admit to him that she suffered from depression. A month later and tired of his evasiveness, Betty caught him before he left for college – which was usually at 10am – and 'said she would go crazy if she could not talk about the only subject that interested her'. So he mollified her by suggesting a discussion that afternoon. 'She is really frightened about all this,' he confided in Tamara, 'and I'm not as skilful as you are, or she knows me better. Last time you were here, she told me that, though you had some foolish utopian ideas about socialism, you were really in agreement with her

---

[78] Frankel to the author, 19 October 1994.
[79] Carr to Freund, 12 November 1968: *RFA:* RF RG GC 1968 401 Carr, E.H.
[80] Carr to Tamara Deutscher, 18 January 1973.

about everything. All this is some deep malaise,' he concluded, 'and parties only do the trick for a few hours.'[81]

Moreover parties only brought out the differences between them:

> The lunch party yesterday was well up to standard – the new (flamboyant) direc-tor of the Fitzwilliam [Museum], [Jaffe,] his retiring (in both senses) predecessor, their respective wives (one simple but pleasant, the other neither), and one or two other bodies. In magnificent but over-furnished rooms in King's . . . . Even I noticed that the food was good and the wine nice (nothing so vulgar as vodka). But the best thing about it was that we arrived at 1.15, and were out at 3. That's what I call a civilized party. Even in my better days I could not bear parties that began at 7.30 and ended at 11.30.[82]

Yet parties, as he noted, worked only a temporary rejuvenating effect on Betty's mind:

> Excitement over the elections, [Dick] Taverne [a Labour MP who stood as an independent] as the national hero who will rally public opinion against the t[rade] u[nion]s and beat the strikes, interspersed with long reflections on the total futility of life; she will spend the rest of her days playing scrabble with her-self – the only rational occupation in this crazy world. She is not happy, but repels any attempt of mine to get near to her. 'That's *my* business'. She lives to talk and argue; and when that stops there's nothing she wants to *do*, no inner core, noth-ing I would call personal life. It's tragic, and I seem helpless. I wonder whether it's not I who am queer. But I have a great need to talk about my problems to some-one who may understand – and there's nobody here.[83]

Living with someone like Carr did not, of course, make any of this easier for her. His work always came first and he was ruthless in pursuit of it, as Anne and Joyce had discovered to their cost. Without betraying any real conscious-ness of his own contribution to the malaise, he told Tamara why they did not get much done on her recent visit to Dales Barn. 'I achieve it only by immur-ing myself in the study and refusing to talk except on urgent practical questions, in working hours. But I'm afraid Betty inwardly, and sometimes out-wardly, resents this.'[84] He was most definitely insensitive to those around him and a chasm was opening up between the two of them that he felt incapable of bridging. They were leading separate inner lives and, given his addiction to writing, he did not have the time, the patience, the inclination nor, perhaps, even the energy to remedy the situation if it required substantial sacrifice on his part, even though it made him unhappy that things remained unchanged.

When they had first married, it was Betty who had complained that he was insufficiently sweet towards her; now the roles were reversed. At some time in

---

[81] Ibid., 19 February 1973.
[82] Ibid., 22 February 1973.
[83] Ibid., 5 March 1973.
[84] Ibid., 28 February 1973.

between that side of the relationship had broken down, as it had before with Joyce. Now he complained: 'Social life is fine (in moderation). But there is also an inner private life shared with another person which is the specifically human part of sex; and this even now I want and need and miss. Nothing intellectual or social makes up for it. But probably,' he concluded defensively, 'I'm being unrealistic, romantic and juvenile (I'm beginning to write in triplets, like Isaiah [Berlin]).'[85] Finally Betty was persuaded to see a psychologist, Dr Sawney. The interview went well. Betty liked her. After many questions, mostly about her background, Sawney said this kind of depression was a familiar phenomenon and could be helped with drugs.[86] Betty was given a prescription and was due to see her again in a fortnight, but very soon her condition deteriorated and she retreated to a nursing-home. When Ted returned from visiting her, he typically sat down to write to Tamara, who had now become his only confidant. Betty was, he was relieved to say, 'cheerful and relaxed. Everything was new and unfamiliar and comfortable, and she was content to stay put and not rush around. In these moods she is delightful, and it's difficult to remember how awful the black moods can be. This makes it all the more harrowing.' On a lighter note, the nursing-home was originally established by a nursing order of nuns. 'Betty imagined that she would be able to indulge in some nice cosy arguments on one of her favourite topics – the basis of morality. But she has already discovered that nursing nuns can be weak on theology.' He wondered whether they were strong on psychology and he was anxious to get hold of Sawney to find out where it was all leading. 'At present I feel bewildered by it all.'[87]

When Betty came home, she seemed less worried by being put on drugs than was Ted. He put this down to philosophical differences: 'like a good liberal, she regards power as something abstract that can be used for "good" ends, e.g. humanitarian objects, maintenance of law and order, while [you and] I would think of it as something used by one group to exercise its rule (sometimes, no doubt, beneficient) over another. This is probably one of the differences in basic assumptions which tend to make political argument difficult and unprofitable.' There were also deep misgivings. 'One thing that worries me about this drug-based psychology is that human drives of different kinds seem to me to be mixed up with one another. I know that I have . . . angularities and troublesomenesses due no doubt to various tensions. But I feel that, if these could in fact be eradicated or relaxed by treatment, other and presumably more constructive drives would disappear with them, so that in the process of becoming comfortably harmless I should also become useless.'[88]

The greater the emotional problems, the more he retreated into his work.

---

[85] Ibid., 28 February 1973.
[86] Ibid., 15 March 1973.
[87] Ibid., 19 March 1973.
[88] Ibid., 23 March 1973.

The *History of Soviet Russia* had become a haven towards which he steered when the seas became too rough. 'I'm sorry if the work seems to add to your worries,' he wrote, 'because for me it's the one thing which is going well and therefore provides comfort and reassurance.' For Tamara, however, the difference in habits of work made her anxious. Although Isaac's publications suggest the wielding of an impressionist brush as against the studied pen and ink detail of Ted's *History*, and Tamara had done a good deal of the research for Isaac, it was Tamara who felt she had to read all the source material painstakingly page by page, and this was simply not how Carr worked. He had given a broad description of his method in *What is History?*:

> The commonest assumption appears to be that the historian divides his work into two sharply distinguishable phases or periods. First, he spends a long preliminary period reading his sources and filling his notebooks with facts: then, when this is over, he puts away his sources, takes out his notebooks and writes his book from beginning to end. This is to me an unconvincing and unplausible picture. For myself, as soon as I have got going on a few of what I take to be the capital sources, the itch becomes too strong and I begin to write – not necessarily at the beginning, but somewhere, anywhere. Thereafter, reading and writing go on simultaneously. The writing is added to, subtracted from, re-shaped, cancelled, as I go on reading. The reading is guided and directed and made fruitful by the writing: the more I write, the more I know what I am looking for, the better I understand the significance and relevance of what I find.

Not surprisingly, researching for someone who operated in this way could be a frustrating and bewildering experience. Tamara described what it was like to be subjected to continuous barrages of requests for more material, having just sent off a pile of research that left her drained:

> just when I was trying to grapple with what was supposed to be Ch'en Tu-hsiu's reports to the Central Committee of the Chinese Party in the summer of 1926, a note would arrive from Cambridge: Carr had just found that he did not have enough details about the reaction of certain Italians to the expulsion of Tasca from the PCI in 1929. At such moments I was glad indeed that, as he had said in his original letter, he 'could no longer work long hours or very fast'.

When he came to stay at Kidderpore Gardens – usually for two days every fortnight – Tamara would put him in her small spare bedroom upstairs overnight, and Carr would be expected to fit into her rather bohemian household as he found it, down to the shots of vodka before dinner. That was scarcely a problem since he could concentrate in almost any conditions. Tamara has described this and the manner the manuscript would take shape in these circumstances:

> Ensconced in his favourite armchair, with a great number of little notes spread on the floor and coffee tables around him, he would go on writing quickly and fluently, undisturbed by interruptions and outside noises. His method of work

presented some difficulties for me. His very first draft of any chapter was barely ten pages long. This is what I know, he would say. Then started the process of 'filling the gaps': a first list of questions would appear and we would discuss where I could find at least some of the answers. Where were the original sources? Were they available in this country? Could we get something from Harvard? From Feltrinelli? Who were the authors who dealt with this topic? – And so on.

On the basis of his research and mine, he would then try to 'fill the gaps' by writing insertions: pages additional to his first draft. These insertions were, of course, of various lengths. One then had to 'insert' new material into the first set of 'insertions': these were mostly slips of flimsy paper of all shapes and sizes with old notes or letters on the reverse, covered with tiny handwriting in pen or pencil, all precariously pinned together. This, of course, played havoc with any attempt to number the pages consecutively. Such was, however, the lucidity of his composition that even when some insertion slips went astray or were temporarily 'lost', it was easy to find their place in the tightly-knit narrative. In this way the initial draft of ten pages or so would grow into a considerable text perhaps ten times the original length. Only one typist, in far-away Scotland, who worked for him for the last twenty-five years of his life, could decipher Ted Carr's manuscript. The typed text would be returned to us for further revision – there were, of course, more gaps to be filled, more questions to be answered, and more insertions pinned on.[89]

They worked well together. But Tamara was never uncritical. She acquired from Isaac a deep suspicion of the official documentation that formed a large part of the source material from which the *grande oeuvre* was to be constructed. Carr worked, as he had done at the Foreign Office, using the official materials that lay to hand, relying upon an acute mind, a none too philanthropic view of human nature, an eye for the telling phrase and some support from the Trotsky archives to buttress his case. Tamara's differences over this could be traced to differences over the manner of writing history, imbued in the course of Isaac's composition of his three-volume biography of Trotsky. Trotsky was, of course, one who – eventually – lost. As we have seen, particularly in the debate over *What is History?*, Carr was not greatly interested in 'losers', although he held Trotsky in some regard. Tamara thus shared with, of all people, Bertram Wolfe, the criticism that Carr could not satisfactorily write the history of the Comintern from the sources of the victorious supporters of Stalin. As Tamara explained:

Brought up in quite a different school in these matters, I was somewhat impatient with what I saw as his excessive preoccupation with constitutions, resolutions, formal programmes, official pronouncements, and so on. I thought that as these were typically all more honoured in the breach than observed in practice, it was not essential to pay so much attention to them. It seemed to me that he was attaching too much weight to the letter and perhaps not enough to the spirit of his documentation . . .

---

[89] T. Deutscher, 'Remembering E.H. Carr', *New Left Review*, 137, January–February 1983, pp. 82–3.

He would listen to my objections with patience, benevolence and an indulgent smile.

But it was, of course, 'one thing to summarize the substance of the speeches made at Party congresses, and quite another to attempt to convey the mood of those who were expelled or debarred . . . . The "subversive" ideas of a minority, especially of a defeated minority, are never as well documented as those of a victorious establishment. To do full justice to these ideas required imagination and empathy.'[90]

Occasionally Tamara felt over-burdened by the strain and by the worry that the information laboriously mined from the pages of *L'Humanité* in the bowels of the British Newspaper Library at Colindale just added up to a mass of undigested facts. This would prompt immediate reassurance by return: 'I know the problem – one gets stuck in a mess of detail which doesn't make much sense, and which one will never be able to use. But it works in the end'.[91] 'As I write, I continually jot down things about which I feel curiosity; some of them are not worth much trouble, and none are [sic] at all urgent. But one somehow builds up the picture out of a lot of trivial details.'[92]

Tamara none the less enjoyed the process of collaboration. It relieved a dreadful loneliness apparent since Isaac's death. It was not that she had no friends – she had an amazing abundance of intimates, as well as her beloved son Martin – nor that she had no intellectual company. Determined to secure Isaac's intellectual legacy, she watched over – in an interested and occasionally motherly, but not condescending, sort of way – the young men who managed and wrote for the *New Left Review* who, with Isaac's demise, had prematurely lost an extraordinary source of inspiration and who always found welcome and unquestioning hospitality at her home. But Carr represented the past in Britain that she and Isaac had become so greatly attached to, and collabora-tion with him unquestionably created an intellectual excitement and enrichment otherwise unavailable.

The crisis with Betty inevitably drove him closer to Tamara. In the autumn of 1973 he began to press his attentions a little further than Tamara was pre-pared to accept. Hitherto the letters, when they did not touch on work, poured out his discomfort at trying – and generally failing – to cope with Betty's depression. The treatment earlier in the year had led to no improvement; she was still seeing the psychologist. Perhaps one should not be surprised, since he himself was a large part of the problem. Her inability to get down to real work was traceable to the end of her active career, as Ted noted; there is an aside in one letter to the effect that 'Retirement has hit Mary [wife of classics Professor Moses Finley] even worse than Betty . . . . This total loss of initiative once the tram-lines are removed is an odd and tragic phenomenon.'[93]

---

[90] Ibid., p. 83.
[91] Carr to Tamara Deutscher, 3 April 1974.
[92] Ibid., 11 June 1974.
[93] Ibid., 15 October 1974.

But it was also true that his relentless devotion to research and writing made Betty feel inadequate. It would never have occurred to him that such a ferocious intellect as hers could be so insecure. The very reputation that had initially attracted and flattered her had become a fearful standard by which her own work might be judged. The fact that he had never read her official history – and why should he? – became a source of deep resentment. Betty was undergoing a kind of intellectual torment as well as an emotional crisis. The devastating onslaught of criticism she could turn on students and books under review were now turned inward, with self-destructive results. What was worse was that she did not discuss this with him; how could she reveal her innermost fears and weaknesses to a man whose respect she still sought, for all their differences? At least partly in ignorance, Ted despaired:

> For long periods she is still as she was five years ago – a bit excitable, lively and intelligent: she has even written a couple of reviews – the first work she has done for months. But the mood changes from hour to hour . . . . Sometimes it's 'those bloody Arabs', more often the miners. Half-dotty phrases such as 'I should love to die on the barricades – a revolution is so exciting' – she sees herself driving a car through the picket lines. Then suddenly: 'If I could play Scrabble all day I should be perfectly happy.' It is terribly sad and distressing – and I feel that it is somehow put on for my benefit. I manage to cope somehow, but I rack my brains for something I could do and find nothing. It's a relief even to write to somebody sane. Forgive me, I know all this is a bit incoherent.'[94]

At times she retreated into a gloomy silence; at others she attacked him: 'The underlying theme, which becomes quite explicit as she goes on, is always the same: "You have a way of life that is satisfactory to you, I don't have a way of life that is satisfactory to me: therefore you are extremely selfish."' On one occasion, after reading a lot of Kafka, Betty explained that although he had (allegedly) ruined the life of the girl he was engaged to, he should be excused on the ground that he was writing a masterpiece. 'Perhaps on the same ground, I too should be excused. Then she got very angry with me because I refused to avail myself of this defence – my only conceivable one – and simply said that I didn't think this kind of argument led anywhere.'[95]

Even where there was humour in his life it was more often than not black, reflecting a renewed bitterness largely absent since the early sixties: '*Stop Press News* – "His Holiness the Dalai Lama" will preach in Cambridge this evening and stay the night in Trinity. Another opportunity for spiritual uplift which I shall miss.' The growing sense of despair fed his appetite for Tamara's company. In late October he began to express feelings of the kind she would rather not hear: 'I'm not naturally a very moody person. I sometimes get frightened of loneliness and of not being able to cope with myself – but that's different. Never, never, do I get cross or angry with you. How could I? I love

---

[94] Ibid., 14 December 1973.
[95] Ibid., 13 December 1974.

you and this is essential to me, and helps to keep me alive. It's true, of course, that the more I see you the more I want to see you. But I accept the . . . necessary limitations . . .'.[96] But Tamara was simply not interested in a relationship that went further than friendship and collaboration. No one could take Isaac's place, and her sound common sense – which always made her a most unusual intellectual – dictated caution where Ted and emotions were concerned. His track record was, after all, pretty awful; and it is striking how his letters to Tamara sound like the letters to Betty sent in the early sixties, even down to the transition to 'epistolatory philandering'.

Tamara did not like even the appearance of anything going on between them. And when one of her friends, on seeing them together, wondered aloud whether something amorous was afoot, Tamara was extremely agitated. She was particularly concerned lest such gossip reach Betty's ears. He claimed innocence. 'I had also consciously or unconsciously assumed . . . that age, however undeservedly, protected me and you in relation to me – from that kind of "On dit . . .". Old age has so many hateful attributes that one should at least be allowed to profit from one of its very few advantages.' As to Betty, she was, he insisted somewhat uncharitably, 'amazingly immune from any interest in, or understanding of, close individual relations or of the emotions that go with them . . .'.[97]

It is an extremely complex issue, as yet unresolved, as to the nature of the inter-relationship between the individual's state of mind (or emotion) and the health of the body. In Carr's case there was a well-attested history of a strong relationship in the first half of his life between attacks of palpitations and the onset of emotional disturbance, ever since 'the woman'.[98] One cannot help wondering whether something similar did not happen in the last decade of his life, not with respect to his heart but with the health of his entire system, its very components; or were these just the normal ravages of old age? In late June 1974 he was complaining of a lot of indigestion, which he immediately diagnosed as psychosomatic; he became afraid to eat and lost weight.[99] Not that he ate much anyway: breakfast consisted of lashings of *café au lait*; a sherry and a digestive biscuit mid-morning if he had visitors, whom he usually received between 10.30 and 11.30; a lunch of cheese, fruit and milk; tea and biscuits in the combination room at around 3.30; and whatever Betty had housekeeper Maria cook for dinner. Early in July he felt something swollen on his neck and went to see his GP, who sent him off to a consultant to remove the growth.[100] This was done at St. Thomas' in London, where they knew all about his blood.[101] They found the growth malignant. Nothing further was

---

96 Ibid.
97 Ibid., 5 October 1974.
98 'I was subject at one time to attacks of palpitation', he recalled, ' – very alarming, but I was always told it was a nervous, not a functional, disorder.' – Ibid., 9 April 1973.
99 Ibid., 23 June 1974.
100 Ibid., 4 July 1974.
101 Ibid., 17 July 1974.

found, but the surgeon botched the job, which left some of the lump in place;[102] in addition and as a precaution he went on to have radium treatment over a couple of weeks.[103]

The frightening reminder of mortality added to the feeling of gloom at Dales Barn and inevitably spilled over into his writing, most particularly the book reviews he produced for the *Times Literary Supplement* for £250 a year. The years of isolation and deprivation of proper employment at the height of the Cold War had made him more intolerant in judging the work of others than he would otherwise have been. And Tamara, for one, used to complain that he never had a good word for the efforts of his colleagues. But the onset of marital strife in the early seventies, and in particular the appearance of the malignant growth in 1974, accentuated his negativity. 'The second half of 1974,' he wrote, 'was the most miserable and painful time I remember.'[104] The main victim of his low spirits was Stephen Cohen, now teaching at Princeton, who had just published an excellent biography of Nikolai Bukharin, the leading light of the Right Opposition to Stalin in the late twenties.

It has to be said that Carr was never taken with Bukharin. Bertram Wolfe had been the first to resuscitate Bukharin's reputation. In *Khrushchev and Stalin's Ghost*, published in 1957, Wolfe republished a long article by Bukharin written in 1929, on the eve of Stalin's denunciation of the right. Wolfe, Carr wrote, 'seems to imply that Bukharin, if he had been left to himself, could have produced some satisfactory and moderate solution of Soviet Russia's economic problem'.[105] Schapiro[106] and Tucker took up Wolfe's stance. This was enough to excite Carr's suspicions. Davies, initially at any rate, favoured a 'Bukharinite' alternative to the Stalinist course eventually adopted in Moscow. Carr called him to task. 'Bukharin,' he wrote, 'was impressionable and more sensitive than most to the difficulties and hardships of industrialization; but his arguments do not strike me as very original or forcible, and he is capable, as in the controversy with Preobrazhensky, of the worst kind of claptrap.'[107] What appealed to others, and what Carr was insensitive to, was perceptively noted by Moshe Lewin: 'for many different reasons, Bukharin is in the stars now, an apostle of a sort of liberal communism in his time, very akin to the gropings for "socialism with a human face" characteristic of East European countries today – may be elsewhere too.'[108]

Carr had been sent an advance copy of Cohen's book, evidently in the hope of extracting words of praise that could appear on the cover. In October 1973

[102] Ibid., 5 August 1974.
[103] Ibid., 13 August 1974.
[104] Ibid., 30 December 1974.
[105] 'De-Stalinization', *Times Literary Supplement*, 17 May 1957.
[106] See Schapiro's review of Deutscher, *The Prophet Unarmed. Trotsky: 1921–1929*, London 1959, in *Political Science Quarterly*, vol. XXV, no.3, pp. 429–31.
[107] Carr to Davies, 29 October 1963.
[108] Lewin to Professor Sigmund (Princeton University), 7 November 1972: *Knopf Papers* – 756.6. Knopf. Eds Cameron Angus (1972–77), Stephen Cohen 1972–73, 1 of 2.

he thanked Angus Cameron on receipt of the biography 'for which I have long been waiting'.[109] He thus had nearly a year to think matters over. The review of Cohen, entitled 'The Legend of Bukharin', appeared on the front page of the *Times Literary Supplement* on 20 September 1974. In a lengthy narrative, he coursed through Bukharin's career, making some sharp jibes en route: 'Unlike any other Bolshevik leader he had a perfectly clean, because perfectly empty, sheet. He alone wears the halo of innocence . . . he was a weak man whose political actions constantly belied his inclinations . . . it was a malign fate which cast so gentle a nature into a maelstrom of revolution.' More to the point, he challenged Bukharin's right to be seen as the leading proponent of a realistic alternative to the policies of rapid industrialization and forced collectiviza-tion of agriculture and the assertion that he would have succeeded if Stalin had not successfully plotted his downfall:

> From 1925 to 1927 what may be reasonably called Bukharin's policy, the gearing of the rate of industrialization to the capacity of the peasant, was quietly pursued.
> . . . By the end of 1927, after two good harvests, the grain was piled up in barns, sheds and any convenient hiding-place. The currency was depreciating; there were few things anyhow to buy. The well-to-do peasant drew his conclusions, and did not bring his grain to the market.
> It was this crisis which dealt the death-blow to Bukharin.

To Cohen this was a difference in perspective that could not have come as a complete surprise; so far, so good. But after a page and a half the tone turns acerbic and the remarks ungenerous. In a long concluding section that praised the author only for his 'thoroughness and accuracy' – which in Carr's lexicon meant the bare minimum as a requirement for a work of history – he turned on Cohen with a vehemence that caused many to shake their heads in surprise and dismay. It almost appeared as if he had, in the course of writing, suddenly noticed the blurb – 'which can scarcely have been prepared without the author's approval' – and then looked to the preface for confirmation: there was the claim that Bukharin rather than Trotsky presented the real challenge to Stalin. This was not accidental. Cohen had written to his publisher of his dis-content with Deutscher's version of history.[110]

Carr was not merely irritated, he was indignant: 'It would be difficult to think of a more fantastic claim.' Cohen had not even mentioned Isaac's name in the preface, but he was, in Carr's view, also claiming that his biography was more important. Yet the two did not begin to compare, he insisted. Isaac Deutscher's biography integrated the life of his hero as 'an integral part of the unfolding of a great historical upheaval. It is this sense of history, of an over-whelming historical background, which is missing in Mr. Cohen.' As to the substance of the allegation, how could one say Bukharin led the fight against

---

[109] Carr to Cameron, 30 October 1973: ibid.
[110] Cohen to Bette Alexander, 4 March 1974: *ibid.*

Stalin and Stalinism? 'For three or four crucial years when Stalin was building up his impregnable hold over the party and the state and beating down the opposition, Bukharin was his zealous henchman.'[111] Bukharin was no fighter, he insisted; and Stalin never treated him as a serious rival. Granted, Bukharin was tried and executed in 1938. 'It was no act of disloyalty to Stalin on the part of Bukharin, but a paranoiac streak of almost motiveless vindictiveness, which caused Stalin to sweep him into the blood-bath of the last great purge trial.' Delivering the final blow with a backhand, he suggested that this attachment to Bukharin was to be explained by the feeble impotence of the American left:

> A second and more agreeable factor may also have been at work in Mr Cohen's assessment of Bukharin – the desire, especially strong among American liberals, to believe that nice men make good political leaders. Cynical observation may throw doubt on this conclusion. In our own century, Lloyd George and Franklin Roosevelt were superb political leaders, but not perhaps very nice men.
>
> George McGovern and Edmund Muskie are exceedingly nice people, imbued with humane ideals and unimpeachable principles. But if a biography of one or other of them fifty years hence seeks to depict his hero as a lost political leader, frustrated only by the devilish machinations of the wicked Richard Nixon, he will be seriously distorting history. And this is what has happened to Mr Cohen over Bukharin.[112]

This was not the only review of a hostile nature. Henry Pachter, a former Comintern hand, delivered a pretty devastating retort in *Dissent* that autumn. But in Carr's case the intemperate tone showed again an uncontrolled tendency, when he was not himself the victim of ostracism and when in acute emotional distress, to decree anathema on other unfortunates who otherwise might have been allies in his longstanding struggle against those one hundred per cent hostile to the Soviet Union. But he did not recognize his mistake; indeed, when he wrote to Tamara and described the review as 'not one of my best efforts',[113] he meant that he had attempted to be too even-handed! The image – all too reminiscent of the ageing A.E. Housman, his erstwhile mentor – of this brilliant but embittered old man dispensing Olympian judgements was certainly not how he saw himself; the sad irony is that he felt weak and vulnerable. 'Stoicism is a hard religion,' he told Tamara, 'unless one has a faith in one's own self-sufficiency and omnipotence which I've never been able to muster.'[114] The truth was he had an extraordinary historical imagination, but he was absolutely incapable of putting himself into other people's shoes; living people, that is.

---

[111] This was a point Cohen vehemently contested in a letter to the *Times Literary Supplement* on 18 October 1974: *Knopf Papers*.

[112] 'The Legend of Bukharin', reprinted in Carr, *From Napoleon to Stalin*, chapter 19. Later, he wrote to Tamara: 'Ken Coates seems to be making a major contribution to the lunacy about Bukharin. Some idiot in the *Times* last week praising Bukharin for having written the 1936 constitution.' Carr to Tamara Deutscher, 14 September 1978.

[113] Ibid., 5 September 1974.

[114] Ibid., 30 December 1974.

The next public and published outburst, again in the *Times Literary Supplement*, appeared early in March 1975. Three months earlier he had returned the proofs: 'It is calculated to offend the maximum number of people. Something of the sour environment must have rubbed off on me. Or just the recklessness of second childhood.'[115] The review is none the less of some interest. 'The View from the Arena' took a brutally dismissive view of *Historians in Politics*, a collection of essays which had been culled from the *Journal of Contemporary History* rather than written for a common purpose, and edited by Walter Laquer and George Mosse. It has some of the knockabout of *What is History?* Carr attacked the editors for not including the most eminent historians who participated in politics. He went on to reflect on the larger historiographical issues. After the First World War the notion of progress was rejected: 'History still had a pattern. But it went round and round, and not on and on.'

Then came Berlin's lecture in 1953: 'Sir Isaiah went perhaps rather further than he intended in seeking to reduce history to a fortuitous jumble of individual actions, good and bad . . . . Practising historians soon learnt the lesson.' This illustrates rather neatly his exaggerated appreciation of Berlin's influence; the counterpart perhaps to Berlin's undue concern at the subversive threat of Carr's pernicious doctrines. He cited Robinson and Gallagher's 'able and much-quoted book' (Gallagher from Trinity) *Africa and the Victorians*, which treated the acquisition of empire as an accidental occurrence. Then there was Stephen Roskill (a Fellow of Churchill College), the biographer of Cabinet secretary Hankey. In a controversy with Arthur Marder in the pages of the *Times Literary Supplement* in December 1974, Roskill had asserted that the historian's job was just to collect and record facts. Nothing could have been more likely to excite Carr's withering scorn as such a display of methodological naivety. 'It is a comfortable doctrine. The historian collects facts. He may even perhaps classify them. But he knows that he can learn nothing from the experience of the past, and that he can draw no conclusions. He is absolved from the onerous burden of thinking.'

There were others who saw economic history in the same terms, as a mere matter of collecting and displaying the right numbers: 'History . . . is a matter not of facts and figures, necessary though these are, but of architecture.' This prompted a conclusion which has a familiar ring, echoing the lament first published in 1930 and illustrative of his firm determination to hold to an optimistic view of an uncertain future: 'Historiography is a function of the society in and for which it works, and reflects its characteristic attitudes. A society which is full of confusion about the present, and has lost faith in the future, will see no more meaning in the past than in its own condition. But, if our society regains its mastery of the present and its vision of the future, it will by the same process renew its insights into the past.'[116]

---

[115] Ibid., 10 January 1975.
[116] 'The View from the Arena', *Times Literary Supplement*, 7 March 1975.

By the end of 1974 he felt 'incredibly older than . . . a year ago'.[117] Tamara accused him of being in a 'deep-freeze'. He agreed: 'I hate being in a deep freeze, even self-imposed, and anyone by whom, or through whom, I am "taken out now and again" is a benefactor.'[118] At Dales Barn the situation continued to deteriorate. When relationships break down money usually rears its ugly head, if not the cause of dispute in the first place. In the New Year Betty raised the issue of their relative contributions to the budget. The house was hers, but he had had the extension built. They had divided daily expenses equally between them. Betty was aggrieved on the grounds that his income was greater – it was in fact one third larger than hers. On the other hand Betty's capital was more than double his. He fought the idea of redistributing costs at his expense, but finally decided to give way only to find that she had backed down. She 'clings passionately to her grievances,' he noted, 'but when anyone proposes a way to remedy them, she loses interest, sees every kind of objection, and won't discuss it'.[119] Then, that summer, she decided to end her visits to the psychologist[120] and became 'more disjointed, impulsive and absent-minded'.[121] Tamara, the reluctant recipient of this stream of depressing domestic detail, finally protested and told him to write 'proper' letters; not that he took much notice. 'What can I tell you that you don't know already? That I like writing to you and hearing your voice on the telephone? I do.'[122]

Betty took a holiday at her friends' in Scotland later that summer – Ted was not welcome after a previous visit – but she returned in no better condition than when she had left. In the inimitable words of the housekeeper, Maria: 'I think Mrs Carr come back worse than before – more excited and worried and panic.' She never had any grasp of financial matters: that was left to her brokers; but her suggestion that they lay in a year's supply of stamps in anticipation of the price rising made him groan. 'There are long patches of clear sky, and one never knows when a storm is coming, or what form it will take.'[123] A trip to India early in 1976 promised some relief for both parties, but while she was away he took the opportunity to talk the servants into presenting a united front on the issue of having her cat, Pandy, put down. Over a year before he had been diagnosed as having an incurable kidney condition which caused him to soil the carpets. But when she returned, the servants, fearing retribution, switched their line and left Ted dangerously exposed. Then Betty 'suddenly announced that she had decided to put Pandy down, and would take him to the vet on Wednesday . . . . It has apparently been so arranged that I shall accompany the cortège, and presumably attend the ceremony. If it

---

[117] Carr to Tamara Deutscher, 23 December 1974.
[118] Ibid., 17 January 1975.
[119] Ibid., 16 May 1975.
[120] Ibid., 4 July 1975.
[121] Ibid., 1 September 1975.
[122] Ibid., 26 September 1975.
[123] Ibid., 30 September 1975.

happens, I shall be branded for ever as the Hitler who sent Pandy to Auschwitz.'[124] He was.

These were the unpromising conditions in which Carr completed his work. The surrounding unhappiness at times spurred him on. 'I'm working quite hard', he wrote, '– a better alternative than gloomy self-critical introspection, which does nobody any good.' 'The trouble is that I get caught up in these esoteric problems', he confessed to Tamara. 'Scholarship? Escapism? Why do I find it so much more enthralling than Mr. Wilson and Mrs. Thatcher – or even Miss World?'[125] He was still vulnerable, however. As he acknowledged in July 1976: 'All these disturbances have rather interfered with work.'[126] He had none the less by then finished the first part of the third volume of *Foundations of a Planned Economy* which, as he freely admitted, could not have been done without Tamara's tireless labours and constant moral support. The volume in its various parts – subsequently published in 1977 – was essentially designed to fill in the backdrop to industrialization. It was nevertheless as full as the industry volumes but, as with the previous editions, the space devoted to diplomacy gave way to enormously detailed coverage of the activities of the Comintern. This is not hard to explain. As he noted, what was 'unique' about Soviet foreign policy was 'the existence of an elaborate and much publicized institution conducting persistently subversive propaganda against potential enemies in the capitalist world'[127] and during the period in question its activities, particularly in China, complicated Moscow's relations with Britain to a serious degree, just short of war.

Yet Carr always tended to play up his view that the 'fear and anger' thus inspired was out of all proportion to reality; a position he had always taken at Riga during the twenties. He took the view along with the majority of liberals in the Foreign Office that, as with revolutionary France after 1815, the revolutionary impulse in Soviet foreign policy would gradually fall away. Thus: 'The passage of time progressively blurred these differences, and brought the purposes and practices of Soviet policy more clearly in line with those of the capitalist world.' It is, however, ironic that he should have published this in 1976 when east – west tension resulting from Soviet support for national liberation movements in the Third World was reaching new and, soon, unprecedented heights in the postwar period. He never believed that the revolution in Russia retained this revolutionary impulse; to him such troublesome activities associated with foreign Communist parties became purely and simply defensive responses governed by unalloyed realpolitik.

But the Comintern's activities at this time, though strikingly irrelevant to his conception of the development of Soviet foreign policy, caught Carr's interest, perhaps like the romantic exiles, for their very futility.

---

[124] Ibid., 9 March 1975.
[125] Ibid.
[126] Ibid., 21 July 1976.
[127] Carr, *Foundations of a Planned Economy*, vol. 3, part I, p. 17.

Furthermore, with the benefit of his own memory of events and with supporting evidence from Gorodetsky, the story of the diplomacy that took
centre stage from the Soviet vantage-point never really captured his interest
and, though beautifully written, gives every appearance of having been disposed of in short order to give time and space to what intrigued him most.
On the one hand, the story of the Comintern showed the utopian futility of
Communist dreams of spreading the revolution abroad. On the other, the
destruction of the left and then the crushing of the right in Moscow were
matched in the international Communist movement by the purging and
replacement of one set of cadres by another, dictated solely by the shifting
domestic political needs of Stalin and his allies. Carr's history of the
Comintern in all these volumes thus caught both sides of his divided mind,
the utopian and the Machiavellian. It is perhaps this, despite the persistent
fragmentation of the narrative into mini-histories of individual parties, that
makes his account so outstanding.

The *History of Soviet Russia* was, after over thirty years' employment, now
finally complete. For so many years he had laboured to the limit in the fear
that his body or, worse still, his mind would give out before the work was complete. The sense of satisfaction must have been palpable. He had become
something of a monument to learning. His splendid new rooms in the Great
Court of Trinity were lined only with his own works (and a bust of Lenin). But
that was a rare display of self-indulgence. Playing to the gallery simply did not
interest him. The BBC were forever phoning only to be told he was unavailable for comment. Scholarship was all that counted. He produced in a matter
of months a summary text, since the *History* itself was 'designed for specialists'. [128]

Although written without direct reference to the larger work, *The Russian
Revolution from Lenin to Stalin* faithfully resumes the story in briefer form.
The only novelty was the discussion of forced collectivization of agriculture:

> The peasant saw the emissaries from Moscow as invaders who had come, not only
> to destroy his cherished way of life, but to reconstitute the conditions of slavery
> from which the first stage of the revolution had freed him. Force was on the side
> of the authorities, and was brutally and ruthlessly applied. The peasant – and not
> only the kulak – was the victim of what looked like naked aggression. What was
> planned as a great achievement ended in one of the great tragedies that left a stain
> on Soviet history.[129]

This represented a new emphasis, as did the comment on Stalin:

> He had already displayed an extraordinary ruthlessness in enforcing his will and
> in crushing all opposition to it. But the full revelation of the quality of his dicta-
> torship still lay ahead. The horrors of the process of collectivization, of the

---

[128] Carr, *The Russian Revolution from Lenin to Stalin 1917–1929*, London 1979, p. vii.
[129] Ibid., p. 162.

concentration camps, of the great show trials, and of the indiscriminate killings, with or without trial, not only of those who had opposed him in the past, but of many who had assisted his rise to power, accompanied by the imposition of a rigid and uniform orthodoxy on the press, on art and literature, on history and on science, and by the suppression of every critical opinion, left a blot which could not be erased by victory in the war or by the sequel.[130]

Carr concluded on the familiar note that Stalin was not merely despot but also westernizer; yet this did not gainsay a very different tone from that struck at the outset of the *History of Soviet Russia*. When asked at this time why the book was entitled the 'Russian' revolution rather than the 'Bolshevik' revolution, his reply was that the revolution was no longer Bolshevik.[131]

With time to fill that even the production of a summary text could not hope to achieve, Carr momentarily played with the idea of writing a sequel to *What is History?* What else could he do? Writing to his publisher in 1958, he had explained that after 1929 'the material dries up, and the would-be historian is reduced largely to guess-work. This I will leave to others. If I have any working capacity left after that, I am more likely to return in order to pick up some of the things I have neglected by the way, than to advance beyond 1929. That, in my view, is definitely the end – or beginning – of a period.'[132] By 1976 he had almost certainly had enough of the 1920s.

New material was beginning to appear from the Moscow archives, albeit through the distorted mirror of Soviet historiography. At Birmingham, Davies had taken the bold and timely decision to pursue collectivization and industrialization into the 1930s. Before long these archives were beginning to re-open. And after a fairly unproductive stint as a research student under Carr, the author had moved to Birmingham and set about writing a history of Soviet foreign policy. A draft paper on the Comintern and the origins of the Popular Front was despatched to Carr for criticism in February 1977. Reflecting the Bulgarian sources, it over-played the role of future general secretary Georgi Dimitrov in the formulation of the new line. Carr was insistent (rightly so) that 'he [Dimitrov] could not have done what he did without powerful backing from Moscow.'[133] At this stage Carr had no thought of tackling the story himself, though many years earlier he had described the Comintern's history as 'one of the most fascinating, if most futile, stories of post-War history, and it leads down many curious and instructive by-paths'.[134] The interest was sustained throughout the writing of his *History of Soviet Russia*. Thus on reaching Moscow the following month, a letter was sent announcing – to the author's consternation – that 'Like you I am taking

[130] Ibid., p. 172.
[131] In conversation with the author. Friend and colleague Francesco Benvenuti alerted me to the shift in title; this prompted my question.
[132] Carr to Lovat Dickson (Macmillan's), 23 July 1958: Macmillan's company archives.
[133] Carr to the author, 22 February 1977.
[134] Review of Franz Borkenau, *The Communist International*, in the *Listener*, 23 February 1939.

some interest in Comintern in the 1930s. I am not sure whether I shall ever get around to this, but I have in mind to trace the bridge to the popular front, i.e. to see what happened between the 6th and 7th Congresses.'[135] It was not unlike sitting blissfully secure in a sail-boat on an apparently placid and empty stretch of water only to hear at the shortest possible notice that a massive oil-tanker had just set its course in precisely the same direction.

---

[135] Carr to the author, 16 March 1977.

=====11=====

'Bloody but Unbowed'

At the age of eighty-five, when most would consider themselves lucky to be alive and in fairly good health, Carr confessed to finding it 'depressing to reflect how much more quickly, and with how much less effort, I used to work'.[1] In his last years he may not have been able to work as hard as before, yet every indication was that his brain was as sharp as ever. The only signs of diminishing capacity were the inability to work after dinner and the increasing habit of mislaying items of importance. His filing system was extraordinary: there was none, merely piles of paper folders containing notes scattered around his spare room in college or in his study at Dales Barn. The fact that he continued to be able to operate this way indicates that lack of short-term memory was an occasional irritation rather than a regular occurrence. It worried him nevertheless. Having seen his friend Piero Sraffa lose his mental faculties – porters used to find him wandering around Great Court unable to remember where he was going – he was very afraid that his mind might give out before his body. In other ways old age came easily to him; he certainly lived long enough to adjust to it. He used to say that as we get older, 'we get more like ourselves': we revert to childhood.[2] Certainly his letters to Tamara Deutscher show he was very aware that this was happening, and he was in many ways content to indulge this weakness. Never normally given to nostalgia, towards the end his mind was increasingly seduced by memories of happier times.

For a considerable period while he was completing the *History of Soviet Russia* Carr deliberately avoided any direct involvement in public controversy concerning current politics. Indeed, those who knew him and admired him as the provocative and stimulating leader writer in the forties regretted that he had devoted so much of his later life to write the kind of history that seemed so devoid of ideas. As we have seen, however, as that project finally drew to a

---

[1] Carr to Tamara Deutscher, 7 November 1977.
[2] In conversation with Tamara Deutscher.

close the urge to speak out, both on the nature of history and the nature of the times, became increasingly apparent in his reviews – now signed – in the *Times Literary Supplement.* This was a way of venting opinions that relieved the frustration of living with someone who shared none of his views and who regularly berated him for holding the views that he had. It also represented a partial return to the role he played in the thirties and the forties, the role he also played in delivering the Trevelyan lectures in 1961. This spirit of rebellion stirred every so often. He railed to Tamara against the 'dictatorship of common-sense'[3] and confessed: 'I have to submit to it because I'm old, because I'm afraid, or because I'm too rooted in the past. I can't be an anarchist. But one is not ever an effective intellectual if one lives all the time in a rational, intellectual world. That kills everything. One needs to feel alive even in order to think.'[4]

Some years earlier he told the *Times Literary Supplement* that, 'as a general rule, . . . I did not want to review books on the current or recent Russian situation . . . .'.[5] The reluctance to deal with current Soviet conditions was essentially from dislike of appearing on the front line faced with an unacceptable dilemma: publicly agree with the bleak assessment of the steadfast retreat from reform in the Soviet Union that was also marked by the rehabilitation of Stalin and thereby serve purposes he had no wish to serve, or publicly deny the truth of what was happening, an option even more unacceptable. He was always eager for news of life in the Soviet Union but, certainly in the last decade, did not wish to hear of the stagnation in every sphere of society that was apparent to any open-minded visitor from the late seventies. On one occasion that the author recalls in May 1977, after listening for a few minutes to an account of the demoralized attitude of Russian youth and rumours of the brutal suppression of strikes, he fell silent: the conversation was now over, and the meeting along with it.

His views were generally expressed in the privacy of correspondence, and even then almost exclusively to Tamara. After the Soviet-led invasion of Czechoslovakia, some Communist parties of western Europe, whose prospects were bleak if overtly dependent on Moscow, began to establish a more independent image, which was tagged Eurocommunism. Simultaneously and despite agreements on strategic arms limitation between Moscow and Washington, the Russians were increasing their support for anti-western revolutionary movements in the Third World and expanding their own military capability beyond the most immediate needs of defence, thereby jeopardizing the fragile détente established at the end of the sixties. Carr never really understood what was going on. He had always underestimated the revolutionary impulse in Soviet foreign policy – 'what *are* they doing in Africa?' was his response to Soviet involvement in Somalia and Ethiopia. At times like

---

[3] Carr to Tamara Deutscher, 21 July 1973.
[4] Ibid., 29 July 1973.
[5] Ibid., 15 October 1970: *DA*, 31.

these, one had the distinct impression that he looked out onto the world from the vantage-point of an ageing Eurocentric Soviet diplomat.[6] He refused to see that the increasing hysteria in the west about Moscow's behaviour was a genuine response to a growing threat across many fronts. At Tamara's he met friends of hers from the New Left, like Perry Anderson, and those now looking to Eurocommunism in the British Communist Party, like Monty Johnstone, who sat on the Isaac Deutscher Memorial Prize committee. But he was privately critical. 'Our poor, unhappy Left! Lenin wanted a revolution and wasn't afraid to say so,' he wrote to Tamara in 1975. 'Our Left wants the fruits of revolution, but without having one.'[7] Over two years later, he was if anything more critical:

the political naivety of the New Left is really shattering. What can one think of 'Euro-Communists' who have produced no programme of their own, but are prepared at the drop of the hat to rub shoulders with declared counter-revolutionaries (anti-Lenin, anti-Marx) and cold warriors? This must be meat and drink to hardliners in the Kremlin. Back to 'the united front from Trotsky to Chamberlain'? At least Trotsky never did that.

Where are we going? There are too many war-mongers around the world at present for conflict. Cannot the New Left go back to Nuclear Disarmament? Also perhaps a bit naive, but healthier.[8]

A letter to Tamara in November 1977 carried a similar message, full of disappointment and saturated with the bitterness and anger that permeated his domestic life:

Yes, I have been absurdly distressed by what I see as the moral collapse of the Left, Old and New. I've never believed in revolution as practical politics in this country. But this is unconditional surrender. Socialism is a pipe-dream of the millennium. So let's all get together under the umbrella of bourgeois democracy, and rally to the defence of the free world against the wicked Russians and the wicked Marxists. It's all of one piece, and it's the capitalists who pay the piper and call the tune. If the Fourth International comes out against this free democratic band-wagon, I'll join it. Otherwise I'll remain in a minority of one.[9]

As editor of the *New Left Review* Anderson thought Carr's views – although out of step with mainstream Marxist thinking – worth airing in the journal. An 'interview' was arranged in the autumn of 1978 for publication; in fact, a written set of questions to which Carr gave a written response. Here he reviewed 'The Left Today'. Answering a question as to the significance of the October revolution, he reiterated much that he had had to say on the fiftieth anniversary at the Harvard conference.

---

[6] In conversation with the author in 1978.
[7] Carr to Tamara Deutscher, 13 June 1975.
[8] Ibid., 7 November 1977.
[9] Ibid., 16 November 1977.

The danger is not that we shall draw a veil over the enormous blots on the record of the Revolution, over its cost in human suffering, over the crimes committed in its name. The danger is that we shall be tempted to forget altogether, and to pass over in silence, its immense achievements . . . the determination, the dedication, the organization, the sheer hard work which in the last sixty years have transformed Russia into a major industrial country and one of the super-powers. Who before 1917 could have predicted or imagined this?

This was not new. But what is so striking, though perhaps at the same time so natural, is that when he spoke of the revolution's achievements Carr's vantage-point was that of an octogenarian Russian, rather than of the younger generation with whom he would normally have identified. 'Most of the members of this new society are grand-children of peasants; some of them are great-grand-children of serfs. They cannot help being conscious of what the Revolution has done for them.'[10]

This comment reminds one of the former Professor of Logic at Moscow University, Alexander Zinoviev, whose mother – formerly a peasant – kept a picture of Stalin on the wall and, when challenged by her son, proceeded to enumerate all the personal advantages that had flowed from the tragedy of collectivizing agriculture. The family had been thrown off the land but all the sons had become urbanized, received higher education and were now prominent in their various professions. Even if that perspective were acceptable – and it was a legitimate one for many Russians to hold – it might seem a curiously inadequate judgement on what the Soviet regime offered and stood for in the 1970s for the succeeding generations, who did not look back and say thank God for the revolution but asked why they could not travel freely abroad, write what they pleased, go on strike when they had grievances, see advertisements on the billboards or get rich quick. Carr had long been out of touch not only with the conduct of international relations and the problems the Soviet Union presented, but even more so with the reality of life within Russian society. The world had moved on.

He made some valid points. The hypocrisy of the British and Americans screaming about human rights in Russia while entertaining and honouring the Shah of Iran and ignoring bloodier repression in countries like China was self-evident, but needed saying. Yet he was excessively alarmist about the 'outburst of national hysteria' concerning Russia, which he saw as 'the symptom of a sick society' unloading its guilt by making scapegoats for its failings. He was certainly right about Eurocommunism: 'If you want to return to Kautsky and denounce the renegade Lenin, fair enough. But why muddy the waters by labelling yourselves communist? In the hitherto accepted terminology you are right-wing social-democrats.' Now they are. He welcomed the New Left and its journal. At the same time, however, he had always felt that 'the jargon of

---

[10] 'The Left Today: An Interview', *New Left Review 111*, Autumn 1978, reprinted in Carr, *From Napoleon to Stalin*, chapter 32.

Althusser, Poulantzas et al.', which regularly featured in the *Review*, had 'done a lot to discredit the study of Marxism in recent years'.[11] In his view what was needed in Britain, 'and in the west generally, is not so much to build up a sect of strict Marxists, as to encourage serious studies by people who, though not themselves committed, recognise Marx's greatness and importance'.[12]

These opinions were generally reserved for correspondence or dinner table conversation. In the interview, Carr none the less ticked off the journal: 'What seems to me incompatible with the spirit of Marxism are scholastically ingenious attempts – such as I have occasionally seen in articles in the NLR – to fit Marxist texts to conditions and problems of which he took no account and which he could not have foreseen. What I should like to see from Marxist intellectuals is less abstract analysis of Marxist texts, and more application of Marxist methods to the examination of social and economic conditions which differentiate our age from his.' If this blow did not fall heavily where it was aimed, the next certainly did. Asked about prospects for revolution in the west he argued that 'the proletariat – meaning, as Marx meant by the term, the organized workers in industry – is not a revolutionary, perhaps even a counter-revolutionary, force.' The fact was that 'the only considerable revolutions achieved since 1917 have been in China and in Cuba, and that revolutionary movements are alive today only in countries where the proletariat is weak or non-existent' and he 'felt tempted to say that the Bolsheviks won their victory in 1917, not in spite of the backwardness of the Russian economy and society, but because of it'.

Carr the realist was in this respect firmly in control over the utopian. Who else was there to fight for change, if not the working-class? 'I am not reassured when I look at the present disarray of the Left, divided into a galaxy of minute warring sects, united only by their failure to attract more than an insignificant fringe of the workers' movement, and by the brave illusion that their prescriptions for revolution represent the interests and ambitions of the workers.' The left was thus left with the choice of either remaining Communist and remaining 'an educational and propagandist group divorced from political action' since it had no 'solid revolutionary base', or 'go into current politics, become social-democrats, frankly recognize and accept the capitalist system, pursue those limited ends which can be achieved within the system, and work for those compromises between employers and workers which serve to maintain it.'

It should occasion no surprise to learn that the interview caused a certain disturbance when it came in to the offices of the *Review* (it is unlikely that Robin Blackburn, for one, agreed with it), but published it was. Another conflict arose; this time on the issue of the Isaac Deutscher Memorial Prize. The main candidate was Rudolf Bahro, an East German dissident Marxist. When Bahro's name was first raised, Carr typically merely skimmed through his book rather inattentively, and wrote favourably about him to Tamara in

---

[11] Carr to the Isaac Deutscher Memorial Prize Committee, 25 June 1979.
[12] Carr to Tamara Deutscher, 16 September 1969: *DA*, 30.

December 1978. But he then changed his mind on a closer inspection and wrote to the members of the Prize Committee:

> The dominant factor in international affairs today is the mounting virulence of the confrontation between east and west. So far as I can see, the Russians for some time past have been avoiding anything that could look provocative. It is the west which is running what I can only call a campaign of hate against the Russians. This appalls and alarms me . . . .
>
> If there were any serious Left movement in England at present, its first duty would be to carry on a vigorous and widespread campaign against this hysterical hostility to the non-capitalist world. It would freely admit the abuses occurring in non-capitalist countries. But it would put them in a fair perspective.
>
> (1) It would insist on the achievement of 1917 in creating the first major non-capitalist economy, and in shaking the capitalist monopoly in Asia and Africa.
>
> (2) It would point out that these abuses are not confined to non-capitalist countries.

He went on: why are the campaigns always against non-capitalist regimes; why are foreign governments always attacked and not our own (Ireland); and why is such a noise made about intellectuals as against ordinary victims? This formed the basis for his argument that the award of the prize to Bahro would play into the hands of these forces against the regimes in eastern Europe. 'I cannot help seeing such things as the Bukharin and Bahro campaigns as "objectively counter-revolutionary"', he added.[13] 'One pebble does not significantly alter the heap,' he wrote. 'Yet, when the heap is being used for such nefarious purposes, it goes against the grain to add even one pebble to it.'[14] The interview with the *New Left Review* had caused Fellows of Trinity to shake their heads in bewilderment. Had Carr disappeared off to the extreme left, perhaps abducted by Tamara Deutscher? The interview and the letter largely represented not a sharp turn to the left but an emotional reaction in defence of the Soviet Union, a sentiment doubtless accentuated by Betty's ranting at home on the subject of Soviet sins; and once she had got hold of Bahro, the temperature rose even higher.

Involvement with the Memorial Prize placed Carr in an anomalous position. He was the only self-confessed non-Marxist on the committee. But that fact never inhibited him from offering candid advice even if it caused offence. Anderson's *Considerations on Western Marxism* made him uneasy. He never much liked the theoretical profile of the *Review*, which was very much Anderson's doing; on the other hand he did not identify with the purely reformist and empiricist Labour left. He agreed that 'people who deride theory and purport to base their conclusions on empirical evidence are the unconscious victims of some probably bad theory.' He also agreed that 'Socialism cannot be attained through reformism, i.e. through the machinery

---

[13] Carr to the Isaac Deutscher Memorial Prize Committee, 9 January 1979.
[14] Ibid.

of bourgeois democracy.' But Anderson had not taken reality into account. 'It is no good theorising about a revolutionary situation without enquiring whether it exists.' And in his view, with Thatcher in power, 'the forces of Socialism' were 'in full retreat' and 'exposed to a damaging counter offensive'; his strategy thus 'relates to a war which nobody in the foreseeable future has either the resources or the will to fight, and is quite irrelevant to the war which is actually being fought under our eyes'.

There were always the lessons of history.

What worries me is not only what is happening in this country today, but my preoccupation with what happened in the 30s. The hard-liners denied that Brüning was a lesser evil than Hitler, and refused to cooperate with the Social Democrats . . . . Trotsky denounced this line from the start, and in the last forty years, I cannot think of any writer who has defended it. Have we all been wrong? And should we really deny that Callaghan is a lesser evil than Thatcher?[15]

What alerted him to this history was his work on the Comintern and the origins of the Popular Front. The critical part of the story is the role of the German Communist Party in undermining the Socialists in their resistance to the rise of Hitler. And as Carr convincingly confirms, it was Stalin who decided to break that resistance because he counted on a revival in German nationalism forestalling the complete reabsorption of Germany into the western camp.[16]

There were curious counterpoints to this posturing. For all the identification with 'progress', his overt sympathy for rebel youth and his delight at shocking more conventional susceptibilities, on a personal level he was perfectly capable of reacting much as any man in his eighties might react. 'The other day,' he wrote to Tamara in late January 1979 half in nostalgia, half in irony, 'undergraduates were throwing snowballs at one another in Great Court – a sight I think I've never seen before; a snow man in New Court is traditional, but has not appeared this time – Manners change, and civilizations decay.'[17] And while contributing to the Marxist wave of the future, he was anxiously debating with his stockbroker where to place his capital. The British economy, along with most of the OECD countries except Japan, was then at the mercy of 'stagflation'. The Labour Government under Callaghan had turned to the International Monetary Fund to help it out of severe difficulties with its balance of payments and had cut social services to meet the obligations imposed upon it. 'There are all the symptoms of a world crisis,' he wrote, 'and this makes our crisis less conspicuous, though not necessarily better. I'm a long-term pessimist, but this is not always a safe guide in the short term.'[18]

---

[15] Note from Carr, dated by Tamara, summer 1980.
[16] Carr, *The Twilight of Comintern, 1930–35*, London 1982.
[17] Carr to Tamara Deutscher, 25 January 1979.
[18] Carr to Paddick, his stockbroker, 11 December 1977.

His pessimism was directed at the British economy, not the future in general. From the early 1940s and for the best part of a decade he had – true to the Victorian principles in which he had been reared – advocated a tightening of the belt during economic reconstruction. But British governments, whether under Churchill, Macmillan or Wilson, sought to bribe the electorate to ensure their stay in power and were totally averse to taking the kind of measures that the Germans and the Japanese had had to take to enhance productive investment at the expense of immediate consumption; the same applied to the United States. 'The set-back in the American economy is no contemporary affair,' he wrote in April 1978; 'like us, the Americans are unable or unwilling to do the unpleasant things necessary to halt the slide.'[19] He saw the pound continuing to decline and therefore looked to foreign destinations for his investment. One likely possibility was the Far East: Hong Kong and Japan. Carr the utopian bemoaned the collapse of the Maoist supremacy in a letter to Tamara Deutscher: 'now I suppose we shall get plenty of de-bunking from headquarters: Taiwan will be out of business. Strange what is happening to the great Chinese revolution.'[20] But Carr the pragmatist had already written to his broker with the new thought that 'a lot of people, as well as the Japanese, are going to benefit from the opening up of trade with China. Have you any ideas?'[21]

When Mrs Thatcher won the election in 1979 he, like many others, seriously underestimated the impact she would have in restoring the capitalist ethic to the faltering British economy which, while it continued to falter and while manufacturing tottered on the brink of collapse, did eventually restore the pound in foreign markets (for a time, anyway). She jacked up interest rates to cut inflation: the very painful measures Carr would surely have otherwise advocated had he still been on *The Times*. In May 1979, he was still very pessimistic, however: 'The conclusion is safety first and a Swiss bank . . . . I have a hunch that I ought to go deeper into Japan, but am frightened to take the plunge.'[22] In June he was, if anything, even more gloomy about Britain's chances: 'The policy of dear money and dear sterling is surely too ruinous for industry to hold up much longer,' he wrote to his broker, adding: 'The process of turning us into an industrially under-developed oil-producing country is too painful.'[23] His solution was to buy gold, or its closest substitute: South African shares. Typically the ethical problem did not arise. To him the idea of boycotting South Africa on a personal level, such as the Anti-Apartheid Movement had long advocated, would have been an act of folly, though the thought had evidently crossed his mind. 'I do not see the regime on the eve of collapse,' he wrote. 'It is immensely strong – not a one-man oligarchy like

---

19 Ibid., 5 April 1978.
20 Carr to Tamara Deutscher, 1 November 1978.
21 Carr to Paddick, 12 September 1978.
22 Ibid., 18 May 1979.
23 Ibid., 2 June 1980.

the Shah.'[24] His broker was not entirely happy with the Far Eastern trend in Carr's portfolio. 'You don't like the Japs any more than I like the South Africans,' he wrote; 'but I don't think this need prevent us from investing in them.'[25]

The fear that had struck him but had been banished in the early seventies suddenly returned in the autumn of 1980. He was by then fully immersed in the completion of *Twilight of Comintern*. To his enormous relief the cancerous growth was successfully dealt with and for a short time his spirits revived, but he felt his strength return only very slowly; his dependence on Tamara Deutscher for progress with his manuscript had increased and was increasing by the day. He became more and more anxious; and when he lost a set of microfilm the author had borrowed for him from the library at Birmingham, he was beside himself with frustration. 'I'm on the road to recovery,' he wrote in an uncharacteristically unguarded moment, 'but it's depressingly slow. I'm just too old.'

Not that there was a trace of degeneration in his work. The draft on the developments that took place in Germany in the early thirties were as immaculate as ever and had been put together with a speed that took the breath away. If this was a sign that he had slowed down, what on earth was his rate of work when at normal speed? The draft chapter he returned on events in Spain between the formation of the republic and the seventh Comintern congress in 1935 – for which the author had supplied the sources available in Spanish – needed proper contextualization, so that the reader would have some sense of conditions in Spain at that time. It occasioned great surprise to receive by return (on the back of a company report from Chartered Consolidated) a short but pithy vignette which showed that his mind was as quick as ever. In customary no nonsense fashion he added: 'don't ask me to make it longer or more detailed: that would destroy the proportions.' The letter then went on to ask still more questions that needed further enquiry and concluding by way of apology: 'Sorry to bother you with so many questions, but I'm still feeling a bit helpless.' His impatience grew, now that his sense of mortality had been so dramatically heightened; Wheeler, his doctor, had given him the all clear, but all he felt he could count on – accurately as it turned out – was 'the possibility . . . that I may have another year or two without further interruption from that source'.[26]

But the problem was not merely a physical one. As ever, his emotions weighed heavily. 'In order to reconstruct my life and work,' he confessed, 'I have first of all to regain the energy and confidence which I had before this disconcerting affair, and that I'm not finding easy, especially in the pessimistic and cynical atmosphere in which I pass so much time.'[27] Betty had meanwhile

---

[24] Ibid.
[25] Ibid., 16 May 1980.
[26] Carr to Tamara Deutscher, 26 November 1980.
[27] Ibid.

suffered an injury and Ted was now worrying about her physical as well as her mental condition. 'This has given her a tremendous shock,' he wrote, adding with some prescience as it turned out, 'and I somehow feel that the whole way of life in Dales Barn is crumbling around us.'[28] He was also worried about himself. 'The fundamental timidity of my character comes out. I'm increasingly dependent on other people, and know that I couldn't cope by myself with any crisis or emergency.'[29]

He had originally hoped to have the manuscript out of the way before the year ended. The illness made for delay, yet he was already weighing up what to do next, driving himself on with relentless persistence. His thoughts returned yet again to the idea of producing a sequel to *What is History?* and he hurriedly drafted an outline introduction for the work, which he sent to Tamara that summer. Picking up where he had left off in 1961, he contrasted the spirit of optimism and belief in the future with which he had ended the lectures with the 'picture of impending doom, sedulously drawn by sensational writers and journalists and transmitted through the media' that had 'penetrated the vocabulary of everyday speech'. This picture was, he asserted, inaccurate and was largely confined to the perspective from western Europe 'and its overseas offshoots'. This was natural. These were the countries that had been the undisputed masters of the world. It was equally unsurprising that 'the epicentre of the disturbance, the seat of the most profound intellectual pessimism' was to be found in Britain; and here he was speaking from the heart: 'nowhere else is the contrast between nineteenth century splendour and twentieth century drabness, between nineteenth century supremacy and twentieth century inferiority, so marked and so painful.'

More specifically, these views emanated from the elite within Britain and other elite countries. 'Of this movement,' he wrote – a section censored by the *Guardian* when published posthumously – 'the main standard-bearers are the intellectuals, the purveyors of the ideas of the ruling social group which they serve . . . .' The book he intended was thus intended as a rebuff to this malaise. As a product of Victorian Britain 'it is difficult for me even today to think in terms of a world in permanent and irretrievable decline. In the following pages I shall try to distance myself from prevailing trends among western intellectuals, and especially those of this country, today, to show how and why I think they have gone astray and to strike out a claim, if not for an optimistic, at any rate for a saner and more balanced outlook on the future.' Unfortunately this was all he ever wrote on this theme. 'I don't think I can go on with the paper I showed you,' he wrote to Tamara on 26 November 1980. 'I can't conjure up the right mood or the necessary energy. It will require a lot of miscellaneous reading and excursions into the University Library – more than I can now manage.'[30]

---

[28] Ibid., 20 February 1981.
[29] Ibid.
[30] Ibid., 26 November 1980.

Perhaps it was more complicated than the reasons he suggested. As when he wrote *The Twenty Years' Crisis*, the extraordinary skills at intellectual dissection and the surgical dispassion could not easily be transformed into healing; he was better at post-mortems than cures. His upbringing drove him to adopt a resolute optimism. The spirit was there; the answers – with the honourable exception of 'The Two Scourges' and the domestic sections of *Conditions of Peace* – were increasingly elusive. As in the late 1930s he proved better at destructive criticism than constructive solutions. Challenged by an increasingly demanding daughter-in-law and an inquisitive son as to whether he 'approved of' revolutions, he wrote: 'This seems to me like asking whether one "approves of" surgery. Some physical diseases can only be cured by drastic surgery. But one has to weigh the risk that this may kill the patient or reduce him to a condition worse than the disease. Personally I have grave doubts whether diseases of our society can be cured by anything short of a revolution. But I recognise that this might destroy such good things as we have left, and produce a still more disastrous situation.' Yet he was not optimistic.

> The prospect of decay seems far more likely than that of revolution. Hardly anyone in this country wants revolution – certainly not the trade unions. People from top to bottom are engaged in an almighty squabble over their respective shares in the diminishing spoils of the system: they don't want to change the system. In some moods I find this reassuring, in others depressing. Some day something new will come out of all this, but perhaps not in your time, and probably not in this country. This country led the world in the 19th century; in the 20th the Americans tried and failed; in the 21st it will be someone else's turn.

This reminds us why Carr searched elsewhere for a solution to the problems of Britain's inexorable decline and had no hesitation in looking abroad for the answer. In a sense his country no longer existed; it had perished in 1914. 'A civilization perished in 1914,' he wrote. 'The Second World War demolished even the ruins which the first had left standing.'[31] He spent the rest of his life looking for a replacement and by the end of 1980 had to reconcile himself to the fact that the search for his unverifiable utopia had so far been in vain. His son and daughter-in-law were happy to see Mrs Thatcher in power and trusted in the capitalist restoration. Carr really understood none of this. 'If you want a feeble compromise to keep things going a little longer,' he wrote, 'Labour is a better bet than Tory. It will not stop the rot (the Tories can't do this either), but it may allow the rot to proceed a little more slowly.' In these circumstances he was in no state to write an optimistic treatise, linking past and present through a fixed faith in a recognizable future.

Instead he decided to carry on the work under way, with a further volume on the 'Slow Death of Comintern' from 1935 to 1943. Doubts still remained,

---

[31] Introduction, *From Napoleon to Stalin*, p. vii.

however. Early in January 1981 he wrote again to Tamara Deutscher to cheer himself up after a particularly depressing weekend. 'The real gloom is in myself,' he confessed.

> I find it difficult to throw off the sense of a machine that is running down. And this leaves me with a dilemma. Can I say 'This is the end – I've done quite a bit in my day and can do no more'? This is too depressing for me to face, so that I'm bound to carry on with the next period. But, realistically, I have to work hard to shake off doubts whether, even with your help, I have the physical strength for the job, and whether I can last out the course – it will take 2–3 years to do properly.[32]

He felt unable, however, to write about anything but work: 'The complexities and perplexities of life are too great.' Continued tension at Dales Barn meant that the stays with John and daughter-in-law Betty increased in number and duration.

On returning home from one such visit early in September Ted wrote to his daughter-in-law thanking them for the 'much needed break, and . . . you in particular for bearing with all my idiosyncrasies'.[33] Of course, the increased number of visits and the greater the length of stay, the more apparent became the vast gulf that separated his way of life and his thinking from theirs. Daughter-in-law Betty made his life there trouble- free. The only problem for Ted was that he was now more exposed to their critical gaze, even down to his phone calls to Tamara. One particular bone of contention was the fact that Betty and John were serious church-goers. Generally the more direct the challenge on any fundamental question the more evasively he responded, but it would have been rude to resist further. Instead he proceeded to dissect the problem. 'I'm afraid I evaded your challenge about God,' he wrote.

> But I was unwilling to embark on so explosive a subject at the fag end of a farewell meal, especially in the presence of [grand-daughter] Liz, whose God seems very different from yours and John's (I don't want to take sides in that one). My short answer would be that one can't be asked to prove a negative, but that I find no evidence whatever for the existence of 'God', whatever meaning one attaches to the word. I'm not even sure that I understand what kind of God you believe in. All Good? All Powerful? Obviously not both. Or is it just a word for the generous, altruistic impulses in human nature (that I could accept)? But in that case why all those miracles? What about the Jewish God? or the God of a central African tribe? The points of similarity and difference between these Gods would be an interesting topic. But the bare question, Does God Exist? strikes me as too floosie [sic] for useful discussion. Really that's all I have to say.[34]

By the spring of 1982 he was correcting the proofs for *Twilight of Comintern*. There were signs of improvement at Dales Barn: 'Betty is at the moment

---

[32] Carr to Tamara Deutscher, 5 January 1981.
[33] Carr to Betty Carr (John's wife), 2 September 1981.
[34] Ibid.

making an effort to see more people, to go to Clare Hall more often etc., and this is a help – I hope it will continue.' But they did not; and he was still fairly gloomy, indeed verging on the apocalyptic. 'It has been a nasty winter all round. What with the wickedness of the Right and the folly of the Left the political scene here is awful. Round the world one sees the cracks developing – Poland, Middle East, Salvador – and doesn't know know what will give first; even China now looks very odd.'[35]

By the time he wrote again over a fortnight later, however, Betty's psychological condition had further deteriorated. 'Yesterday the situation was helped by the re-emergence of that strange guru [Sir] Martin Roth [Professor of Psychiatry and Fellow of Trinity]. He has schemes for dealing with Betty's problems, but has not yet unveiled them. I don't know how she will take them, and I cannot be very optimistic. This self-hatred, hatred of the world, hatred of the human race is terribly deep.'[36] As before, Ted did not see the extent to which he was a catalyst to the continuing depression Betty had fallen into, though he had himself earlier been to see Roth after his chronic indigestion indicated a psychosomatic response to nervous tension. He found Roth fascinating, having long taken an interest in Freud whom he regarded with Marx and Darwin as the key thinkers of the modern age. Needless to say, the fascination was reciprocated.

By the end of April cancer had returned and he was scheduled for further radiotherapy. Not surprisingly his fears returned; he felt like a guinea-pig, subjected to medical experimentation. 'I see what is happening to these top doctors,' he wrote to Tamara.

> The advance of medical science has transformed them into scientists conducting experiments on this human body. Like all scientists, they are passionately interested in the success of their experiments, and this tends to make them – I won't say forget but – relegate to second place the interests of the patient whose body it is, so that one can imagine their triumphantly curing the disease, and their discovering that they have inadvertently killed the patient or reduced him to idiocy. They have not yet reached that stage with me – far from it. But I begin to understand the concept, and find it frightening.[37]

In and out of Addenbrooke's he worked on as before, but was confined to the Evelyn Nursing Home courtesy of his private health insurance. He had also finally reached a point of no return with Betty. During the first week in May, he had decided that he could take no more of her depression and her tirades; almost certainly concluding that her mental condition was contributing to his further physical deterioration. That same day Betty told John and his wife that she could no longer contemplate his return to Dales Barn. Ted could be as pugnacious as ever, though, and asked Betty for his share of

---

[35] Carr to Tamara Deutscher, 2 March 1982.
[36] Ibid., 19 March 1982.
[37] Ibid., 26 April 1982.

the proceeds from the resulting sale of Dales Barn, given that he had paid for the extension. This led to a shouting match, and this demand was fortunately dropped when John talked him out of the idea, though the damage had already been done; Betty's bitterness was unnecessarily aroused and renewed.

He tried to stay on in the Evelyn, insisting to John – who had come up with suggested residential homes – that he had 'friends with influence' who could ensure his continued presence there. Going to see him on 16 May it came as some surprise to be asked to visit the house to dispose of his papers, mostly a collection of press-cuttings: 'put them on the bonfire', he suggested. He also wanted his small library of books and journals handed over to Birmingham University's Centre for Russian and East European Studies. Betty was not there.

Ted's next letter from the Evelyn on 16 June indicated that his 'friends' had greater limits to their influence than he believed. 'I need an institution which will provide some nursing care, reasonable company, and not cut off entirely from Trinity. It's a terrible problem.'[38] He wanted a further trip to Barton to dispose of other books and journals so that he could house the minimal amount in his rooms in Great Court. And he was unusually effusive in his gratitude for any help that could be given: 'I need it very much just now.'[39] On the second trip to Barton, the Portuguese servant Maria was at the door. When reminded of how sad it all was, she naturally thought this was a reference to her having to find alternative employment. Betty was there, flustered, wary, and attempted, without great success, to brew cups of coffee. The atmosphere was funereal.

He continued to work despite the emotional stress and the acute discomfort involved in therapy. He soon had to move. The first nursing-home, near St. Ives, proved too distant from college, but the conditions were adequate to his minimal needs, the owners were kind and friendly. 'A few of the inmates seem intelligent, but I can't yet really judge.' He met one old inmate of ninety-four who had been a shining light in the International Labour Organization in the days when Ted was in Geneva. 'The old gentleman is deaf,' he noted, 'but can talk sensibly about the old days. Whether he is still living in the modern world I don't know.'[40]

He had now shelved the idea of attempting the whole period 1935–43, though he had written scattered sections of text in his usual haphazard manner, including a fierce and eloquent characterization of Stalin's terror. For the time being he lowered his sights to completion of the section on the Spanish civil war and turning that into a self-contained text. 'In my least optimistic moments, I still think I can probably hold on long enough to complete this, though not perhaps with all the polish I might wish.'[41] The result, *The*

---

[38] Carr to the author, 16 June 1982.
[39] Ibid.
[40] Carr to Tamara Deutscher, 20 July 1982.
[41] ibid., no date but sometime between 20 July and 30 August 1982.

Comintern and the Spanish Civil War, which was prepared for publication only posthumously, is certainly not as polished as it would have been had he lived a few months more, but it added important new detail on Stalin's policy, most particularly the determined crushing of the burgeoning revolution in Spain. In this sense the book is very Orwellian, which almost certainly reflects Tamara's influence as much as Carr's reading of the sources.[42] She insisted he quote *Homage to Catalonia* and use Koestler's memoirs. 'I read Koestler,' he replied, 'but he was preoccupied by his imprisonment under Franco, and didn't seem to me to contribute anything. But if there's anything you think I ought to say, I'll say it.'[43]

Work on the history kept him going. But he made a futile attempt to get Betty to take him back. She, having faced the separation and having dismissed the servants and made arrangements to let the annexe to the house, was not having any of it, distressed though she was at his condition. He was living in gloom and isolation. His eyes were deteriorating. The occulist was not encouraging and left him with the feeling that he would need a magnifying glass to read ordinary print before long. Others were, of course, rushing around attempting to alleviate the burden. Tamara would drive up from London. Step-daughter Rachel came down from Hinckley. Grand-daughter Liz was there as well. John set about trying to find alternative accommodation. But Carr felt desperately alone, cut off from his customary existence, from the routine at Trinity, from direct access to the library. He sorely missed his occasional lunchtime chats with fellows such as Peter Laslett and visitors from around the world who dropped in for the morning sherry and digestive biscuits at 10.30 or took tea with him at half past three. The end was too obviously approaching. In these bleak circumstances he wrote a poignant note to Tamara on 9 August 1982: '80th anniversary of the coronation of Edward VII, postponed from June for the removal of his appendix. I was on a family holiday at Exmouth, and remember the decorations and fireworks. Why could we not have gone on living for ever and ever in that innocent world?'

Finally a home was found, run by relatives of the owners of his current lodgings, on Gresham Road, by Parker's Piece in the centre of Cambridge, to which he moved at the end of the month. His new quarters had the advantage of accessibility 'to people, to Trinity, to the hospital', though the inmates were 'no less dilapidated' than at Houghton. He wanted Tamara to come down to see him on 6 September and take him over to Addenbrooke's for his examination. He knew he was asking for a lot, but 'this may be a traumatic occasion – the prognostications aren't very encouraging – and I would infinitely rather face it with someone whom I feel close to me than in a taxi or a hospital bus. I lack your independence and fortitude (also your relative

---

[42] E.H. Carr, *The Comintern and the Spanish Civil War,* London 1983, edited by T. Deutscher.
[43] Carr to Tamara Deutscher, 20 July 1982.

youth).' It was a sad letter. 'Yes,' he wrote,' you are of course right to say that
my emotional life has always been a bit askew – due, if any purpose is served
by revealing this now, to my singular upbringing. So long as I was vigorous and
active, I seemed to control it, or perhaps to smother it in intense intellectual
activity. But now I'm old and feeble, it has caught up with me. I'm lonely, and
deeply unhappy.'[44]

He was due for a barium test towards the end of the month and was told by
Roth that Wheeler, the doctor, expected to take him into hospital afterwards.
As far as Ted was concerned, he did not want to linger on the edge any more.
'I told Wheeler long ago that, if the cancer attacked again, I could not be
exposed to another dose of radiation, and that the only thing would be to
fade me out as painlessly and quickly as possible.'[45] His loneliness was unsup-
portable. He was only too conscious he had to keep mentally active. A further
letter to Tamara towards the end of September showed his spirits had revived;
the barium test had not shown any recurrence of the cancer.

Although physically very tired – the radiotherapy in April still left unpleasant after-effects and he was being treated for anaemia along with everything
else – the concern 'to measure and document' still predominated. Indeed he
all but asked to be pressured by his helpers, to keep himself busy. 'How long
it will take before my little volume [on the Comintern and the Spanish Civil
War] is complete depends on how much work you and Jonathan [the
author] make me do.' 'Once I've got rid of Spain, I suppose I shall go on
with the rest as before,' he continued. 'Some of the earlier chapters are in
shape, and I can see the general outline up to Munich – autumn 1938; my
thinking at present has not gone beyond that.' Tamara was drafting a section
on the Polish Communist Party up to its dissolution on Stalin's instructions
in 1938 and he wanted her to move on to the British Party. 'Sooner or later
I must brace myself to deal with the Far East, which is both interesting and
important.' At the same time he felt that his health could deteriorate again
at any moment: 'it seems unlikely that this vile disease, having attacked me
twice at a two-year interval, will now remain quiescent for any length of time.
So I can't look forward to the future with any great confidence.'[46]

A further move now took place, to a home found by Betty Behrens where
the innovative owner had decided to accept only the mentally active from the
elderly; this was on Queen Edith's Way. Carr was sceptical, since relatives
'usually look after the infirm aged till they become senile; it's only then that
they send them to the "homes"'. But he was desperate to get out of the 'present awful surroundings'. Betty still visited him from time to time.

But, after a period during which she did seem to be making an effort, and seeing
a few people, she has now relapsed into total misery. The barn is being sold for a

---

[44] Ibid., 30 August 1982.
[45] Ibid., 9 September 1982.
[46] Ibid., 27 September 1982.

higher price than the agents expected. But she is now full of gloom about the prospect of selling the house and cottage. Nor does she know where she then wants to go. The other day the stately homes seemed to have reappeared; she now knows they are awful, but what is she to do? A sad picture, I feel myself surrounded by sadness.[47]

Ted eventually moved on 17 October to the luxury of a double-room as the sole occupant of the new home. But he was deteriorating again. A succession of nosebleeds proved troubling, worrying and depressing, and his last letter to Tamara on the twenty-second typically ended a discussion of work with arrangements for her next visit and the thought that 'I seem to need you even more than ever at present' given his family's natural preoccupation with their own pressing affairs.[48] He died soon after her visit, on 4 November 1982. He was taken into Addenbrooke's overnight for another blood transfusion. But he wanted no more administered and told Dr Wheeler so. In the ambulance on the way back to the home he started to haemorrhage but insisted he wanted to continue the journey. On arrival he fell unconscious and slipped away quietly to the sound of classical music on Radio Three.

Carr's remarkable and controversial intellectual legacy lives on. He was always a fighter and one of the most acute minds of his generation. He touched and inspired the early careers of some notable intellects, from the right as well as the centre and the left. He took a key part in framing the debate on postwar Britain. He pioneered research in Soviet history. The early, lightly ironical biographical works still give great pleasure. His *What is History?* is still read in schools and universities around the world. His was a fascinating mind, even in its darkest interiors. His writing, at its best, is enormously stimulating to read, even where one disagrees with the direction it sweeps one into, as in his leaders on *The Times*. The hopes that originally inspired the *History of Soviet Russia* most certainly crashed to the ground with the collapse of the Soviet Union less than a decade after his death. He wrote it as an act of faith. No one could have accomplished so much on such a scale without such inspiration. The faith may have proved misplaced, but the work that resulted has a value apart from the motivation which inspired it.

It may yet be too early to draw a final balance sheet on the Russian revolution and the regime that it created. The true trajectory of that great country is still undetermined. How will future generations of Russians judge that most dramatic and arguably one of the most brutal episodes in their history? It created widespread literacy but then stifled expression. It built mammoth industries that enabled a war to be won and the extermination camps of central and eastern Europe to be liberated but also enabled half a continent to be conquered and much of the rest of the world to be threatened. But we are here primarily concerned with a man who, for all his apparent Olympian

---

[47] Ibid.
[48] Ibid., 22 October 1982.

detatchment, could not cope with the turbulent world of emotion, whose
secure bases of belief were thrown out of orbit by an incoming mass of frightening power, namely the First World War; a man unable to return to his past,
but always unable to live by intellect alone. The best epitaph was deftly coined
by the Cambridge classicist Moses Finley: 'It was sad to open yesterday's paper
and be confronted with the news of Ted's death, and also in a way surprising:
one does not expect a force of nature to come to an end.'[49]

---

[49] Finley to Betty Behrens, 6 November 1982.

Index